M000277130

IMPLEMENTING DERIVATIVES MODELS

WILEY SERIES IN FINANCIAL ENGINEERING

Series Editor: Jack Marshall
Managing Director of the International Association of Financial Engineers

Derivatives Demystified: Using Structured Financial Products
John C. Braddock

Derivatives for Decision Makers: Strategic Management Issues
George Crawford and Bidyut Sen

Interest-Rate Option Models
Riccardo Rebonato

Derivatives Handbook: Risk Management and Control
Robert J. Schwartz and Clifford Smith, Jr.

Dynamic Hedging: Managing Vanilla and Exotic Options
Nassim Taleb

IMPLEMENTING DERIVATIVES MODELS

Les Clewlow and Chris Strickland

The Financial Options Research Centre,
Warwick Business School, University of Warwick,
England

Centre for Financial Mathematics,
Australian National University, Canberra,
Australia

School of Finance and Economics,
University of Technology, Sydney,
Australia

Instituto de Estudios Superiores de Administración
Caracas, Venezuela

JOHN WILEY & SONS

Chichester • New York • Weinheim • Brisbane • Singapore • Toronto

Copyright © Les Clewlow and Chris Strickland
Published in 1998 by John Wiley & Sons Ltd,
Baffins Lane, Chichester,
West Sussex PO19 IUD, England

National 01243 779777
International (+44) 1243 779777
e-mail (for orders and customer service enquiries): cs-books@wiley.co.uk
Visit our Home Page on http://www.wiley.co.uk
or http://www.wiley.com

Reprinted January 1999, February 2000, July 2001, March 2002

All Rights Reserved. No part of this publication may be reproduced, stored in a retrieval system, or transmitted, in any form or by any means, electronic, mechanical, photocopying, recording, scanning or otherwise, except under the terms of the Copyright, Designs and Patents Act 1988 or under the terms of a licence issued by the Copyright Licensing Agency, 90 Tottenham Court Road, London, UK, W1P 9HE, without the permission in writing of the Publisher or the copyright owner.

Les Clewlow and Chris Strickland have asserted their right under the Copyright, Designs and Patents Act 1988, to be identified as the author of this work.

Library of Congress Cataloging-in-Publication Data

Clewlow, Les.
Implementing derivatives models / Les Clewlow and Chris Strickland.
p. cm. — (Wiley series in financial engineering)
Includes bibliographical references and index.
ISBN 0-471-96651-7 (cloth : alk. paper)
1. Derivative securities-Mathematical models. I. Strickland, Chris. II. Title. III. Series.
HG6024.A3C584 1998
332.64'.5-dc21 97-36998
CIP

British Library Cataloguing in Publication Data

A catalogue record for this book is available from the British Library

ISBN 0-471-96651-7
ISBN 13: 978-0-471-96651-7

Contents

PART TWO: IMPLEMENTING INTEREST RATE MODELS

Preface

Our objective in writing *Implementing Derivatives Models* is to explain, in detail, how to efficiently implement a wide range of models and methods for pricing and hedging derivative securities. Whilst there are a number of excellent books on the theoretical basis of derivatives, the best of which we think is John Hull's *Options, Futures and Other Derivative Securities* (Hull (1996)), we felt there was a serious gap in the area of the implementation of a theoretical model as a usable tool. We hope that this book fills that gap. The intention is that any reader with a basic knowledge of mathematics and computer programming will, with the help of this book, be able to implement all of the most important and common models, to a level where they are usable in a real research or trading environment. The models and methods we have included are those which our academic and practical experience advising financial institutions and practitioners has indicated are the most widely used. We have attempted to make the implementations completely transparent, there are no "missing bits" here. To help achieve our goal we have created our own simple pseudo computer language, the syntax of which is outlined in the notation section, and have used this to give complete implementations of many of the models and methods. The reader should be able to easily translate these pseudo-code implementations into any computer language. Furthermore, in addition to the pseudo-code, we provide numerical examples of the important computations which occur in the pseudo-code so the reader can check every stage in their implementation of a particular model or algorithm.

The book is divided into two main sections. In the first, which comprises Chapters one through to five, we concentrate on models and methods which are generally applied in FX, equity and commodity markets or markets other than fixed income. However many of the numerical techniques, in particular Monte Carlo simulation, can be used to price interest rate based derivatives. Our descriptions and examples are generally based on the classical Black and Scholes [1973] world but we clearly indicate how these can be generalised where appropriate. We begin in Chapter 1 by outlining the model for asset prices that forms the basis for this first section, deriving the fundamental partial differential equation that describes the evolution of all derivatives whose payoff is dependent on a single underlying asset following geometric Brownian motion (GBM) and time. In Chapter 2 we describe the binomial model of asset prices and show how European and American derivatives can be priced and hedged efficiently in binomial trees. After introducing the basic idea of the binomial model we spend some time discussing its generalisations as this forms an important stepping stone into the following chapters. We describe how the binomial model can be adapted to incorporate time-varying volatility, pricing path dependent options, and to pricing options which depend on more than a single underlying asset. Chapter 3 generalises the tree analysis to more flexible trinomial trees and their natural extension to finite difference methods, which are becoming increasingly important as an efficient way of pricing and hedging complex path dependent and American featured options. In this chapter we describe the implementation of explicit, implicit, and Crank–Nicolson finite difference methods, as well as the Alternating Direction Implicit method for pricing options which depend on multiple state variables.

The subject of Chapter 4 is Monte-Carlo simulation, an extemely simple and flexible method for pricing a wide range of European style derivatives. Most users of simulation are aware, however, that Monte Carlo simulation is computationally inefficient in its basic form, typically requiring hundreds of thousands of simulations to achieve reasonable accuracy. We therefore concentrate in this chapter on describing variance reduction techniques that can reduce the computation times needed by factors of a thousand or more. The methodology is extended to multiple stochastic factors and we also show how a variety of path dependent options can be valued in this framework, finishing with a discussion on the generation of standard normal random numbers and quasi-random numbers or deterministic sequences. Finally, for the first section, we generalise the discussion of binomial and trinomial trees to that of implied trees which involves making the constant parameters, of the earlier chapters, time dependent in order to calibrate the tree to the market prices of traded standard options. We then show how the implied trees can be used to price and hedge European and American exotic options.

The second section of the book describes methods for implementing models constructed specifically for pricing interest rate derivatives. Chapter six first introduces the markets, our notation and the structure of the standard interest rate derivative instruments — coupon bond options, swaptions, caps, floors and collars. We then describe the market convention for pricing these instruments using the Black (1976) model and finally discuss interest rate models, such as Vasicek (1977) and Cox, Ingersoll and Ross (1985) which weren't designed to price derivatives consistent with the observed market yield and yield volatility information. In Chapter 7 we introduce the idea of term structure consistent models — models that were built to be consistent with an observed yield curve. We focus on those models which provide analytical solutions for pure discount bond options (e.g. Ho–Lee and Hull–White). The models which have this analytical tractability are often popular with practitioners because of the computational ease with which they can be calibrated to a range of market interest rate derivative prices — although they may not necessarily fit the market data very well.

Chapter 8 details the building of binomial trees for the short rate which is normally the preferred technique for implementing the Black–Derman–Toy models. We show how the tree can be built for this model in such a way that it is consistent with firstly the observed yield curve and then the observed yield and volatility curves. We also show how to price a number of interest rate derivatives using the trees, including discount bond and coupon bond options. In Chapter 9 we extend the short rate tree building procedures to trinomial trees which are applicable to a wide range of models, including the well-known models of Hull–White, and Black–Karasinski, but also provides a very general method for constructing a large variety of short rate models. We again describe the construction of the trees to be consistent with yield and volatility data and show how to price derivatives within the tree. Finally in Chapter 10, we briefly introduce some procedures for the efficient implementation of interest rate models in the Heath–Jarrow–Morton framework.

A book of this kind can never be complete but we hope that we have made reasonable choices in selecting the content for this first edition. Obvious omissions are specific methods for large numbers of state variables including numerical integration techniques, multifactor short rate models, more details on Heath, Jarrow and Morton and related models such as Brace, Gatarek and Musiela. We are very keen to receive comments on any aspect of the book such as the choice of content, notation, pseudo-code, numerical examples, missing models or methods, etc.

Finally, although writing this book was extremely hard work it was also very enjoyable and we have learned an immense amount in the process. We hope the reader finds this book a useful addition to their library.

Acknowledgements

The number of people who have contributed in some way to this book through colloborative research or stimulating discussions are too numerous to mention — we apologise to those we don't mention by name. Specific people we would like thank either as colleagues or friends and in many cases both are; Silio David Aparicio, Antreas Athanassopoulos, Joan Ballantine, Andrew Carverhill, Nigel and Brian Collins, Gail Dean, Ana María Fernandez, David Heath, Stewart Hodges, Phil Hudson, Harry Kat, Chee Kian Lee, Glenn Kentwell, Asha Leer, Ed Levy, Javier Llanos, Christopher May, Ian Merker, Kin Pang, Ana Pascoa, Eckard Platen, Fiona Rennie, Delia Richardson, Mike Roffey, Maria Schmidt, Michael Selby, Andrea Taylor, Maria Eugenia Tinedo, Harry Tsivanidis, Louise Walker. Russell Grimwood and Mark Wong read the entire manuscript and found many typos. All remaining errors are our own.

LC would like most of all to thank and dedicate this book to his mom, dad, brother, sister and grandparents.

CS would like to thank and dedicate this book to his mum, dad and grandmothers, and to the memory of his grandfathers.

Notation

GENERAL NOTATIONAL COMMENTS

Continuous time variables will sometimes be subscripted with a time variable.

Discrete time and/or state variables such as those referring to a node in a tree will be subscripted first by the time index and then by the indices indicating the level of the state variables.

ALPHABETICAL INDEX OF NOTATION

N/A indicates not applicable

Symbol	Description	Pseudo-code equivalent
t	time	`t`
K	strike or exercise price of a contingent claim	`K`
T	maturity date of contingent claim — usually current date will be 0 and so T will also be time to maturity	`T`
S	asset price	`S, St`
μ	drift of S	
σ	volatility of S — usually instantaneous standard deviation of returns.	`sig`
r	instantaneous continuously compounded interest rate OR (in short rate trees) continuous or simply compounded interest rate over one time step	`r`

δ	continuous dividend yield on an asset	`div`
$c(K, T)$	European call price with strike price K and time to maturity T	`call`
$p(K, T)$	European put price with strike price K and time to maturity T	`put`
C	contingent claim price	`Ov`
$\mathrm{E}[]$	expectation operator	N/A
dS	infinitesimal increment in asset S	N/A
dr	infinitesimal increment in short rate	N/A
dt	infinitesimal increment of time	N/A
dz, dw	infinitesimal increment in a standard Wiener process during dt	N/A
x	natural logarithm of S ($\ln(S)$)	`x`
ν	risk neutral drift of x	`nu`
Δt	small increment of time	`dt`
Δx	small increment in x	`dx`
u	size of proportional upward move of stochastic variable or subscript indicating upward move of a stochastic variable	`u`
d	size of proportional downward move of stochastic variable or subscript indicating downward move of a stochastic variable	`d`
m	subscript indicating a central (between upward and downward) move of a stochastic variable	`m`
p	probability of transition in a tree — subscripted by combinations of u, m and d to indicate the direction of the transition	`p`

N	number of time steps in tree or simulation	`N`
N_j	number of nodes above and below current level of asset price in finite difference lattice	`Nj`
M	number of simulations	`M`
i	time step index	`i`
j, k	usually a state variable level index	`j,k`
H	barrier level	`H`
X_{rebate}	cash rebate associated with barrier option	`Xrebate`
ρ	correlation of two Wiener processes	`rho`
cv	control variate	`cv`
$\mathbf{1}_{\text{condition}}$	indicator function	`if condition then statement else statement`
Σ	covariance matrix	N/A
Γ	eigenvector matrix	N/A
Λ	diagonal eigenvalue matrix	N/A
Q	state price	`Q`
$F_{i,j,k}$	path dependent variable value k at node i, j	`F[i,j,k]`
$n_{i,j}$	number of path dependent variable values at node i, j	`n[i,j]`
$P(t, s)$	price at time t of a discount bond which matures at time s, with $t \leq S$.	`P`
$R(t, s)$	continuously compounded yield on $P(t, s)$	`R`
$f(t, s)$	instantaneous forward rate at time t for time s	N/A
$f(t, T, s)$	foward rate at time t for the period T to s	`f`
$c(t, T, s)$	price at time t of a European call option maturing at time T on an s-maturity bond	N/A

$p(t, T, s)$	price at time t of a European put option maturing at time T on an s-maturity bond	N/A
$\sigma(r)$	volatility of the short rate	sig
$\nu(t, s)$	volatility at time t of the s-maturity pure discount bond	N/A
$\sigma_R(t, s)$	volatility of the s-maturity spot rate	sigR
$\sigma_f(t, s)$	volatility of the s-maturity instantaneous forward rate	N/A
CB	price of a coupon bond maturing at s, which pays c_i at time s_i	B
$c_{CB}(t, T, \{s_i\})$	price of a European call option at time t with maturity date T on a coupon bearing bond which pays c_i at time $s_i \geq T$	N/A
$p_{CB}(t, T, \{s_i\})$	price of a European put option at time t with maturity date T on a coupon bearing bond which pays c_i at time $s_i \geq T$	N/A
R_{swap}	swap rate	Rswap
R_{fswap}	forward swap rate	Rfswap
R_{cap}	level of interest rate cap	Rcap
R_{floor}	level of interest rate floor	Rfloor
$\Delta\tau$	cap and swap reset frequency	N/A
$P_F(t, T, s)$	forward bond price between T and s	N/A
P_U	price of pure discount bond seen from node U	Pu
P_D	price of pure discount bond seen from node D	Pd
R_U	yield on pure discount bond seen from node U	Ru
R_D	yield on pure discount bond seen from node D	Rd
Q_U	state price seen from node U	Qu

Q_D	state price seen from node D	`Qd`
$r_{i,j}$	short rate at node (i, j)	`r[i,j]`
$d_{i,j}$	one period discount factor at node (i, j)	`d[i,j]`
N_s	number of time steps in short rate tree until maturity of the bond	`Ns`
N_T	Number of time steps in short rate tree until maturity of the option	`NT`
$Ps_{i,j}$	Value of the s-maturity bond at node (i, j)	`Ps[i,j]`
$B_{i,j}$	Value of a fixed rate bond at node (i, j)	`B[i,j]`
$\mu_{i,j}$	drift rate of r at node (i, j)	`mu[i,j]`
$p_{u,i,j}$	probability associated with the upward branch emanating from node (i, j)	`pu[i,j]`
$p_{m,i,j}$	probability associated with the middle branch emanating from node (i, j)	`pm[i,j]`
$p_{d,i,j}$	probability associated with the downward branch emanating from node (i, j)	`pd[i,j]`
exp(x)	e^x	`exp(x)`
sqrt(x)	$\sqrt{x}$	`sqrt(x)`
$N(x)$	Standard cumulative normal distribution function evaluated at x	`N(x)`

Pseudo-code Syntax

i, j subscripts to algebraic variables become [i, j]

$x\hat{}y$ indicates x raised to the power y

initialise_parameters indicates a routine which initialises all variables not explicitly initialised in the pseudo code routine

{ } encloses comments

x[i,j, ...] is an array-type variable

for ⟨variable⟩ = ⟨expression1⟩ to|downto ⟨expression2⟩ step ⟨expression3⟩ do
    ⟨statements⟩
next ⟨variable⟩

⟨statements⟩ are repeated for values of ⟨variable⟩ from ⟨expression1⟩ to ⟨expression2⟩ in increments of ⟨expression3⟩.

If step ⟨expression3⟩ is omitted step 1 is assumed.

if ⟨condition⟩ then ⟨statement1⟩ else ⟨statement2⟩

If ⟨condition⟩ is true then ⟨statement1⟩ is performed, if ⟨condition⟩ is not true then ⟨statement2⟩ is performed.

subroutine ⟨name⟩ (⟨variable⟩, ...)

Where ⟨name⟩ (⟨variable1⟩, ...) occurs the statements enclosed by subroutine ⟨name⟩ (⟨variable2⟩, ...) and end are performed with ⟨variable2⟩ being replaced by ⟨variable1⟩, etc.

PART ONE

Implementing Models in a Generalised Black–Scholes World

1

The Black–Scholes World, Option Pricing and Numerical Techniques

1.1 INTRODUCTION

We begin in this first chapter by looking at the mathematical foundations that underlie all of the other chapters in this section. We also discuss the need for numerical techniques in pricing and hedging derivatives when analytical solutions are unavailable. It is not our intention to be concerned with mathematical rigor in this chapter (for rigorous mathematical treatments see for example Duffie (1992) or Øksendal (1995)) but rather to provide the underlying intuition behind the assumptions that are made in a generalised Black and Scholes (1973) world and show how these combine to determine derivative prices. From the perspective of any derivative model the most important assumption that is made concerns the mathematical description of how the asset price underlying the derivative evolves randomly through time. We therefore begin by looking at a general description of how random variables evolve.

1.2 A MODEL FOR ASSET PRICES

A variable whose value changes randomly through time is said to follow a stochastic process. Most models of asset price behaviour for pricing derivatives are formulated in a continuous time framework by assuming a stochastic differential equation (SDE) describing the stochastic process followed by the asset price. For example, the most well-known assumption made about asset price behaviour, which was made by Black and Scholes (1973), is geometric Brownian motion (GBM). A non-dividend paying asset, S, following GBM is governed by the following SDE:

$$dS = \mu S\,dt + \sigma S\,dz \tag{1.1}$$

where μ and σ are known constants and dS represents the change in the level of the asset price over a small interval of time dt. Dividing through by S we obtain:

$$\frac{dS}{S} = \mu\,dt + \sigma\,dz \tag{1.2}$$

From equation (1.2) we see that the percentage change or return in the asset price, dS/S, has two components. The first component says that during the small interval of time dt

the average return on the asset is $\mu\, dt$, this is deterministic and the parameter μ is known as the drift. Added to this drift term is a random component made up of a change, dz, in a random variable z, and a parameter σ, which is generally referred to as the volatility of the asset.

The random variable z, or equivalently the change dz, is called a Wiener or Brownian motion process. Two key properties define a Wiener process: firstly dz is normally distributed with mean zero and variance dt or standard deviation of $\sqrt{dt}$, and secondly the values of dz over two different, non-overlapping increments of time are independent. Equations (1.1) or (1.2) are examples of an Itô process, as the drift and volatility only depend on the current value of the variable (the asset price) and time. In general the stochastic differential equation for a variable S following an Itô's process is

$$dS = \mu(S, t)\, dt + \sigma(S, t)\, dz \tag{1.3}$$

where the functions $\mu(S, t)$ and $\sigma(S, t)$ are general functions for the drift and volatility. Many models for the behaviour of asset prices assume that the future evolution of the asset depends only on its present level and not on the path taken to reach that level (this assumption can be justified by weak form market efficiency, see Hull, 1996). A stochastic process possessing this property is known as Markovian.

From the assumption about the behaviour of the asset price we can deduce the stochastic process followed by any derivative security whose pay-off is dependent on that asset. Then, using the key idea of Black–Scholes of constructing a riskless portfolio, we can obtain a partial differential equation governing the price of the derivative security.

1.3 THE BLACK–SCHOLES PARTIAL DIFFERENTIAL EQUATION

The stochastic differential equation for the asset price S is the starting-point for any derivative model. A derivative whose value C depends on asset price S at time t (for example a European call option) can be thought of as a function $C(t, S)$ of the random asset price and time. In order to be able to work with random variables and functions of random variables we need to use stochastic calculus. One of the most important results in stochastic calculus is Itô's lemma which tells us how to compute the stochastic processes followed by functions of stochastic variables.

Itô's lemma states that the process followed by $C(t, S)$, where S obeys equation (1.3) is given by

$$dC = \left(\frac{\partial C}{\partial S}\mu(t, S) + \frac{\partial C}{\partial t} + \frac{1}{2}\frac{\partial^2 C}{\partial S^2}\sigma^2(t, S)\right) dt + \left(\frac{\partial C}{\partial S}\sigma(t, S)\right) dz \tag{1.4}$$

For example if S follows the process given by equation (1.1) then C evolves according to the process:

$$dC = \left(\frac{\partial C}{\partial S}\mu S + \frac{\partial C}{\partial t} + \frac{1}{2}\frac{\partial^2 C}{\partial S^2}\sigma^2 S^2\right) dt + \left(\frac{\partial C}{\partial S}\sigma S\right) dz \tag{1.5}$$

In the same way as for equation (1.1) the process for C has two components which can be interpreted as drift and volatility terms. The drift term is deterministic, involving the drift and volatility parameters of the asset price process and the partial differentials of C with respect to S and t. The important point to notice from equation (1.5) is that the source of randomness, dz, is exactly the same as that in the asset price process.

Because both the process for the asset and the process for the derivative have the same source of uncertainty it is possible to combine the two securities in a portfolio in such a way as to eliminate that uncertainty. Consider a portfolio P consisting of a short position in the option and a long position of $\partial C/\partial S$ units of the underlying asset. The value of the portfolio is therefore:

$$P = -C + \frac{\partial C}{\partial S} S \tag{1.6}$$

The value of the portfolio changes as the value of the asset, and hence the option value, changes. The change in the value of the portfolio over the period of time dt is described by

$$dP = -dC + \frac{\partial C}{\partial S} dS \tag{1.7}$$

Substituting for dC and dS in equation (1.7) and using equations (1.1) and (1.5) we obtain

$$dP = -\left(\frac{\partial C}{\partial S}\mu S + \frac{\partial C}{\partial t} + \frac{1}{2}\frac{\partial^2 C}{\partial S^2}\sigma^2 S^2\right) dt - \frac{\partial C}{dS}\sigma S\, dz + \frac{\partial C}{dS}(\mu S\, dt + \sigma S\, dz) \tag{1.8}$$

Collecting terms involving dt and dz together we get

$$dP = -\frac{\partial C}{\partial S}\mu S\, dt - \frac{\partial C}{\partial t} dt - \frac{1}{2}\frac{\partial^2 C}{\partial S^2}\sigma^2 S^2 dt + \frac{\partial C}{dS}\mu S\, dt - \frac{\partial C}{dS}\sigma S\, dz + \frac{\partial C}{\partial S}\sigma S\, dz \tag{1.9}$$

Finally, simplifying gives

$$dP = -\left(\frac{\partial C}{\partial t} + \frac{1}{2}\sigma^2 S^2 \frac{\partial^2 C}{\partial S^2}\right) dt \tag{1.10}$$

The change in the value of the portfolio during dt is independent of the source of randomness dz. The portfolio is therefore riskless and in equilibrium it must earn the riskless rate of interest r which we can write as

$$\frac{dP}{P} = \frac{-\left(\frac{\partial C}{\partial t} + \frac{1}{2}\sigma^2 S^2 \frac{\partial^2 C}{\partial S^2}\right) dt}{-C + \frac{\partial C}{\partial S} S} = r\, dt \tag{1.11}$$

Rearranging this formula leads to the well-known Black–Scholes partial differential equation:

$$\begin{gathered} -\left(\frac{\partial C}{\partial t} + \frac{1}{2}\sigma^2 S^2 \frac{\partial^2 C}{\partial S^2}\right) dt = r\left(-C + \frac{\partial C}{\partial S} S\right) dt \\ \frac{\partial C}{\partial t} + rS\frac{\partial C}{\partial S} + \frac{1}{2}\sigma^2 S^2 \frac{\partial^2 C}{\partial S^2} - rC = 0 \end{gathered} \tag{1.12}$$

Note that in the above analysis we did not make any assumptions about the pay-off to the derivative C, and so equation (1.12) therefore holds for any derivative whose pay-off depends only on S and t. For example it holds for standard European call and put options, as well as for American options, lookback options and barrier options. The analytical Black–Scholes formulae for standard European call (c) and put (p) options are the result of solving this partial differential equation with the appropriate boundary conditions. If the maturity date of the option is given by T and the strike price is given by K then these boundary conditions can be expressed as

$$C_T = \max(0, S_T - K)$$

for a call option and

$$C_T = \max(0, K - S_T)$$

for a put option, where the subscripts denote the time T values of S and C. Apart from the fundamental assumption describing the asset price movements, other assumptions that we implicitly made when deriving equation (1.12) are that the short selling of securities with full use of the proceeds is permitted, there are no transaction costs, all securities are infinitely divisible, no dividends are paid during the life of the derivative security, the riskless rate of interest is constant and the same for all maturities, and that security trading is continuous.

Perhaps surprisingly, the expected return on the asset (μ) does not appear in the Black–Scholes partial differential equation. This allowed Black and Scholes in their 1973 paper to use a very powerful argument; since the expected return on the asset does not appear in the Black–Scholes partial differential equation the value of the derivative must be independent of investor risk preferences.[1] We can therefore assume any risk preferences we want in the valuation of the derivative or, put another way, we can assume the drift of the asset price is anything we want. If we assume risk neutrality, i.e. all investors are risk neutral, then all assets earn the riskless rate of interest, and we can rewrite equation (1.1) replacing μ by r thereby obtaining

$$dS = rS\,dt + \sigma S\,dz \tag{1.13}$$

If the asset pays out a continuous dividend yield at a rate δ per annum, then the drift rate is reduced by this payout and the process becomes

$$dS = (r - \delta)S\,dt + \sigma S\,dz \tag{1.14}$$

The implication of this risk-neutral pricing is that the present value of any future random cash flow (e.g. the pay-off to an option) is given by the expected value of the random future value discounted at the riskless rate. This leads to the so-called expectations approach to option valuation, e.g. for a European call option:

$$C = E_t^*[e^{-\int_t^T r_u\,du} \max(0, S_T - K)] \tag{1.15}$$

where $E_t^*[.]$ is the expectation at time t, the valuation date, under the risk-neutral probabilities. Notice that because we have assumed interest rates are constant we can rewrite equation (1.15) as

$$C = e^{-r(T-t)} E_t^*[\max(0, S_T - K)] \tag{1.16}$$

If interest rates were stochastic then we would have to use equation (1.15).

The following chapters of this first section describe how key numerical tools can be implemented to solve equations (1.12) or (1.15). In the process we will introduce important generalisations which give more realistic models for pricing and hedging derivatives. The remaining sections of this chapter discuss some more key ideas and indicate how numerical techniques arise.

1.4 THE BLACK–SCHOLES FORMULA

In the previous section we saw that the value of the option is its expected pay-off, in a risk-neutral world, discounted at the riskless rate. We can replace the expectation term in equation (1.16) by the integral across all the possible asset prices at the maturity of the option, of the product of the payoff at each asset price and the probability of each price occurring. For a European call option this gives

$$C = e^{-r(T-t)} \int_0^\infty \max(0, S_T - K) g(S_T)\, dS_T \tag{1.17}$$

where $g(S_T)$ is the probability density function of the terminal asset price. If S follows the process given by equation (1.14) then we can apply Itô's lemma to obtain the process for $x = \ln(S)$

$$dx = \left(r - \delta - \tfrac{1}{2}\sigma^2\right) dt + \sigma\, dz \tag{1.18}$$

The drift and volatility in equation (1.18) are constant, i.e. they do not depend on x. Since dz is normally distributed with mean zero and variance dt, it follows that dx is normally distributed with mean $(r - \delta - \frac{1}{2}\sigma^2)dt$ and variance $\sigma^2 dt$. Therefore the natural logarithm of S at time T is normally distributed with the following characteristics:

$$\ln S_T \sim N\left(\ln S + \left(r - \delta - \tfrac{1}{2}\sigma^2\right)(T - t), \sigma\sqrt{T - t}\right) \tag{1.19}$$

This result allows us to solve equation (1.17) (see for example Hull, 1996) to obtain the Black–Scholes equation for a European call:

$$c = S\, e^{-\delta(T-t)} N(d_1) - K\, e^{-r(T-t)} N(d_2) \tag{1.20}$$

where

$$d_1 = \frac{\ln\left(\dfrac{S}{K}\right) + \left(r - \delta + \dfrac{1}{2}\sigma^2\right)(T - t)}{\sigma\sqrt{T - t}}$$

$$d_2 = d_1 - \sigma\sqrt{T - t}$$

The corresponding equation for a European put is

$$p = K\, e^{-r(T-t)} N(-d_2) - S\, e^{-\delta(T-t)} N(-d_1) \tag{1.21}$$

1.5 HEDGING AND THE BLACK–SCHOLES FORMULA

For options traders possibly the most important issue is the management of the risk of an option position. This typically involves dynamically trading a portfolio of assets in order

TABLE 1.1 Standard Hedge Sensitivities or Greeks

Delta	$\frac{\partial C}{\partial S}$
Gamma	$\frac{\partial^2 C}{\partial S^2}$
Vega or lambda	$\frac{\partial C}{\partial \sigma}$
Theta	$\frac{\partial C}{\partial t}$
Rho	$\frac{\partial C}{\partial r}$

to neutralise sources of risk in a way which is closely related to the riskless portfolio we created in section 1.3 in order to derive the Black–Scholes formula.

We saw in section 1.3 that in order to hedge an option position against small changes in the underlying asset price we must take a position in the underlying asset equal to $-\partial c/\partial S$. The quantity $\partial c/\partial S$ is called the option delta. For the Black–Scholes call formula (1.20) there is an analytical expression for delta:

$$\frac{\partial c}{\partial S} = e^{-\delta(T-t)}N(d_1) \tag{1.22}$$

If we have written a European call option we need to take a position of $-e^{-\delta(T-t)}N(d_1)$ units of the underlying asset in order to hedge the option. This hedge is only valid for an infinitesimally small period of time — in order to maintain a riskless portfolio the position in the underlying asset (delta) must be continuously rebalanced. Options traders routinely calculate sensitivities of the option price to other variables and parameters (even though these are assumed constant by the model). The standard hedge sensitivities or "greeks" are given in Table 1.1.

Traders will typically construct portfolios of options which have desired sensitivities to particular variables or parameters. For example they may construct a portfolio of options in which all the sensitivities except vega are zero because they believe they have a better forecast of the future volatility than the market.

1.6 THE NEED FOR NUMERICAL TECHNIQUES

The Black and Scholes formulae are used widely by market participants due to their simplicity and level of analytical tractability. However, they are only applicable for standard European call and put options and, if the user wants to price something more complicated, more computationally intensive numerical techniques have to be applied. For example, for American options, and other options where there are early exercise opportunities, the value of the option is worth more than its European counterpart by an amount equal to the early exercise premium. In order to value American-style options we need to use numerical techniques such as binomial and trinomial trees and finite difference schemes.

For many "path-dependent" options, of which lookbacks, Asians, and barriers are probably the best known, the pay-off to the option at maturity is some known function of the path that the asset takes before the maturity date. Although for some of these instruments there exist closed-form solutions for the price of the option, the specifications of the contracts that are traded in practice do not often allow this level of analytical tractability. For example, the closed-form formulas in existence assume that the underlying price is monitored on a continuous basis, whereas it is usual for the observation frequency to be at discrete intervals and at most daily. In order to take these real market considerations into account we again need to turn to numerical techniques.

Other areas in which analytical formulae are not possible involve the pricing of options whose payoff depends on multiple random factors, for example options on multiple assets or models which incoporate stochastic volatility and/or interest rates. Monte Carlo simulation provides a simple and flexible method for pricing these types of instruments, as well as allowing the incorporation of more realistic price processes, such as jumps in asset prices.

The description of these techniques are the subject of the remaining chapters of this first section.

ENDNOTE

1. In equilibrium it is the average investor's risk preferences which determine the expected return or drift of asset prices.

2

The Binomial Method

2.1 INTRODUCTION

THE binomial option pricing model was first introduced by Sharpe (1978) and in detail by Cox, Ross and Rubinstein (1979) (CRR). The primary practical use for the binomial model was and still is for pricing American-style options. Since it is never optimal to exercise early an American call option on an asset that does not pay dividends[1] they can be valued using the Black–Scholes formula. But, for American put options and American call options on assets that pay dividends, early exercise can be optimal depending on the level of the underlying asset. The price of these options has no closed-form solution, and so numerical procedures must be used to solve the Black–Scholes partial differential equation. The binomial model provides a simple and intuitive numerical method for valuing American style options and it can also be extended to price more complex options. We begin our discussion of the binomial model by looking at non-dividend paying assets.

2.2 A BINOMIAL MODEL FOR A NON-DIVIDEND PAYING ASSET

The binomial model assumes that the underlying asset price follows a binomial process, that is at any time the asset price can only change to one of two possible values. Under this assumption the asset price has a binomial distribution.

Consider an asset with a current price of S which follows a binomial process. That is, during a time period Δt the asset price can go up to uS or down to dS, we refer to this as the multiplicative binomial process. The parameters u and d determine the average behaviour and the volatility of the asset. Consider also a call option on this asset which matures at the end of the time period Δt, Figure 2.1 illustrates the asset prices and call option prices. These are the first two branches of a binomial tree starting from its root node which represents today and evolving out in time by one time step. In the same way as with the Black and Scholes model in Chapter 1, we can set up a riskless portfolio consisting of the underlying asset and the call option. Consider a long position of Δ units of the asset and a short position of one call option. We want the value of the portfolio to be the same regardless of whether the asset price goes up or down over the period Δt:

$$-C_{\mathrm{u}} + \Delta uS = -C_{\mathrm{d}} + \Delta dS \tag{2.1}$$

Rearranging we obtain

$$\Delta = \frac{C_{\mathrm{u}} - C_{\mathrm{d}}}{(u-d)S} \tag{2.2}$$

FIGURE 2.1 Binomial Model of an Asset Price and Call Option

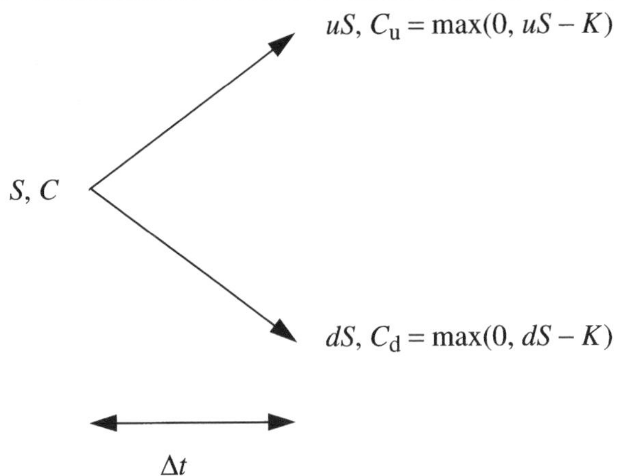

Since this portfolio is riskless it must earn the riskless rate of interest r (continuously compounded)

$$(-C_{\mathrm{u}} + \Delta uS) = e^{r\Delta t}(-C + \Delta S) \tag{2.3}$$

Substituting into equation (2.3) for ΔS, using equation (2.2) and rearranging for the call price at the start of the period C, we obtain

$$C = e^{-r\Delta t}\left(\frac{e^{r\Delta t} - d}{u - d}C_{\mathrm{u}} + \frac{u - e^{r\Delta t}}{u - d}C_{\mathrm{d}}\right) \tag{2.4}$$

Defining

$$p = \frac{e^{r\Delta t} - d}{u - d}$$

we can rewrite the above equation in the simpler form:

$$C = e^{-r\Delta t}(pC_{\mathrm{u}} + (1 - p)C_{\mathrm{d}}) \tag{2.5}$$

This is the price of a call option with one period to maturity. In order to value a put we simply have to change the pay-off condition, that is, the values of C_{u} and C_{d}, to those for a put

$$C_{\mathrm{u}} = \max(0, K - uS)$$
$$C_{\mathrm{d}} = \max(0, K - dS)$$

Note that in the same way as for the Black–Scholes model the actual probabilities of the stock moving up or down are never used in deriving the option price — the option price is independent of the expected return of the stock. The option price is therefore independent of the risk preferences of investors which allows us to interpret p and $(1-p)$ as risk-neutral probabilities. Equation (2.4) can therefore be interpreted as taking discounted expectations of future pay-offs under the risk-neutral probabilities. This gives us a very simple way of calculating the risk-neutral probabilities directly from the asset price, the return of which we can now assume is the riskless rate

$$uSp + dS(1-p) = S\,e^{r\Delta t} \tag{2.6}$$

Rearranging leads, as before, to

$$p = \frac{e^{r\Delta t} - d}{u - d} \tag{2.7}$$

To price options with more than one period to go to maturity we extend the binomial tree outwards for the required number of periods to the maturity date of the option. For example, for an option which matures in four periods of time, Figure 2.2 illustrates the binomial tree we obtain.

We will refer to a state in the tree as a node and label the nodes (i, j), where i indicates the number of time steps from time zero and j indicates the number of upward movements the asset price has made since time zero. Therefore the level of the asset price at node (i, j) is $S_{i,j} = Su^j d^{i-j}$ and the option price will be $C_{i,j}$. Note in particular that $j = 0$ at the lowest node at every time step and in going from one node to another via a downward branch j remains the same since the number of upward moves which have occurred has not changed. In general we will assume we have N time steps in total, where the Nth time step corresponds to the maturity date of the option. As with the one period example, we note that the value of the option at the maturity date is known, it is simply the pay-off, for example for a call option

$$C_{N,j} = \max(0, S_{N,j} - K) \tag{2.8}$$

FIGURE 2.2 A Four-step Binomial Tree for an Asset

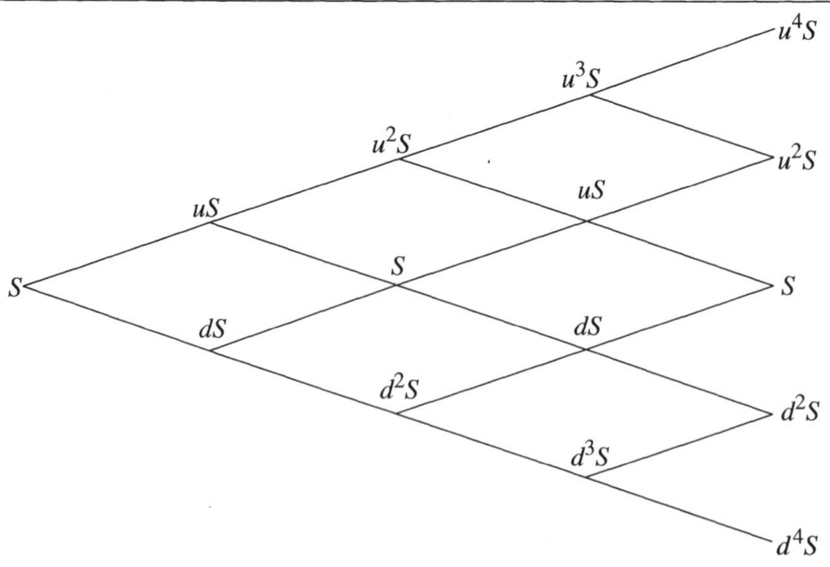

We have shown above that the value of the option at any node in the tree is its discounted expected future value, therefore at every node in the tree before maturity we have

$$C_{i,j} = e^{-r\Delta t}(pC_{i+1,j+1} + (1-p)C_{i+1,j}) \tag{2.9}$$

Using equations (2.8) and (2.9) we can compute the value of the option at every node at time step $N-1$. We can then reapply equation (2.9) at every node at every time step, working backwards through the tree, to compute the value of the option at every node in the tree. This procedure computes the value of the European option at every node in the tree. In order to compute the value of an American option we simply compare, at every node, the value of the option if exercised with the value if not exercised and set the option value at that node equal to the greater of the two. For example for an American put option we have

$$C_{i,j} = \max(e^{-r\Delta t}(pC_{i+1,j+1} + (1-p)C_{i+1,j}), K - S_{i,j}) \tag{2.10}$$

To illustrate the procedures, Figure 2.3 gives a pseudo-code implementation for the valuation of a European call in a multiplicative binomial tree.

Note firstly that we can precompute the one step discount factor (disc). Secondly, the asset prices at maturity can be efficiently computed because every node differs from the one below by a factor u/d. Also we do not have to store the entire binomial tree either for the asset price or the option price. We only need the asset prices at the final (maturity) time in order to evaluate the maturity condition. In stepping back through the tree we

FIGURE 2.3 Pseudo-code for Multiplicative Binomial Tree Valuation of a European Call

```
initialise_parameters { K, T, S, r, N, u, d }

{ precompute constants }

dt = T/N
p = (exp(r*dt)-d)/(u-d)
disc = exp(-r*dt)

{ initialise asset prices at maturity time step N }

St[0] = S*d^N
for j = 1 to N do St[j] = St[j-1]*u/d

{ initialise option values at maturity }

for j = 0 to N do C[j] = max( 0.0 , St[j] - K )

{ step back through the tree }

for i = (N-1) downto 0 do
  for j = 0 to i do
    C[j] = disc * ( p*C[j+1] + (1-p)*C[j] )

European_call = C[0]
```

can overwrite the previous time steps option values with the current values as they are computed.

Example : Multiplicative Binomial Tree Valuation of a European Call

We price a one-year maturity, at-the-money European call option with the current asset price at 100. The binomial tree has three time steps and up and down proportional jumps of 1.1 and 0.9091 respectively. The continuously compounded interest rate is assumed to be 6 per cent per annum, i.e. $K = 100$, $T = 1$, $S = 100$, $r = 0.06$, $N = 3$, $u = 1.1$, and $d = 1/u = 0.9091$. Figure 2.4 illustrates the numerical results, where nodes in the tree are represented by the boxes in which the upper value is the asset price and the lower value is the option price.

Firstly the constants; $\Delta t(dt)$, p, and $disc$ are precomputed:

$$\Delta t = \frac{T}{N} = \frac{1}{3} = 0.3333$$

$$p = \frac{e^{r\times\Delta t} - d}{u-d} = \frac{e^{0.06\times 0.3333} - 0.9091}{1.1 - 0.9091} = 0.5820$$

$$disc = e^{-r\times\Delta t} = e^{-0.06\times 0.3333} = 0.9802$$

Then the asset prices at maturity are computed, for example the asset price at node (3, 0) is computed as

FIGURE 2.4 Multiplicative Binomial Tree Valuation of a European Call

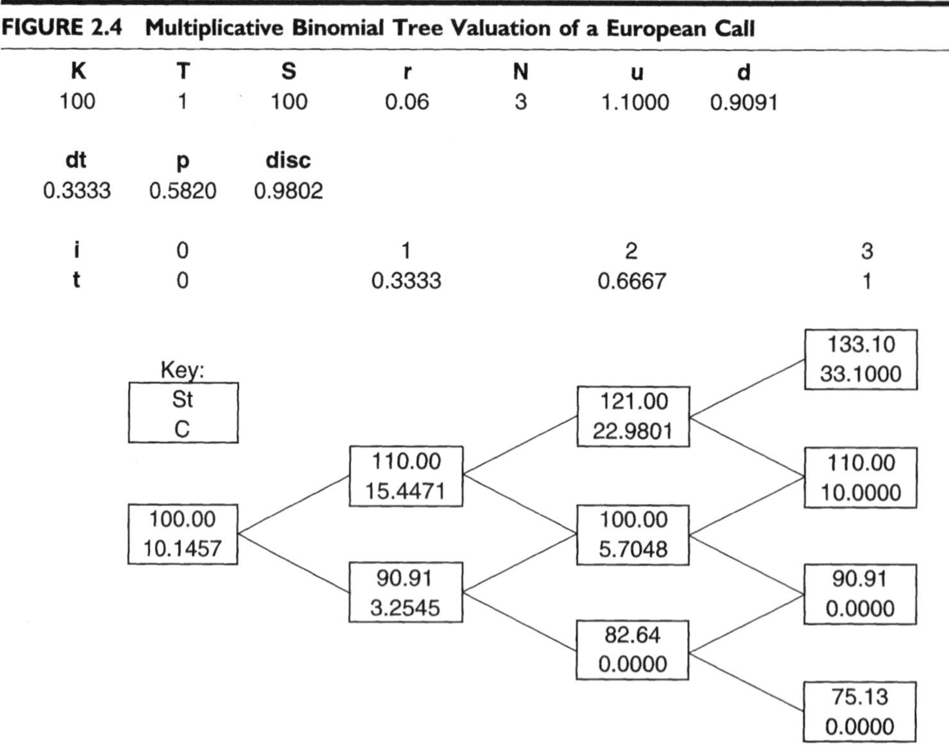

$$S_{3,0} = S \times d^N = 100 \times 0.9091^3 = 75.13$$

The other asset prices are computed from this, for example at node (3, 2) the asset is computed as

$$S_{3,2} = S_{3,1} \times \frac{u}{d} = 90.91 \times \frac{11}{0.9091} = 110.00$$

Next the option values at maturity are computed, for node (3, 2) we have

$$C_{3,2} = \max(0, S_{3,2} - K) = \max(0, 110.00 - 100.00) = 10.00$$

Finally we perform discounted expectations back through the tree. For node (2, 2) we have

$$\begin{aligned} C_{2,2} &= disc \times (p \times C_{3,3} + (1-p) \times C_{3,2}) \\ &= 0.9802 \times (0.5820 \times 33.1000 + (1 - 0.5820) \times 10.0000) = 22.9801 \end{aligned}$$

Figure 2.5 presents the pseudo-code for the valuation of an American put by the multiplicative binomial model. The changes made from the code for the European call are in bold.

The first change from Figure 2.3 is to the pay-off, which becomes that for a put. Secondly, in order to apply the early exercise condition we must adjust the asset prices

FIGURE 2.5 Pseudo-code for Multiplicative Binomial Tree Valuation of an American Put

```
initialise_parameters { K, T, S, r, N, u, d }

{ precompute constants }

dt = T/N
p = (exp(r*dt)-d)/(u-d)
disc = exp(-r*dt)

{ initialise asset prices at maturity time step N }

St[0] = S*d^N
for j = 1 to N do St[j] = St[j-1]*u/d

{ initialise option values at maturity }

for j = 0 to N do C[j] = max( 0.0 , K - St[j] )

{ step back through the tree applying the
  early exercise condition }

for i = (N-1) downto 0 do
  for j = 0 to i do
    C[j] = disc * ( p*C[j+1] + (1-p)*C[j] )
    St[j] = St[j]/d
    C[j] = max( C[j] , K - St[j] )
  next j
next i

American_put = C[0]
```

so they apply to the current time step. Since the asset prices are indexed by the number of up jumps, as we step backwards, for each index level, the asset price must have had one less down jump. Finally, the early exercise condition is added.

Example : Multiplicative Binomial Tree Valuation of an American Put

We price a one-year maturity, at-the-money American put option with the current asset price at 100. The binomial tree has three time steps and up and down proportional jumps of 1.1 and 0.9091 respectively. The continuously compounded interest rate is assumed to be 6 per cent per annum, i.e. $K = 100$, $T = 1$, $S = 100$, $r = 0.06$, $N = 3$, $u = 1.1$ and $d = 1/u = 0.9091$. Figure 2.6 illustrates the numerical results, where nodes in the tree are represented by the boxes in which the upper value is the asset price and the lower value is the option price.

Firstly the constants; $\Delta t\ (dt)$, p, and $disc$ are precomputed:

$$\Delta t = \frac{T}{N} = \frac{1}{3} = 0.3333$$

$$p = \frac{e^{r\times\Delta t} - d}{u - d} = \frac{e^{0.06\times 0.3333} - 0.9091}{1.1 - 0.9091} = 0.5820$$

$$disc = e^{-r\times\Delta t} = e^{-0.06\times 0.3333} = 0.9802$$

FIGURE 2.6 Multiplicative Binomial Tree Valuation of an American Put

K	T	S	r	N	u	d
100	1	100	0.06	3	1.1	0.9091

dt	p	disc
0.3333	0.5820	0.9802

i	0	1	2	3
t	0	0.3333	0.6667	1

Key: St / C

			133.10 0.0000
		121.00 0.0000	
	110.00 1.5261		110.00 0.0000
100.00 4.6546		100.00 3.7247	
	90.91 9.2356		90.91 9.0909
		82.64 17.3554	
			75.13 24.8685

Then the asset prices at maturity are computed, for example the asset price at node (3, 0) is computed as

$$S_{3,0} = S \times d^N = 100 \times 0.9091^3 = 75.13$$

The other asset prices are computed from this, for example at node (3, 2) the asset is computed as

$$S_{3,2} = S_{3,1} \times \frac{u}{d} = 90.91 \times \frac{11}{0.9091} = 110.00$$

Next the option values at maturity are computed, for node (3, 1) we have

$$C_{3,1} = \max(0, K - S_{3,1}) = \max(0, 100.00 - 90.91) = 9.0909$$

Finally we perform discounted expectations back through the tree. For node (2, 0) we have:

$$\begin{aligned} C_{2,0} &= disc \times (p \times C_{3,1} + (1-p) \times C_{3,0}) \\ &= 0.9802 \times (0.5820 \times 9.0909 + (1 - 0.5820) \times 24.8685) = 15.3754 \end{aligned}$$

We then compute the asset price as

$$S_{2,0} = \frac{S_{3,0}}{d} = \frac{75.13}{0.9091} = 82.64$$

and apply the early exercise test:

$$C_{2,0} = \max(C_{2,0}, K - S_{2,0}) = \max(15.3754, 100 - 82.64) = 17.3554$$

We have not yet said anything about how to choose u and d to capture the volatility of the asset price and how to choose the time period Δt. In order to do this we will describe in the following section a more general approach to constructing binomial trees which will allow us to create more sophisticated trees later in this and subsequent chapters.

2.3 A GENERAL FORMULATION OF THE BINOMIAL MODEL

The binomial model is an approximation to the true behaviour of a real asset price. In Chapter 1 we described the two key properties of an asset price — its average behaviour or drift and its randomness or volatility. These properties can be captured by the mean and variance of changes in the asset price over a particular interval of time. Therefore, a reasonable way to proceed, in computing the parameters u and d and the probability p, is so that the mean and variance of the discrete binomial process match those of the risk-neutral process of the asset price over the time step of the binomial tree. As we stated in the introduction (section 2.1), the binomial model was originally constructed to price American-style options. It seems natural, therefore, to construct the binomial tree so as to be consistent with the Black–Scholes model for European options, and therefore to choose u, d and p to match the risk-neutral mean and variance of the GBM process:

$$dS = rS\,dt + \sigma S\,dz \tag{2.11}$$

This is the standard approach for choosing the binomial parameters. However, since there are three parameters and we are only trying to match two values we have a free choice for one of the parameters. Cox, Ross and Rubinstein (1979) (CRR) chose the probabilities to be one-half which leads to

$$\begin{aligned} u &= \exp\left(\left(r - \tfrac{1}{2}\sigma^2\right)\Delta t + \sigma\sqrt{\Delta t}\right) \\ d &= \exp\left(\left(r - \tfrac{1}{2}\sigma^2\right)\Delta t - \sigma\sqrt{\Delta t}\right) \\ p &= \tfrac{1}{2} \end{aligned} \tag{2.12}$$

Jarrow and Rudd (1983) (JR) set the jump sizes to be equal, which leads to the probabilities being unequal:

$$\begin{aligned} u &= \exp\left(\sigma\sqrt{\Delta t}\right) \\ d &= \exp\left(-\sigma\sqrt{\Delta t}\right) \\ p &= \frac{1}{2} + \frac{r - \frac{1}{2}\sigma^2}{2\sigma}\sqrt{\Delta t} \end{aligned} \tag{2.13}$$

A problem with these formulations is that the approximation is only good over a small time interval, we cannot freely choose arbitrarily large time steps. In order to solve this problem and to obtain a more general and flexible formulation which is consistent with later chapters we reformulate the model in terms of the natural logarithm of the asset price ($x = \ln(S)$). The natural logarithm of the asset price under GBM is normally distributed with a constant mean and variance. Applying Itô's lemma the continuous time risk-neutral process for x can be shown to be

$$\begin{aligned} dx &= \nu\, dt + \sigma\, dz \\ \nu &= r - \tfrac{1}{2}\sigma^2 \end{aligned} \tag{2.14}$$

The discrete time binomial model for x is illustrated in Figure 2.7. The variable x can either go up to a level of $x + \Delta x_u$ with a probability of p_u or down to a level of

FIGURE 2.7 Binomial Model of the Natural Logarithm of an Asset

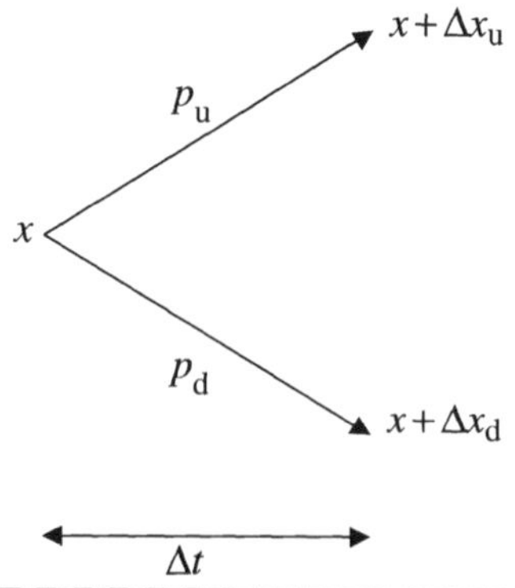

$x + \Delta x_\mathrm{d}$ with a probability of $p_\mathrm{d} = 1 - p_\mathrm{u}$. We describe this as the additive binomial process. We now equate the mean and variance of the binomial process for x with the mean and variance of the continuous time process over the time interval Δt. This leads to the following equations:

$$\begin{aligned} E[\Delta x] &= p_\mathrm{u}\Delta x_\mathrm{u} + p_\mathrm{d}\Delta x_\mathrm{d} = \nu\Delta t \\ E[\Delta x^2] &= p_\mathrm{u}\Delta x_\mathrm{u}^2 + p_\mathrm{d}\Delta x_\mathrm{d}^2 = \sigma^2\Delta t + \nu^2\Delta t^2 \end{aligned} \tag{2.15}$$

We also have that $p_\mathrm{u} + p_\mathrm{d} = 1$ and therefore have three equations in four unknowns, or equivalently we can trivially substitute $p_\mathrm{d} = 1 - p_\mathrm{u}$ and obtain two equations in three unknowns. So, as we have already mentioned, we have a "free" choice for one of the parameters. The two obvious choices, analogous to those made by CRR and JR, are to set the probabilities to be equal to one-half or to set the jump sizes to be equal. Equal probabilities of one-half leads to the following:

$$\begin{aligned} \tfrac{1}{2}\Delta x_\mathrm{u} + \tfrac{1}{2}\Delta x_\mathrm{d} &= \nu\Delta t \\ \tfrac{1}{2}\Delta x_\mathrm{u}^2 + \tfrac{1}{2}\Delta x_\mathrm{d}^2 &= \sigma^2\Delta t + \nu^2\Delta t^2 \end{aligned} \tag{2.16}$$

which gives

$$\begin{aligned} \Delta x_\mathrm{u} &= \tfrac{1}{2}\nu\Delta t + \tfrac{1}{2}\sqrt{4\sigma^2\Delta t - 3\nu^2\Delta t^2} \\ \Delta x_\mathrm{d} &= \tfrac{3}{2}\nu\Delta t - \tfrac{1}{2}\sqrt{4\sigma^2\Delta t - 3\nu^2\Delta t^2} \end{aligned} \tag{2.17}$$

Equal jump sizes lead to

$$\begin{aligned} p_\mathrm{u}(\Delta x) + p_\mathrm{d}(-\Delta x) &= \nu\Delta t \\ p_\mathrm{u}\Delta x^2 + p_\mathrm{d}\Delta x^2 &= \sigma^2\Delta t + \nu^2\Delta t^2 \end{aligned} \tag{2.18}$$

which gives

$$\begin{aligned} \Delta x &= \sqrt{\sigma^2\Delta t + \nu^2\Delta t^2} \\ p_\mathrm{u} &= \frac{1}{2} + \frac{1}{2}\frac{\nu\Delta t}{\Delta x} \end{aligned} \tag{2.19}$$

This latter solution was proposed by Trigeorgis (1992) (TRG) and on average has slightly better accuracy than the CRR, JR and the general formulation with equal probabilities (EQP). Figure 2.8 shows a comparison of the convergence of the four methods for typical choices of the parameters.

Figure 2.8 shows that the convergence behaviour of all the methods is quite complicated. It is also unsatisfactory in the sense that the error can actually increase with an increase in the number of time steps. The finite difference methods we describe in Chapter 3 solve this problem.

2.4 IMPLEMENTATION OF THE GENERAL BINOMIAL MODEL

The general additive binomial model has a similar structure to that of the multiplicative model in section 2.2. The nodes in the tree will be identified by a pair of indices (i, j),

FIGURE 2.8 The Price of an American Put Option Computed by the Binomial Method as a Function of the Number of Time Steps

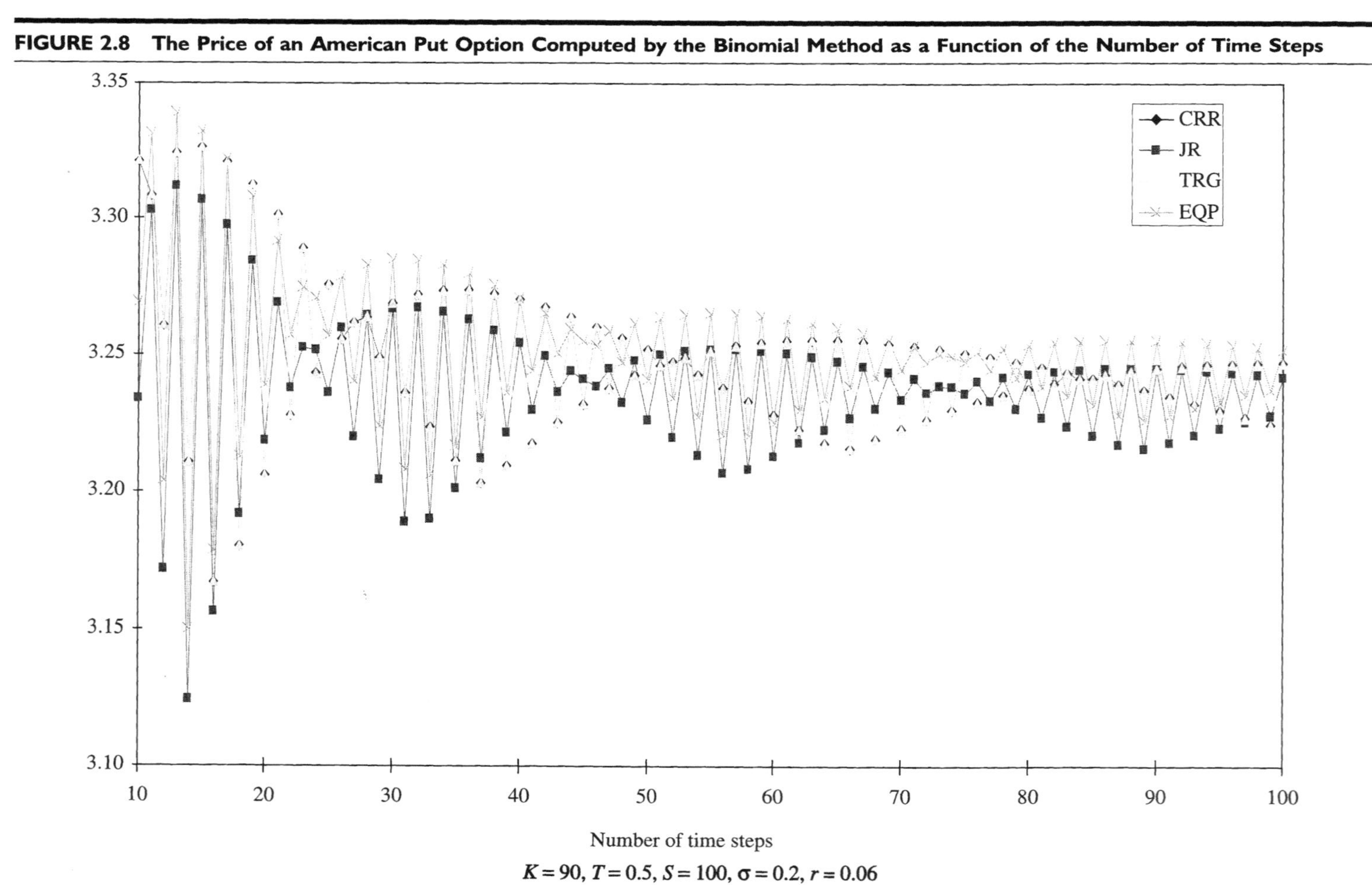

$j = 0, 1, \ldots, i$ such that the node is i periods in the future and the asset has made j upwards moves to reach that node. Therefore the level of the asset price at node (i, j) is given by

$$S_{i,j} = \exp(x_{i,j}) = \exp(x + j\Delta x_u + (i - j)\Delta x_d) \tag{2.20}$$

The option price, as before, will be $C_{i,j}$ and again we will assume we have N time steps in total, where the Nth time step corresponds to the maturity date of the option. Figure 2.9 illustrates the structure of the general additive binomial tree.

Firstly, we illustrate the basic algorithm for valuation of a European call by the general additive binomial model. Figure 2.10 gives the pseudo-code implementation which is identical to the pseudo-code for the multiplicative model except for the initialisation of the parameters and asset price array.

Example : General Additive Binomial Tree Valuation of an European Call

We price a one-year maturity, at-the-money European call option with the current asset price at 100 and volatility of 20 per cent. The continuously compounded interest rate is assumed to be 6 per cent per annum and the binomial tree has three time steps, i.e. $K = 100$, $T = 1$, $S = 100$, $\sigma = 0.20$, $r = 0.06$, $N = 3$. Figure 2.11 illustrates the results of the calculations, where nodes in the tree are represented by the boxes in which the upper value is the asset price and the lower value is the option price.

FIGURE 2.9 The General Additive Binomial Tree

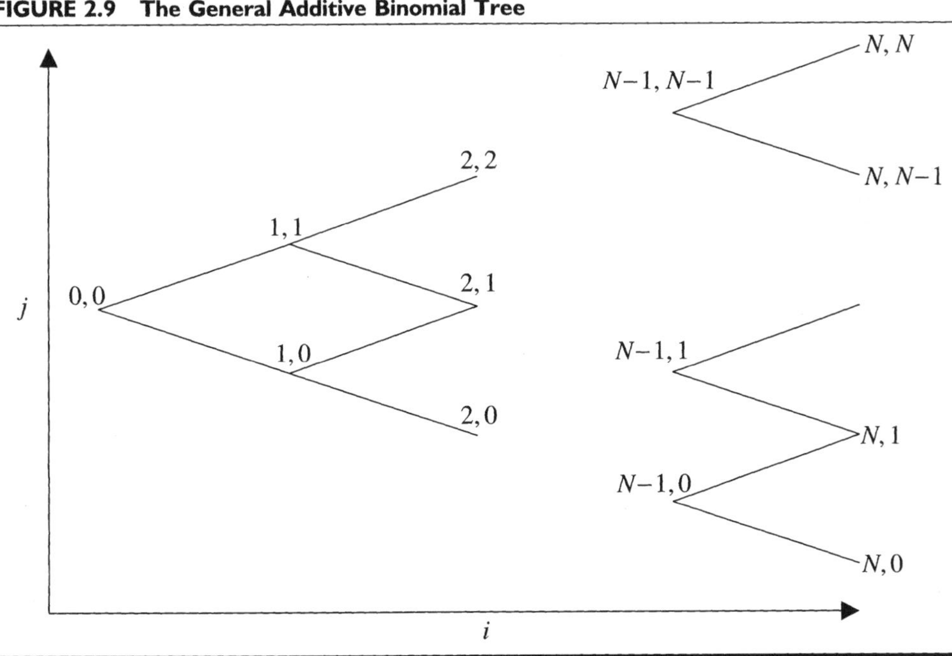

FIGURE 2.10 Pseudo-code for General Additive Binomial Valuation of a European Call

```
initialise_parameters { K, T, S, sig, r, N }

{ set coefficients - Trigeorgis }

dt = T/N
nu = r - 0.5*sig^2
dxu = sqrt( sig^2*dt + (nu*dt)^2 )
dxd = -dxu
pu = 1/2 + 1/2*( nu*dt/dxu )
pd = 1 - pu

{ precompute constants }

disc = exp(-r*dt)

{ initialise asset prices at maturity N }

St[0] = S*exp(N*dxd)
for j = 1 to N do St[j] = St[j-1]*exp( dxu-dxd )

{ initialise option values at maturity }

for j = 0 to N do C[j] = max( 0.0 , St[j] - K )

{ step back through the tree }

for i = (N-1) downto 0 do
  for j = 0 to i do
    C[j] = disc * ( pu*C[j+1] + pd*C[j] )

European_call = C[0]
```

Firstly the constants are precomputed (symbols in parentheses denote pseudo code equivalent): $\Delta t(dt)$, $\nu(nu)$, $\Delta x_{\mathrm{u}}(dxu)$, $\Delta x_{\mathrm{d}}(dxd)$, $p_{\mathrm{u}}(pu)$, $p_{\mathrm{d}}(pd)$, and *disc*:

$$\Delta t = \frac{T}{N} = \frac{1}{3} = 0.3333$$

$$\nu = r - \tfrac{1}{2}\sigma^2 = 0.06 - \tfrac{1}{2}0.20^2 = 0.0400$$

$$\Delta x_{\mathrm{u}} = \sqrt{\sigma^2 \times \Delta t + (\nu \times \Delta t)^2} = \sqrt{0.20^2 \times 0.3333 + (0.0400 \times 0.3333)^2} = 0.1162$$

$$\Delta x_{\mathrm{d}} = -\Delta x_{\mathrm{u}} = -0.1162$$

$$p_{\mathrm{u}} = \frac{1}{2} + \frac{1}{2}\left(\frac{\nu \times \Delta t}{\Delta x_{\mathrm{u}}}\right) = \frac{1}{2} + \frac{1}{2}\left(\frac{0.040 \times 0.3333}{0.1162}\right) = 0.5574$$

$$p_{\mathrm{d}} = 1 - p_{\mathrm{u}} = 1 - 0.5574 = 0.4426$$

$$disc = \exp(-r \times \Delta t) = \exp(-0.06 \times 0.3333) = 0.9802$$

FIGURE 2.11 General Additive Binomial Tree Valuation of an European Call

K	T	S	sig	rate	N
100	1	100	0.2	0.06	3

dt	nu	dxu	dxd	pu	pd	disc
0.3333	0.0400	0.1162	−0.1162	0.5574	0.4426	0.9802

i	0	1	2	3
t	0	0.3333	0.6667	1

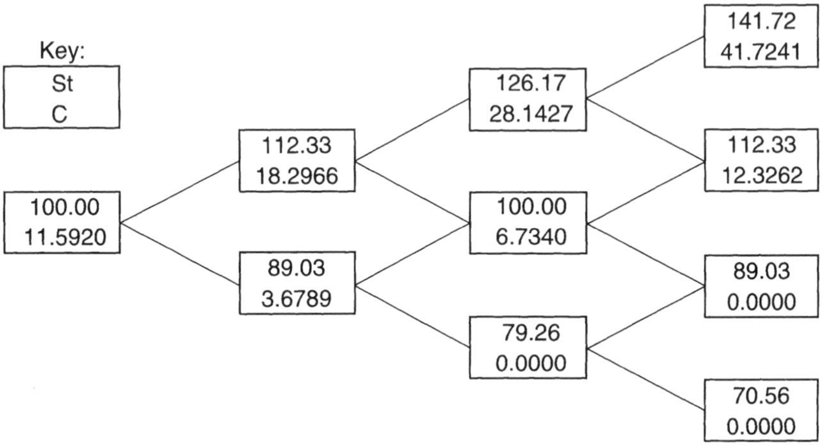

Key:
St
C

	i = 0	i = 1	i = 2	i = 3
				141.72 41.7241
			126.17 28.1427	
		112.33 18.2966		112.33 12.3262
	100.00 11.5920		100.00 6.7340	
		89.03 3.6789		89.03 0.0000
			79.26 0.0000	
				70.56 0.0000

Then the asset prices at maturity are computed, for example the asset price at node (3, 0) is computed as

$$S_{3,0} = S \times \exp(N \times \Delta x_{\mathrm{d}}) = 100 \times e^{(3\times(-0.1162))} = 70.56$$

The other asset prices are computed from this, for example the asset price at node (3, 2) is computed as

$$S_{3,2} = S_{3,1} \times e^{(\Delta x_{\mathrm{u}} - \Delta x_{\mathrm{d}})} = 89.03 \times e^{(0.1162-(-0.1162))} = 112.33$$

Next the option values at maturity are computed. For node (3, 2) we have

$$C_{3,2} = \max(0, S_{3,2} - K) = \max(0, 112.33 - 100) = 12.326$$

Finally we perform discounted expectations back through the tree. For node (2, 2) we have

$$\begin{aligned} C_{2,2} &= disc \times (p_{\mathrm{u}} \times C_{3,3} + p_{\mathrm{d}} \times C_{3,2}) \\ &= 0.9802 \times (0.5574 \times 41.7241 + 0.4426 \times 12.3262) = 28.1427 \end{aligned}$$

Figure 2.12 gives the pseudo-code algorithm for the valuation of an American put in the general additive binomial tree. Here we also introduce some simple optimisations

FIGURE 2.12 Pseudo-code for General Additive Binomial Valuation of an American Put

```
initialise_parameters { K, T, S, sig, r, N }

{ set coeffients - Trigeorgis }

dt = T/N
nu = r - 0.5*sig^2
dxu = sqrt( sig^2*dt + (nu*dt)^2 )
dxd = -dxu
pu = 1/2 + 1/2*( nu*dt/dxu )
pd = 1 - pu

{ precompute constants }

disc = exp(-r*dt)
dpu = disc*pu
dpd = disc*pd
edxud = exp( dxu - dxd )
edxd = exp( dxd )

{ initialise asset prices at maturity N }

St[0] = S*exp( N*dxd )
for j = 1 to N do St[j] = St[j-1]*edxud

{ initialise option values at maturity }

for j = 0 to N do C[j] = max( 0.0 , K - St[j] )

{ step back through the tree applying the
  early exercise condition }

for i = (N-1) downto 0 do
  for j = 0 to i do

    C[j] = dpd*C[j] + dpu*C[j+1]

    { adjust asset price to current time step }
    St[j] = St[j]/edxd

    { Apply the early exercise condition }
    C[j] = max( C[j] , K - St[j] )

  next j
next i

American_put = C[0]
```

to improve the efficiency. Firstly, the probabilities can be premultiplied by the discount factor (disc) saving one multiplication at every node. Secondly, by precomputing the proportional difference between the asset price levels (edxud) the asset price array can be computed using only one call to exp().

The changes from the corresponding European code are highlighted in bold. The calculation of the asset price array is more efficient, the pay-off condition is changed to that for a put, the asset price array is adjusted for the current time step, and the early exercise condition is applied.

Example : General Additive Binomial Tree Valuation of an American Put

We price a one-year maturity, at-the-money American put option with the current asset price at 100 and volatility of 20 per cent. The continuously compounded interest rate is assumed to be 6 per cent per annum and the binomial tree has three time steps, i.e. $K = 100$, $T = 1$, $S = 100$, $\sigma = 0.20$, $r = 0.06$, $N = 3$. Figure 2.13 illustrates the results of the calculations, where nodes in the tree are represented by the boxes in which the upper value is the asset price and the lower value is the option price.

Firstly the constants are precomputed: $\Delta t(dt)$, $\nu(nu)$, $\Delta x_u(dxu)$, $\Delta x_d(dxd)$, $p_u(pu)$, $p_d(pd)$, *disc, dpu, dpd, edxud, edxd*:

$$\Delta t = \frac{T}{N} = \frac{1}{3} = 0.3333$$

$$\nu = r - \tfrac{1}{2}\sigma^2 = 0.06 - \tfrac{1}{2}0.20^2 = 0.0400$$

$$\Delta x_u = \sqrt{\sigma^2 \times \Delta t + (\nu \times \Delta t)^2)} = \sqrt{0.20^2 \times 0.3333 + (0.0400 \times 0.3333)^2} = 0.1162$$

$$\Delta x_d = -\Delta x_u = -0.1162$$

$$p_u = \frac{1}{2} + \frac{1}{2}\left(\frac{\nu \times \Delta t}{\Delta x_u}\right) = \frac{1}{2} + \frac{1}{2}\left(\frac{0.040 \times 0.3333}{0.1162}\right) = 0.5574$$

$$p_d = 1 - p_u = 1 - 0.5574 = 0.4426$$

$$dpu = disc \times p_u = 0.9802 \times 0.5574 = 0.5463$$

$$dpd = disc \times p_d = 0.9802 \times 0.4426 = 0.4339$$

$$edxud = e^{(\Delta x_u - \Delta x_d)} = e^{(0.1162-(-0.1162))} = 1.2617$$

$$edxd = e^{\Delta x_d} = e^{-0.1162} = 0.8903$$

Then the asset prices at maturity are computed, for example the asset price at node (3, 0) is computed as

$$S_{3,0} = S \times \exp(N \times \Delta x_d) = 100 \times \exp(3 \times (-0.1162)) = 70.56$$

The other asset prices are computed from this, for example the asset price at node (3, 2) is computed as

$$S_{3,2} = S_{3,1} \times e^{(\Delta x_u - \Delta x_d)} = 89.03 \times e^{(0.1162-(-0.1162))} = 112.33$$

FIGURE 2.13 General Additive Binomial Tree Valuation of an American Put

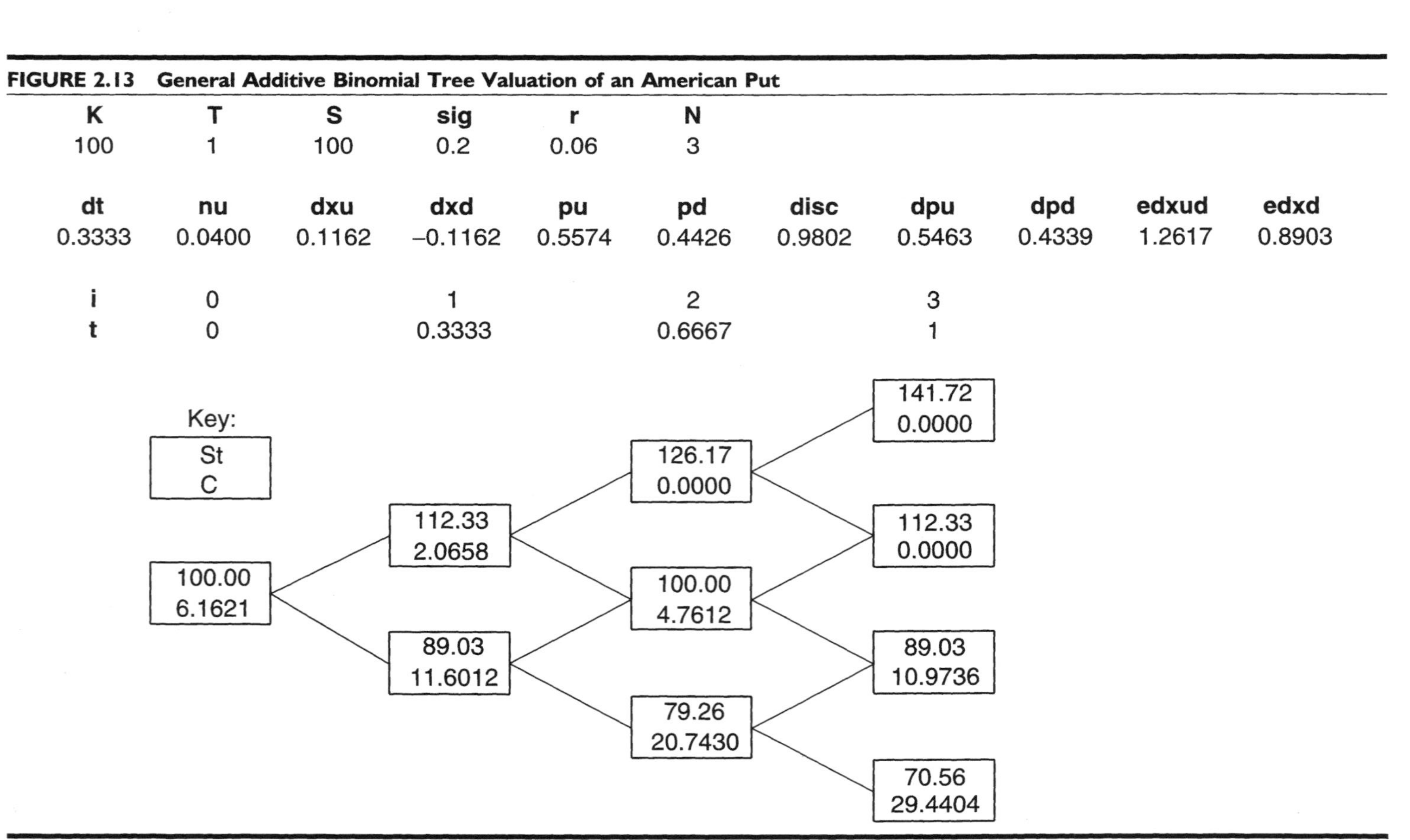

Next the option values at maturity are computed. For node (3, 1) we have

$$C_{3,1} = \max(0, K - S_{3,1}) = \max(0, 100 - 89.03) = 10.974$$

Finally we perform discounted expectations back through the tree. For node (2, 0) we have:

$$\begin{aligned} C_{2,0} &= dpu \times C_{3,1} + dpd \times C_{3,0} \\ &= 0.5463 \times 10.9736 + 0.4339 \times 29.4404 = 18.7691 \end{aligned}$$

We then compute the asset price as

$$S_{2,0} = \frac{S_{3,0}}{edxd} = \frac{70.56}{0.8902} = 79.26$$

and apply the early exercise test:

$$C_{2,0} = \max(C_{2,0}, K - S_{2,0}) = \max(18.7691, 100 - 79.26) = 20.7430$$

For this general case where the up and down jumps may not be equal, we must adjust the asset price vector as we step backwards through the tree. This is necessary because we need the asset prices at each time step in order to apply the early exercise condition for the American option. If we restrict ourselves to equal up and down jumps in the asset price $\Delta x = \Delta x_u = \Delta x_d$ we can obtain a much more efficient algorithm. In order to achieve the more efficient implementation we change the structure of the binomial tree slightly; the new structure is illustrated in Figure 2.14.

FIGURE 2.14 The Equal Jumps General Additive Binomial Tree

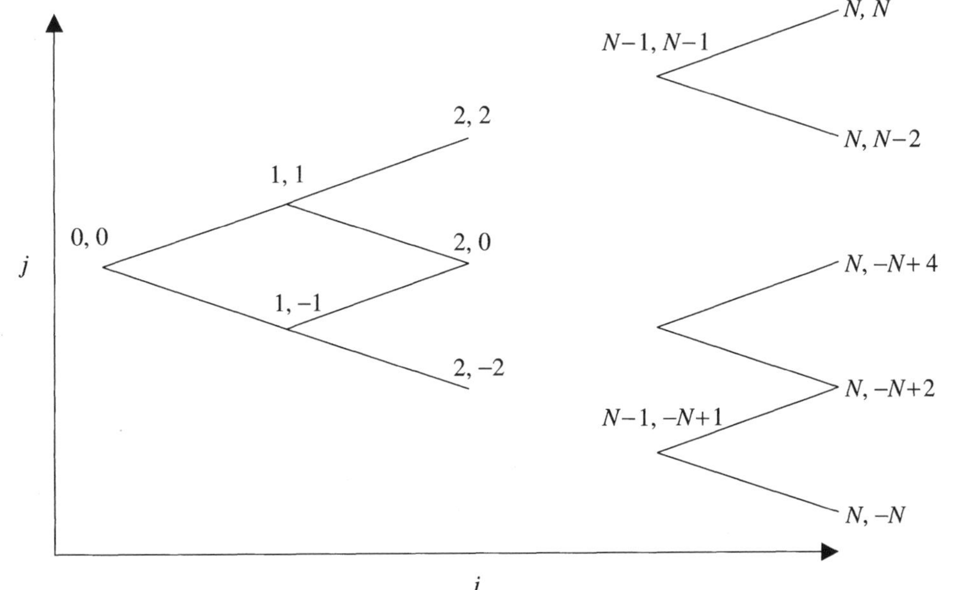

The only change from Figure 2.9 is the way the levels of the asset price are indexed. The index j no longer refers to the number of up jumps to reach a particular asset price, instead it indicates the level of the asset price

$$S_{i,j} = \exp(x_{i,j}) = \exp(x + j\Delta x) \tag{2.21}$$

The pseudo-code algorithm for an American put is given in Figure 2.15 with the changes highlighted in bold.

The important point to note in Figure 2.15 is that the j index now steps by two at each time step. This is because j now indicates the level of the asset price rather than the number of upward branches which have occurred and between each pair of nodes at a given time step there is an asset level which is not considered (see Figure 2.14).

FIGURE 2.15 Pseudo-code for the Equal Jump General Additive Binomial Valuation of an American Put

```
initialise_parameters { K, T, S, sig, r, N }

{ set coeffients - Trigeorgis }

dt = T/N
nu = r - 0.5*sig^2
dx = sqrt( sig^2*dt + (nu*dt)^2 )
pu = 1/2 + 1/2*( nu*dt/dx )
pd = 1 - pu

{ precompute constants }

disc = exp(-r*dt)
dpu = disc*pu
dpd = disc*pd
edx = exp( dx )

{ initialise asset prices at maturity N }

St[-N] = S*exp( -N*dx )
for j = -N+1 to N do St[j] = St[j-1]*edx

{ initialise option values at maturity }

for j = -N to N step 2 do C[j] = max( 0.0 , K - St[j] )

{ step back through the tree applying early exercise }

for i = N-1 downto 0 do
  for j = -i to +i step 2 do
    C[j] = dpd*C[j] + dpu*C[j+1]
    C[j] = max( C[j] , K - St[j] )
  next j
next i

American_put = C[0]
```

Finally, the accuracy of the binomial method can be improved by using the Black–Scholes formula to compute the prices of the option at time step $N-1$, rather than using discounted expectations back from time step N with the pay-off values. However, this technique can make the binomial method significantly slower.

2.5 COMPUTING HEDGE SENSITIVITIES

As important as computing price of an option is computing the standard hedge sensitivities; *delta*, *gamma*, *vega*, *theta* and *rho*. The calculation of *delta*, *gamma* and *theta* is straightforward since they can be approximated by finite difference ratios in a binomial tree. One estimate of the *delta* of an option is given by[2]

$$delta = \frac{\partial C}{\partial S} \approx \frac{\Delta C}{\Delta S} = \frac{C_{1,1} - C_{1,0}}{S_{1,1} - S_{1,0}} \tag{2.22}$$

For example, using the American put numerical example illustrated in Figure 2.13, we have

$$delta = \frac{2.066 - 11.601}{112.33 - 89.03} = -0.40923$$

Notice that with this approximation the asset and the option prices are one time step into the future. This may be regarded as the *delta* one time step in the future. Similarly, an estimate of the *gamma* is

$$gamma = \frac{\partial^2 C}{\partial S^2} \approx \frac{[(C_{2,2} - C_{2,1})/(S_{2,2} - S_{2,1})] - [(C_{2,1} - C_{2,0})/(S_{2,1} - S_{2,0})]}{\frac{1}{2}(S_{2,2} - S_{2,0})} \tag{2.23}$$

For example, again using the numerical example illustrated in Figure 2.13, we have

$$\begin{aligned} gamma &= \frac{[(0.000 - 4.761)/(126.17 - 100.00)] - [(4.761 - 20.743)/(100.00 - 79.26)]}{\frac{1}{2}(126.17 - 79.26)} \\ &= 0.0250975 \end{aligned}$$

This can be regarded as an estimate two time steps into the future. To obtain estimates of *delta* and *gamma* at the current time we build the tree starting from two time steps back from today. Figure 2.16 illustrates the start of the tree, where the current value of the option is $C_{0,1}$.

We do not actually have to build the tree starting two time steps back from today as this is inefficient. All we do is extend the tree at the upper and lower edges by one node. So in Figure 2.16 at time zero we add the nodes (0, 2) and (0, 0). An estimate of *delta* can now be obtained from

$$delta = \frac{C_{0,2} - C_{0,0}}{S_{0,2} - S_{0,0}} \tag{2.24}$$

and *gamma* by

$$gamma = \frac{\partial^2 C}{\partial S^2} \approx \frac{[(C_{0,2} - C_{0,1})/(S_{0,2} - S_{0,1})] - [(C_{0,1} - C_{0,0})/(S_{0,1} - S_{0,0})]}{\frac{1}{2}(S_{0,2} - S_{0,0})} \tag{2.25}$$

FIGURE 2.16 A Binomial Tree Starting Two Time Steps Back From Today

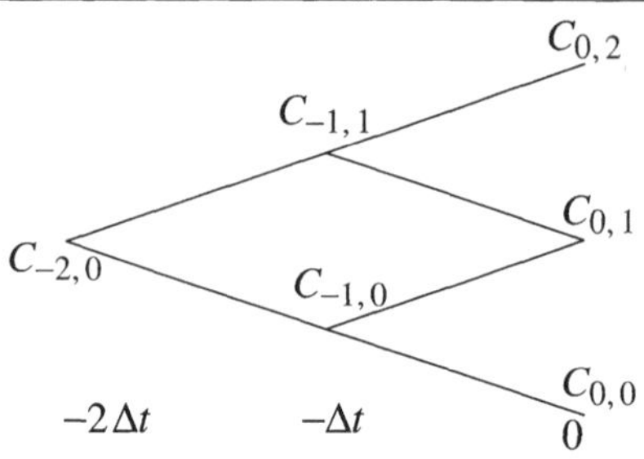

Vega and *rho* can be computed by re-evaluation of the price for small changes in the volatility and the interest rate respectively:

$$vega = \frac{\partial C}{\partial \sigma} \approx \frac{C(\sigma + \Delta\sigma) - C(\sigma - \Delta\sigma)}{2\Delta\sigma} \tag{2.26}$$

$$rho = \frac{\partial C}{\partial r} \approx \frac{C(r + \Delta r) - C(r - \Delta r)}{2\Delta r} \tag{2.27}$$

where, for example, $C(\sigma+\Delta\sigma)$ is the value computed using an initial volatility of $\sigma+\Delta\sigma$, where $\Delta\sigma$ is a small fraction of σ, e.g. $\Delta\sigma = 0.001\sigma$.

2.6 THE BINOMIAL MODEL FOR ASSETS PAYING A CONTINUOUS DIVIDEND YIELD

If the underlying asset pays a continuous dividend yield at a rate of δ per unit time then, as we saw in Chapter 1, in a Black–Scholes world the stochastic differential equation governing its evolution is

$$dS = (r - \delta)S\,dt + \sigma S\,dz \tag{2.28}$$

To a reasonable approximation assets that fit into this category include: options on (broad-based) stock indices, where δ represents the dividend yield on the index; options on foreign exchange rates, where δ represents the foreign exchange rate; options on futures contracts, where δ is equal to the risk-free rate ensuring that the contract has a zero risk-neutral drift; and options on commodities, where δ is interpreted as the convenience yield on the commodity.

It is straightforward to take into account a continuous dividend yield in the binomial model. We simply replace r by $r - \delta$ wherever it appears in the formulae for the probabilities and jump sizes. For example the general additive formulation equal jump size formulae become

$$\begin{aligned} \Delta x &= \sqrt{\sigma^2 \Delta t + \nu^2 \Delta t^2} \\ p_u &= \frac{1}{2} + \frac{1}{2}\frac{\nu \Delta t}{\Delta x} \\ \nu &= r - \delta - \tfrac{1}{2}\sigma^2 \end{aligned} \tag{2.29}$$

2.7 THE BINOMIAL MODEL WITH A KNOWN DISCRETE PROPORTIONAL DIVIDEND

If the asset pays a known discrete proportional dividend at a known time in the future then adjusting the binomial tree to take account of the dividend is again straightforward. Let $\hat{\delta}$ now be the known proportional dividend or the proportional amount by which the asset price decreases on the dividend date τ. Assume also that the dividend date corresponds to one of the dates in the binomial tree[3]. The binomial tree structure is shown in terms of the asset price in Figure 2.17.

If the time $i\Delta t$ is prior to the ex-dividend date then the nodes remain unchanged. If the time $i\Delta t$ is on or after the date on which the asset pays the dividend, then the value of the asset at node (i, j) becomes $S(1 - \hat{\delta})u^j d^{i-j}$, where

$$u = \exp(\Delta x_{\mathrm{u}}), d = \exp(\Delta x_{\mathrm{d}})$$

Example : Additive Binomial Tree Valuation of an American Put with a Known Discrete Proportional Dividend

We price a one-year maturity, at-the-money American put option with the current asset price at 100 and volatility of 20 per cent. The continuously compounded interest rate is assumed to be 6 per cent per annum and the binomial tree has three time steps. The asset is assumed to pay a discrete proportional dividend of 3 per cent after eight months, i.e. $K = 100$, $T = 1$, $S = 100$, $\sigma = 0.20$, $r = 0.06$, $\hat{\delta}(\mathrm{dvh}) = 0.03$, $\tau = 0.66667$, $N = 3$. Figure 2.18 illustrates the results of the calculations, where nodes in the tree are represented by the boxes in which the upper value is the asset price and the lower value is the option price.

FIGURE 2.17 Binomial Tree Adjusted for a Known Discrete Proportional Dividend

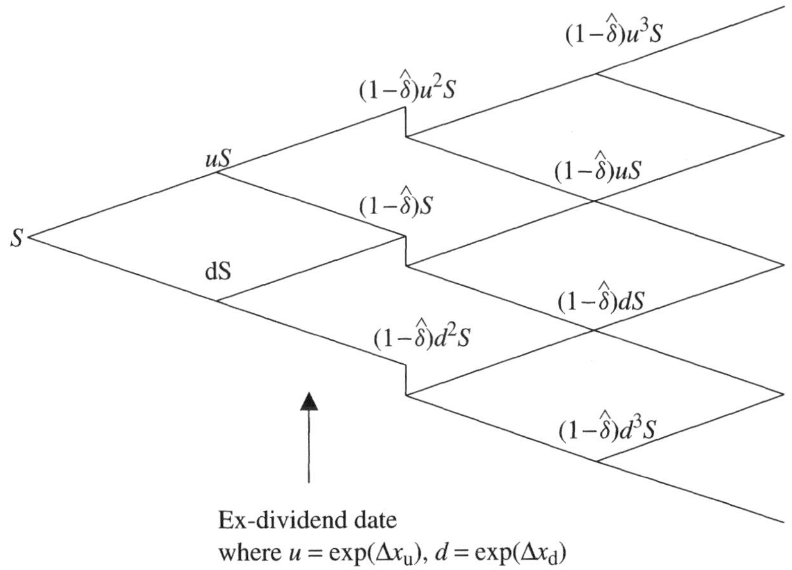

FIGURE 2.18 Additive Binomial Tree Valuation of an American Put with a Known Discrete Proportional Dividend

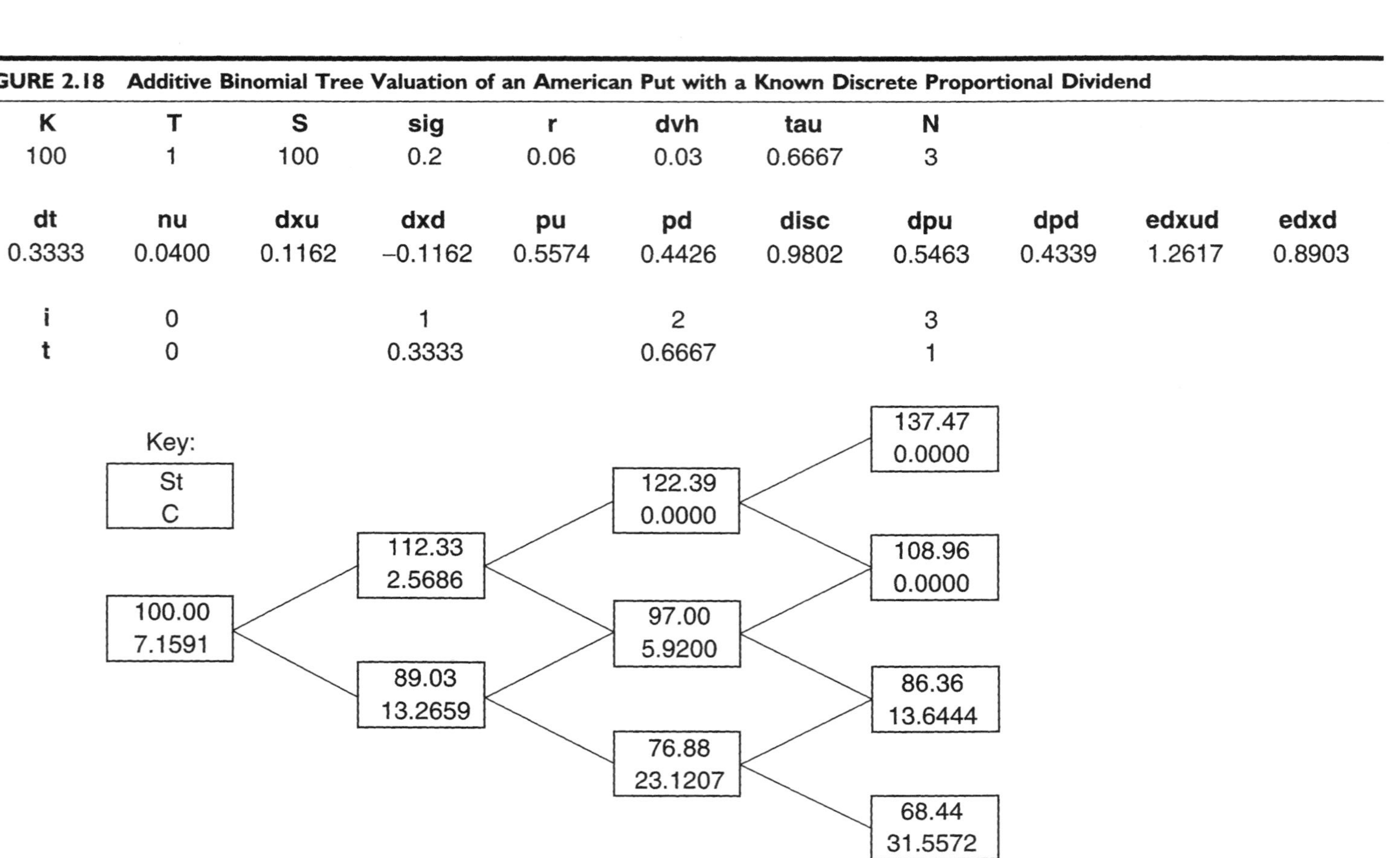

Firstly the constants are precomputed; $\Delta t(dt)$, $\nu(nu)$, $\Delta x_{\text{u}}(dxu)$, $\Delta x_{\text{d}}(dxd)$, $p_{\text{u}}(pu)$, $p_{\text{d}}(pd)$, *disc, dpu, dpd, edxud, edxd*:

$$\Delta t = \frac{T}{N} = \frac{1}{3} = 0.3333$$

$$\nu = r - \tfrac{1}{2}\sigma^2 = 0.06 - \tfrac{1}{2}0.20^2 = 0.0400$$

$$\Delta x_{\text{u}} = \sqrt{\sigma^2 \times \Delta t + (\nu \times \Delta t)^2)} = \sqrt{0.20^2 \times 0.3333 + (0.0400 \times 0.3333)^2} = 0.1162$$

$$\Delta x_{\text{d}} = -\Delta x_{\text{u}} = -0.1162$$

$$p_{\text{u}} = \frac{1}{2} + \frac{1}{2}\left(\frac{\nu \times \Delta t}{\Delta x_{\text{u}}}\right) = \frac{1}{2} + \frac{1}{2}\left(\frac{0.040 \times 0.3333}{0.1162}\right) = 0.5574$$

$$p_{\text{d}} = 1 - p_{\text{u}} = 1 - 0.5574 = 0.4426$$

$$dpu = disc \times p_{\text{u}} = 0.9802 \times 0.5574 = 0.5463$$

$$dpd = disc \times p_{\text{d}} = 0.9802 \times 0.4426 = 0.4339$$

$$edxud = e^{(\Delta x_{\text{u}} - \Delta x_{\text{d}})} = e^{(0.1162-(-0.1162))} = 1.2617$$

$$edxd = e^{\Delta x_{\text{d}}} = e^{-0.1162} = 0.8903$$

Then the asset prices at maturity are computed. The asset price at node (3, 0) is computed as

$$S_{3,0} = S \times (1 - \hat{\delta})e^{N \times \Delta x_{\text{d}}} = 100 \times (1 - 0.03)e^{3\times(-0.1162)} = 68.44$$

The other asset prices are computed from this value. Consider node (3, 2) the asset price is computed as

$$S_{3,2} = S_{3,1} \times edxud = 86.36 \times 1.2617 = 108.96$$

Next the option values at maturity are computed. For node (3, 1) we have

$$C_{3,1} = \max(0, K - S_{3,1}) = \max(0, 100 - 86.36) = 13.6444$$

Finally, perform discounted expectations back through the tree applying the early exercise test. For node (2, 0) we have

$$C_{2,0} = dpu \times C_{3,1} + dpd \times C_{3,0} = 0.5463 \times 13.6444 + 0.4339 \times 31.5572 = 21.1466$$

We then compute the asset price as

$$S_{2,0} = \frac{S_{3,0}}{edxd} = \frac{68.44}{0.8903} = 76.88$$

and apply the early exercise test:

$$C_{2,0} = \max(C_{2,0}, K - S_{2,0}) = \max(21.1466, 100 - 76.88) = 23.1207$$

For node (1, 0) we have

$$C_{1,0} = dpu \times C_{2,1} + dpd \times C_{2,0} = 0.5463 \times 5.9200 + 0.4339 \times 23.1207 = 13.2659$$

We then compute the asset price as

$$S_{1,0} = \frac{S_{2,0}}{edxd \times (1 - \hat{\delta})} = \frac{76.88}{0.8903 \times (1 - 0.03)} = 89.03$$

and apply the early exercise test:

$$C_{1,0} = \max(C_{1,0}, K - S_{1,0}) = \max(13.2659, 100 - 89.03) = 13.2659$$

2.8 THE BINOMIAL MODEL WITH A KNOWN DISCRETE CASH DIVIDEND

If the asset pays a known cash dividend then the situation is more difficult as the binomial tree becomes non-recombining for nodes after the ex-dividend date. Suppose that the asset pays a dividend as a cash amount D at a time τ such that $k\Delta t < \tau < (k+1)\Delta t$. Figure 2.19 illustrates the structure of the binomial tree.

If the time $i\Delta t$ is prior to the dividend date then the nodes remain unchanged. If the time $i\Delta t$ is on or after the date on which the asset pays the dividend then the value of the asset at node (i, j) becomes

$$S \exp(\Delta x_{\mathrm{u}})^j \exp(\Delta x_{\mathrm{d}})^{i-j} - D$$

Therefore at time $(k+m)\Delta t$ there are $m(k+1)$ nodes rather than $k+m+1$.

We can overcome this problem and obtain a recombining tree by making a particular assumption about the volatility of the asset price. Suppose that the asset price, S_t, has two components, a part that is uncertain, $\tilde{S}_t$, and a certain part that is the present value

FIGURE 2.19 Binomial Tree Adjusted for a Known Discrete Cash Dividend

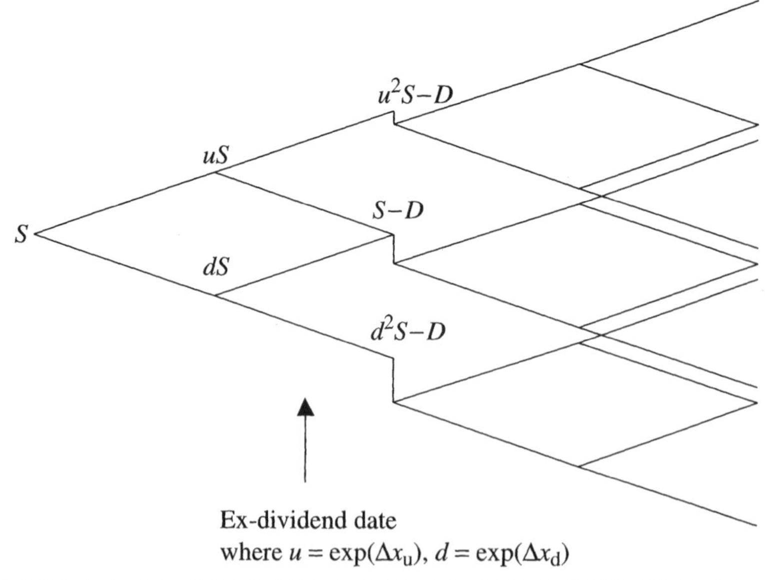

of the future dividend stream. The value of $\tilde{S}_t$ is given by

$$\tilde{S}_t = S_t \quad \text{when } t > \tau$$

and

$$\tilde{S}_t = S_t - De^{-r(\tau-t)} \quad \text{when } t \leq \tau$$

Define $\tilde{\sigma}$ as the volatility of $\tilde{S}_t$ and assume it is constant. The binomial tree parameters p_{u}, p_{d}, Δx_{u}, Δx_{d} are calculated in the usual way but with σ replaced by $\tilde{\sigma}$. The binomial tree is then constructed in the same way as before. The value of the asset is given by

$$\tilde{S}_t \exp(\Delta x_{\mathrm{u}})^j \exp(\Delta x_{\mathrm{d}})^{i-j} + De^{-r(\tau-t)}$$

when $t = i\Delta t < \tau$ and

$$\tilde{S}_t \exp(\Delta x_{\mathrm{u}})^j \exp(\Delta x_{\mathrm{d}})^{i-j}$$

when $t = i\Delta t \geq \tau$.

Example : Additive Binomial Tree Valuation of an American Put with a Known Discrete Cash Dividend

We price a one-year maturity, at-the-money American put option with the current asset price at 100 and volatility of 20 per cent. The continuously compounded interest rate is assumed to be 6 per cent per annum and the binomial tree has three time steps. The asset is assumed to pay a discrete cash dividend of 3 after six months i.e. $K = 100$, $T = 1$, $S = 100$, $\sigma = 0.20$, $r = 0.06$, $N = 3$, $D(\text{Div}) = 3$, $\tau = 0.5$. Figure 2.20 illustrates the results of the calculations, where nodes in the tree are represented by the boxes in which the upper value is the asset price and the lower value is the option price.

Firstly the constants are precomputed: $\Delta t(dt)$, $\nu(nu)$, $\Delta x_{\mathrm{u}}(dxu)$, $\Delta x_{\mathrm{d}}(dxd)$, $p_{\mathrm{u}}(pu)$, $p_{\mathrm{d}}(pd)$, *disc, dpu, dpd, edxud, edxd*:

$$\Delta t = \frac{T}{N} = \frac{1}{3} = 0.3333$$

$$\nu = r - \tfrac{1}{2}\sigma^2 = 0.06 - \tfrac{1}{2}0.20^2 = 0.0400$$

$$\Delta x_{\mathrm{u}} = \sqrt{\sigma^2 \times \Delta t + (\nu \times \Delta t)^2} = \sqrt{0.20^2 \times 0.3333 + (0.0400 \times 0.3333)^2} = 0.1162$$

$$\Delta x_{\mathrm{d}} = -\Delta x_{\mathrm{u}} = -0.1162$$

$$p_{\mathrm{u}} = \frac{1}{2} + \frac{1}{2}\left(\frac{\nu \times \Delta t}{\Delta x_{\mathrm{u}}}\right) = \frac{1}{2} + \frac{1}{2}\left(\frac{0.040 \times 0.3333}{0.1162}\right) = 0.5574$$

$$p_{\mathrm{d}} = 1 - p_{\mathrm{u}} = 1 - 0.5574 = 0.4426$$

$$dpu = disc \times p_{\mathrm{u}} = 0.9802 \times 0.5574 = 0.5463$$

$$dpd = disc \times p_{\mathrm{d}} = 0.9802 \times 0.4426 = 0.4339$$

$$edxud = e^{(\Delta x_{\mathrm{u}} - \Delta x_{\mathrm{d}})} = e^{(0.1162-(-0.1162))} = 1.2617$$

$$edxd = e^{\Delta x_{\mathrm{d}}} = e^{-0.1162} = 0.8903$$

FIGURE 2.20 Additive Binomial Tree Valuation of an American Put with a Known Discrete Cash Dividend

K	T	S	sig	r	Div	tau	N			
100	1	100	0.2	0.06	3.00	0.5	3			
dt	**nu**	**dxu**	**dxd**	**pu**	**pd**	**disc**	**dpu**	**dpd**	**edxud**	**edxd**
0.3333	0.0400	0.1162	–0.1162	0.5574	0.4426	0.9802	0.5463	0.4339	1.2617	0.8903
i	0		1		2		3			
t	0		0.3333		0.6667		1			

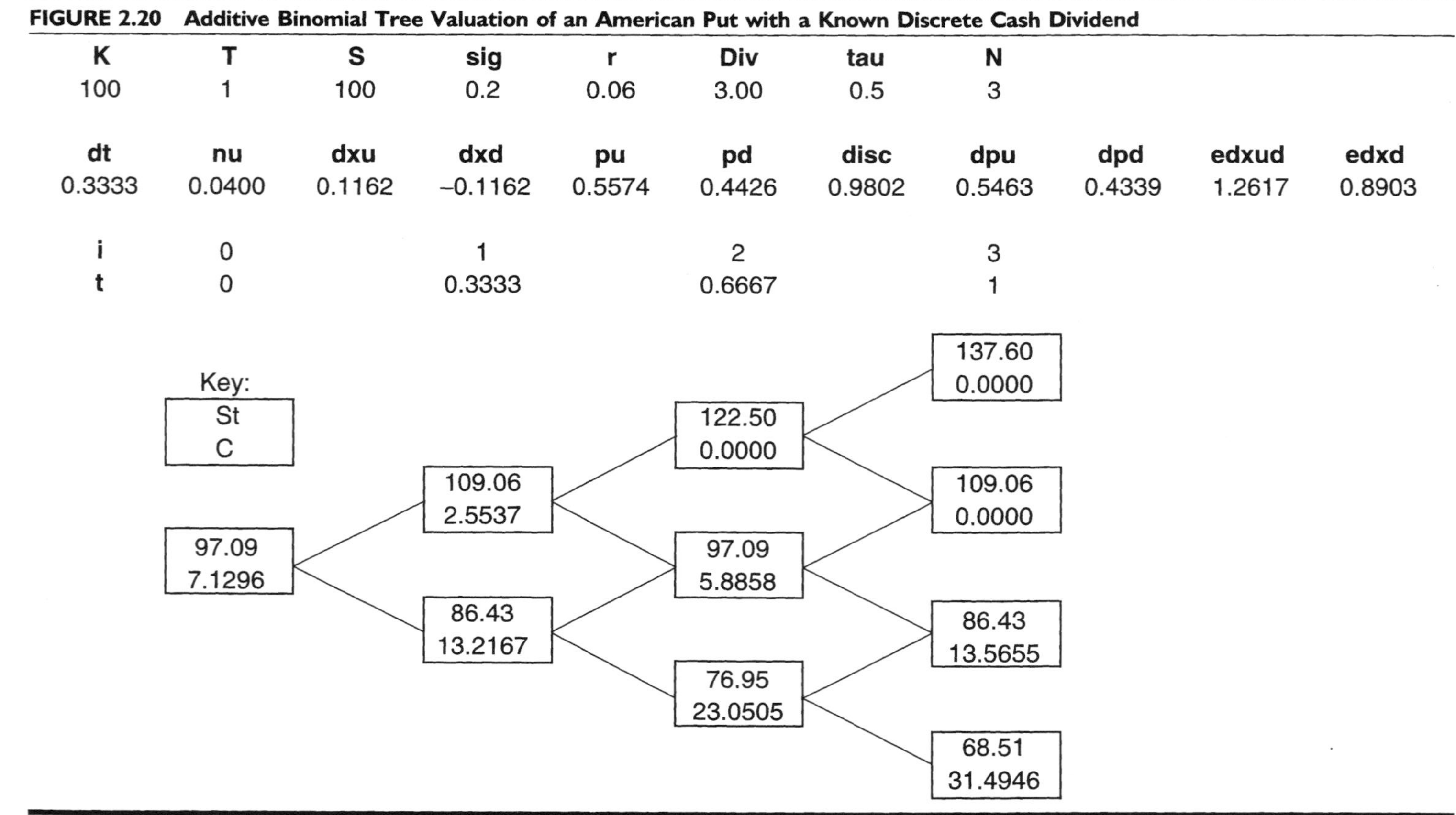

Then the asset prices at maturity are computed. The asset price at node (3, 0) is computed as

$$S_{3,0} = (S - D \times e^{-r\times\tau})e^{N\times\Delta x_d} = (100 - 3.0 \times e^{-0.06\times 0.5})e^{3\times(-0.1162)} = 68.51$$

where $(S - D \times e^{-r\times\tau})$ is the current value of $\tilde{S}$. The other asset prices are computed from this value, the node (3,2) asset price is computed as

$$S_{3,2} = S_{3,1} \times edxud = 86.43 \times 1.2617 = 109.06$$

Next the option values at maturity are computed. For node (3, 1) we have:

$$C_{3,1} = \max(0, K - S_{3,1}) = \max(0, 100 - 86.43) = 13.5655$$

Finally we perform discounted expectations back through the tree applying the early exercise test. For node (2, 0) we have

$$C_{2,0} = dpu \times C_{3,1} + dpd \times C_{3,0} = 0.5463 \times 13.5655 + 0.4339 \times 31.4946 = 21.0763$$

We then compute the asset price as

$$S_{2,0} = \frac{S_{3,0}}{edxd} = \frac{68.51}{0.8903} = 76.95$$

and apply the early exercise test:

$$C_{2,0} = \max(C_{2,0}, K - S_{2,0}) = \max(21.0763, 100 - 76.95) = 23.0505$$

For node (1, 0) we have

$$C_{1,0} = dpu \times C_{2,1} + dpd \times C_{2,0} = 0.5463 \times 5.8858 + 0.4339 \times 23.0505 = 13.2167$$

We then compute the asset price as

$$S_{1,0} = \frac{S_{2,0}}{edxd} + D \times e^{-r(\tau-t)} = \frac{76.95}{0.8903} + 3.00 \times e^{-0.06(0.5-0.3333)} = 89.40$$

and apply the early exercise test:

$$C_{1,0} = \max(C_{1,0}, K - S_{1,0}) = \max(13.2167, 100 - 89.40) = 13.2167$$

2.9 ADAPTING THE BINOMIAL MODEL TO TIME VARYING VOLATILITY

A common requirement in practice is the incorporation of time varying volatility (and to a lesser extent interest rates) into a model. This arises for example when implied volatilities are obtained from the market prices of options. In order to price other options consistently with the market the model must be consistent with these observed volatilities. This can be achieved with the binomial model (although we will see in Chapter 3 that it is simpler to achieve with trinomial trees).

The simplest and most robust way to adapt the binomial model to time-varying volatility is to fix the space step and vary the probabilities and time step. This ensures that the binomial tree recombines. If we fix the space step at Δx and have a time-varying volatility σ_i and interest rate r_i for time step i, which leads to time varying probabilities p_i, time step Δt_i, and risk-neutral drift ν_i, equations (2.15) become

$$\begin{aligned} p_i \Delta x - (1 - p_i)\Delta x &= \nu_i \Delta t_i \\ p_i \Delta x^2 + (1 - p_i)\Delta x^2 &= \sigma_i^2 \Delta t_i + \nu_i^2 \Delta t_i^2 \end{aligned} \tag{2.30}$$

which leads to

$$\begin{aligned} \Delta t_i &= \frac{1}{2\nu_i^2}\left(-\sigma_i^2 \pm \sqrt{\sigma_i^4 + 4\nu_i^2 \Delta x^2}\right) \\ p_i &= \frac{1}{2} + \frac{\nu_i \Delta t_i}{2\Delta x} \end{aligned} \tag{2.31}$$

If Δx is set according to

$$\Delta x = \sqrt{\overline{\sigma}^2 \overline{\Delta t} + \overline{\nu}^2 \overline{\Delta t}^2} \tag{2.32}$$

where

$$\overline{\sigma} = \frac{1}{N}\sum_{i=1}^{N} \sigma_i \quad \text{and} \quad \overline{\nu} = \frac{1}{N}\sum_{i=1}^{N} \nu_i$$

then $\overline{\Delta t}$ will be approximately the average time step which is obtained when the tree is built. Figure 2.21 illustrates the typical parameters obtained and Figure 2.22 illustrates the binomial tree obtained using this method.

The input parameters are the interest rate r_i which varies between approximately 4 and 6 per cent and the volatility σ_i which varies between approximately 14 and 17 per cent over the total time period which is approximately one year.

The problem with this method is that the time steps are now constrained by the interest rates and volatilities and we are no longer free to choose them to correspond, for example, to option exercise dates or cashflow dates. In Figure 2.22 the time step varies between

FIGURE 2.21 Typical Time-varying Binomial Tree Parameters

i	r_i	σ_i	ν_i	Δt_i	p_i
0	0.059292	0.14103	0.049347	0.116065	0.559184
1	0.040042	0.173789	0.024941	0.077396	0.519947
2	0.040604	0.146126	0.029927	0.109148	0.533754
3	0.051304	0.162250	0.038141	0.088505	0.534882
4	0.058875	0.166929	0.044943	0.083516	0.538786
5	0.058571	0.166925	0.044639	0.083527	0.538528
6	0.046959	0.129180	0.038616	0.138586	0.555300
7	0.052179	0.136914	0.042806	0.123411	0.554588
8	0.050334	0.142216	0.040221	0.114708	0.547675
9	0.054212	0.159661	0.041466	0.091283	0.539114

FIGURE 2.22 Typical Binomial Tree With Time Varying Interest Rate and Volatility

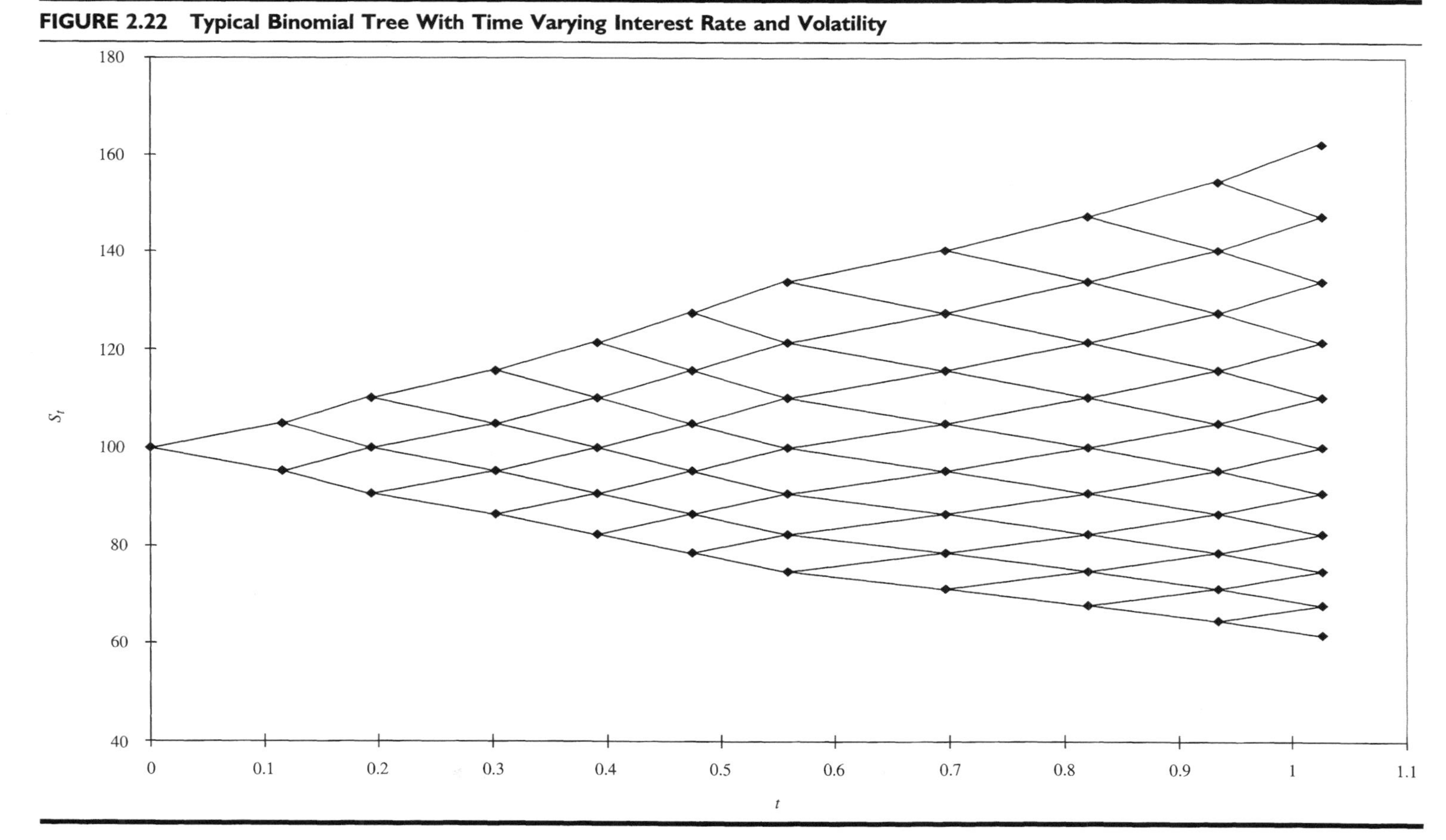

approximately 0.08 and 0.14 of a year. This inconvenient variation in the time step can clearly be seen in Figure 2.22. The trinomial tree methods we describe in Chapter 3 solve this problem.

2.10 PRICING PATH-DEPENDENT OPTIONS

Trees (or lattices) can be used to price path-dependent American style exotic options. Binomial trees are not ideal because of the problems with accuracy, convergence and the simplicity of the binomial tree structure which we have discussed in the previous sections. However, the simplicity of the structure does make the method clear so we will introduce the ideas here and refer the reader to Chapter 5 for more detailed examples.

As a simple first example of the method and the problems which can be encountered we describe the pricing of an American down-and-out call option. This is a standard American call option except that if the asset price falls below a predetermined level H, the barrier level, then the option ceases to exist, or knocks out, and pays off nothing[4]. Figure 2.23 illustrates three example paths of the asset price.

Path 1 does not go below the barrier level and finishes above the strike price and therefore pays off, path 2 does not go below the barrier level, but finishes below the strike price and therefore pays off zero and finally path 3 goes below the barrier and therefore pays off nothing even though it finishes above the strike price. The valuation of this option in a binomial tree is similar to that for the American put option in section 2.4, the only difference is that the value of the option at every node below the barrier is set to zero. These sections are highlighted in bold in Figure 2.24 which gives the pseudo-code implementation.

FIGURE 2.23 Example Asset Paths for a Down-and-Out Call Option

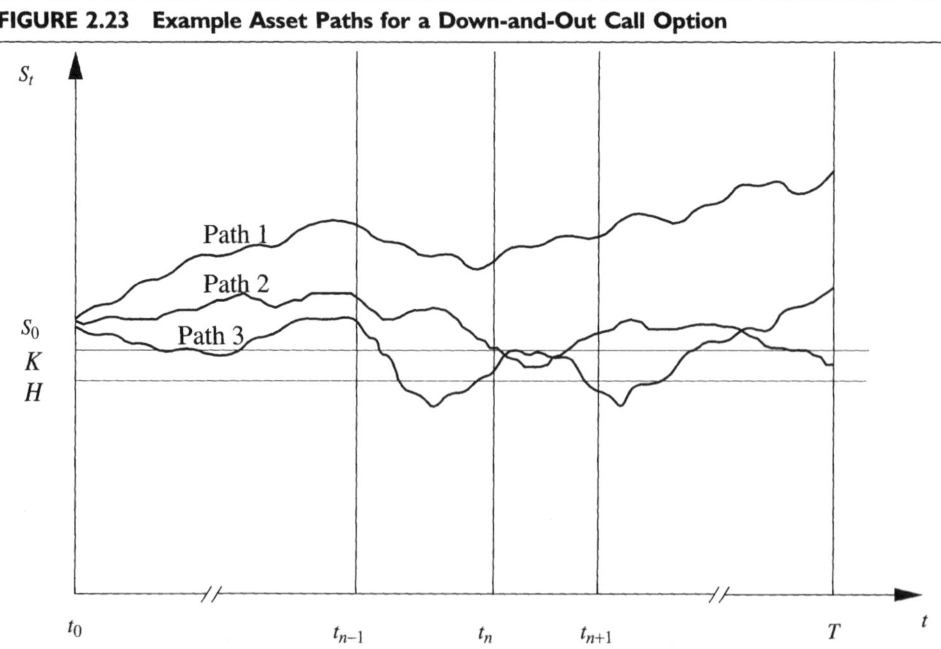

FIGURE 2.24 Pseudo-code for General Additive Binomial Valuation of an American Down-and-Out Call

```
initialise_parameters { K, T, S, sig, r, H, N }

{ set coefficients - Trigeorgis }

dt = T/N
nu = r - 0.5*sig^2
dxu = sqrt( sig^2*dt + (nu*dt)^2 )
dxd = -dxu
pu = 1/2 + 1/2*( nu*dt/dxu )
pd = 1 - pu

{ precompute constants }

disc = exp(-r*dt)
dpu = disc*pu
dpd = disc*pd
edxud = exp( dxu - dxd )
edxd = exp( dxd )

{ initialise asset prices at maturity N }

St[0] = S*exp( N*dxd )
for j = 1 to N do St[j] = St[j-1]*edxud

{ initialise option values at maturity }

for j = 0 to N do
  if ( St[j] > H ) then
    C[j] = max( 0.0 , St[j] - K )
  else
    C[j] = 0.0
next j

{ step back through the tree applying the barrier and early
  exercise condition }

for i = (N-1) downto 0 do
  for j = 0 to i do

  { adjust asset price to current time step }
  St[j] = St[j]/edxd

  if ( St[j] > H ) then

    C[j] = dpd*C[j] + dpu*C[j+1]

    { Apply the early exercise condition }
    C[j] = max( C[j] , St[j] - K )
```

(continues)

FIGURE 2.24 (*continued*)

```
    else

      C[j] = 0.0

    next j
  next i

  American_Down_and_Out_Call = C[0]
```

Example : Additive Binomial Tree Valuation of an American Down-and-Out Call

We price a one year maturity, at-the-money American down-and-out call option with the current asset price at 100 and volatility of 20 per cent. The barrier is set at 95, the continuously compounded interest rate is 6 per cent per annum and the binomial tree has three time steps, i.e. $K = 100$, $T = 1$, $S = 100$, $\sigma = 0.20$, $r = 0.06$, $H = 95$, $N = 3$. Figure 2.25 illustrates the results of the calculations, where nodes in the tree are represented by the boxes in which the upper value is the asset price and the lower value is the option price.

Firstly the constants are precomputed: $\Delta t(dt)$, $\nu(nu)$, $\Delta x_u(dxu)$, $\Delta x_d(dxd)$, $p_u(pu)$, $p_d(pd)$, *disc*, *dpu*, *dpd*, *edxud*, *edxd*:

$$\Delta t = \frac{T}{N} = \frac{1}{3} = 0.3333$$

$$\nu = r - \tfrac{1}{2}\sigma^2 = 0.06 - \tfrac{1}{2}0.20^2 = 0.0400$$

$$\Delta x_u = \sqrt{\sigma^2 \times \Delta t + (\nu \times \Delta t)^2)} = \sqrt{0.20^2 \times 0.3333 + (0.0400 \times 0.3333)^2} = 0.1162$$

$$\Delta x_d = -\Delta x_u = -0.1162$$

$$p_u = \frac{1}{2} + \frac{1}{2}\left(\frac{\nu \times \Delta t}{\Delta x_u}\right) = \frac{1}{2} + \frac{1}{2}\left(\frac{0.040 \times 0.3333}{0.1162}\right) = 0.5574$$

$$p_d = 1 - p_u = 1 - 0.5574 = 0.4426$$

$$dpu = disc \times p_u = 0.9802 \times 0.5574 = 0.5463$$

$$dpd = disc \times p_d = 0.9802 \times 0.4426 = 0.4339$$

$$edxud = e^{(\Delta x_u - \Delta x_d)} = e^{(0.1162-(-0.1162))} = 1.2617$$

$$edxd = e^{\Delta x_d} = e^{-0.1162} = 0.8903$$

Then the asset prices at maturity are computed, for example the asset price at node (3, 0) is computed as

$$S_{3,0} = S \times e^{N \times \Delta x_d} = 100 \times e^{3\times(-0.1162)} = 70.56$$

FIGURE 2.25 Additive Binomial Tree Valuation of an American Down-and-Out Call

K	T	S	sig	r	H	N
100	1	100	0.2	0.06	95	3

dt	nu	dxu	dxd	pu	pd	disc	dpu	dpd	edxud	edxd
0.3333	0.0400	0.1162	–0.1162	0.5574	0.4426	0.9802	0.5463	0.4339	1.2617	0.8903

i	0	1	2	3
t	0	0.3333	0.6667	1

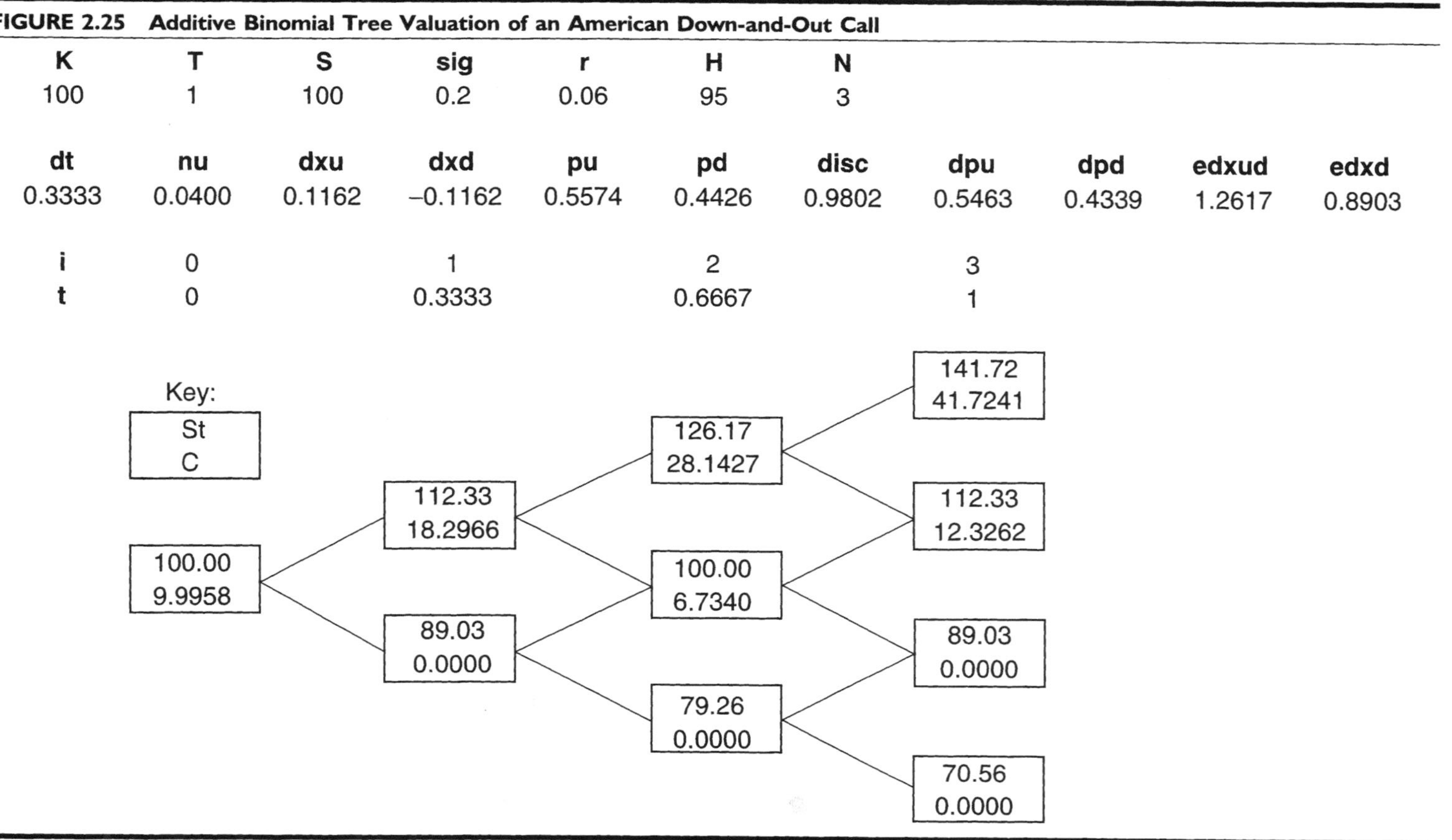

The other asset prices are computed from this, for example the asset price at node (3, 2) is computed as

$$S_{3,2} = S_{3,1} \times e^{(\Delta x_u - \Delta x_d)} = 89.03 \times e^{0.1162-(-0.1162))} = 112.33$$

Next the option values at maturity are computed. For node (3, 1) we have $S_{3,1} < H$, i.e. $89.03 < 95$ and therefore $C_{3,1} = 0.0$. For node (3, 2) we have $S_{3,2} > H$, i.e. $112.33 > 95$ and therefore

$$C_{3,2} = \max(0, S_{3,2} - K) = \max(0, 112.33 - 100) = 12.3262$$

Finally we perform discounted expectations back through the tree, applying the barrier condition. For example at node (1, 0) we have $S_{1,0} < H$, i.e. $89.03 < 95$, therefore $C_{1,0} = 0.0$.

2.11 THE MULTIDIMENSIONAL BINOMIAL METHOD

If we want to price options whose pay-off depends on more than one asset, for example options on the maximum or minimum of a basket of equity indices, then we must model all the assets simultaneously. This can be done by modelling the assets in a multidimensional binomial tree[5]. Consider the case of an option which pays off based on the values of two assets, S_1 and S_2 , which follow correlated GBMs

$$dS_1 = (r - \delta_1)S_1 dt + \sigma_1 S_1 dz_1 \tag{2.33}$$

$$dS_2 = (r - \delta_2)S_2 dt + \sigma_2 S_2 dz_2 \tag{2.34}$$

where the two assets have correlation ρ, i.e. $dz_1 dz_2 = \rho\, dt$ and the other symbols have their usual meaning.

We can model the joint evolution of S_1 and S_2 with a two-variable binomial lattice. The first step of a simple multiplicative two variable binomial tree is illustrated in Figure 2.26.

We now have four branches instead of two at every node, corresponding to the four possible combinations of the two assets going up or down. This tree can be extended in exactly the same way as the single asset tree in section 2.2. In order to specify the jump sizes and probabilities we equate the means, variances and correlations for the binomial process with those of the continuous time process. As with the single asset binomial tree it is easier to work in terms of the processes for the natural logarithms of the asset prices:

FIGURE 2.26 Multiplicative Two-Variable Binomial Process

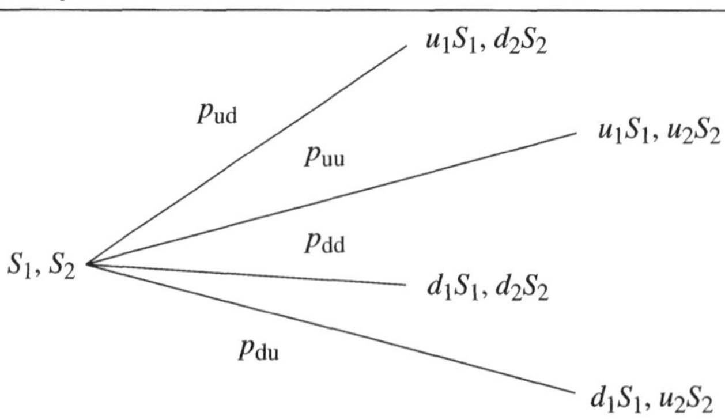

FIGURE 2.27 Additive Two-variable Binomial Process

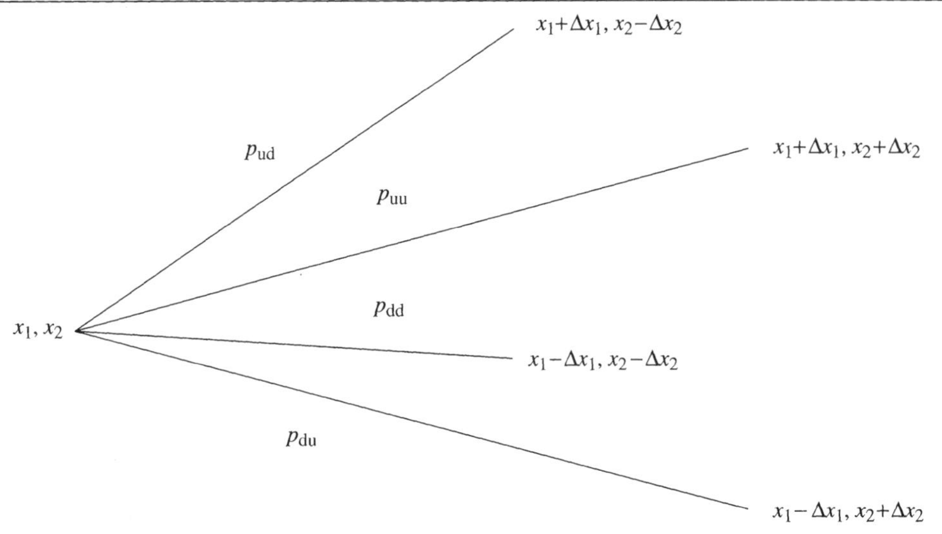

$$dx_1 = \nu_1 dt + \sigma_1 dz_1 \tag{2.35}$$

$$dx_2 = \nu_2 dt + \sigma_2 dz_2 \tag{2.36}$$

where $\nu_1 = r - \delta_1 - \frac{1}{2}\sigma_1^2$ and $\nu_2 = r - \delta_2 - \frac{1}{2}\sigma_2^2$. Figure 2.27 shows the first step of the additive two-asset binomial tree, where we have chosen equal up and down jump sizes for each asset. The probabilities (p_{uu}, p_{ud}, p_{du}, p_{dd}) and the jump sizes (equal up and down jumps) (Δx_1, Δx_2) are chosen to match the means and variances of the risk-neutral process:

$$E[\Delta x_1] = (p_{uu} + p_{ud})\Delta x_1 - (p_{du} + p_{dd})\Delta x_1 = \nu_1 \Delta t \tag{2.37}$$

$$E[\Delta x_1^2] = (p_{uu} + p_{ud})\Delta x_1^2 - (p_{du} + p_{dd})\Delta x_1^2 = \sigma_1^2 \Delta t \tag{2.38}$$

$$E[\Delta x_2] = (p_{uu} + p_{du})\Delta x_2 - (p_{ud} + p_{dd})\Delta x_2 = \nu_2 \Delta t \tag{2.39}$$

$$E[\Delta x_2^2] = (p_{uu} + p_{du})\Delta x_2^2 - (p_{ud} + p_{dd})\Delta x_2^2 = \sigma_2^2 \Delta t \tag{2.40}$$

$$E[\Delta x_1 \Delta x_2] = (p_{uu} - p_{ud} - p_{du} - p_{dd})\Delta x_1 \Delta x_2 = \rho\sigma_1\sigma_2 \Delta t \tag{2.41}$$

and we have that the probabilities must sum to one

$$p_{uu} + p_{ud} + p_{du} + p_{dd} = 1 \tag{2.42}$$

The solution[6] to this system of equations is

$$\Delta x_1 = \sigma_1 \sqrt{\Delta t} \tag{2.43}$$

$$\Delta x_2 = \sigma_2 \sqrt{\Delta t} \tag{2.44}$$

$$p_{uu} = \frac{1}{4} \frac{(\Delta x_1 \Delta x_2 + \Delta x_2 \nu_1 \Delta t + \Delta x_1 \nu_2 \Delta t + \rho\sigma_1\sigma_2\Delta t)}{\Delta x_1 \Delta x_2} \tag{2.45}$$

$$p_{ud} = \frac{1}{4} \frac{(\Delta x_1 \Delta x_2 + \Delta x_2 \nu_1 \Delta t - \Delta x_1 \nu_2 \Delta t - \rho\sigma_1\sigma_2\Delta t)}{\Delta x_1 \Delta x_2} \tag{2.46}$$

$$p_{\text{du}} = \frac{1}{4}\frac{(\Delta x_1 \Delta x_2 - \Delta x_2 v_1 \Delta t + \Delta x_1 v_2 \Delta t - \rho\sigma_1\sigma_2\Delta t)}{\Delta x_1 \Delta x_2} \tag{2.47}$$

$$p_{\text{dd}} = \frac{1}{4}\frac{(\Delta x_1 \Delta x_2 - \Delta x_2 v_1 \Delta t - \Delta x_1 v_2 \Delta t + \rho\sigma_1\sigma_2\Delta t)}{\Delta x_1 \Delta x_2} \tag{2.48}$$

Nodes in this tree are referred to by (i, j, k) which indicates the node at time step i, level j in asset 1 and level k in asset 2, i.e.

$$S_{1,i,j,k} = S_1 \exp(j\Delta x_1) \quad \text{and} \quad S_{2,i,j,k} = S_2 \exp(k\Delta x_2)$$

This tree therefore has the same structure as the equal jump size tree in section 2.4, but with two asset prices so at each time step nodes are separated by two space steps and the space indices will step by two.

As an example of using the two-variable binomial tree we consider an American spread option on the difference between the two assets S_1 and S_2 with strike price K which has the pay-off

$$\max(0, S_{1,T} - S_{2,T} - K)$$

Figure 2.28 gives a pseudo-implementation of this example. Note that the probabilities have been multiplied by the one step discount factor for efficiency.

FIGURE 2.28 Pseudo-code for American Spread Call Option by Two-variable Binomial

```
initialise_parameters { K, T, S1, S2, sig1, sig2, div1, div2, rho, r, N }

{ precompute constants }

dt = T/N
nu1 = r - div1 - 0.5*sig1^2
nu2 = r - div2 - 0.5*sig2^2
dx1 = sig1*sqrt(dt)
dx2 = sig2*sqrt(dt)
disc = exp(-r*dt)

puu = ( dx1*dx2 + ( dx2*nu1 + dx1*nu2 + rho*sig1*sig2 )*dt )/
      ( 4*dx1*dx2 ) * disc
pud = ( dx1*dx2 + ( dx2*nu1 - dx1*nu2 - rho*sig1*sig2 )*dt )/
      ( 4*dx1*dx2 ) * disc
pdu = ( dx1*dx2 + ( -dx2*nu1 + dx1*nu2 - rho*sig1*sig2 )*dt )/
      ( 4*dx1*dx2 ) * disc
pdd = ( dx1*dx2 + ( -dx2*nu1 - dx1*nu2 + rho*sig1*sig2 )*dt )/
      ( 4*dx1*dx2 ) * disc

edx1 = exp( dx1 )
edx2 = exp( dx2)

{ initialise asset prices at time step N }

S1t[-N] = S1*exp( -N*dx1 )
S2t[-N] = S2*exp( -N*dx2 )
for j = -N+1 to N do
```

FIGURE 2.28 (continued)

```
  S1t[j] = S1t[j-1]*edx1
  S2t[j] = S2t[j-1]*edx2
next j

{ initialise option values at maturity }

for j = -N to N step 2 do
  for k = -N to N step 2 do
    C[j, k] = max( 0.0 , S1t[j] - S2t[k] - K )

{ step back through the tree applying early exercise }

for i = N-1 downto 0 do
  for j = -i to i step 2 do
    for k = -i to i step 2 do

      C[j, k] = pdd*C[j-1, k-1] + pud*C[j+1, k-1] +
                pdu*C[j-1, k+1] + puu*C[j+1, k+1]

    C[j, k] = max( C[j, k] , S1t[j] - S2t[k] - K )

    next k
  next j
next i

American_spread_option = C[0, 0]
```

Example : American Spread Call Option by Two-variable Binomial

We price a one-year maturity, American spread call option with a strike price of 1, current asset prices of 100, volatilities of 20 and 30 per cent, continuous dividend yields of 3 and 4 per cent and a correlation of 50 per cent. The continuously compounded interest rate is assumed to be 6 per cent per annum and the binomial tree has three time steps, i.e. $K = 1$, $T = 1$, $S_1 = 100$, $S_2 = 100$, $\sigma_1 = 0.20$, $\sigma_2 = 0.30$, $d_1 = 0.03$, $d_2 = 0.04$, $\rho = 0.50$, $r = 0.06$, $N = 3$. Figure 2.29 illustrates the results of the calculations, where nodes in the tree are represented by the grids of boxes and the asset prices by the separate rows and columns of boxes.

Firstly the constants are precomputed: $\Delta t(dt)$, $\nu_1(nu1)$, $\nu_2(nu2)$, $\Delta x_1(dx1)$, $\Delta x_2(dx2)$, *disc*, $p_{uu}(puu)$, $p_{ud}(pud)$, $p_{du}(pdu)$, $p_{dd}(pdd)$, *edx1, and edx2*:

$$\Delta t = \frac{T}{N} = \frac{1}{3} = 0.3333$$

$$\nu_1 = r - \delta_1 - \tfrac{1}{2}\sigma_1^2 = 0.06 - 0.03 - \tfrac{1}{2}0.20^2 = 0.0100$$

$$\nu_2 = r - \delta_2 - \tfrac{1}{2}\sigma_2^2 = 0.06 - 0.04 - \tfrac{1}{2}0.30^2 = -0.0250$$

$$\Delta x_1 = \sigma_1\sqrt{\Delta t} = 0.2\sqrt{0.3333} = 0.1155$$

FIGURE 2.29 American Spread Call Option by Two-variable Binomial

K	T	S_1	S_2	sig1	sig2	div1	div2	rho	r	N	
1	1	100	100	0.2	0.3	0.03	0.04	0.50	0.06	3	
dt	**nu1**	**nu2**	**dx_1**	**dx_2**	**disc**	**puu**	**pud**	**pdu**	**pdd**	**edx1**	**edx2**
0.3333	0.0100	−0.0250	0.1155	0.1732	0.9802	0.3629	0.1414	0.1037	0.3723	1.1224	1.1891

i 0
t 0

S2t							
168.14							
141.40							
118.91							
100.00				10.04479			
84.10							
70.72							
59.47							
S1t	70.72	79.38	89.09	100.00	112.24	125.98	141.40

i 1
t 0.333333

S2t							
168.14							
141.40							
118.91			0.9635		6.7420		
100.00							
84.10			9.4563		28.1353		
70.72							
59.47							
S1t	70.72	79.38	89.09	100.00	112.24	125.98	141.40

i 2
t 0.666667

S2t							
168.14							
141.40		0.0000		0.0000		3.0381	
118.91							
100.00		0.5653		5.3263		25.8626	
84.10							
70.72		9.3123		28.2778		54.2561	
59.47							
S1t	70.72	79.38	89.09	100.00	112.24	125.98	141.40

i 3
t 1

S2t							
168.14	0.0000		0.0000		0.0000		0.0000
141.40							
118.91	0.0000		0.0000		0.0000		21.4873
100.00							
84.10	0.0000		3.9982		27.1436		56.3017
70.72							
59.47	10.2473		28.6198		51.7652		80.9233
S1t	70.72	79.38	89.09	100.00	112.24	125.98	141.40

$$\Delta x_2 = \sigma_2 \sqrt{\Delta t} = 0.3\sqrt{0.3333} = 0.1732$$

$$disc = \exp(-r \times \Delta t) = 0.9802$$

The probabilities multiplied by *disc* are:

$$p_{\mathrm{uu}} = \frac{(\Delta x_1 \times \Delta x_2 + (\Delta x_2 \times \nu_1 + \Delta x_1 \times \nu_2 + \rho \times \sigma_1 \times \sigma_2) \times \Delta t)}{(4 \times \Delta x_1 \times \Delta x_2)} \times disc$$

$$= \frac{\left\{\begin{array}{c}(0.1154 \times 0.1732 + (0.1732 \times 0.01 + 0.1154 \times (-0.0250) \\ + 0.5 \times 0.2 \times 0.3) \times 0.3333)\end{array}\right\}}{(4 \times 0.1154 \times 0.1732)} \times 0.9802$$

$$= 0.3629$$

$$p_{\text{ud}} = \frac{(\Delta x_1 \times \Delta x_2 + (\Delta x_2 \times v_1 - \Delta x_1 \times v_2 - \rho \times \sigma_1 \times \sigma_2) \times \Delta t)}{(4 \times \Delta x_1 \times \Delta x_2)} \times disc$$

$$= \frac{\left\{\begin{array}{c}(0.1154 \times 0.1732 + (0.1732 \times 0.01 - 0.1154 \times (-0.0250) \\ - 0.5 \times 0.2 \times 0.3) \times 0.3333)\end{array}\right\}}{(4 \times 0.1154 \times 0.1732)} \times 0.9802$$

$$= 0.1414$$

$$p_{\text{du}} = \frac{(\Delta x_1 \times \Delta x_2 + (-\Delta x_2 \times v_1 + \Delta x_1 \times v_2 - \rho \times \sigma_1 \times \sigma_2) \times \Delta t)}{(4 \times \Delta x_1 \times \Delta x_2)} \times disc$$

$$= \frac{\left\{\begin{array}{c}(0.1154 \times 0.1732 + (-0.1732 \times 0.01 + 0.1154 \times (-0.0250) \\ - 0.5 \times 0.2 \times 0.3) \times 0.3333)\end{array}\right\}}{(4 \times 0.1154 \times 0.1732)} \times 0.9802$$

$$= 0.1037$$

$$p_{\text{dd}} = \frac{(\Delta x_1 \times \Delta x_2 + (-\Delta x_2 \times v_1 - \Delta x_1 \times v_2 + \rho \times \sigma_1 \times \sigma_2) \times \Delta t)}{(4 \times \Delta x_1 \times \Delta x_2)} \times disc$$

$$= \frac{\left\{\begin{array}{c}(0.1154 \times 0.1732 + (-0.1732 \times 0.01 \\ - 0.1154 \times (-0.0250) + 0.5 \times 0.2 \times 0.3) \times 0.333)\end{array}\right\}}{(4 \times 0.1154 \times 0.1732)} \times 0.9802$$

$$= 0.3723$$

$$edx1 = e^{\Delta x_1} = e^{0.1154} = 1.1224$$

$$edx2 = e^{\Delta x_2} = e^{0.1732} = 1.1891$$

Then the asset prices at maturity are computed (these are the same for every time step). The asset price 1 at node (3, −3, −3) is computed as

$$S_{1,3,-3,-3} = S_1 \times e^{-N \times \Delta x_1} = 100 \times e^{-3 \times 0.1154} = 70.72$$

and asset price 2 at node (3, −3, −3) is computed as

$$S_{2,3,-3,-3} = S_2 \times e^{-N \times \Delta x_2} = 100 \times e^{-3 \times 0.1732} = 59.47$$

The other asset prices are computed from this, e.g. node (3, −2, −2) asset price 1 is computed as

$$S_{1,3,-2,-2} = S_{1,3,-3,-2} \times edx1 = 70.72 \times 1.1224 = 79.38$$

Next the option values at maturity are computed. For node (3, 1, −1) we have

$$C_{3,1,-1} = \max(0, S_{1,3,1,-1} - S_{2,3,1,-1} - K) = \max(0, 112.24 - 84.10 - 1) = 27.144$$

FIGURE 2.30 Convergence of the Two-variable Binomial Method

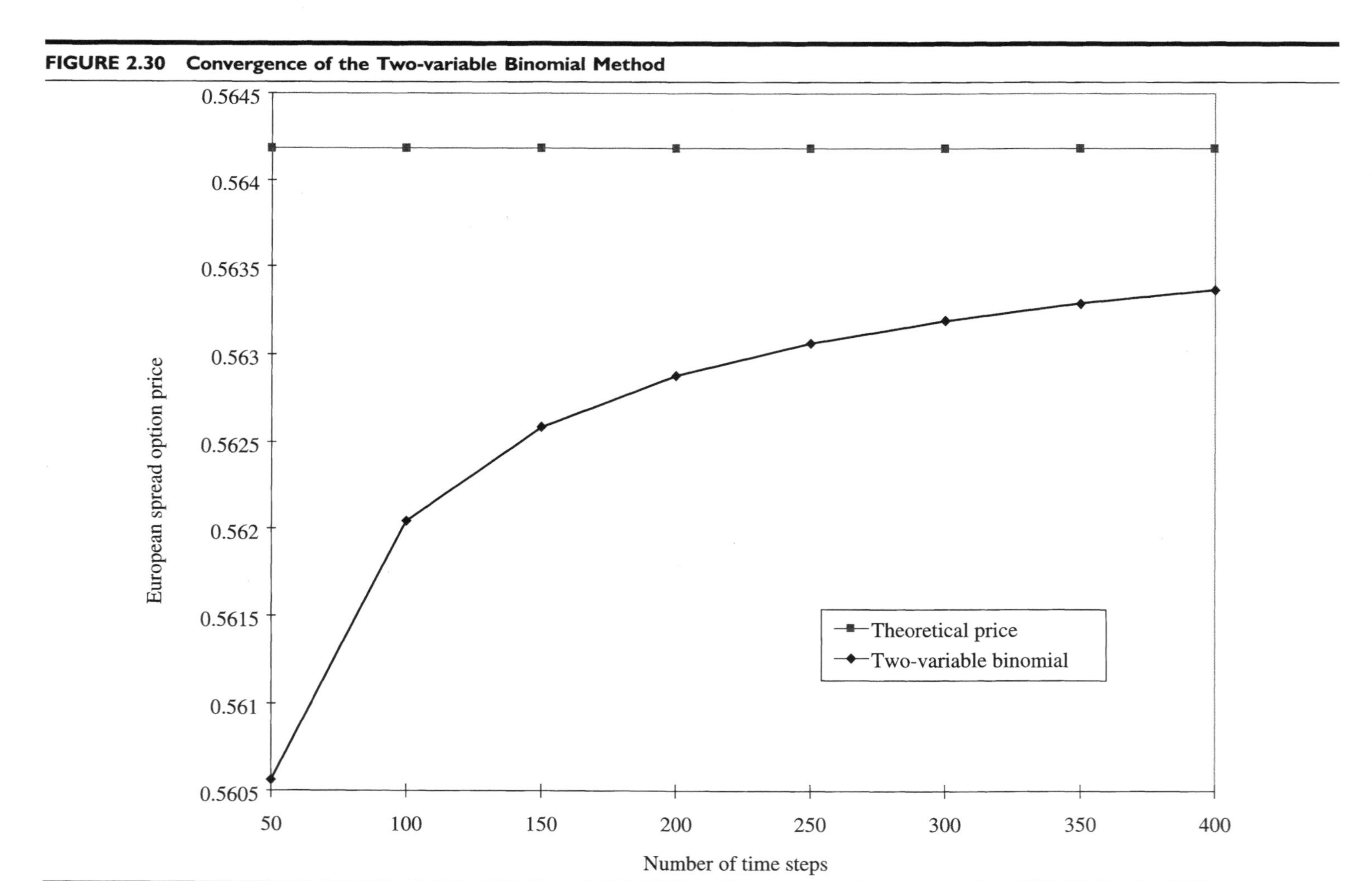

Finally we perform discounted expectations back through the tree applying the early exercise test. For node (2, 0, 0) we have

$$C_{2,0,0} = p_{dd} \times C_{3,-1,-1} + p_{ud} \times C_{3,1,-1} + p_{du} \times C_{3,-1,1} + p_{uu} \times C_{3,1,1}$$
$$= 0.3723 \times 3.998 + 0.1414 \times 27.144 + 0.1037 \times 0.000 + 0.3629 \times 0.000 = 5.3269$$

then applying the early exercise test we have

$$C_{2,0,0} = \max(C_{2,0,0}, S_{1,2,0,0} - S_{2,2,0,0} - K) = \max(5.3269, 100 - 100 - 1) = 5.3269$$

Unfortunately the binomial model is even less efficient for two variables than for one variable. Figure 2.30 illustrates the convergence of the price of an example European spread option (for which we can compute an accurate value by numerical integration) as a function of the number of time steps.

It can be seen that convergence cannot be achieved with a reasonable number of time steps. To achieve efficient pricing for more than one variable problems implicit methods must be used. These are discussed in Chapter 3.

2.12 SUMMARY

In this chapter we have introduced the binomial model of asset prices and shown how it can be generalised and used for pricing American-style options. We then described in detail how the binomial model can be efficiently implemented and how hedge ratios can be computed. An important consideration in option pricing is whether the underlying asset has an associated income or dividend stream, we therefore discussed methods for dealing with asset paying various forms of dividend streams. These methods are quite general and can be applied to the trinomial trees and finite difference methods in Chapters 3 and 5. Finally, we showed how the binomial method can be extended to deal with time-varying volatility, path-dependent options and options whose payoff depends on more than one asset. However, these types of problems can be far more efficiently dealt with using trinomial tree and finite difference methods.

ENDNOTES

1. Strictly, American call options on assets paying a dividend less than or equal to zero can be valued using the Black–Scholes formula.
2. The indexing for the nodes in this section refer to the general additive tree — see Figure 2.9.
3. If this is not the case then we can apply an appropriately inflated amount to the nearest date in the tree after the dividend date. With trinomial trees it is straightforward to arrange for the tree dates to match important dates such as dividends (see Chapter 3).
4. Sometimes the option will pay a predetermined cash rebate, X_{rebate}, when the option knocks out, we deal with this case in Chapter 5.
5. These methods were introduced by Boyle (1988) and Boyle, Evnine and Gibbs (1989), see also Kamrad and Ritchken (1991).
6. Computer algebra packages are useful for solving systems of equation such as these.

3

Trinomial Trees and Finite Difference Methods

3.1 INTRODUCTION

We saw in Chapter 1 that pricing options in the Black–Scholes world requires solving the partial differential equation which the option price satisfies. In Chapter 2 we showed that option prices could be obtained by building a discrete time and state binomial model of the asset price and applying discounted expectations. In this chapter we first generalise the binomial model to a trinomial tree model and then we show that solving the partial differential equation by the explicit finite difference method (introduced by Schwartz, 1977) is equivalent to performing discounted expectations in a trinomial tree. Finally, we describe the implementation of more efficient implicit (Brennan and Schwartz, 1978) and Crank–Nicolson (Courtadon, 1982) finite difference methods and the extension of the procedures to multi-asset problems.

3.2 A TRINOMIAL TREE MODEL OF THE ASSET PRICE

The stochastic differential equation for the risk-neutral geometric Brownian motion (GBM) model of an asset price paying a continuous dividend yield (see Chapter 1, section 1.3) is

$$dS = (r - \delta)S\,dt + \sigma S\,dz \tag{3.1}$$

As in the case of the binomial model it is more convenient to work in terms of $x = \ln(S)$

$$dx = \nu\,dt + \sigma\,dz, \text{ where } \nu = r - \delta - \tfrac{1}{2}\sigma^2 \tag{3.2}$$

Consider a trinomial model of the asset price in which, over a small time interval Δt, the asset price can go up by Δx (the space step), stay the same or go down by Δx, with probabilities p_{u}, p_{m} and p_{d} respectively. This is depicted in terms of x in Figure 3.1.

The drift and volatility parameters of the continuous time process are now captured by Δx, p_{u}, p_{m} and p_{d}. We will see later that Δx cannot be chosen independently of Δt and that a good choice is $\Delta x = \sigma\sqrt{3\Delta t}$. The relationship between the parameters of the continuous time process and the trinomial process is obtained by equating the mean and variance over the time interval Δt and requiring that the probabilities sum to one:

$$E[\Delta x] = p_{\mathrm{u}}(\Delta x) + p_{\mathrm{m}}(0) + p_{\mathrm{d}}(-\Delta x) = \nu\Delta t \tag{3.3}$$

$$E[\Delta x^2] = p_u(\Delta x^2) + p_{\mathrm{m}}(0) + p_{\mathrm{d}}(\Delta x^2) = \sigma^2\Delta t + \nu^2\Delta t^2 \tag{3.4}$$

$$p_{\mathrm{u}} + p_{\mathrm{m}} + p_{\mathrm{d}} = 1 \tag{3.5}$$

FIGURE 3.1 Trinomial Tree Model of an Asset Price

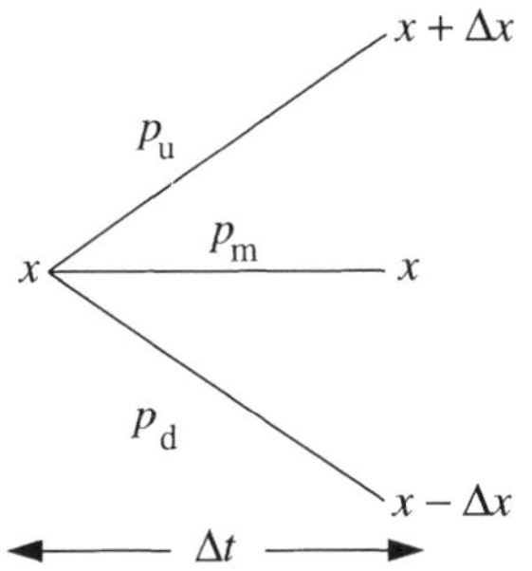

Solving equations (3.3) to (3.5) gives

$$p_u = \frac{1}{2}\left(\frac{\sigma^2 \Delta t + \nu^2 \Delta t^2}{\Delta x^2} + \frac{\nu \Delta t}{\Delta x}\right) \tag{3.6}$$

$$p_m = 1 - \frac{\sigma^2 \Delta t + \nu^2 \Delta t^2}{\Delta x^2} \tag{3.7}$$

$$p_d = \frac{1}{2}\left(\frac{\sigma^2 \Delta t + \nu^2 \Delta t^2}{\Delta x^2} - \frac{\nu \Delta t}{\Delta x}\right) \tag{3.8}$$

The trinomial process in Figure 3.1 can be extended to form a trinomial tree. The result is depicted in Figure 3.2 where i is the time step and j is the level of the asset price relative to the initial asset price, i.e. at node (i, j) we have $t = i\Delta t$, and $S_{i,j} = S\exp(j\Delta x)$. Using the same notation as Chapter 2, we will represent the value of an option at node (i, j) by $C_{i,j}$ and time step N will correspond to the maturity date of the option, i.e. $T = N\Delta t$. The values of the option at the final time step are determined by its pay-off, for example for a call option

$$C_{N,j} = \max(0, S_{N,j} - K) \tag{3.9}$$

FIGURE 3.2 A Trinomial Tree

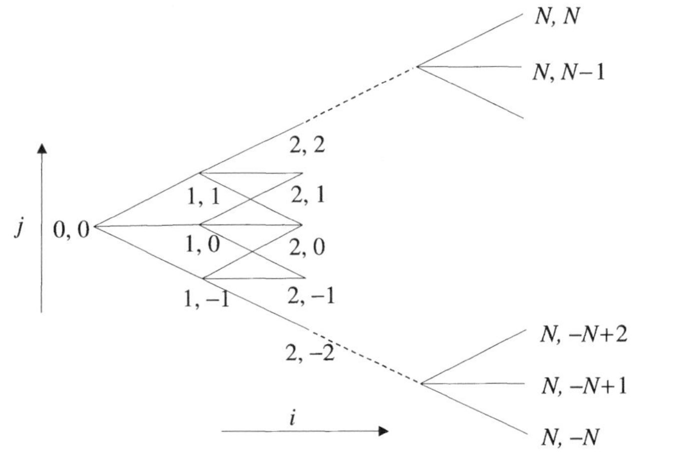

We have seen in Chapters 1 and 2 that we can compute option values as discounted expectations in a risk-neutral world,[1] therefore the values of the option at earlier nodes can be computed as discounted expectations

$$C_{i,j} = e^{-r\Delta t}(p_u C_{i+1,j+1} + p_m C_{i+1,j} + p_d C_{i+1,j-1}) \tag{3.10}$$

The trinomial tree has many advantages over the binomial tree. Firstly, because there are three possible future movements over each time rather than two the trinomial tree provides a much better approximation to the continuous time process than the binomial tree for the same number of time steps. More importantly, the trinomial tree is easier to work with because of its more regular grid and is more flexible, allowing relatively easy extension to time-varying drift and volatility parameters.

The pseudo-code implementation of the trinomial tree using equation (3.10) for the pricing of a European call option is shown in Figure 3.3.

FIGURE 3.3 Pseudo code for a European Call Option by Trinomial Tree

```
initialise_parameters { K, T, S, sig, r, div, N, dx }

{ precompute constants }

dt = T/N
nu = r - div - 0.5 * sig^2
edx = exp(dx)
pu = 0.5*( (sig^2*dt+nu^2*dt^2)/dx^2 + nu*dt/dx )
pm = 1.0 - (sig^2*dt+nu^2*dt^2)/dx^2
pd = 0.5*( (sig^2*dt+nu^2*dt^2)/dx^2 - nu*dt/dx )
disc = exp(-r*dt)

{ initialise asset prices at maturity }

St[-N] = S*exp(-N*dx)
for j = -N+1 to N do St[j] = St[j-1]*edx

{ initialise option values at maturity }

for j = -N to N do C[N,j] = max( 0 , St[j] - K )

{ step back through lattice }

for i = N-1 downto 0 do

  for j = -i to i do
  C[i,j] = disc*(pu*C[i+1,j+1] + pm*C[i+1,j] + pd*C[i+1,j-1])

next i

European_call = C[0,0]
```

Example : Pricing a European Call Option in a Trinomial Tree

We price a one-year maturity, at-the-money European call option with the current asset price at 100 and volatility of 20%. The continuously compounded interest rate is assumed to be 6 per cent per annum, the asset pays a continuous dividend yield of 3 per cent per annum, the trinomial tree has three time steps and the space step is 0.2; $K = 100$, $T =$ one year, $S = 100$, $\sigma = 0.2$, $r = 0.06$, $\delta = 0.03$, $N = 3$, $\Delta x = 0.2$. Figure 3.4 illustrates the numerical results, notice the asset price is no longer shown stored at the node since the asset price levels do not change with the time step.

Firstly the constants: $\Delta t(dt)$, $\nu(nu)$, edx, $p_{\mathrm{u}}(pu)$, $p_{\mathrm{m}}(pm)$, $p_{\mathrm{d}}(pd)$, and *disc* are precomputed:

$$\Delta t = \frac{T}{N} = \frac{1}{3} = 0.3333$$

$$\nu = r - \delta - \tfrac{1}{2}\sigma^2 = 0.06 - 0.03 - 0.5 \times 0.02^2 = 0.01$$

$$\mathrm{edx} = \exp(\Delta x) = \exp(0.2) = 1.2214$$

$$p_{\mathrm{u}} = \frac{1}{2}\left(\frac{\sigma^2 \Delta t + \nu^2 \Delta t^2}{\Delta x^2} + \frac{\nu \Delta t}{\Delta x}\right)$$

$$= \frac{1}{2}\left(\frac{0.2^2 \times 0.3333 + 0.01^2 \times 0.3333^2}{0.2^2} + \frac{0.01 \times 0.3333}{0.2}\right) = 0.1751$$

FIGURE 3.4 Pricing a European Call Option in a Trinomial Tree

K	T	S	sig	r	div	N	dx
100	1	100	0.2	0.06	0.03	3	0.2

dt	nu	edx	pu	pm	pd	disc
0.3333	0.0100	1.2214	0.1751	0.6664	0.1585	0.9802

	i	0	1	2	3
j	St, t	0	0.3333	0.6667	1
3	182.21				82.2119
2	149.18			49.6782	49.1825
1	122.14		24.0802	22.9051	22.1403
0	100.00	8.4253	6.4148	3.8008	0.0000
−1	81.87		0.6525	0.0000	0.0000
−2	67.03			0.0000	0.0000
−3	54.88				0.0000

$$p_{\rm m} = 1 - \left(\frac{\sigma^2\Delta t + v^2\Delta t^2}{\Delta x^2}\right) = 1 - \left(\frac{0.2^2 \times 0.3333 + 0.01^2 \times 0.3333^2}{0.2^2}\right)$$
$$= 0.6664$$
$$p_{\rm d} = \frac{1}{2}\left(\frac{\sigma^2\Delta t + v^2\Delta t^2}{\Delta x^2} - \frac{v\Delta t}{\Delta x}\right)$$
$$= \frac{1}{2}\left(\frac{0.2^2 \times 0.3333 + 0.01^2 \times 0.3333^2}{0.2^2} - \frac{0.01 \times 0.3333}{0.2}\right) = 0.1585$$
$$disc = \exp(-r\Delta t) = \exp(-0.06 \times 0.3333) = 0.9802$$

Then the asset prices at maturity are computed (these apply to every time step). The asset price at node (3, −3) is computed as

$$S_{3,-3} = S \times \exp(-N \times \Delta x) = 100 \times \exp(-3 \times 0.2) = 54.88$$

then the other asset prices are computed from this. For example at node (3, −2) the asset price is given by

$$S_{3,-2} = S_{3,-2} \times \text{edx} = 54.88 \times 1.2214 = 67.03$$

Next the option values at maturity are computed. For node (3, 2) we have

$$C_{3,2} = \max(0, S_{3,2} - K) = \max(0, 149.1825 - 100.00) = 49.1825$$

Finally we perform discounted expectations back through the tree. For node (2, 1) we have

$$C_{2,1} = disc \times (p_u \times C_{3,2} + p_m \times C_{3,1} + p_d \times C_{3,0})$$
$$= 0.9802 \times (0.1751 \times 49.1825 + 0.6664 \times 22.1403 + 0.1585 \times 0.0000) = 22.9051$$

3.3 EXTENDING THE TREE INTO A GRID

Imagine we now take the trinomial tree in Figure 3.2 and add extra nodes above and below the tree so that we have $2N_j + 1, N_j \geq N$ nodes at every time step i rather than $2i + 1$. Figure 3.5 shows the resulting rectangular grid which we obtain.

However, at time step i, given all option values at $i+1$ we cannot compute the bottom and top option values ($C_{i,-N_j}$ and C_{i,N_j}) using discounted expectations since this would require knowing option values $C_{i+1,-N_j-1}$ and C_{i+1,N_j+1} which we do not have. With no additional information we can only compute the region indicated by the dashed branches using discounted expectations. At time zero we have $2(N_j - N) + 1$ option values rather than just a single value with the original trinomial tree.

In order to be able to compute the remainder of the grid we must add extra boundary conditions which determine the behaviour of the option price as a function of the asset price for high and low values of the asset price. For example, for a European call option,

FIGURE 3.5 A Trinomial Tree in a Rectangular Grid

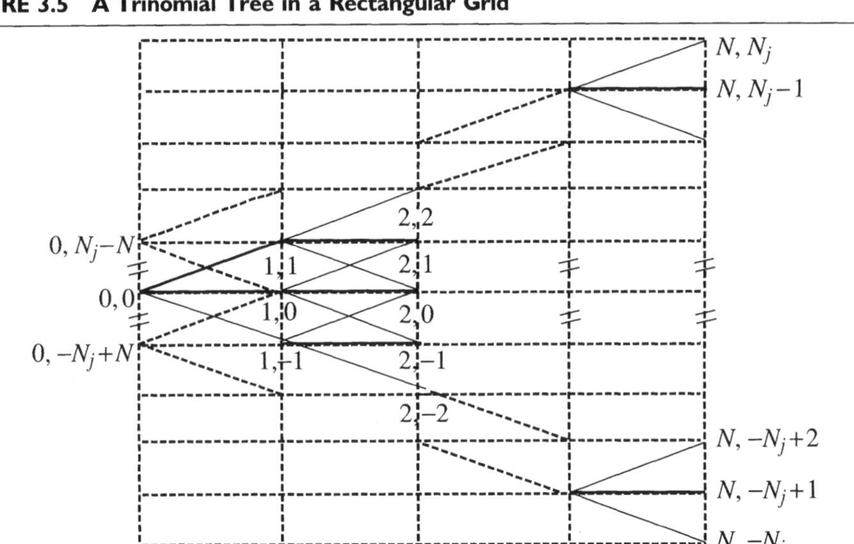

we have

$$\frac{\partial C}{\partial S} = 1 \quad \text{for } S \text{ large} \tag{3.11}$$

$$\frac{\partial C}{\partial S} = 0 \quad \text{for } S \text{ small} \tag{3.12}$$

In terms of the grid equations (3.11) and (3.12) become

$$\frac{C_{i,N_j} - C_{i,N_j-1}}{S_{i,N_j} - S_{i,N_j-1}} = 1 \quad \text{for } S \text{ large} \tag{3.13}$$

$$\frac{C_{i,-N_j+1} - C_{i,-N_j}}{S_{i,-N_j+1} - S_{i,-N_j}} = 0 \quad \text{for } S \text{ small} \tag{3.14}$$

Equations (3.13) and (3.14) allow us to compute the option values at the bottom and top of the grid ($C_{i,-N_j}$ and C_{i,N_j}) from the values one space step inside the grid. The values $C_{i-N_j+1}, \ldots, C_{i,N_j-1}$ can be computed at each time step by the discounted expectation formula (3.10).

There is an alternative derivation of the model we have just described from which we obtain the explicit finite difference method. This is the subject of the next section.

3.4 THE EXPLICIT FINITE DIFFERENCE METHOD

The idea behind finite difference methods is to simplify the PDE by replacing the partial differentials with finite differences. We will begin by describing the application of the explicit finite difference method to the Black–Scholes PDE (see Chapter 1, section 1.3),

$$-\frac{\partial C}{\partial t} = \frac{1}{2}S^2\sigma^2\frac{\partial^2 C}{\partial S^2} + (r-\delta)S\frac{\partial C}{\partial S} - rC \tag{3.15}$$

As was pointed out in Chapter 1, this PDE governs the price of all European and American options whose pay-off depends on a single asset which follows GBM. Different options are defined by their boundary conditions, in later sections of this chapter we will look at generalisations of this PDE to more state variables and in Chapter 5 we discuss more general diffusion processes governing the state variables.

In terms of $x = \ln(S)$, equation (3.15) becomes

$$-\frac{\partial C}{\partial t} = \frac{1}{2}\sigma^2\frac{\partial^2 C}{\partial x^2} + \nu\frac{\partial C}{\partial x} - rC \tag{3.16}$$

Equation (3.16) is a PDE with constant coefficients, i.e. they do not depend on x or t, which makes the application of finite difference methods much easier.

In a similar way to the trinomial tree, when implementing finite difference methods, we imagine time and space divided up into discrete intervals (Δt and Δx), this is the finite difference grid or lattice.

To obtain the explicit finite difference method we approximate equation (3.16) using a forward difference[2] for $\partial C/\partial t$ and central differences for $\partial^2 C/\partial x^2$ and $\partial C/\partial x$. Therefore, in terms of the grid we obtain

$$-\frac{C_{i+1,j} - C_{i,j}}{\Delta t} = \frac{1}{2}\sigma^2\frac{C_{i+1,j+1} - 2C_{i+1,j} + C_{i+1,j-1}}{\Delta x^2} + \nu\frac{C_{i+1,j+1} - C_{i+1,j-1}}{2\Delta x} - rC_{i+1,j} \tag{3.17}$$

which can be rewritten as

$$C_{i,j} = p_\mathrm{u}C_{i+1,j+1} + p_\mathrm{m}C_{i+1,j} + p_\mathrm{d}C_{i+1,j-1} \tag{3.18}$$

$$p_\mathrm{u} = \Delta t\left(\frac{\sigma^2}{2\Delta x^2} + \frac{\nu}{2\Delta x}\right) \tag{3.19}$$

$$p_\mathrm{m} = 1 - \Delta t\frac{\sigma^2}{\Delta x^2} - r\Delta t \tag{3.20}$$

$$p_\mathrm{d} = \Delta t\left(\frac{\sigma^2}{2\Delta x^2} - \frac{\nu}{2\Delta x}\right) \tag{3.21}$$

Equation (3.18) is equivalent to taking discounted expectations. This can be seen by taking a slightly different approximation to the PDE in which the last term in equation (3.17) is approximated by the value at node (i, j) rather than $(i+1, j)$

$$-\frac{C_{i+1,j} - C_{i,j}}{\Delta t} = \frac{1}{2}\sigma^2\frac{C_{i+1,j+1} - 2C_{i+1,j} + C_{i+1,j-1}}{\Delta x^2} + \nu\frac{C_{i+1,j+1} - C_{i+1,j-1}}{2\Delta x} - rC_{i,j} \tag{3.22}$$

which can be rewritten as

$$C_{i,j} = \frac{1}{1+r\Delta t}(p_\mathrm{u}C_{i+1,j+1} + p_\mathrm{m}C_{i+1,j} + p_\mathrm{d}C_{i+1,j-1}) \tag{3.23}$$

$$p_\mathrm{u} = \frac{1}{2}\Delta t\left(\frac{\sigma^2}{\Delta x^2} + \frac{\nu}{\Delta x}\right) \tag{3.24}$$

$$p_{\mathrm{m}} = 1 - \Delta t \frac{\sigma^2}{\Delta x^2} \tag{3.25}$$

$$p_{\mathrm{d}} = \frac{1}{2}\Delta t \left(\frac{\sigma^2}{\Delta x^2} - \frac{\nu}{\Delta x} \right) \tag{3.26}$$

where $1/(1 + r\Delta t)$ is an approximation of $1/e^{r\Delta t}$. Therefore the explicit finite difference method is equivalent to approximating the diffusion process by a discrete trinomial process. It can be shown (see Brennan and Schwartz, 1978) that the variance of the discrete process is a downward-biased approximation of the continuous GBM process with an upper bound of σ^4 to the bias.

Figure 3.6 illustrates the relationship between the grid values in equation (3.18). The pseudo-code implementation of the explicit finite difference method using equation (3.18) for the pricing of a European call option is given in Figure 3.7.

Example : Pricing a European Call Option by Explicit Finite Difference Method

We price a one-year maturity, at-the-money European call option with the current asset price at 100 and volatility of 20 per cent. The continuously compounded interest rate is assumed to be 6 per cent per annum, the asset pays a continuous dividend yield of 3 per cent per annum, the trinomial tree has three time steps and the space step is 0.2; $K = 100$, $T = 1$ year, $S = 100$, $\sigma = 0.2$, $r = 0.06$, $\delta = 0.03$, $N = 3$, $N_j = 3$, $\Delta x = 0.2$. Figure 3.8 illustrates the numerical results.

Firstly the constants $\Delta t(dt)$, $\nu(nu)$, edx, $p_{\mathrm{u}}(pu)$, $p_{\mathrm{m}}(pm)$, $p_{\mathrm{d}}(pd)$ are precomputed:

$$\Delta t = \frac{T}{N} = \frac{1}{3} = 0.3333$$

$$\nu = r - \delta - \frac{1}{2}\sigma^2 = 0.06 - 0.03 - 0.5 \times 0.02^2 = 0.01$$

FIGURE 3.6 The Explicit Finite Difference Method

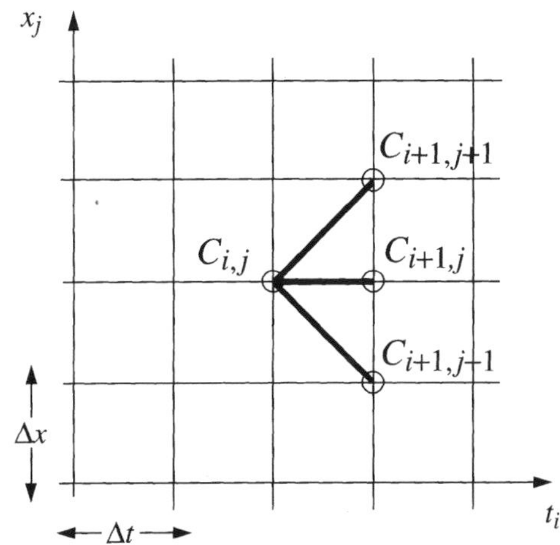

FIGURE 3.7 Pseudo-code for a European Call Option by Explicit Finite Difference Method

```
initialise_parameters { K, T, S, sig, r, div, N, Nj, dx }

{ precompute constants }

dt = T/N
nu = r - div - 0.5 * sig^2
edx = exp(dx)
pu = 0.5*dt*( (sig/dx)^2 + nu/dx )
pm = 1.0 - dt*(sig/dx)^2 - r*dt
pd = 0.5*dt*( (sig/dx)^2 - nu/dx )

{ initialise asset prices at maturity }

St[-Nj] = S*exp(-Nj*dx)
for j = -Nj+1 to Nj do St[j] = St[j-1]*edx

{ initialise option values at maturity }

for j = -Nj to Nj do C[N,j] = max( 0 , St[j] - K )

{ step back through lattice }

for i = N-1 downto 0 do

  for j = -Nj+1 to Nj-1 do
    C[i,j] =
      pu*C[i+1,j+1] + pm*C[i+1,j] + pd*C[i+1,j-1]

  { boundary conditions }

  C[i,-Nj] = C[i,-Nj+1]

  C[i,Nj] = C[i,Nj-1] + (St[Nj]-St[Nj-1])

next i

European_call = C[0,0]
```

$$edx = \exp(\Delta x) = \exp(0.2) = 1.2214$$

$$p_{\mathrm{u}} = \frac{1}{2}\Delta t\left(\left(\frac{\sigma}{\Delta x}\right)^2 + \frac{\nu}{\Delta x}\right) = \frac{1}{2} \times 0.3333 \times \left(\left(\frac{0.2}{0.2}\right)^2 + \frac{0.01}{0.2}\right) = 0.1750$$

$$p_{\mathrm{m}} = 1 - \Delta t\left(\frac{\sigma}{\Delta x}\right)^2 - r\Delta t = 1 - 0.3333 \times \left(\frac{0.2}{0.2}\right)^2 - 0.06 \times 0.3333 = 0.6467$$

$$p_{\mathrm{d}} = \frac{1}{2}\Delta t\left(\left(\frac{\sigma}{\Delta x}\right)^2 - \frac{\nu}{\Delta x}\right) = \frac{1}{2} \times 0.3333 \times \left(\left(\frac{0.2}{0.2}\right)^2 - \frac{0.01}{0.2}\right) = 0.1583$$

FIGURE 3.8 Numerical Example for a European Call Option by Explicit Finite Difference Method

K	T	S	sig	r	div	N	Nj	dx
100	1	100	0.2	0.06	0.03	3	3	0.2

dt	nu	edx	pu	pm	pd
0.3333	0.0100	1.2214	0.1750	0.6467	0.1583

	i	0	1	2	3
j	St, t	0	0.3333	0.6667	1
3	182.21	83.9151	83.2738	82.7267	82.2119
2	149.18	50.8857	50.2444	49.6973	49.1825
1	122.14	25.4319	24.1349	22.9243	22.1403
0	100.00	8.5455	6.5173	3.8745	0.0000
−1	81.87	1.5790	0.6780	0.0000	0.0000
−2	67.03	0.1187	0.0000	0.0000	0.0000
−3	54.88	0.1187	0.0000	0.0000	0.0000

Then the asset prices at maturity are computed (these apply to every time step). The asset price at node $(3, -3)$ is computed as

$$S_{3,-3} = S \times \exp(-N \times \Delta x) = 100 \times \exp(-3 \times 0.2) = 54.88$$

then the other asset prices are computed from this. For example at node $(3, -2)$ the asset price is given by

$$S_{3,-2} = S_{3,-2} \times edx = 54.8812 \times 1.2214 = 67.03$$

Next the option values at maturity are computed. For node $(3, 2)$ we have

$$C_{3,2} = \max(0, S_{3,2} - K) = \max(0, 149.18 - 100) = 49.1825$$

Finally we perform discounted expectations back through the tree. For node $(2, 1)$ we have:

$$\begin{aligned} C_{2,1} &= p_{\mathrm{u}} \times C_{3,2} + p_{\mathrm{m}} \times C_{3,1} + p_{\mathrm{d}} \times C_{3,0} \\ &= 0.1750 \times 49.1825 + 0.6467 \times 22.1403 + 0.1583 \times 0.0000 = 22.9243 \end{aligned}$$

FIGURE 3.9 Pseudo-code for an American Put Option by Explicit Finite Difference Method

```
initialise_parameters { K, T, S, sig, r, div, N, Nj, dx }

{ precompute constants }

dt = T/N
nu = r - div - 0.5 * sig^2
edx = exp (dx)
pu = 0.5*dt*( (sig/dx)^2 + nu/dx )
pm = 1.0 - dt*(sig/dx)^2 - r*dt
pd = 0.5*dt*( (sig/dx)^2 - nu/dx )

{ initialise asset prices at maturity }

St[-Nj] = S*exp(-Nj*dx)
for j = -Nj+1 to Nj do St[j] = St[j-1]*edx

{ initialise option values at maturity }

for j = -Nj to Nj do C[0,j] = max( 0 , K - St[j] )

{ step back through lattice }

for i = N-1 downto 0 do

  for j = -Nj+1 to Nj-1 do
    C[1,j] = pu*C[0,j+1] + pm*C[0,j] + pd*C[0,j-1]

  { boundary conditions }

  C[1,-Nj] = C[1,-Nj+1] + (St[-Nj+1]-St[-Nj])

  C[1,Nj] = C[1,Nj-1]

  { apply early exercise condition }

  for j = -Nj to Nj do
    C[0,j] = max( C[1,j] , K - St[j] )

next i

American_put = C[0,0]
```

The pseudo-code implementation of the explicit finite difference method using equation (3.18) for the pricing of an American put option is given in Figure 3.9 (the changes from the European call pseudo-code in Figure 3.7 are highlighted in bold). The first highlighted change is the maturity condition for a put option. Secondly, we have introduced a storage efficiency improvement. The option value array $C[,]$ only has two time indices, zero and one, rather than zero up to N. Index one is used to temporarily store the discounted expectation and then the boundary conditions and early exercise test store the appropriate value in time index zero.

Example : Pricing an American Put Option in a Trinomial Tree

We price a one-year maturity, at-the-money American put option with the current asset price at 100 and volatility of 20 per cent. The continuously compounded interest rate is assumed to be 6 per cent per annum, the asset pays a continuous dividend yield of 3 per cent per annum, the trinomial tree has three time steps and the space step is 0.2; $K = 100$, $T = 1$ year, $S = 100$, $\sigma = 0.2$, $r = 0.06$, $\delta = 0.03$, $N = 3$, $N_j = 3$, $\Delta x = 0.2$. Figure 3.10 illustrates the numerical results.

Firstly the constants; $\Delta t(dt)$, $\nu(nu)$, edx, $p_u(pu)$, $p_m(pm)$, $p_d(pd)$ are precomputed:

$$\Delta t = \frac{T}{N} = \frac{1}{3} = 0.3333$$

FIGURE 3.10 Numerical Example for an American Put Option by Explicit Finite Difference Method

K	T	S	sig	r	div	N	Nj	dx
100	1	100	0.2	0.06	0.03	3	3	0.2

dt	nu	edx	pu	pm	pd
0.3333	0.0100	1.2214	0.1750	0.6467	0.1583

j	i / St, t	0 / 0	1 / 0.3333	2 / 0.6667	3 / 1
3	182.21	0.0720 0.0720	0.0000 0.0000	0.0000 0.0000	0.0000
2	149.18	0.0720 0.0720	0.0000 0.0000	0.0000 0.0000	0.0000
1	122.14	1.0422 1.0422	0.4544 0.4544	0.0000 0.0000	0.0000
0	100.00	6.0058 6.0058	4.7261 4.7261	2.8701 2.8701	0.0000
–1	81.87	17.7691 18.1269	17.4443 18.1269	16.9420 18.1269	18.1269
–2	67.03	31.6353 32.9680	31.6353 32.9680	31.6353 32.9680	32.9680
–3	54.88	43.7862 45.1188	43.7862 45.1188	43.7862 45.1188	45.1188

*discounted expectation or boundary condition

*
C

$$\nu = r - \delta - \tfrac{1}{2}\sigma^2 = 0.06 - 0.03 - 0.5 \times 0.02^2 = 0.01$$

$$edx = \exp(\Delta x) = \exp(0.2) = 1.2214$$

$$p_{\mathrm{u}} = \frac{1}{2}\Delta t\left(\left(\frac{\sigma}{\Delta x}\right)^2 + \frac{\nu}{\Delta x}\right) = \frac{1}{2} \times 0.3333 \times \left(\left(\frac{0.2}{0.2}\right)^2 + \frac{0.01}{0.2}\right) = 0.1750$$

$$p_{\mathrm{m}} = 1 - \Delta t\left(\frac{\sigma}{\Delta x}\right)^2 - r\Delta t = 1 - 0.3333 \times \left(\frac{0.2}{0.2}\right)^2 - 0.06 \times 0.3333 = 0.6467$$

$$p_{\mathrm{d}} = \frac{1}{2}\Delta t\left(\left(\frac{\sigma}{\Delta; x}\right)^2 - \frac{\nu}{\Delta x}\right) = \frac{1}{2} \times 0.3333 \times \left(\left(\frac{0.2}{0.2}\right)^2 - \frac{0.01}{0.2}\right) = 0.1583$$

Then the asset prices at maturity are computed (these apply to every time step). The asset price at node (3, −3) is computed as:

$$S_{3,-3} = S \times \exp(-N \times \Delta x) = 100 \times \exp(-3 \times 0.2) = 54.88$$

then the other asset prices are computed from this. For example at node (3, −2) the asset price is given by

$$S_{3,-2} = S_{3,-2} \times edx = 54.8812 \times 1.2214 = 67.03$$

Next the option values at maturity are computed. For node (3, −2) we have:

$$C_{3,-2} = \max(0, K - S_{3,-2}) = \max(0, 100 - 67.03) = 32.9680$$

Finally we perform discounted expectations back through the tree. For node (2, −1) we have

$$\begin{aligned} C_{2,-1} &= p_{\mathrm{u}} \times C_{3,0} + p_{\mathrm{m}} C_{3,-1} + p_{\mathrm{d}} \times C_{3,-2} \\ &= 0.1750 \times 0.0000 + 0.6467 \times 18.1269 + 0.1583 \times 32.9680 = 16.9420 \end{aligned}$$

Applying the early exercise test we have

$$C_{2,-1} = \max(C_{2,-1}, K - S_{2,-1}) = \max(16.9420, 100 - 81.8731) = 18.1269$$

The accuracy of this method is $O(\Delta x^2 + \Delta t)$ which means that if we halve $\Delta x^2 + \Delta t$ we halve the error. Therefore to halve the error we must halve the time step, but only need to reduce the space step by a factor of $1/\sqrt{2}$.

3.5 STABILITY AND CONVERGENCE

It is very important to ensure that the probabilities p_{u}, p_{m} and p_{d} are positive and that the stability and convergence condition mentioned in section 3.2 is satisfied:

$$\Delta x \geq \sigma\sqrt{3\Delta t} \tag{3.27}$$

Imagine that C represents the exact solution of the PDE and O represents the exact solution of the finite difference equation. The difference $C - O$ is called the discretisation error and is caused by approximating the partial derivatives by finite differences. It can generally be reduced by using smaller space and time steps. Now let $\tilde{O}$ represent the actual numerically computed solution. The difference $\tilde{O} - O$ is called the round-off error and is caused by representing real numbers to finite precision. A finite difference method is convergent if the discretisation error tends to zero as the space and time steps tend to zero, and it is stable if the round-off error is small and remains bounded for all time.

Consider equations (3.19), (3.20) and (3.21) for the trinomial tree probabilities. If the volatility becomes small relative to the interest rate then p_{d} can become negative. Furthermore, if the volatility becomes large then the condition (3.27) can be violated and this can lead to p_{m} becoming negative, although this is not the only reason for instability and lack of convergence (see Press *et al.*, 1992 or Smith, 1975). Figure 3.11 illustrates how the probabilities vary as a function of σ for typical parameter values.

Let us consider what a reasonable number of time steps to use would be for the example of Figure 3.11 with a typical volatility of 25 per cent ($\sigma = 0.25$). A reasonable range of asset price values at the maturity date of the option is three standard deviations either side of the mean and a reasonable number of asset price values is 100 ($2N_j + 1 = 100$). This allows us to calculate the space step required:

$$\Delta x = 6\sigma\sqrt{T}/100 = 0.015 \tag{3.28}$$

If we now apply the condition (3.27) we obtain

$$\Delta t \leq \frac{1}{3}\left(\frac{\Delta x}{\sigma}\right)^2 = 0.0012 \tag{3.29}$$

This leads to a requirement of more than 833 time steps per year. In fact we can substitute for Δx in equation (3.29) using equation (3.28), replacing the 6 by n_{SD} (number of standard deviations), and rearrange to obtain a formula for the number of time steps required:

$$N = \frac{T}{\Delta t} \geq 3\left(\frac{2N_j + 1}{n_{\mathrm{SD}}}\right)^2 \tag{3.30}$$

Since we will typically want the ratio of the number of asset values to the number of standard deviations

$$\left(\frac{2N_j + 1}{n_{\mathrm{SD}}}\right)$$

to be at least 15 to have a good approximation to the asset price distribution, then we have immediately the requirement for the number of time steps to be at least 675.

3.6 THE IMPLICIT FINITE DIFFERENCE METHOD

Consider now approximating the transformed Black–Scholes PDE (3.16) by replacing the space derivatives with central differences at time step i rather than at $i + 1$. This gives

$$-\frac{C_{i+1,j} - C_{i,j}}{\Delta t} = \frac{1}{2}\sigma^2\frac{C_{i,j+1} - 2C_{i,j} + C_{i,j-1}}{\Delta x^2} + \nu\frac{C_{i,j+1} - C_{i,j-1}}{2\Delta x} - rC_{i,j} \tag{3.31}$$

which can be rewritten as

$$p_{\mathrm{u}}C_{i,j+1} + p_{\mathrm{m}}C_{i,j} + p_{\mathrm{d}}C_{i,j-1} = C_{i+1,j} \tag{3.32}$$

FIGURE 3.11 Explicit Finite Difference Probabilities as a Function of Sigma

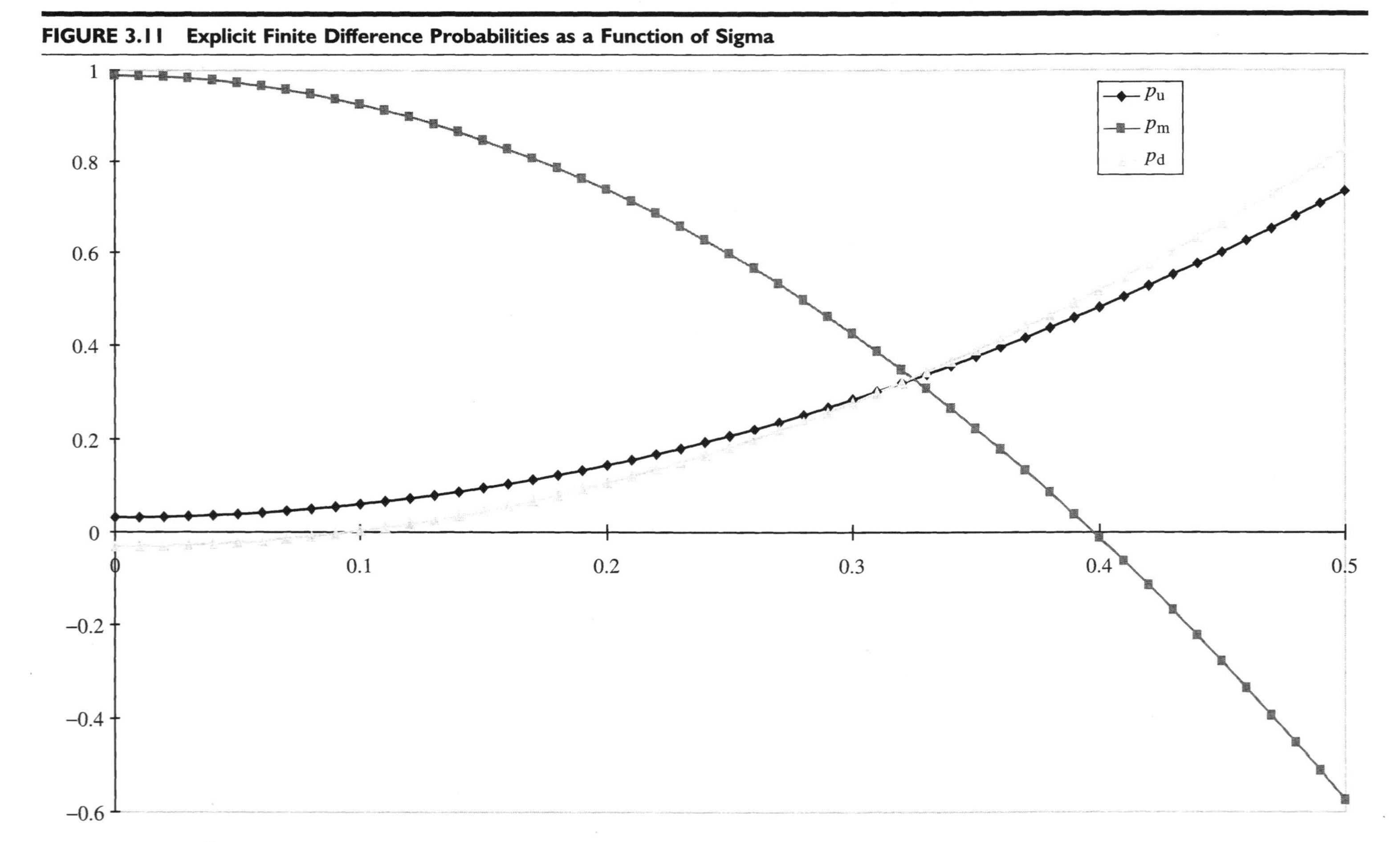

$$p_{\mathrm{u}} = -\frac{1}{2}\Delta t\left(\frac{\sigma^2}{\Delta x^2} + \frac{\nu}{\Delta x}\right) \tag{3.33}$$

$$p_{\mathrm{m}} = 1 + \Delta t\frac{\sigma^2}{\Delta x^2} + r\Delta t \tag{3.34}$$

$$p_{\mathrm{d}} = -\frac{1}{2}\Delta t\left(\frac{\sigma^2}{\Delta x^2} - \frac{\nu}{\Delta x}\right) \tag{3.35}$$

Figure 3.12 illustrates the relationship between the grid values in equation (3.32).

Each equation (3.32) for $j = -N_j + 1, \ldots, N_j - 1$ cannot be solved individually for the option values at time step i as they could for the explicit finite difference method. Instead they must be considered, together with the boundary conditions,

$$C_{i,N_j} - C_{i,N_{j-1}} = \lambda_U \tag{3.36}$$

$$C_{i,-N_j+1} - C_{i,-N_j} = \lambda_L \tag{3.37}$$

to be a system of $2N_j + 1$ linear equations which implicitly determine the $2N_j + 1$ option values at time step i. The boundary condition parameters λ_U and λ_L are determined by the type of option being valued, for example for a call we have (compare with equations (3.13) and (3.14))

$$\lambda_U = S_{i,N_j} - S_{i,N_j-1} \tag{3.38}$$

$$\lambda_L = 0 \tag{3.39}$$

This set of equations has a special structure which is called tridiagonal. Each equation has two variables in common with the equation above and below. This can clearly be

FIGURE 3.12 The Implicit Finite Difference Method

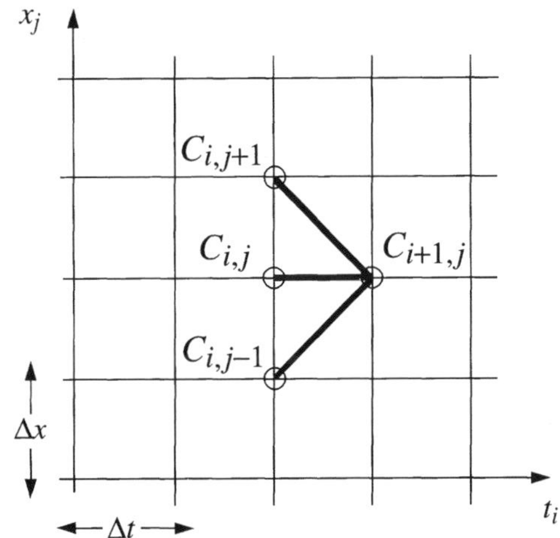

seen by writing the set of equations in matrix form:

$$\begin{vmatrix} 1 & -1 & 0 & \dots & \dots & \dots & 0 \\ p_{\rm u} & p_{\rm m} & p_{\rm d} & 0 & \dots & \dots & 0 \\ 0 & p_{\rm u} & p_{\rm m} & p_{\rm d} & 0 & \dots & 0 \\ \dots & \dots & \dots & \dots & \dots & \dots & \dots \\ 0 & \dots & 0 & p_{\rm u} & p_{\rm m} & p_{\rm d} & 0 \\ 0 & \dots & \dots & 0 & p_{\rm u} & p_{\rm m} & p_{\rm d} \\ 0 & \dots & \dots & \dots & 0 & 1 & -1 \end{vmatrix} \begin{vmatrix} C_{i,N_j} \\ C_{i,N_j-1} \\ C_{i,N_j-2} \\ \dots \\ C_{i,-N_j+2} \\ C_{i,-N_j+1} \\ C_{i,-N_j} \end{vmatrix} = \begin{vmatrix} \lambda_U \\ C_{i+1,N_j-1} \\ C_{i+1,N_j-2} \\ \dots \\ C_{i+1,-N_j+2} \\ C_{i+1,-N_j+1} \\ \lambda_L \end{vmatrix} \tag{3.40}$$

This tridiagonal matrix equation can be solved very efficiently. Beginning with the boundary condition equation $j = -N_j$ this equation is rearranged to obtain

$$C_{i,-N_j} = C_{i,-N_j+1} - \lambda_L \tag{3.41}$$

This is then substituted into the equation above ($j = -N_j + 1$) to obtain

$$p_{\rm u} C_{i,-N_j+2} + p_{\rm m} C_{i,-N_j+1} + p_{\rm d}(C_{i,-N_j+1} - \lambda_L) = C_{i+1,-N_j+1} \tag{3.42}$$

which can be rewritten as

$$p_{\rm u} C_{i,-N_j+2} + p'_{\rm m} C_{i,-N_j+1} = p' \tag{3.43}$$

where

$$p'_{\rm m} = p_{\rm m} + p_{\rm d} \quad \text{and} \quad p' = C_{i+1,-N_j+1} + p_d \lambda_L$$

Therefore the original equation for $j = -N_j + 1$ with three unknowns has become equation (3.43) with only two unknowns. Equation (3.43) can be rearranged to obtain

$$C_{i,-N_j+1} = \frac{p' - p_{\rm u} C_{i,-N_j+2}}{p'_{\rm m}} \tag{3.44}$$

which can be substituted into the equation for $j = -N_j + 2$ to obtain

$$p_{\rm u} C_{i,-N_j+3} + p'_{\rm m} C_{i,-N_j+2} = p' \tag{3.45}$$

where

$$p'_{\rm m} = p_{\rm m} - \frac{p_{\rm u}}{p'_{{\rm m},-N_j+1}} p_{\rm d},\ p' = C_{i+1,-N_j+2} - \frac{p'_{-N_j+1}}{p'_{{\rm m},-N_j+1}} p_d$$

and we have added subscripts to the p's to indicate they apply to the equation for $j = -N_j + 1$. This process of substitution can be repeated all the way up to $j = N_j - 1$ where we obtain:[3]

$$p_{\rm u} C_{i,N_j} + p'_{\rm m} C_{i,N_j-1} = p' \tag{3.46}$$

Now using equation (3.44) and the boundary condition equation for $j = N_j$

$$C_{i,N_j} - C_{i,N_j-1} = \lambda_U \tag{3.47}$$

we can solve for both C_{i,N_j} and C_{i,N_j-1}. Using the next equation down for $j = N_j - 2$ and C_{i,N_j-1} we can obtain C_{i,N_j-2}. This process of substitution can be repeated all the way down to $j = -N_j$, at which point the tridiagonal system of equations (3.40) has been solved.[4]

The pseudo-code implementation of the implicit finite difference method for the pricing of a American put option is given in Figure 3.13.

FIGURE 3.13 Pseudo-code for an American Put Option by Implicit Finite Difference Method

```
initialise_parameters { K, T, S, sig, r, div, N, Nj, dx }

{ precompute constants }

dt = T/N
nu = r - div - 0.5 * sig^2
edx = exp(dx)
pu = -0.5*dt*( (sig/dx)^2 + nu/dx )
pm = 1.0 + dt*(sig/dx)^2 + r*dt
pd = -0.5*dt*( (sig/dx)^2 - nu/dx )

{ initialise asset prices at maturity }

St[-Nj] = S*exp(-Nj*dx)
for j = -Nj+1 to Nj do St[j] = St[j-1]*edx

{ initialise option values at maturity }

for j = -Nj to Nj do C[0,j] = max( 0 , K - St[j] )

{ compute derivative boundary condition }

lambda_L = -1 * ( St[-Nj+1] - St[-Nj] )
lambda_U = 0.0

{ step back through lattice }

for i = N-1 downto 0 do

  solve_implicit_tridiagonal_system( C, pu, pm, pd,
    lambda_L, lambda_U )

  { apply early exercise condition }

  for j = -Nj to Nj do
    C[0,j] = max( C[1,j] , K - St[j] )

next i

American_put = C[0,0]

{-----------------------------------------------------------------}
                                                       (continues)
```

FIGURE 3.13 ***(continued)***

```
subroutine solve_implicit_tridiagonal_system( C, pu, pm, pd,
  lambda_L, lambda_U )

{ substitute boundary condition at j = -Nj into j = -Nj+1 }

pmp[-Nj+1] = pm + pd
pp[-Nj+1] = C[0,-Nj+1] + pd*lambda_L

{ eliminate upper diagonal }

for j = -Nj+2 to Nj-1 do
  pmp[j] = pm - pu*pd/pmp[j-1]
  pp[j] = C[0,j] - pp[j-1]*pd/pmp[j-1]
next j

{ use boundary condition at j = Nj and equation at j = Nj-1 }

C[1,Nj] = (pp[Nj-1] + pmp[Nj-1]*lambda_U)/(pu + pmp[Nj-1])
C[1,Nj-1] = C[1,Nj] - lambda_U

{ back-substitution }

for j = Nj-2 downto -Nj do
  C[1,j] = ( pp[j] - pu*C[1,j+1] )/pmp[j]
next j

return
```

Example : Pricing an American Put Option by Implicit Finite Difference Method

We price a one-year maturity, at-the-money American put option with the current asset price at 100 and volatility of 20 per cent. The continuously compounded interest rate is assumed to be 6 per cent per annum, the asset pays a continuous dividend yield of 3 per cent per annum, the trinomial tree has three time steps and the space step is 0.2; $K = 100$, $T = 1$ year, $S = 100$, $\sigma = 0.2$, $r = 0.06$, $\delta = 0.03$, $N = 3$, $N_j = 3$, $\Delta x = 0.2$. Figure 3.14 illustrates the numerical results.

Firstly the constants; $\Delta t(dt)$, $\nu(nu)$, edx, $p_u(pu)$, $p_m(pm)$, $p_d(pd)$ are precomputed:

$$\Delta t = \frac{T}{N} = \frac{1}{3} = 0.3333$$

$$\nu = r - \delta - \tfrac{1}{2}\sigma^2 = 0.06 - 0.03 - 0.5 \times 0.02^2 = 0.01$$

$$edx = \exp(\Delta x) = \exp(0.2) = 1.2214$$

$$p_u = -\frac{1}{2}\Delta t\left(\left(\frac{\sigma}{\Delta x}\right)^2 + \frac{\nu}{\Delta x}\right) = \frac{1}{2} \times 0.3333 \times \left(\left(\frac{0.2}{0.2}\right)^2 + \frac{0.01}{0.2}\right) = -0.1750$$

FIGURE 3.14 Numerical Example for an American Put Option by Implicit Finite Difference Method

K	T	S	sig	r	div	N	Nj	dx
100	1	100	0.2	0.06	0.03	3	3	0.2

dt	nu	edx	pu	pm	pd
0.3333	0.0100	1.2214	−0.1750	1.3533	−0.1583

j	i St, t	0 0		1 0.3333		2 0.6667		3 1
3	182.21	0.2386 0.2386		0.1120 0.1120		0.0330 0.0330		0.0000
2	149.18	0.2386 0.2386	1.3325 0.2762	0.1120 0.1120	1.3325 0.1296	0.0330 0.0330	1.3325 0.0382	0.0000
1	122.14	1.0684 1.0684	1.3325 1.3819	0.6248 0.6248	1.3325 0.8129	0.2458 0.2458	1.3325 0.3218	0.0000
0	100.00	4.9221 4.9221	1.3325 6.3718	3.6637 3.6637	1.3325 4.7726	2.0646 2.0646	1.3325 2.7080	0.0000
−1	81.87	17.7509 18.1269	1.3301 22.7500	17.5854 18.1269	1.3301 22.7500	17.3750 18.1269	1.3301 22.7500	18.1269
−2	67.03	31.7977 32.9680	1.1950 34.8919	31.7735 32.9680	1.1950 34.8919	31.7427 32.9680	1.1950 34.8919	32.9680
−3	54.88	43.9486 45.1188		43.9243 45.1188		43.8935 45.1188		45.1188

*solution of tridiagonal system

pmp pp	* C

$$p_{\mathrm{m}} = 1 + \Delta t \left(\frac{\sigma}{\Delta x}\right)^2 + r\Delta t = 1 + 0.3333 \times \left(\frac{0.2}{0.2}\right)^2 + 0.06 \times 0.3333 = 1.3533$$

$$p_{\mathrm{d}} = -\frac{1}{2}\Delta t\left(\left(\frac{\sigma}{\Delta x}\right)^2 - \frac{\nu}{\Delta x}\right) = -\frac{1}{2} \times 0.3333 \times \left(\left(\frac{0.2}{0.2}\right)^2 - \frac{0.01}{0.2}\right) = -0.1583$$

Then the asset prices at maturity are computed (these apply to every time step). The asset price at node $(3, -3)$ is computed as

$$S_{3,-3} = S \times \exp(-N \times \Delta x) = 100 \times \exp(-3 \times 0.2) = 54.88$$

then the other asset prices are computed from this. For example at node $(3, -2)$ the asset price is given by

$$S_{3,-2} = S_{3,-2} \times edx = 54.8812 \times 1.2214 = 67.03$$

Next the option values at maturity are computed. For node (3, −2) we have

$$C_{3,-2} = \max(0, K - S_{3,-2}) = \max(0, 100 - 67.032) = 32.9680$$

Finally we step back through the tree applying the early exercise condition. Stepping back through the tree involves solving the tridiagonal system of equations. Firstly we eliminate the upper diagonal. For node (2, −2) we have

$$\begin{aligned} p'_{\mathrm{m},-2} &= p_{\mathrm{m}} + p_{\mathrm{d}} = 1.3533 + (-0.1583) = 1.1950 \\ p'_{-2} &= C_{3,-2} + p_{\mathrm{d}} \times \lambda_{\mathrm{L}} \\ &= 32.9680 + (-0.1583) \times ((-1) \times (67.03 - 54.88)) = 34.8919 \end{aligned}$$

For node (2, −1) we have

$$p'_{\mathrm{m},-1} = p_{\mathrm{m}} - \frac{p_{\mathrm{u}}}{p_{\mathrm{m},-2}} p_{\mathrm{d}} = 1.3533 - (-0.1750) \times (-0.1583)/1.1950 = 1.3301$$

$$p'_{-1} = C_{3,-1} - \frac{p'_{-2}}{p_{\mathrm{m}-2}} p_{\mathrm{d}} = 18.1269 - 34.8919 \times (-0.1583)/1.1950 = 22.7500$$

Then we back-substitute, for example node (2, 0) we have

$$C_{2,0} = \frac{p'_0 - p_{\mathrm{u}} C_{2,1}}{p'_{\mathrm{m},0}} = (2.7080 - (-0.1750) \times 0.2458)/1.3325 = 2.0646$$

Finally applying the early exercise test we have

$$C_{2,0} = \max(C_{2,0}, K - S_{2,0}) = \max(2.0646, 100 - 100.00) = 2.0646$$

The accuracy of this method is $O(\Delta x^2 + \Delta t)$, and more importantly it is unconditionally stable and convergent. So whilst it has the same order of accuracy as the explicit finite difference method we have more freedom to trade-off accuracy for speed by decreasing the time steps because we do not have to worry about a stability and convergence condition. Note that we can no longer interpret p_{u}, p_{m} and p_{d} directly as probabilities, indeed p_{u} and p_{d} will typically be negative and p_{m} will be greater than one. However, it can be shown that the implicit finite difference approximation is equivalent to a generalised discrete stochastic process in which the asset price may jump to every node on the grid at the next time step. The variance of the discrete process is an upward-biased approximation to the continuous time GBM (see Brennan and Schwartz, 1978).

3.7 THE CRANK–NICOLSON FINITE DIFFERENCE METHOD

The Crank–Nicolson method is a refinement of the implicit finite difference method. It is a so-called fully centred method, because it replaces the space and time derivatives with finite differences centred at an imaginary time step at $(i + \frac{1}{2})$. If we do this we obtain the following finite difference equation:

$$
\begin{aligned}
-\frac{C_{i+1,j}-C_{i,j}}{\Delta t} \\
&= \frac{1}{2}\sigma^2\left(\frac{(C_{i+1,j+1}-2C_{i+1,j}+C_{i+1,j-1})+(C_{i,j+1}-2C_{i,j}+C_{i,j-1})}{2\Delta x^2}\right) \\
&\quad +\nu\left(\frac{(C_{i+1,j+1}-C_{i+1,j-1})+(C_{i,j+1}-C_{i,j-1})}{4\Delta x}\right)-r\left(\frac{C_{i+1,j}+C_{i,j}}{2}\right)
\end{aligned}
\tag{3.48}
$$

which can be rewritten as

$$p_{\mathrm{u}}C_{i,j+1}+p_{\mathrm{m}}C_{i,j}+p_{\mathrm{d}}C_{i,j-1}=-p_{\mathrm{u}}C_{i+1,j+1}-(p_{\mathrm{m}}-2)C_{i+1,j}-p_{\mathrm{d}}C_{i+1,j-1} \tag{3.49}$$

$$p_{\mathrm{u}}=-\frac{1}{4}\Delta t\left(\frac{\sigma^2}{\Delta x^2}+\frac{\nu}{\Delta x}\right) \tag{3.50}$$

$$p_{\mathrm{m}}=1+\Delta t\frac{\sigma^2}{2\Delta x^2}+\frac{r\Delta t}{2} \tag{3.51}$$

$$p_{\mathrm{d}}=-\frac{1}{4}\Delta t\left(\frac{\sigma^2}{\Delta x^2}-\frac{\nu}{\Delta x}\right) \tag{3.52}$$

Figure 3.15 illustrates the relationship between the grid values in equation (3.49).

FIGURE 3.15 The Crank–Nicolson Finite Difference Method

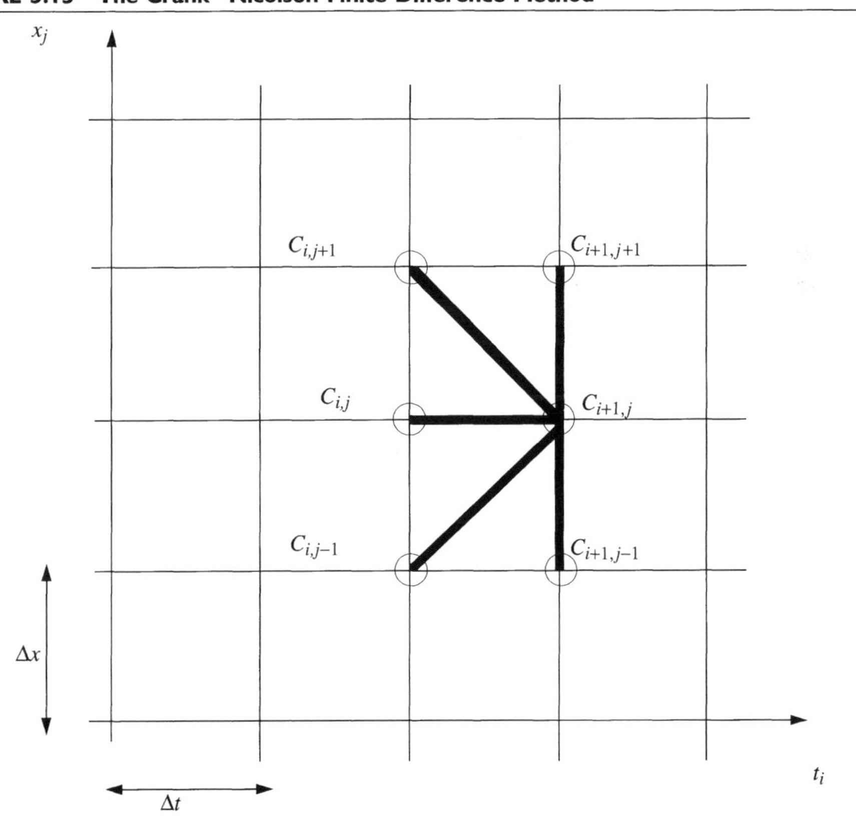

The right-hand side of equation (3.49) is made up of known option values and the known constant coefficients p_u, p_m, p_d and can therefore be considered a known constant. So the set of equations (3.49) for $j = -N_j+1, \ldots, N_j-1$, together with the boundary conditions,

$$C_{i,N_j} - C_{i,N_j-1} = \lambda_U \tag{3.53}$$

$$C_{i,-N_j+1} - C_{i,-N_j} = \lambda_L \tag{3.54}$$

make up a tridiagonal system of equations similar to the implicit finite difference method. This system of equations can be solved very efficiently (see section 3.6). The pseudo-code implementation of the Crank–Nicolson finite difference method for the pricing of an American put option is very similar to that for the implicit finite difference method in section 3.6 (the differences are highlighted in bold) and is given in Figure 3.16.

FIGURE 3.16 Pseudo-code for an American Put Option by the Crank–Nicolson Finite Difference Method

```
initialise_parameters { K, T, S, sig, r, div, N, Nj, dx }

{ precompute constants }

dt = T/N
nu = r - div - 0.5 * sig^2
edx = exp(dx)
pu = -0.25*dt*( (sig/dx)^2 + nu/dx )
pm = 1.0 + 0.5*dt*(sig/dx)^2 + 0.5*r*dt
pd = -0.25*dt*( (sig/dx)^2 - nu/dx )

{ initialise asset prices at maturity }

St[-Nj] = S*exp(-Nj*dx)
for j = -Nj+1 to Nj do St[j] = St[j-1]*edx

{ initialise option values at maturity }

for j = -Nj to Nj do C[0,j] = max( 0 , K - St[j] )

{ compute derivative boundary condition }

lambda_L = -1 * ( St[-Nj+1] - St[-Nj] )
lambda_U = 0.0

{ step back through lattice }

for i = N-1 downto 0 do

  solve_Crank_Nicolson_tridiagonal_system( C, pu, pm, pd,
    lambda_L, lambda_U )

  { apply early exercise condition }

  for j = -Nj to Nj do
```

FIGURE 3.16 ***(continued)***

```
    C[0,j] = max( C[1,j] , K - St[j] )
next i

American_put = C[0,0]

{---------------------------------------------------------------------}

subroutine solve_Crank_Nicolson_tridiagonal_system( C,
  pu, pm, pd, lambda_L, lambda_U )

{ substitute boundary condition at j = -Nj into j = -Nj+1 }

pmp[-Nj+1] = pm + pd
pp[-Nj+1] = -pu*C[0,-Nj+2]-(pm-2)*C[0,-Nj+1]-pd*C[0,-Nj]
            + pd*lambda_L

{ eliminate upper diagonal }

for j = -Nj+2 to Nj-1 do
  pmp[j] = pm - pu*pd/pmp[j-1]
  pp[j] = -pu*C[0,j+1]-(pm-2)*C[0,j]-pd*C[0,j-1]
          - pp[j-1]*pd/pmp[j-1]
next j

{ use boundary condition at j = Nj and equation at j = Nj-1 }

C[1,Nj] = (pp[Nj-1] + pmp[Nj-1]*lambda_U)/(pu + pmp[Nj-1])
C[1,Nj-1] = C[1,Nj] - lambda_U

{ back-substitution }

for j = Nj-2 downto -Nj do
  C[1,j] = ( pp[j] - pu*C[1,j+1] )/pmp[j]
next j

return
```

Figure 3.17 gives a numerical example, the calculations are virtually identical to those for the implicit finite difference method.The accuracy of this method is

$$O\left(\Delta x^2+\left(\frac{\Delta t}{2}\right)^2\right)$$

and it is unconditionally stable and convergent. The Crank–Nicolson method converges much faster than the implicit or explicit finite difference methods. As in the case of the implicit finite difference method we can no longer interpret p_u, p_m and p_d as probabilities, p_u and p_d will typically be negative and p_m will be greater than one. It can be shown that the Crank–Nicolson finite difference approximation is equivalent to a generalised discrete stochastic process in which the asset price may jump to every node on the grid at the

FIGURE 3.17 Numerical Example for an American Put Option by the Crank–Nicolson Finite Difference Method

K	T	S	sig	r	div	N	Nj	dx
100	1	100	0.2	0.06	0.03	3	3	0.2

dt	nu	edx	pu	pm	pd
0.3333	0.0100	1.2214	−0.0875	1.1767	−0.0792

j	i St/t	0 0		1 0.3333		2 0.6667		3 1
3	182.21	0.1686 0.1686		0.0620 0.0620		0.0117 0.0117		0.0000
2	149.18	0.1686 0.1686	1.1707 0.1826	0.0620 0.0620	1.1707 0.0672	0.0117 0.0117	1.1707 0.0127	0.0000
1	122.14	1.0488 1.0488	1.1707 1.2131	0.5568 0.5568	1.1707 0.6465	0.1616 0.1616	1.1707 0.1882	0.0000
0	100.00	5.4184 5.4184	1.1707 6.2518	4.1237 4.1237	1.1707 4.7791	2.3896 2.3896	1.1707 2.7834	0.0000
−1	81.87	17.7458 18.1269	1.1704 20.2947	17.5193 18.1269	1.1704 20.1430	17.2110 18.1269	1.1704 19.9339	18.1269
−2	67.03	31.7233 32.9680	1.0975 33.2636	31.7053 32.9680	1.0975 33.2636	31.6807 32.9680	1.0975 33.2636	32.9680
−3	54.88	43.8742 45.1188		43.8561 45.1188		43.8315 45.1188		45.1188

*solution of tridiagonal system

pmp pp	* C

next time step and the variance of the discrete process is an unbiased approximation to the continuous time GBM process (see Courtadon, 1982).

3.8 COMPUTING HEDGE SENSITIVITIES

The calculation of the standard hedge sensitivities; *delta, gamma, vega, theta* and *rho* is as important as computing price of an option. For *delta*, *gamma*, and *theta* this is straightforward since they can be approximated by finite difference ratios in a trinomial tree. An estimate of the *delta* of an option is given by

$$delta = \frac{\partial C}{\partial S} \approx \frac{C_{0,j+1} - C_{0,j-1}}{S_{0,j+1} - S_{0,j-1}} \tag{3.55}$$

Similarly an estimate of *gamma* is

$$gamma = \frac{\partial^2 C}{\partial S^2} \approx \frac{\left(\dfrac{C_{0,j+1} - C_{0,j}}{S_{0,j+1} - S_{0,j}}\right) - \left(\dfrac{C_{0,j} - C_{0,j-1}}{S_{0,j} - S_{0,j-1}}\right)}{\frac{1}{2}(S_{0,j+1} - S_{0,j-1})} \tag{3.56}$$

and theta:

$$theta = \frac{\partial C}{\partial t} \approx \frac{C_{1,j} - C_{0,j}}{\Delta t} \tag{3.57}$$

Vega and *rho* can be computed by re-evaluation of the price for small changes in the volatility and the interest rate respectively:

$$vega = \frac{\partial C}{\partial \sigma} \approx \frac{C(\sigma + \Delta\sigma) - C(\sigma - \Delta\sigma)}{2\Delta\sigma} \tag{3.58}$$

$$rho = \frac{\partial C}{\partial r} \approx \frac{C(r + \Delta r) - C(r - \Delta r)}{2\Delta r} \tag{3.59}$$

where $C(\sigma + \Delta\sigma)$ is the value computed using an initial volatility of $\sigma + \Delta\sigma$, where $\Delta\sigma$ is a small fraction of σ e.g. $\Delta\sigma = 0.001\sigma$.

3.9 OPTIONS ON MORE THAN ONE ASSET

In Chapter 2, section 2.11 we showed how the binomial method could be extended to price options whose payoff depends on more than one asset. In the case of two assets, examples include options on the difference between the two assets (spread options), and options on the maximum or minimum of the two assets. Finite difference methods in general can be extended to deal with multiple state variables. However, if we have 100 grid points in one space dimension, then with two space dimensions we will have 100×100 grid points and therefore 100 times as much computation. In order to obtain reasonable computation times, much smaller grid sizes must be used and therefore implicit methods are even more desirable for problems with more than one state variable. However, they become quite complex to implement and the details are beyond the scope of this chapter. In section 3.10 we illustrate the general procedure for a two-state variable problem, highlighting the important steps. For most derivative pricing problems the alternating direction implicit (ADI) gives a good trade-off between accuracy, efficiency and tractability. There are more efficient methods, but the complexity of their implementation is beyond the present scope of this book (see for example Smith, 1975 and Press *et al.*, 1992).

3.10 THE ALTERNATING DIRECTION IMPLICIT METHOD

Consider the case of an option which pays off based on the values of two assets, S_1 and S_2, which follow the correlated GBMs:

$$dS_1 = (r - \delta_1)S_1\,dt + \sigma_1 S_1\,dz_1 \tag{3.60}$$

$$dS_2 = (r - \delta_2)S_2\,dt + \sigma_2 S_2\,dz_2 \tag{3.61}$$

where the two assets have correlation ρ i.e. $dz_1 \cdot dz_2 = \rho\,dt$.

The PDE which governs the price of the option is given by (see Cox, Ingersoll, and Ross, 1985)

$$\begin{aligned} -\frac{\partial C}{\partial t} &= (r - \delta_1)S_1\frac{\partial C}{\partial S_1} + (r - \delta_2)S_2\frac{\partial C}{\partial S_2} \\ &\quad + \frac{1}{2}\sigma_1^2 S_1^2\frac{\partial^2 C}{\partial S_1^2} + \frac{1}{2}\sigma_2^2 S_2^2\frac{\partial^2 C}{\partial S_2^2} + \rho\sigma_1 S_1\sigma_2 S_2\frac{\partial^2 C}{\partial S_1 \partial S_2} - rC \end{aligned} \tag{3.62}$$

If we directly apply the Crank–Nicolson method to equation (3.62) we obtain a system of $(2N_j - 1)(2N_k - 1)$ linear equations each containing the nine unknown option values at time step i. Together with the $2(2N_j - 1) + 2(2N_k + 1)$ boundary conditions we have a system of $(2N_j + 1)^*(2N_k + 1)$ linear equations[5] for the $(2N_j + 1)(2N_k + 1)$ unknown option values. These no longer have a simple structure and must be solved using sparse matrix methods (see for example Press *et al.*, 1992). The ADI method is an adaptation of the Crank–Nicolson method which allows us to obtain simple tridiagonal matrix equations.

Before we can apply the ADI method to equation (3.62) we must transform it into the form of a standard diffusion equation. Firstly, we transform to the natural logarithms of the asset prices $x_1 = \ln(S_1)$ and $x_2 = \ln(S_2)$, which gives a PDE with constant coefficients:

$$-\frac{\partial C}{\partial t} = v_1\frac{\partial C}{\partial x_1} + v_2\frac{\partial C}{\partial x_2} + \frac{1}{2}\sigma_1^2\frac{\partial^2 C}{\partial x_1^2} + \frac{1}{2}\sigma_2^2\frac{\partial^2 C}{\partial x_2^2} + \rho\sigma_1\sigma_2\frac{\partial^2 C}{\partial x_1 \partial x_2} - rC \tag{3.63}$$

where $v_1 = r - \delta_1 - \frac{1}{2}\sigma_1^2$ and $v_2 = r - \delta_2 - \frac{1}{2}\sigma_2^2$.

Secondly, the ADI method cannot handle the mixed second-order derivative in equation (3.63) involving the correlation between the assets. We must therefore transform to space variables which are uncorrelated. This can be achieved by computing the eigenvectors and eigenvalues of the covariance matrix of x_1 and x_2:

$$\underbrace{\left(\begin{pmatrix} e_{11} \\ e_{12} \end{pmatrix} \begin{pmatrix} e_{21} \\ e_{22} \end{pmatrix}\right)}_{\text{eigenvectors}} \underbrace{\begin{pmatrix} \lambda_1 & 0 \\ 0 & \lambda_2 \end{pmatrix}}_{\text{eigenvalues}} \begin{pmatrix} e_{11} & e_{12} \\ e_{21} & e_{22} \end{pmatrix} = \underbrace{\begin{pmatrix} \sigma_1^2 & \rho\sigma_1\sigma_2 \\ \rho\sigma_1\sigma_2 & \sigma_2^2 \end{pmatrix}}_{\text{covariance matrix}} \tag{3.64}$$

The eigenvectors give the linear combinations of x_1 and x_2 which are uncorrelated:

$$\begin{aligned} y_1 &= e_{11}x_1 + e_{12}x_2 \\ y_2 &= e_{21}x_1 + e_{22}x_2 \\ \alpha_1 &= e_{11}v_1 + e_{12}v_2 \\ \alpha_2 &= e_{21}v_1 + e_{22}v_2 \\ dy_1 &= \alpha_1\,dt + \sqrt{\lambda_1}\,dw_1 \\ dy_2 &= \alpha_2\,dt + \sqrt{\lambda_2}\,dw_2 \end{aligned} \tag{3.65}$$

where dw_1, dw_2 are uncorrelated Brownian motions. Under this transformation the PDE (equation (3.63)) becomes

$$-\frac{\partial C}{\partial t} = \alpha_1\frac{\partial C}{\partial y_1} + \alpha_2\frac{\partial C}{\partial y_2} + \frac{1}{2}\lambda_1\frac{\partial^2 C}{\partial y_1^2} + \frac{1}{2}\lambda_2\frac{\partial^2 C}{\partial y_2^2} - rC \tag{3.66}$$

Now the ADI method does not handle the zeroth (rC) and first-order terms

$$\left(\alpha_1\frac{\partial C}{\partial y_1} + \alpha_2\frac{\partial C}{\partial y_2}\right)$$

very well. These can be removed with the transformation

$$C(y_1, y_2, t) = \exp(a_1 y_1 + a_2 y_2 + a_3 t) U(y_1, y_2, t) \tag{3.67}$$

Applying this transformation to equation (3.66) and setting the coefficients of the resulting zeroth and first-order terms to zero we obtain

$$-\frac{\partial U}{\partial t} = \frac{1}{2}\lambda_1 \frac{\partial^2 U}{\partial y_1^2} + \frac{1}{2}\lambda_2 \frac{\partial^2 U}{\partial y_2^2} \tag{3.68}$$

and

$$a_1 = -\frac{\alpha_1}{\lambda_1},\ a_2 = -\frac{\alpha_2}{\lambda_2},\ a_3 = \frac{\alpha_1^2}{2\lambda_1} + \frac{\alpha_2^2}{2\lambda_2} + r \tag{3.69}$$

Finally, we transform so that the coefficients of the two second-order terms are equal using

$$y_2' = \sqrt{\frac{\lambda_1}{\lambda_2}}\, y_2 \tag{3.70}$$

which gives

$$-\frac{\partial U}{\partial t} = \frac{1}{2}\lambda_1 \left(\frac{\partial^2 U}{\partial y_1^2} + \frac{\partial^2 U}{\partial y_2'^2} \right) \tag{3.71}$$

The ADI method can be applied to equation (3.71) which is in the form of a standard two-dimensional diffusion equation. The ADI method replaces the partial derivatives by their Crank–Nicolson style finite difference approximations in two stages. Firstly, the derivatives with respect to y_1 are replaced by finite difference approximations at time step $i + \frac{1}{2}$, whilst the derivatives with respect to y_2' are approximated by finite differences at time step $i + 1$. This gives the following finite difference equation:

$$-\frac{U_{i+1,j,k} - U_{i+\frac{1}{2},j,k}}{\frac{1}{2}\Delta t} = \frac{1}{2}\lambda_1 \left(\frac{\left(U_{i+\frac{1}{2},j+1,k} - 2U_{i+\frac{1}{2},j,k} + U_{i+\frac{1}{2},j-1,k}\right)}{\Delta y_1^2} + \frac{(U_{i+1,j,k+1} - 2U_{i+1,j,k} + U_{i+1,j,k-1})}{\Delta y_2'^2} \right) \tag{3.72}$$

which can be rewritten as

$$p_u U_{i+\frac{1}{2},j+1,k} + p_m U_{i+\frac{1}{2},j,k} + p_d U_{i+\frac{1}{2},j-1,k} = -\frac{2}{\Delta t} U_{i+1,j,k} - \frac{1}{2}\lambda_1 \left(\frac{(U_{i+1,j,k+1} - 2U_{i+1,j,k} + U_{i+1,j,k-1})}{\Delta y_2'^2} \right) \tag{3.73}$$

$$p_u = \frac{\lambda_1}{2\Delta y_1^2} \tag{3.74}$$

$$p_m = -\frac{2}{\Delta t} - \frac{\lambda_1}{\Delta y_1^2} \tag{3.75}$$

$$p_d = \frac{\lambda_1}{2\Delta y_1^2} \tag{3.76}$$

Secondly, the derivatives with respect to y_2' are replaced by finite difference approximations at time step i, whilst the derivatives with respect to y_1 are approximated by finite differences at time step $i+\frac{1}{2}$. This gives the following finite difference equation:

$$-\frac{U_{i+\frac{1}{2},j,k} - U_{i,j,k}}{\frac{1}{2}\Delta t} = \frac{1}{2}\lambda_1 \left(\frac{\left(U_{i+\frac{1}{2},j+1,k} - 2U_{i+\frac{1}{2},j,k} + U_{i+\frac{1}{2},j-1,k}\right)}{\Delta y_1^2} + \frac{\left(U_{i,j,k+1} - 2U_{i,j,k} + U_{i,j,k-1}\right)}{\Delta y_2'^2} \right) \tag{3.77}$$

which can be rewritten as

$$p_{\mathrm{u}} U_{i.j,k+1} + p_{\mathrm{m}} U_{i,j,k} + p_{\mathrm{d}} U_{i,j,k-1} = -\frac{2}{\Delta t} U_{i+\frac{1}{2},j,k} - \frac{1}{2}\lambda_1 \left(\frac{\left(U_{i+\frac{1}{2},j+1,k} - 2U_{i+\frac{1}{2},j,k} + U_{i+\frac{1}{2},j-1,k}\right)}{\Delta y_1'^2} \right) \tag{3.78}$$

$$p_{\mathrm{u}} = \frac{\lambda_1}{2\Delta y_2'^2} \tag{3.79}$$

$$p_{\mathrm{m}} = -\frac{2}{\Delta t} - \frac{\lambda_1}{\Delta y_2'^2} \tag{3.80}$$

$$p_{\mathrm{d}} = \frac{\lambda_1}{2\Delta y_2'^2} \tag{3.81}$$

Equations (3.64) and (3.69) are tridiagonal systems of equations. Each step individually is unstable and non-convergent, but together they are unconditionally stable and convergent.

3.11 SUMMARY

In this chapter we described the generalisation of the binomial tree model to the trinomial tree model and then the extension of the trinomial tree into a lattice or grid of nodes. From this we went on to discuss the refinement of the approach to explicit, implicit and Crank–Nicolson finite difference methods. Finally, we described the efficient computation of hedge sensitivities and the extension of the Crank–Nicolson method to options which depend on more than one asset.

ENDNOTES

1. Strictly, we can must show that we can construct a riskless hedge. There is a technical difficulty with the trinomial process in that it is not possible to construct a riskless hedge using just the asset and cash because there are now three possible future states of the world. The solution to this is to show that the trinomial process is equivalent to solving the Black–Scholes partial

differential equation (PDE) by the explicit finite difference method and thus converges to the continuous time limit.

2. The term "forward" is with respect to the direction in which the computations are being made on the grid.
3. This procedure is called elimination of the upper diagonal. Alternatively, we could start at $j = N_j$ and work downwards, eliminating the lower diagonal in a similar way.
4. This procedure is called back-substitution.
5. Where N_k is analogous to N_j, i.e. the number of nodes either side of the current level of S_2.

4

Monte Carlo Simulation

4.1 INTRODUCTION

MANY complex derivatives exist for which analytical formulae are not possible, Monte Carlo simulation (first used by Boyle, 1977) provides a simple and flexible method for valuing these types of instruments. It can deal easily with multiple random factors; for example options on multiple assets, random volatility or random interest rates. Monte Carlo simulation also allows the incorporation of more realistic asset price processes, such as jumps in asset prices, and more realistic market conditions such as the discrete fixing of exotic path-dependent options. It can also give insights into the effectiveness of a hedge. However, Monte Carlo simulation is computationally inefficient in its basic form. In this chapter, after first introducing the Monte Carlo simulation methods, we show how to improve its efficiency using control variates and quasi-random numbers (deterministic sequences). We also describe in detail how Monte Carlo simulation can be used to value complex path-dependent options. The interested reader is recommended to study Ripley (1987) for a general discussion of stochastic simulation.

4.2 VALUATION BY SIMULATION

In Chapter 1 it was shown that the value of an option is the risk-neutral expectation of its discounted pay-off. We can obtain an estimate of this expectation by computing the average of a large number of discounted payoffs. Consider a European-style option which pays C_T at the maturity date T. Firstly, we simulate the risk-neutral processes for the state variables from their values today, time zero to the maturity date T and compute the pay-off of the contingent claim, $C_{T,j}$ for this simulation (j). Then we discount this pay-off using the simulated short-term interest rate sequence:

$$C_{0,j} = \exp\left(-\int_0^T r_u\,du\right) C_{T,j} \tag{4.1}$$

In the case of constant interest rates equation (4.1) simplifies to

$$C_{0,j} = \exp(-rT)C_{T,j}$$

The simulations are repeated many (say M) times and the average of all the outcomes is taken

$$\hat{C}_0 = \frac{1}{M}\sum_{j=1}^{M} C_{0,j} \tag{4.2}$$

where $\hat{C}_0$ is an estimate of the true value of the option C_0, but with an error due to the fact that it is an average of randomly generated samples and so is itself random. A measure of the error is the standard deviation of $\hat{C}_0$ which is called the standard error SE(.) and can be estimated as the sample standard deviation of $C_{0,j}$ divided by the square root of the number of samples (see Hines and Montgomery, 1980, for an introduction to probability and statistics).

$$\mathrm{SE}(\hat{C}_0) = \frac{\mathrm{SD}(C_{0,j})}{\sqrt{M}} \tag{4.3}$$

where

$$\mathrm{SD}(C_{0,j}) = \sqrt{\frac{1}{M-1}\sum_{j=1}^{M}\left(C_{0,j} - \hat{C}_0\right)^2}$$

Let us look at a simple, specific example in detail; a standard European call option in the Black–Scholes world. Here interest rates are constant and so, as noted above, the discounting term in (4.1) becomes $\exp(-rT)$. This is the same for all simulations and so can be taken out of equation (4.1) and applied once to the average obtained using equation (4.2). In order to implement Monte Carlo simulation we need to simulate the geometric Brownian motion (GBM) process for the underlying asset[1]

$$dS_t = (r - \delta)S_t\,dt + \sigma S_t\,dz_t \tag{4.4}$$

The best way to simulate a variable following GBM is via the process for the natural logarithm of the variable which follows arithmetic Brownian motion and is normally distributed. Let $x_t = \ln(S_t)$ then we have

$$dx_t = \nu\,dt + \sigma\,dz_t, \qquad \nu = r - \delta - \tfrac{1}{2}\sigma^2 \tag{4.5}$$

Equation (4.5) can be discretised[2] by changing the infinitesimals dx, dt and dz into small changes Δx, Δt and Δz

$$\Delta x = \nu\Delta t + \sigma\Delta z \tag{4.6}$$

This representation involves no approximation because it is actually the solution of the SDE (4.5) which we can write as

$$x_{t+\Delta t} = x_t + \nu\Delta t + \sigma(z_{t+\Delta t} - z_t) \tag{4.7}$$

In terms of the asset price S we have

$$S_{t+\Delta t} = S_t \exp(\nu\Delta t + \sigma(z_{t+\Delta t} - z_t)) \tag{4.8}$$

where z_t would normally be defined as being equal to zero. The random increment $z_{t+\Delta t} - z_t$ has mean zero and a variance of Δt, it can therefore be simulated by random samples of $\sqrt{\Delta t}\varepsilon$, where ε is a sample from a standard normal distribution.[3] Equation (4.8) therefore provides a way of simulating values of S_t. We divide the time period over which we wish to simulate S_t, in this case $(0, T)$, into N intervals such that $\Delta t = T/N$. We can then generate values of S_t at the end of these intervals, $t_i = i\Delta t$, $i = 1, \ldots, N$ using equation (4.7) as follows:

$$S_{t_i} = \exp(x_{t_i}), \qquad x_{t_i} = x_{t_{i-1}} + \nu\Delta t + \sigma\sqrt{\Delta t}\varepsilon_i \tag{4.9}$$

FIGURE 4.1 Simulated Asset Price Paths in the Black–Scholes World

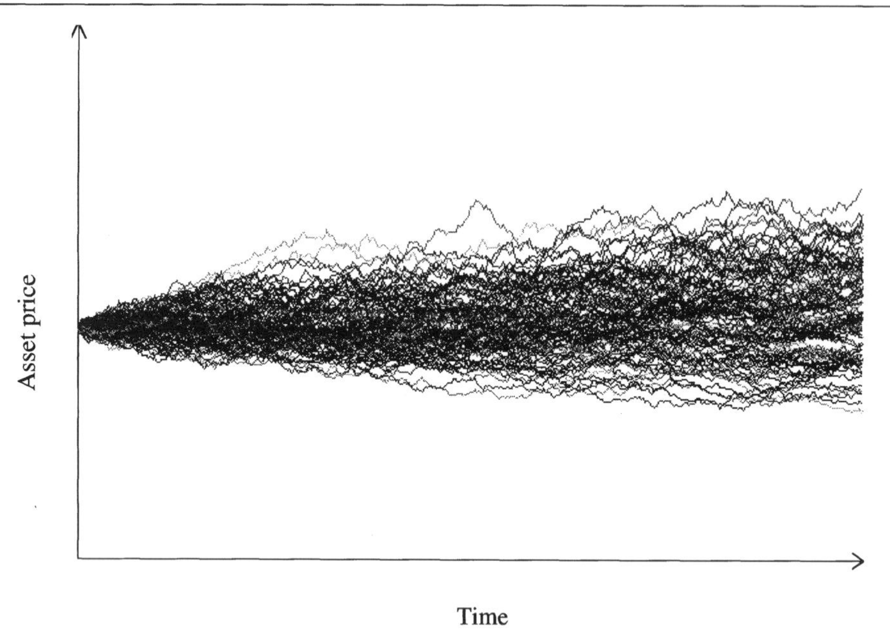

Figure 4.1 illustrates a set of $M = 100$ simulated paths using (4.9) repeatedly with typical parameter values for a stock: $S = 100$, $\sigma = 20$ per cent, $r = 6$ per cent, $T = 1$ year, $N = 365$. For each simulated path we compute the pay-off of the call option $\max(0, S_T - K)$. To obtain the estimate of the call price we simply take the discounted average of these simulated pay-offs

$$\hat{C}_0 = \exp(-rT)\frac{1}{M}\sum_{j=1}^{M}\max(0, S_{T,j} - K) \tag{4.10}$$

Note that for this simple example, since we have the solution of the underlying SDE (equation (4.7)), we can generate the samples of S_T directly without simulating the entire path as shown in Figure 4.1. This is not the case in general, as we will see later; normally we can only obtain an approximate discretisation of the SDE which must be simulated with relatively small time steps. Figure 4.2 gives a pseudo-code implementation of the Monte Carlo valuation of a European call option.

Once again, note that to compute the European call option estimate under GBM we can set $N = 1$, but this is not the case in general.

Example : Pricing a European Call Option by Monte Carlo Simulation

We price a one-year maturity, at-the-money European call option with the current asset price at 100 and volatility of 20 per cent. The continuously compounded interest rate is assumed to be 6 per cent per annum, the asset pays a continuous dividend yield of 3 per cent per annum. The simulation has 10 time steps and 100 simulations; $K = 100$, $T = 1$

FIGURE 4.2 Pseudo-code for Monte Carlo Valuation of a European Call Option in a Black–Scholes World

```
initialise_parameters { K, T, S, sig, r, div, N, M }

{ precompute constants }

dt = T/N
nudt = (r-div-0.5*sig^2)*dt
sigsdt = sig*sqrt(dt)
lnS = ln(S)

sum_CT = 0
sum_CT2 = 0

for j = 1 to M do { for each simulation }

lnSt = lnS

  for i = 1 to N do { for each time step }
    ε = standard_normal_sample
    lnSt = lnSt + nudt + sigsdt*ε { evolve the stock price }
  next i

  ST = exp(lnSt)
  CT = max( 0 , ST - K )
  sum_CT = sum_CT + CT
  sum_CT2 = sum_CT2 + CT*CT

next j

call_value = sum_CT/M*exp(-r*T)
SD = sqrt( ( sum_CT2 - sum_CT*sum_CT/M )*exp(-2*r*T)/(M-1) )
SE = SD/sqrt(M)
```

year, $S = 100$, $\sigma = 0.2$, $r = 0.06$, $\delta = 0.03$, $N = 10$, $M = 100$. Figure 4.3 illustrates the numerical results, the simulated paths of $\ln(S_t)(i = 1, \ldots, 10)$ are only shown for $j = 1, \ldots 5$ and $j = 95, \ldots, 100$. The corresponding standard normal random numbers ε are shown in the table below the table of $\ln(S_t)$ values in Figure 4.3.

Firstly, the constants; Δt (dt), $\nu\Delta(nudt)$, $\sigma\sqrt{\Delta t}(sigsdt)$, and $\ln(S)(lnS)$ are precomputed:

$$\Delta t = \frac{T}{N} = \frac{1}{10} = 0.1$$

$$nudt = (r - \delta - \tfrac{1}{2}\sigma^2)\Delta t = (0.06 - 0.03 - 0.5 \times 0.2^2) \times 0.1 = 0.001$$

$$sigsdt = \sigma\sqrt{\Delta t} = 0.2\sqrt{0.1} = 0.0632$$

$$lnS = \ln(S) = 4.6052$$

Then for each simulation $j = 1$ to M, where $M = 100$, $\ln(S_t)$ is initialised to lnS:

$$\ln(S_t) = 4.6052$$

FIGURE 4.3 Numerical Example for Monte Carlo Valuation of a European Call Option in a Black–Scholes World

K	T	S	sig	r	div	N	M	sum_CT	sum_CT2	SD
100	1	100	0.2	0.06	0.03	10	100	996.49	26610.7	12.22457

dt	nudt	sigsdt	lnS	call_value	SE
0.1	0.0010	0.0632	4.6052	9.3846	1.2225

lnSt

j \ i	0	1	2	3	4	5	6	7	8	9	10	ST	CT	CT*CT
1	4.6052	4.6030	4.6257	4.6738	4.6512	4.6666	4.5619	4.5864	4.5521	4.4840	4.6521	104.81	4.8070	23.11
2	4.6052	4.6862	4.6749	4.5386	4.4745	4.4546	4.4901	4.5206	4.4977	4.4618	4.4993	89.95	0.0000	0.00
3	4.6052	4.6430	4.6144	4.6184	4.6770	4.7225	4.7489	4.7402	4.7507	4.7275	4.7983	121.30	21.2996	453.67
4	4.6052	4.6188	4.6297	4.5106	4.5404	4.4814	4.4843	4.4984	4.5072	4.5060	4.4590	86.40	0.0000	0.00
5	4.6052	4.6807	4.7067	4.6915	4.7176	4.7258	4.7810	4.8131	4.8516	4.7885	4.8243	124.49	24.4939	599.95
95	4.6052	4.6121	4.6291	4.6968	4.6099	4.6949	4.5597	4.5229	4.6530	4.6761	4.6349	103.02	3.0211	9.13
96	4.6052	4.6331	4.6620	4.7152	4.7603	4.8091	4.8847	4.8218	4.7674	4.7796	4.8012	121.65	21.6545	468.92
97	4.6052	4.5729	4.7010	4.6682	4.7704	4.8236	4.9556	4.8797	4.9385	4.9607	4.9938	147.49	47.4931	2255.59
98	4.6052	4.5910	4.6111	4.6929	4.6479	4.7125	4.8040	4.9143	4.9915	4.9884	4.9925	147.30	47.3012	2237.41
99	4.6052	4.5634	4.5047	4.4652	4.4984	4.5028	4.5370	4.4913	4.5071	4.4906	4.4065	81.98	0.0000	0.00
100	4.6052	4.5189	4.5183	4.4599	4.5276	4.6812	4.6191	4.5996	4.5985	4.7130	4.7282	113.09	13.0941	171.46

ε

j \ i	1	2	3	4	5	6	7	8	9	10
1	−0.0497	0.3425	0.7442	−0.3723	0.2277	−1.6708	0.3709	−0.5581	−1.0924	2.6422
2	1.2660	−0.1948	−2.1717	−1.0290	−0.3296	0.5444	0.4668	−0.3777	−0.5831	0.5763
3	0.5818	−0.4677	0.0476	0.9110	0.7042	0.4014	−0.1541	0.1510	−0.3833	1.1032
4	0.1999	0.1557	−1.8976	0.4551	−0.9486	0.0294	0.2076	0.1225	−0.0347	−0.7592
5	1.1781	0.3955	−0.2564	0.3978	0.1129	0.8569	0.4924	0.5929	−1.0130	0.5489
95	0.0938	0.2533	1.0545	−1.3899	1.3276	−2.1535	−0.5969	2.0413	0.3494	−0.6672
96	0.4258	0.4411	0.8249	0.6971	0.7571	1.1791	−1.0113	−0.8750	0.1762	0.3261
97	−0.5256	2.0098	−0.5352	1.6003	0.8254	2.0709	−1.2152	0.9144	0.3343	0.5075
98	−0.2396	0.3012	1.2779	−0.7271	1.0051	1.4321	1.7281	1.2042	−0.0647	0.0485
99	−0.6757	−0.9440	−0.6416	0.5091	0.0544	0.5256	−0.7383	0.2339	−0.2779	−1.3456
100	−1.3793	−0.0259	−0.9388	1.0538	2.4134	−0.9981	−0.3233	−0.0339	1.7945	0.2252

Then for each time step $i = 1$ to N, where $N = 10$, $\ln(S_t)$ is simulated. For example for $j = 1$ and $i = 1$ (dropping the i and j subscripts):

$$\ln(S_t) = \ln(S_t) + nudt + sigsdt \times \varepsilon$$

$$\ln(S_t) = 4.6052 + 0.001 + 0.0632 \times (-0.0497) = 4.6030$$

At $i = 10$

$$S_T = \exp(\ln(S_t)) = \exp(4.6521) = 104.81$$

$$C_T = \max(0, S_T - K) = \max(0, 104.81 - 100) = 4.8070$$

The sum of the values of C_T and the squares of the values of C_T are accumulated:

$$\sum_{j=1}^{M} C_{T,j} = 996.488 \text{ (sum\_CT)} \quad \text{and} \quad \sum_{j=1}^{M} (C_{T,j})^2 = 26610.7 \text{(sum\_CT2)}$$

The estimate of the option value $\hat{C}_0$ (call_value) is then given by

$$\hat{C}_0 = 996.488/100 \times \exp(-0.06 \times 1) = 9.3846$$

The standard deviation (SD) is given by

$$\text{SD} = \frac{\sqrt{\sum_{j=1}^{M} (C_{T,j})^2 - \frac{1}{M}\left(\sum_{j=1}^{M} C_{T,j}\right)^2} \exp(-2rT)}{M - 1}$$

$$= \frac{\sqrt{26610.73 - \frac{1}{100}(996.488)^2} \exp(-2 \times 0.06 \times 1)}{100 - 1} = 12.2246$$

and so the standard error (SE) is

$$\text{SE} = \frac{\text{SD}}{\sqrt{M}} = 12.2246/10 = 1.22246$$

Unfortunately, in order to get an acceptably accurate estimate of the option price a very large number of simulations has to be performed, typically in the order of millions ($M > 1\,000\,000$). This problem can be dealt with by using variance reduction methods. These methods work on exactly the same principle as that of hedging an option position, that is that the pay-off of a hedged portfolio will have a much smaller variability than an unhedged pay-off. This corresponds to the variance (or equivalently standard error) of a simulated hedge portfolio being much smaller than that of the unhedged pay-off. We will stress this interpretation throughout this chapter.

4.3 ANTITHETIC VARIATES AND VARIANCE REDUCTION

Imagine that you have written an option on an asset S_1 and simultaneously are able to write an option on an asset S_2 which is perfectly negatively correlated with S_1, and which currently has exactly the same price as S_1. That is S_1 and S_2 satisfy the stochastic differential equations

$$dS_{1,t} = rS_{1,t}\,dt + \sigma S_{1,t}\,dz_t \tag{4.11}$$

$$dS_{2,t} = rS_{2,t}\,dt - \sigma S_{2,t}\,dz_t \tag{4.12}$$

The value of these two options are indentical since the price and volatility of the two assets are identical. However, the variance of the pay-off of a portfolio consisting of the two options is much less than the variance of the pay-off of each individual option since, roughly speaking, when one option pays off the other does not and vice versa. It may not be obvious at first why this leads to a smaller variance and so we give some intuition. Figure 4.4 illustrates the pay-off of a written call option on a lognormally distributed asset and the probability distribution of the payoff.

The variance (or variability) of the pay-off is very high because of the large spike of probability which corresponds to all the asset prices below the strike price. The hedge portfolio we have just described removes this spike and so reduces the variance of the pay-off.

This technique of creating a hypothetical asset which is perfectly negatively correlated with the original asset is called antithetic variance reduction and the created asset is called an antithetic variate. Implementation of this technique is very simple, for example, consider pricing a European call option. Our simulated pay-offs are

$$C_{T,j} = \max(0, S\exp(\nu T + \sigma\sqrt{T}(\varepsilon_j)) - K) \tag{4.13}$$

We can simulate the pay-offs to the option on the perfectly negatively correlated asset as

$$\overline{C}_{T,j} = \max(0, S\exp(\nu T + \sigma\sqrt{T}(-\varepsilon_j)) - K) \tag{4.14}$$

In other words we simply replace ε_j by $-\varepsilon_j$ in the equation for the simulation of the asset. We then take the average of the two pay-offs as the pay-off for that simulation. Note that, not only do we obtain a much more accurate estimate from M pairs of $(C_{T,j}, \overline{C}_{T,j})$ than from $2M$ of $C_{T,j}$, but it is also computationally cheaper to generate the pair $(C_{T,j}, \overline{C}_{T,j})$ than two instances of $C_{T,j}$. This method also ensures that the mean of the normally

FIGURE 4.4 Pay-off of Written Call Option and Probability Distribution of the Pay-off

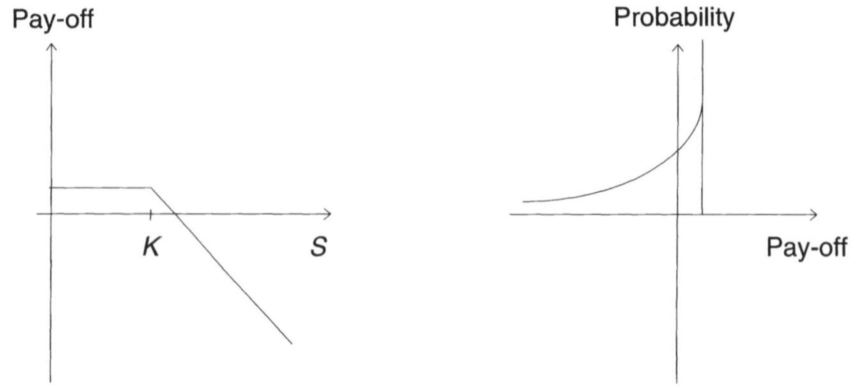

FIGURE 4.5 Pseudo-code for Monte Carlo Valuation of a European Call Option in a Black–Scholes World with Antithetic Variance Reduction

```
initialise_parameters { K, T, S, sig, r, div, N, M }

{ precompute constants }

dt = T/N
nudt = (r-div-0.5*sig^2)*dt
sigsdt = sig*sqrt(dt)
lnS = ln(S)

sum_CT = 0
sum_CT2 = 0

for j = 1 to M do { for each simulation }

lnSt1 = lnS
lnSt2 = lnS

  for i = 1 to N do { for each time step }
    ε = standard_normal_sample
    lnSt1 = lnSt1 + nudt + sigsdt*(ε)
    lnSt2 = lnSt2 + nudt + sigsdt*(-ε)
  next i

  St1 = exp(lnSt1)
  St2 = exp(lnSt2)
  CT = 0.5*( max( 0 , St1 - K ) + max( 0 , St2 - K ) )
  sum_CT = sum_CT + CT
  sum_CT2 = sum_CT2 + CT*CT

next j

call_value = sum_CT/M*exp(-r*T)
SD = sqrt( ( sum_CT2 - sum_CT*sum_CT/M )*exp(-2*r*T)/(M-1) )
SE = SD/sqrt(M)
```

distributed samples ε is exactly zero which also helps to improve the simulation. Figure 4.5 gives a pseudo-code implementation of the Monte Carlo valuation of a European call option with antithetic variance reduction. The differences from Figure 4.2 are highlighted in bold.

Example : Pricing a European Call Option by Monte Carlo Simulation with Antithetic Variance Reduction

We price a one-year maturity, at-the-money European call option with the current asset price at 100 and volatility of 20 per cent. The continuously compounded interest rate is assumed to be 6 per cent per annum, the asset pays a continuous dividend yield of 3 per cent per annum. The simulation has one time step and 100 simulations; $K = 100$, $T = 1$ year, $S = 100$, $\sigma = 0.2$, $r = 0.06$, $\delta = 0.03$, $N = 1$, $M = 100$. Figure 4.6 illustrates

FIGURE 4.6 Numerical Example for Monte Carlo Valuation of a European Call Option in a Black–Scholes World with Antithetic Variance Reduction

K	T	S	sig	r	div	N	M	sum_CT	sum_CT2	SD
100	1	100	0.2	0.06	0.03	1	100	1140.37	20790.8	8.3521
dt	**nudt**	**sigsdt**	**lnS**					**call_value**	**SE**	
1	0.0100	0.2000	4.6052					10.7396	0.8352	
j	ε	**lnSt1**	**lnSt2**	**ST1**	**ST2**	**CT**	**CT*CT**			
1	−0.8265	4.4499	4.7805	85.62	119.16	9.5807	91.79			
2	−0.6445	4.4863	4.7441	88.79	114.90	7.4508	55.51			
3	−0.9527	4.4246	4.8057	83.48	122.21	11.1033	123.28			
4	−1.8013	4.2549	4.9754	70.45	144.81	22.4057	502.01			
5	2.4056	5.0963	4.1341	163.41	62.43	31.7067	1005.32			
95	2.3200	5.0792	4.1512	160.64	63.51	30.3210	919.36			
96	1.9226	4.9997	4.2306	148.37	68.76	24.1840	584.87			
97	−0.6575	4.4837	4.7467	88.56	115.20	7.5995	57.75			
98	−1.0324	4.4087	4.8217	82.16	124.17	12.0849	146.05			
99	−0.3316	4.5488	4.6815	94.52	107.93	3.9656	15.73			
100	−0.4677	4.5216	4.7087	91.99	110.91	5.4542	29.75			

the numerical results, the simulated asset prices are only shown for $j = 1, \ldots 5$ and $j = 95, \ldots, 100$. Note that in this example there is only one time step ($N = 1$) because we only need to simulate asset prices at the maturity date of the option.

Firstly, the constants: $\Delta t\,(dt)$, $\nu\Delta t\,(nudt)$, $\sigma\sqrt{\Delta t}\,(sigsdt)$ and $\ln(S)(lnS)$ are precomputed:

$$\Delta t = \frac{T}{N} = \frac{1}{1} = 1$$

$$nudt = (r - \delta - \tfrac{1}{2}\sigma^2)\Delta t = (0.06 - 0.03 - 0.5 \times 0.2^2) \times 1 = 0.01$$

$$sigsdt = \sigma\sqrt{\Delta t} = 0.2\sqrt{1} = 0.2$$

$$\ln S = \ln(S) = 4.6052$$

Then for each simulation $j = 1$ to M, where $M = 100$, $\ln(S_{1,t})$ and $\ln(S_{2,t})$ are initialised to $\ln(S) = 4.6052$. Then $\ln(S_{1,t})$ and $\ln(S_{2,t})$ are simulated, for example for $j = 1$ and $i = 1$:

$$\ln(S_{1,t}) = 4.6052 + 0.010 + 0.2 \times (-0.8265) = 4.4499$$

$$\ln(S_{2,t}) = 4.6052 + 0.010 + 0.2 \times (0.8265) = 4.7805$$

$$S_{1,T} = \exp(4.4499) = 85.62$$

$$S_{2,T} = \exp(4.7805) = 119.16$$

Computing the pay-off at maturity gives:

$$C_T = 0.5 \times (\max(0, 85.62 - 100) + \max(0, 119.16 - 100)) = 9.5807$$

The sum of the values of C_T and the squares of the values of C_T are accumulated:

$$\sum_{j=1}^{M} C_{T,j} = 1140.37 \quad \text{and} \quad \sum_{j=1}^{M} (C_{T,j})^2 = 20790.8$$

The estimate of the option value $\hat{C}_0$ (call_value) is then given by

$$\hat{C}_0 = 1140.366/100 \times \exp(-0.06 \times 1) = 10.7396$$

This technique can be easily applied to virtually any Monte Carlo simulation to improve the efficiency. In the next section we describe more advanced variance reduction methods based on the hedging analogy.

4.4 CONTROL VARIATES AND HEDGING

The general approach of using hedges as control variates was first described by Clewlow and Carverhill (1994).[4] Consider the case of writing a European call option. Figure 4.4 illustrated the pay-off and its probability distribution. The distribution of this pay-off has a large standard deviation, and so if we try and estimate the call value as the mean of a number of Monte Carlo simulations then the standard error of the mean will be large.

FIGURE 4.7 Probability Distribution of the Pay-off Written Call Option after Delta Hedging

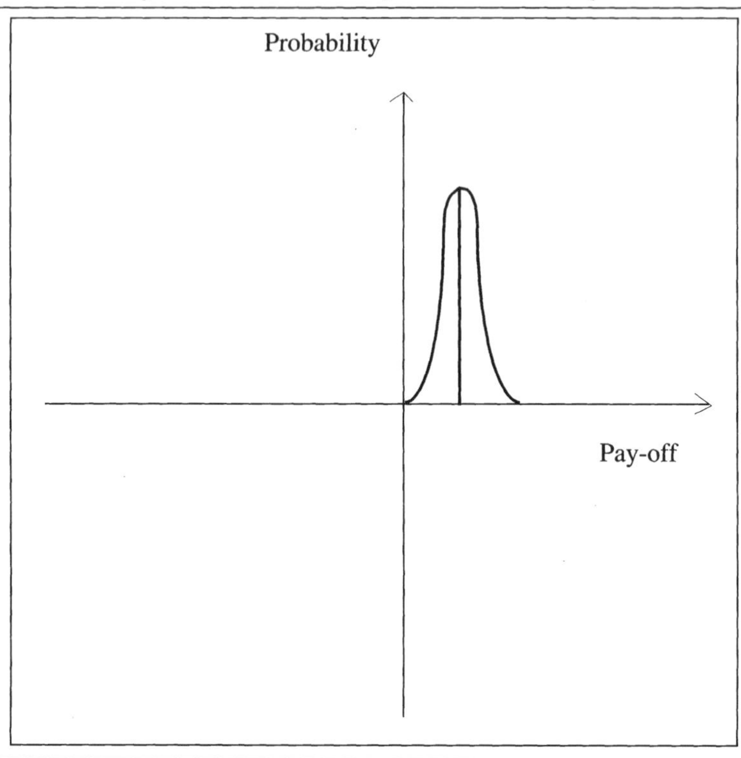

Consider the effect of delta hedging the call option. Figure 4.7 illustrates the probability distribution of the pay-off after delta hedging

The pay-off of the hedged portfolio has a much smaller standard deviation, this is of course the whole point of the delta hedge. Let us consider the mechanics of a discretely rebalanced delta hedge in detail. The delta hedge consists of a holding of $\partial C/\partial S$ in the asset which is rebalanced at discrete intervals, t_i, $i = 0, \ldots, N$. The changes in the value of the hedge as the asset price changes randomly offset the changes in the option value. Because the hedge is rebalanced at discrete time intervals it is not perfect, but for reasonably frequent rebalancing we expect it to be very good. The hedging procedure consists of selling the option, putting the premium in the bank and rebalancing the holding in the asset at discrete intervals with resultant cash flows into and out of the bank account. At the maturity date the hedge, consisting of the cash account plus the asset, closely replicates the pay-off of the option. We can express this mathematically as follows:

$$C_{t_0} e^{r(T-t_0)} - \left[\sum_{i=0}^{N} \left(\frac{\partial C_{t_i}}{\partial s} - \frac{\partial C_{t_{i-1}}}{\partial s} \right) S_{t_i} e^{r(T-t_i)} \right] = C_T + \eta \tag{4.15}$$

where $\partial C_{t-1}/\partial S = 0$. The first term in equation (4.15) is the premium received for writing the option, inflated at the riskless rate to the maturity date, the second term represents the cash flows from rebalancing the hedge at each date t_i and the third term is the pay-off of the option C_T and the hedging error η. The expression in square brackets is the delta hedge. Expanding the summation term in the square brackets in equation (4.15) gives

$$\frac{\partial C_{t_0}}{\partial S}S_{t_0}e^{r(T-t_0)} + \frac{\partial C_{t_1}}{\partial S}S_{t_1}e^{r(T-t_1)} + \cdots + \frac{\partial C_{t_{N-1}}}{\partial S}S_{t_{N-1}}e^{r(T-t_{N-1})} + \frac{\partial C(t_N)}{\partial s}S_{t_N}$$
$$-\frac{\partial C_{t_0}}{\partial S}S_{t_1}e^{r(T-t_1)} - \frac{\partial C_{t_1}}{\partial S}S_{t_2}e^{r(T-t_2)} - \cdots - \frac{\partial C_{t_{N-1}}}{\partial S}S_{t_N} \quad (4.16)$$

Rewriting equation (4.16) grouping terms with $\partial C_{t_i}/\partial S$ at the same time step:

$$-\frac{\partial C_{t_0}}{\partial S}(S_{t_1} - S_{t_0}e^{r\Delta t})e^{r(T-t_1)} - \frac{\partial C_{t_1}}{\partial S}(S_{t_2} - S_{t_1}e^{r\Delta t})e^{r(T-t_2)}\ldots$$
$$-\frac{\partial C_{t_{N-1}}}{\partial S}(S_{t_N} - S_{t_{N-1}}e^{r\Delta t}) + \frac{\partial C_{t_N}}{\partial S}S_{t_N} \quad (4.17)$$

If we assume that the final term in (4.17) is zero, which corresponds to not buying the final delta amount of the asset, but simply liquidating the holding from the previous rebalancing date into cash, then the hedged portfolio becomes

$$C_{t_0}e^{r(T-t_0)} + \left[\sum_{i=0}^{N-1}\frac{\partial C_{t_i}}{\partial S}(S_{t_{i+1}} - S_{t_i}e^{r\Delta t})e^{r(T-t_{i+1})}\right] = C_T + \eta \quad (4.18)$$

The expression in square brackets, which is the delta hedge, we call a delta-based martingale control variate (cv_1). This can be seen by writing it as follows:

$$cv_1 = \sum_{i=0}^{N-1}\frac{\partial C_{t_i}}{\partial S}(S_{t_{i+1}} - E[S_{t_i}])e^{r(T-t_{i+1})} \quad (4.19)$$

Thus, the expectation or mean of cv_1 will be zero. Rearranging equation (4.18) we have

$$C_{t_0}e^{r(T-t_0)} = C_T - \left[\sum_{i=0}^{N-1}\frac{\partial C_{t_i}}{\partial S}(S_{t_{i+1}} - E[S_{t_i}])e^{r(T-t_{i+1})}\right] + \eta \quad (4.20)$$

and we can interpret equation (4.20) as saying that the expectation of the pay-off plus the hedge is equal to the initial premium inflated to the maturity date at the riskless rate of interest. Therefore if we simulate the payoff and the hedge and compute the mean of these we will obtain an estimate of the option value but with a much smaller variance. This can be more easily visualised by plotting the payoff against the control variate cv_1 resulting from a Monte Carlo simulation. This is done in Figure 4.8 for European call option with parameter values; $K = 100$, $T = 1.0$, $S = 100$, $\sigma = 0.2$, $r = 0.06$, $\delta = 0.03$. The Monte Carlo simulation has been repeated for a number of different rebalancing intervals (or Monte Carlo time steps) corresponding to monthly, weekly and daily time steps ($N = 12$, $N = 52$, and $N = 250$) with $M = 1000$.

Figure 4.8 shows that the combination of the initial premium inflated at the riskless rate of interest plus the control variate cv_1 which is the cash accumulated by the delta hedging process is approximately equal to the pay-off of the option. The hedge gets better as the time step is decreased or equivalently as the hedge is rebalanced more often. Therefore, with this method the key to obtaining accurate prices is to have small time steps rather than a large number of simulations. In the terminology of Monte Carlo simulation, cv_1 is

FIGURE 4.8 Black–Scholes Monte Carlo Simulation with Delta-based Control Variate

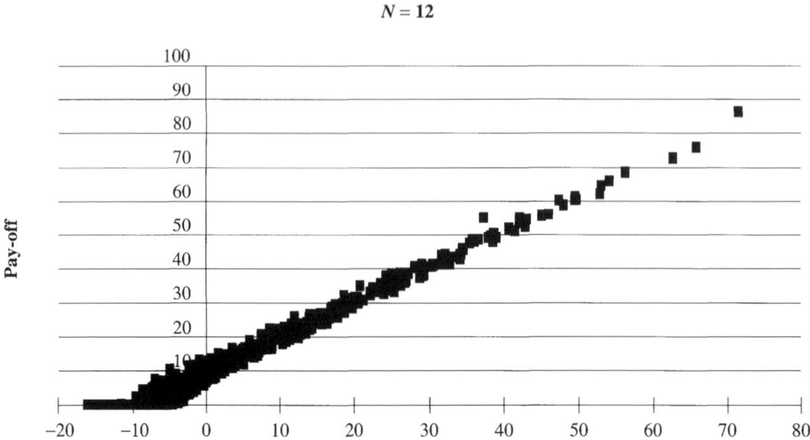

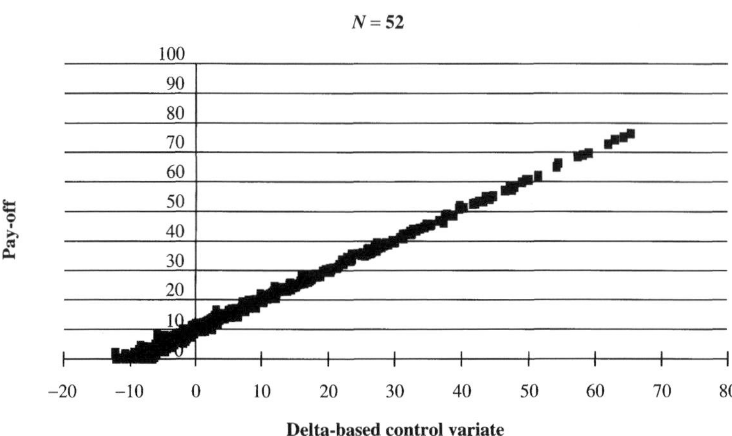

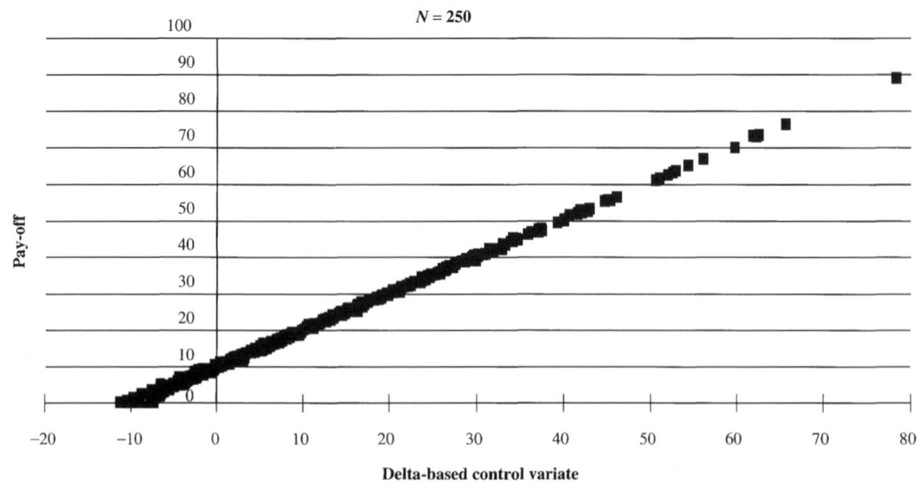

a control variate, a random variable, whose expected value we know, which is correlated with the variable we are trying to estimate (in our case the option value). In this case the known mean of cv_1 is zero. In the same way as for cv_1 we can construct other control variates equivalent to other hedges. For example, a *gamma* hedge

$$cv_2 = \sum_{i=0}^{N-1} \frac{\partial^2 C_{t_i}}{\partial S^2}((\Delta S_{t_i})^2 - E[(\Delta S_{t_i})^2])e^{r(T-t_{i+1})} \tag{4.21}$$

where $\mathrm{E}[(\Delta S_{t_i})^2] = S_{t_i}^2(e^{(2r+\sigma^2)\Delta t_i} - 2e^{r\Delta t_i} + 1)$.

For the general case of a European option paying off C_T at time T, setting $t_0 = 0$ and with m control variates, equation (4.20) becomes

$$C_0 e^{rT} = C_T - \sum_{k=1}^{m} \beta_k cv_k + \eta \tag{4.22}$$

where the β factors are included to account for the sign of the hedge, for errors in the hedges due to the discrete rebalancing and only having approximate hedge sensitivities (i.e. *delta, gamma*, etc.). This is important for the practical implementation of this method. In reality we will be using Monte Carlo to value an option for which we do not have an analytical expression. Therefore we will not have analytical expressions for the hedge sensitivities; however, we are quite likely to have an analytical formula for a similar option. For example we might be valuing a path-dependent option which is similar to a lookback option where we have analytical expressions for continuously fixed lookback options under the Black–Scholes assumptions. Therefore we can use the hedge sensitivities from the analytical lookback formula in the control variates to value the more complex option. We describe this example in detail in the next section.

We rewrite equation (4.22) as follows:

$$C_T = \beta_0 + \sum_{k=1}^{m} \beta_k cv_k + \eta \tag{4.23}$$

where $\beta_0 = C_0 e^{rT}$ is the forward price of the option. We can interpret equation (4.23) as a linear equation relating the pay-off of the option to the control variates via the β coefficients. If we perform M simulations we can regard the pay-offs and control variates $(C_{T,j}, cv_{1,j}, \ldots, cv_{m,j};\ j = 1, \ldots, M)$ as samples from this linear relationship with noise. The noise comes from the discrete rebalancing and the imperfect sensitivities. We can then obtain an estimate of the "true" relationship by least-squares regression. The least-squares estimate of the β is

$$\beta = (X'X)^{-1}X'Y \tag{4.24}$$

where $\beta = (\beta_0, \beta_1, \ldots, \beta_m)$, X is a matrix whose rows correspond to each simulation and are $(1, cv_{1,j}, \ldots, cv_{m,j})$ and Y is the vector of simulated pay-offs (the "dash" denotes transpose). The matrices $X'X$ and $X'Y$ can be accumulated as the simulation proceeds as follows:

$$(X'X)_{k,l,j+1} = (X'X)_{k,l,j} + cv_{k,j+1}cv_{l,j+1} \tag{4.25}$$

$$(X'Y)_{k,j+1} = (X'Y)_{k,j} + cv_{k,j+1}C_{T,j+1} \tag{4.26}$$

where k and l index the rows and columns of the matrix and j is the time step as usual. It is important to note that since the pay-offs and control variates are not jointly normally distributed then the estimate of β will be biased. This is particularly important for the forward value of the option β_0, as we do not want biased estimates of the option value. This problem is easily overcome by precomputing the β_k; $k = 1, \ldots, m$ by the least-squares regression method or fixing them at some appropriate value for the type of hedge. All options can then be priced, keeping the β's fixed, by simply taking the mean of the hedged portfolio under a different set of simulated paths. This is our recommended method for implementing this technique.

There is one other subtle but important aspect of the hedge control variate idea. If we form a control variate delta hedge for a variable which in the analytical model is stochastic and which in the simulation is following the same process as in the model, then the control variate hedge is simply replicating the model option. In this case it is much more efficient to form a static hedge portfolio which is long the option we want to price and short the analytical model option. We then value the difference between the two options using the Monte Carlo simulation which has much smaller variance than the option we want to price; we use this idea in section 4.9 to value an Asian option. However, a control variate hedge for a variable which is a constant parameter in the analytical model, but which is stochastic in the simulation, cannot be simplified. The analytical model does not price any possible pay-offs due to randomness of this variable. However, using the sensitivity from the analytical model in the simulation will approximately hedge the risk and therefore help reduce the variability of the Monte Carlo estimate. We use this method in section 4.10 to value a lookback option under stochastic volatility.

4.5 MONTE CARLO SIMULATION WITH CONTROL VARIATES

In this section we illustrate the use of control variates with a series of examples based on a European call option. For our first example we consider the Monte Carlo valuation of a European call option with a *delta*-based control variate. Figure 4.9 gives the pseudo-code algorithm.

The code which has been added from the simple Monte Carlo example in Figure 4.2 is highlighted in bold. Notice also that the method of simulating the asset price is slightly different. Since we need the asset price at each time step we simulate this directly rather than its natural logarithm. The variable **erddt** allows us to compute $E[S_i]$ in equation (4.19) efficiently. We set **beta1** $= -1$ which is the appropriate value for this example where we have the exact delta. The **delta** variable is computed as the Black–Scholes delta, by the function Black_ Scholes_delta ($S_t, t, K, T, \sigma, r, \delta$), at the start of the time step, i.e. before the asset price has been evolved and the control variate is then accumulated after the asset price has been evolved . The pay-off of the hedged portfolio is computed after the end of the time step loop and at the end the mean and standard error of this are computed. Since the mean of the control variate is zero, the mean gives us an estimate of the option price, but the standard error is greatly reduced by the control variate hedge. Figure 4.10 gives a numerical example.

FIGURE 4.9 Pseudo-code for Monte Carlo Valuation of a European Call Option in a Black–Scholes World with a *Delta*-based Control Variate

```
initialise_parameters { K, T, S, sig, r, div, N, M }

{ precompute constants }

dt = T/N
nudt = (r-div-0.5*sig^2)*dt
sigsdt = sig*sqrt(dt)
erddt = exp((r-div)*dt)

beta1 = -1

sum_CT = 0
sum_CT2 = 0

for j = 1 to M do { for each simulation }

  St = S
  cv = 0

  for i = 1 to N do { for each time step }

   t = (i-1)*dt
   delta = Black_Scholes_delta(St,t;K,T,sig,r,div)
   ε = standard_normal_sample
   Stn = St*exp( nudt + sigsdt*ε )
   cv = cv + delta*(Stn-St*erddt)
   St = Stn
  next i

  CT = max( 0 , St - K ) + beta1*cv
  sum_CT = sum_CT + CT
  sum_CT2 = sum_CT2 + CT*CT

next j

call_value = sum_CT/M*exp(-r*T)
SD = sqrt( ( sum_CT2 - sum_CT*sum_CT/M )*exp(-2*r*T)/(M-1) )
SE = SD/sqrt(M)
```

Example : Pricing a European Call Option by Monte Carlo Simulation with a Delta-based Control Variate

We price a one-year maturity, at-the-money European call option with the current asset price at 100 and volatility of 20 per cent. The continuously compounded interest rate is assumed to be 6 per cent per annum, the asset pays a continuous dividend yield of 3 per cent per annum. The simulation has 10 time steps and 100 simulations; $K = 100$, $T = 1$

FIGURE 4.10 Monte Carlo Valuation of a European Call Option in a Black–Scholes World with a *Delta*-based Control Variate

K	T	S	sig	r	div	N	M		sum_CT		sum_CT2		SD
100	1	100	0.2	0.06	0.03	10	100		963.1277		9670.3		1.879193
dt	**nudt**	**sigsdt**	**erddt**		**beta1**				**call_value**		**SE**		
0.1	0.0010	0.0632	1.0030		-1				9.070396		0.1879		
j=100													
i	0	1	2	3	4	5	6	7	8	9	10		
t	0	0.1	0.2	0.3	0.4	0.5	0.6	0.7	0.8	0.9	1		
ε	0	0.3766	0.4430	0.3302	0.2286	−0.6488	1.2000	−1.0518	−0.8125	1.0052	−1.1513		
St	100	102.51	105.53	107.87	109.55	105.25	113.66	106.45	101.22	107.97	100.49	**CT**	**CT*CT**
delta	0.5810	0.6264	0.6834	0.7304	0.7690	0.6944	0.8686	0.7536	0.5941	0.8991	1.0000	7.0029	49.04
cv	0.0000	1.2853	2.9830	4.3621	5.3525	1.7938	7.4153	0.8576	−3.3255	0.5050	−6.5133		

year, $S = 100$, $\sigma = 0.2$, $r = 0.06$, $\delta = 0.03$, $N = 10$, $M = 100$. Figure 4.10 illustrates the numerical results for the simulation of the path for $j = 100$.

Firstly, the constants; Δt (dt), $\nu\Delta t$ $(nudt)$, $\sigma\sqrt{\Delta t}$ $(sigsdt)$, $\exp((r-\delta)\Delta t)$ $(erddt)$ and β_1 $(beta1)$ are precomputed:

$$\begin{aligned}
\Delta t &= \frac{T}{N} = \frac{1}{10} = 0.1 \\
nudt &= \left(r - \delta - \tfrac{1}{2}\sigma^2\right)\Delta t = (0.06 - 0.03 - 0.5 \times 0.2^2) \times 0.1 = 0.001 \\
sigsdt &= \sigma\sqrt{\Delta t} = 0.2\sqrt{0.1} = 0.0632 \\
erddt &= \exp(-(r-\delta)\Delta t) = \exp(-(0.06 - 0.03) \times 0.1) = 1.0030 \\
lnS &= \ln(S) = 4.6052 \\
\beta_1 &= -1
\end{aligned}$$

Then for each simulation $j = 1$ to M, where $M = 100$, S_t is initialised to $S = 100$ and the control variate $cv = 0$. Then for each time step $i = 1$ to N, where $N = 10$, delta is computed, S_t is simulated and the control variate cv is accumulated. For example for $j = 100$ and $i = 0$, $delta = 0.58101$, this is the $delta$ which is used at $i = 1$ for accumulating the control variate. At $i = 1$ we have:

$$\begin{aligned}
S_t &= S \times \exp(nudt + sigsdt \times \varepsilon) \\
&= 100 \times \exp(0.0010 + 0.06325 \times 0.37656) = 102.513
\end{aligned}$$

$$cv = cv + \text{delta} \times (S_t - S \times erddt) = 0 + 0.5810 \times (102.513 - 100 \times 1.0030) = 1.2853$$

After the i loop we have

$$\begin{aligned}
C_T &= \max(0, S_T - K) + \beta_1 \times cv \\
&= \max(0, 100.49 - 100) + (-1) \times (-6.5133) = 7.0029
\end{aligned}$$

The sum of the values of C_T and the squares of the values of C_T are accumulated in sum_CT and sum_CT2, giving sum_CT = 963.128 and sum_CT2 = 9670.3. The estimate of the option value is then given by

$$\hat{C}_0 = \text{sum\_CT/M} \times \exp(-r \times T) = 963.128/100 \times \exp(-0.06 \times 1) = 9.0704$$

It is straightforward to combine the antithetic and control variate methods, we simply accumulate control variates for the standard and antithetic asset paths. Figure 4.11 illustrates the pseudo-code for combining antithetics with delta-based control variates for a European call option. The lines which have been added from Figure 4.9 are highlighted in bold. Note that in the calculation of the pay-off of the hedged portfolio (CT) both cv1 and cv2 are multiplied by beta1 and then added together. Therefore we do not need separate variables for the standard and antithetic control variates, they could both be accumulated in cv1. This method is used in the final example.

Example : Pricing a European Call Option by Monte Carlo Simulation with Antithetic and Delta-based Control Variates

We price a one-year maturity, at-the-money European call option with the current asset price at 100 and volatility of 20 per cent. The continuously compounded interest rate is

FIGURE 4.11 Pseudo-code for Monte Carlo Valuation of a European Call Option in a Black–Scholes World with Antithetic and *Delta*-based Control Variates

```
initialise_parameters { K, T, S, sig, r, div, N, M }

{ precompute constants }

dt = T/N
nudt = (r-div-0.5*sig^2)*dt
sigsdt = sig*sqrt(dt)
erddt = exp((r-div)*dt
beta1 = -1

sum_CT = 0
sum_CT2 = 0

for j = 1 to M do { for each simulation }

  St1 = S
  St2 = S
  cv1 = 0
  cv2 = 0

  for i = 1 to N do { for each time step }

    t = (i-1)*dt
    delta1 = Black_Scholes_delta(St1,t;K,T,sig,r,div)
    delta2 = Black_Scholes_delta(St2,t;K,T,sig,r,div)
    ε = standard_normal_sample
    Stn1 = St1*exp( nudt + sigsdt*(ε) )
    Stn2 = St2*exp( nudt + sigsdt*(-ε) )
    cv1 = cv1 + delta1*(Stn1-St1*erddt)
    cv2 = cv2 + delta2*(Stn2-St2*erddt)
    St1 = Stn1
    St2 = Stn2

  next i

 CT = 0.5*( max( 0 , St1 - K ) + beta1*cv1 +
            max( 0 , St2 - K ) + beta1*cv2 )
  sum_CT = sum_CT + CT
  sum_CT2 = sum_CT2 + CT*CT

next j

call_value = sum_CT/M*exp(-r*T)
SD = sqrt( ( sum_CT2 - sum_CT*sum_CT/M )*exp(-2*r*T)/(M-1) )
SE = SD/sqrt(M)
```

assumed to be 6 per cent per annum, the asset pays a continuous dividend yield of 3 per cent per annum. The simulation has 10 time steps and 100 simulations: $K = 100$, $T = 1$ year, $S = 100$, $\sigma = 0.2$, $r = 0.06$, $\delta = 0.03$, $N = 10$, $M = 100$. Figure 4.12 illustrates the numerical results for the simulation of the path for $j = 100$.

FIGURE 4.12 Monte Carlo Valuation of a European Call Option in a Black–Scholes World with Antithetic and *Delta*-based Control Variates

K	**T**	**S**	**sig**	**r**	**div**	**N**	**M**		**sum_CT**		**sum_CT2**		**SD**
100	1	100	0.2	0.06	0.03	10	100		962.75		9597.3		1.7153
dt	**nudt**	**sigsdt**	**erddt**		**beta1**				**call_value**		**SE**		
0.1	0.0010	0.0632	1.0030		−1				9.0669		0.1715		
j = 100													
i	0	1	2	3	4	5	6	7	8	9	10		
t	0	0.1	0.2	0.3	0.4	0.5	0.6	0.7	0.8	0.9	1		
ε	0	0.7987	0.0516	0.4174	−0.2495	0.2289	−0.2836	−0.2831	−1.5826	−0.5560	0.0549		
St1	100	105.29	105.74	108.67	107.08	108.75	106.92	105.13	95.21	92.01	92.43	CT	CT*CT
St2	100	95.17	94.95	92.57	94.14	92.88	94.66	96.46	106.72	110.65	110.38	7.3631	54.22
delta1	0.581012	0.6760	0.6871	0.7442	0.7242	0.7677	0.7450	0.7171	0.3291	0.1077	0.0000		
delta2	0.581012	0.4774	0.4625	0.3922	0.4147	0.3594	0.3866	0.4201	0.7946	0.9506	1.0000		
cv1	0	2.8967	2.9868	4.7865	3.3569	4.3332	2.6804	1.1059	−6.2332	−7.3799	−7.3653		
cv2	0	−2.9812	−3.2203	−4.4537	−3.9483	−4.5882	−4.0503	−3.4620	0.7272	3.5954	3.0194		

The calculations are identical for {delta1, Stn1, cv1} and {delta2, Stn2, cv2} as for {delta, Stn, cv} in Figure 4.10. The only other difference is the computation of the pay-off:

$$C_T = 0.5 \times (\max(0, S_{1,t} - K) + \beta_1 \times cv_1 + \max(0, S_{2,t} - K) + \beta_1 \times cv_2)$$

The final example using a European call option combines antithetic, *delta*- and *gamma*-based control variates, the pseudo-code appearing in Figure 4.13.

FIGURE 4.13 Pseudo-code for Monte Carlo Valuation of a European Call Option in a Black–Scholes World with Antithetic, *Delta*- and *Gamma*-based Control Variates

```
initialise_parameters { K, T, S, sig, r, div, N, M }

{ precompute constants }

nudt = (r-div-0.5*sig^2)*dt
sigsdt = sig*sqrt(dt)
erddt = exp((r-div)*dt
egamma = exp((2*(r-div)+sig^2)*dt)-2*erddt+1
beta1 = -1
beta2 = -0.5

sum_CT = 0
sum_CT2 = 0

for j = 1 to M do { for each simulation }

 St1 = S
 St2 = S
 cv1 = 0
 cv2 = 0

 for i = 1 to N do { for each time step }

  { compute hedge sensitivities }
  t = (i-1)*dt
  delta1 = Black_Scholes_delta(St1,t;K,T,sig,r,div)
  delta2 = Black_Scholes_delta(St2,t;K,T,sig,r,div)
  gamma1 = Black_Scholes_gamma(St1,t;K,T,sig,r,div)
  gamma2 = Black_Scholes_gamma(St2,t;K,T,sig,r,div)

  { evolves asset prices }
  ε = standard_normal_sample
  Stn1 = St1*exp( nudt + sigsdt*(ε) )
  Stn2 = St2*exp( nudt + sigsdt*(-ε) )

  { accumulate control variates }
  cv1 = cv1 + delta1*(Stn1-St1*erddt) +
              delta2*(Stn2-St2*erddt)
  cv2 = cv2 + gamma1*((Stn1-St1)^2-St1^2*egamma) +
              gamma2*((Stn2-St2)^2-St2^2*egamma)
  St1 = Stn1
  St2 = Stn2
next i
```

FIGURE 4.13 (continued)

```
CT = 0.5*( max( 0 , St1 - K ) + max( 0 , St2 - K ) +
        beta1*cv1 + beta2*cv2 )

 sum_CT = sum_CT + CT
 sum_CT2 = sum_CT2 + CT*CT

next j

call_value = sum_CT/M*exp(-r*T)
SD = sqrt( ( sum_CT2 - sum_CT*sum_CT/M )*exp(-2*r*T)/(M-1) )
SE = SD/sqrt(M)
```

Example : Pricing a European Call Option by Monte Carlo Simulation with Antithetic, *Delta*- and *Gamma*-based Control Variates

We price a one-year maturity, at-the-money European call option with the current asset price at 100 and volatility of 20 per cent. The continuously compounded interest rate is assumed to be 6 per cent per annum, the asset pays a continuous dividend yield of 3 per cent per annum. The simulation has 10 time steps and 100 simulations; $K = 100$, $T = 1$ year, $S = 100$, $\sigma = 0.2$, $r = 0.06$, $\delta = 0.03$, $N = 10$, $M = 100$. Figure 4.14 illustrates the numerical results for the simulation of the path for $j = 100$. The calculations are very similar to the previous examples (compare also the pseudo-code implementations).

Table 4.1 illustrates the typical standard errors and computation times which can be achieved for example by the application of antithetic, delta- and gamma-based control variates to the valuation of a standard European call option in a Black–Scholes world.

TABLE 4.1 Typical Standard Errors and Relative Computation Times for the Monte Carlo Valuation of a European Call Option in a Black–Scholes World with Antithetic, *Delta*- and *Gamma*-based Control Variates

Strike price		100
Time to maturity		1 year
Initial asset price		100
Volatility		20%
Riskless interest rate		6%
Continuous dividend yield		3%
Number of time steps		52
Number of simulations		1000
Standard European call value		9.1352
	Standard error	Relative computation time
Simple estimate	0.4348	1.00
With antithetic variate	0.2253	1.29
With control variates	0.0072	3.64
Combined variates	0.0048	6.43

FIGURE 4.14 Monte Carlo Valuation of a European Call Option in a Black–Scholes World with *Delta*- and *Gamma*-based Control Variates

K	**T**	**S**	**sig**	**r**	**div**	**N**	**M**		**sum_CT**		**sum_CT2**		**SD**
100	1	100	0.2	0.06	0.03	10	100		981.87		9662.2		0.4390
dt	**nudt**	**sigsdt**	**erddt**	**egamma**	**beta1**	**beta2**			**call_value**		**SE**		
0.1	0.0010	0.063246	1.0030	0.004041	−1	−0.5			9.2469		0.043898		
j = 100													
i	0	1	2	3	4	5	6	7	8	9	10		
t	0	0.1	0.2	0.3	0.4	0.5	0.6	0.7	0.8	0.9	1		
ε	0	−0.0944	−1.4005	−1.0658	0.4191	−0.9075	2.9757	0.0462	−0.5343	−1.3023	−0.7867		
St1	100	99.50	91.16	85.30	87.68	82.87	100.14	100.53	97.29	89.68	85.42	CT	CT*CT
St2	100	100.70	110.14	117.93	114.96	121.88	101.07	100.88	104.45	113.53	119.44	10.93887	119.66
delta1	0.581012	0.5680	0.3754	0.2246	0.2517	0.1229	0.5603	0.5683	0.4198	0.0501	0.0000		
delta2	0.581012	0.5917	0.7589	0.8656	0.8476	0.9284	0.5886	0.5805	0.7208	0.9785	1.0000		
cv1	0	-0.2308	0.2653	3.6309	1.2304	5.5206	−12.0463	−12.2874	−12.4048	−9.3998	−4.1767		
gamma1	0.018762	0.0201	0.0229	0.0208	0.0233	0.0173	0.0307	0.0353	0.0447	0.0182	0.0000		
gamma2	0.018762	0.0196	0.0148	0.0097	0.0121	0.0066	0.0299	0.0349	0.0355	0.0063	0.0000		
cv2	0	−1.5026	0.0338	0.2245	−0.7289	−0.9820	6.1436	3.6703	1.6087	3.8441	3.4760		

In this example the total standard error is reduced by a factor of 90. To achieve this order of variance reduction in the simple Monte Carlo method would require increasing the number of simulations by a factor of 8100, that is, 8.1 million simulations with a computation time of approximately 3.15 hours. However, this is a slightly unrealistic example because we have the delta and gamma analytically, and so the hedge works perfectly in the limit as the time step is decreased to zero. In following sections we describe more realistic examples.

4.6 COMPUTING HEDGE SENSITIVITIES

The standard hedge sensitivities, *delta, gamma, vega, theta* and *rho* can be computed by approximating them by finite difference ratios;

$$delta = \frac{\partial C}{\partial S} \approx \frac{C(S+\Delta S) - C(S-\Delta S)}{2\Delta S} \tag{4.27}$$

$$gamma = \frac{\partial^2 C}{\partial S^2} \approx \frac{C(S+\Delta S) - 2C(S) + C(S-\Delta S)}{\Delta S^2} \tag{4.28}$$

$$vega = \frac{\partial C}{\partial \sigma} \approx \frac{C(\sigma+\Delta\sigma) - C(\sigma-\Delta\sigma)}{2\Delta\sigma} \tag{4.29}$$

$$theta = \frac{\partial U}{\partial t} \approx \frac{C(t+\Delta t) - C(t)}{\Delta t} \tag{4.30}$$

$$rho = \frac{\partial C}{\partial r} \approx \frac{C(r+\Delta r) - C(r-\Delta r)}{2\Delta r} \tag{4.31}$$

where $C(S+\Delta S)$ is the Monte Carlo estimate using an initial asset price of $S+\Delta S$, and ΔS is a small fraction of S, e.g. $\Delta S = 0.001S$ and the other $C(.)$'s are defined similarly. Note that every price $C(.)$ in equations (4.27)–(4.31) should be computed using the same set of random numbers. If this is not done then the random error in the prices from the Monte Carlo simulation can be a large proportion of the price differences in the numerator of the finite difference ratios leading to very large errors in the sensitivity estimates. By using the same random numbers the pricing errors will tend to cancel out.

A more efficient way to compute *delta* and from this *gamma* is by applying the discounted expectations approach. We can express the standard European call *delta* as follows:

$$delta = \frac{\partial C}{\partial S} = \frac{\partial}{\partial S}\left(e^{-rT}E\left[(S_T - K)\mathbf{1}_{S_T>K}\right]\right) \tag{4.32}$$

where $S_T = S\exp(\nu T + \sigma z_T)$ and $\mathbf{1}_{S_T>K}$ is the indicator function which is one if $S_T > K$ and zero otherwise. Substituting S_T in equation (4.32) and differentiating we obtain

$$delta = e^{-rT}E[\exp(\nu T + \sigma z_T)\mathbf{1}_{S_T>K}] \tag{4.33}$$

So to compute *delta* by Monte Carlo simulation we simulate the asset price as usual and compute the discounted expectation of an instrument which pays off $\exp(\nu T + \sigma z_T)$ if $S_T > K$ and zero otherwise. Figure 4.15 gives a pseudo-code implementation of this method.

FIGURE 4.15 Pseudo-code for Monte Carlo Calculation of a European Call Option Delta in a Black–Scholes World

```
initialise_parameters { K, T, S, sig, r, div, M }

{ precompute constants }

dt = T
nudt = (r-div-0.5*sig^2)*dt
sigsdt = sig*sqrt(dt)
lnS = ln(S)

sum_CT = 0
sum_CT2 = 0

for j = 1 to M do { for each simulation }

  ε = standard_normal_sample
  e = exp( nudt + sigsdt*ε )

  ST = S*e

  if ( ST > K ) then
    CT = e
  else
    CT = 0

  sum_CT = sum_CT + CT
  sum_CT2 = sum_CT2 + CT*CT

next j

delta_value = sum_CT/M*exp(-r*T)
SD = sqrt( ( sum_CT2 - sum_CT*sum_CT/M )*exp(-2*r*T)/(M-1) )
SE = SD/sqrt(M)
```

Example : Computing a European Call Option Delta by Monte Carlo Simulation

We compute the delta of a one year maturity, at-the-money European call option with the current asset price at 100 and volatility of 20 per cent. The continuously compounded interest rate is assumed to be 6 per cent per annum, the asset pays a continuous dividend yield of 3 per cent per annum. The simulation has one time step and 100 simulations; $K = 100$, $T = 1$ year, $S = 100$, $\sigma = 0.2$, $r = 0.06$, $\delta = 0.03$, $N = 1$, $M = 100$. Figure 4.16 illustrates the numerical results for the simulation of paths $j = 1, \ldots, 5$ and $95, \ldots, 100$.

Firstly, the constants; $\Delta t(dt)$, $\nu\Delta t$ $(nudt)$, $\sigma\sqrt{\Delta t}$ $(sigsdt)$ are precomputed:

$$\Delta t = \frac{T}{N} = \frac{1}{1} = 1$$

$$nudt = (r - \delta - \tfrac{1}{2}\sigma^2)\Delta t = (0.06 - 0.03 - 0.5 \times 0.2^2) \times 1 = 0.01$$

$$sigsdt = \sigma\sqrt{\Delta t} = 0.2\sqrt{1} = 0.2$$

FIGURE 4.16 Monte Carlo Calculation of a European Call Option Delta in a Black–Scholes World

K	T	S	sig	r	div	N	M	sum_CT	sum_CT2	SD
100	1	100	0.2	0.06	0.03	1	100	60.3992	77.98	0.6097
dt	**nudt**	**sigsdt**						**delta_value**	**SE**	
1	0.0100	0.2000						0.5688	0.0610	
j	ε	**e**	**ST**	**CT**	**CT*CT**					
1	−0.8265	0.8562	85.6152	0.0000	0.0000					
2	−0.6445	0.8879	88.7892	0.0000	0.0000					
3	−0.9527	0.8348	83.4816	0.0000	0.0000					
4	−1.8013	0.7045	70.4504	0.0000	0.0000					
5	2.4056	1.6341	163.4134	1.6341	2.6704					
95	2.3200	1.6064	160.6420	1.6064	2.5806					
96	1.9226	1.4837	148.3680	1.4837	2.2013					
97	−0.6575	0.8856	88.5599	0.0000	0.0000					
98	−1.0324	0.8216	82.1617	0.0000	0.0000					
99	−0.3316	0.9452	94.5232	0.0000	0.0000					
100	−0.4677	0.9199	91.9860	0.0000	0.0000					

Then for each simulation $j = 1$ to M, where $M = 100$, the exponential term e is simulated, S_T and C_T are computed, and the sums sum_CT and sum_CT2 are accumulated. For $j = 1$ we have

$$e = \exp(nudt + sigsdt \times \varepsilon) = \exp(0.010 + 0.2 \times (-0.8265)) = 0.8562$$

$$S_T = S \times e = 100 \times 0.8562 = 85.62$$

$$S_T < K \text{ therefore } C_T = 0.$$

For $j = 5$ we have

$$e = \exp(nudt + sigsdt \times \varepsilon) = \exp(0.01 + 0.2 \times (2.4056)) = 1.6341$$

$$S_T = S \times e = 100 \times 1.6341 = 163.41$$

$$S_T > K \text{ therefore } C_T = e = 1.6341.$$

The sum of the values of C_T and the squares of the values of C_T are accumulated in sum_CT and sum_CT2, giving sum_CT = 60.399 and sum_CT2 = 78.0. The estimate of the delta value is then given by

$$delta = \text{sum\_CT/M} \times \exp(-r \times T) = 60.399/100 \times \exp(-0.06 \times 1) = 0.5688$$

The antithetic and control variate methods can be applied in the same way as for the Monte Carlo valuation of the option itself.

This technique cannot be used for the calculation of *gamma* because differentiating equation (4.33) again leads to the expectation of a Dirac delta function which cannot easily be evaluated by Monte Carlo simulation. We can, however, use a finite difference ratio in terms of *delta*

$$gamma = \frac{\partial^2 C}{\partial S^2} \approx \frac{delta(S + \Delta S) - delta(S - \Delta S)}{2\Delta S} \tag{4.34}$$

4.7 MULTIPLE STOCHASTIC FACTORS

One of the main uses of Monte Carlo simulation is for pricing options under multiple stochastic factors. For example pricing options whose pay-off depends on multiple asset prices, or with stochastic volatility or interest rates. For example, consider a European spread option on the difference between two assets (e.g. stock indices) S_1 and S_2, which follow GBM:[5]

$$dS_1 = (r - \delta_1)S_1\,dt + \sigma_1 S_1\,dz_1 \tag{4.35}$$

$$dS_2 = (r - \delta_2)S_2\,dt + \sigma_2 S_2\,dz_2 \tag{4.36}$$

The first complication we have is that it is quite likely that we will want S_1 and S_2 to be correlated to some degree ρ. That is, the Brownian motions dz_1 and dz_2 have instantaneous correlation ρ ($dz_1.dz_2 = \rho dt$). In order to price the option by simulation we use the solutions of the SDEs to simulate the asset prices, as in section 4.2:

$$S_{1,T} = S_1 \exp(\nu_1 T + \sigma_1 z_{1,T}) \tag{4.37}$$

where $\nu_1 = r - \delta_1 - \frac{1}{2}\sigma_1^2$ and

$$S_{2,T} = S_2 \exp(\nu_2 T + \sigma_2 z_{2,T}) \tag{4.38}$$

where $\nu_2 = r - \delta_2 - \frac{1}{2}\sigma_2^2$. However, here we need to generate the variates z_1 and z_2 from a standard bivariate normal distribution with correlation ρ. This is easily achieved by generating independent standard normal variates ε_1 and ε_2 and combining them as follows:

$$z_1 = \varepsilon_1 \tag{4.39}$$

$$z_2 = \rho\varepsilon_1 + \sqrt{1-\rho^2}\varepsilon_2 \tag{4.40}$$

The general procedure for generating n correlated normal variates is described in section 4.11.

The Monte Carlo procedure is exactly the same as that for the standard European call in section 4.2 except that we simulate the two asset processes and from this the pay-off of the spread option ($\max(0, S_1 - S_2 - K)$). Figure 4.17 gives the pseudo-code implementation.

Example : Pricing a European Spread Call Option by Monte Carlo Simulation

We price a one-year maturity, European spread call option with a strike price of 1, current asset prices of 100, volatilities of 20 and 30 per cent, continuous dividend yields of 3 and 4 per cent and a correlation of 50 per cent. The continuously compounded interest rate is assumed to be 6 per cent per annum and the simulation has one time step and 100 simulations, i.e. $K = 1$, $T = 1$, $S_1 = 100$, $S_2 = 110$, $\sigma_1 = 0.20$, $\sigma_2 = 0.30$, $d_1 = 0.03$, $d_2 = 0.04$, $\rho = 0.50$, $r = 0.06$, $N = 1$, $M = 100$. Figure 4.18 illustrates the results of the calculations for the simulation of paths $j = 1, \ldots, 5$ and $95, \ldots, 100$.

Firstly, the constants; Δt (dt), $\nu_1\Delta t$ ($nu1\,dt$), $\nu_2\Delta t$ ($nu2\,dt$), $\sigma_1\sqrt{\Delta t}$ ($sig\,1\,sdt$), $\sigma_2\sqrt{\Delta t}$ ($sig\,2\,sdt$), $\sqrt{1-\rho^2}$ ($srho$) are precomputed:

$$\Delta t = \frac{T}{N} = \frac{1}{1} = 1$$

$$nu1dt = (r - \delta_1 - \tfrac{1}{2}\sigma_1^2)\Delta t = (0.06 - 0.03 - 0.5 \times 0.2^2) \times 1 = 0.01$$

$$nu2dt = (r - \delta_2 - \tfrac{1}{2}\sigma_2^2)\Delta t = (0.06 - 0.04 - 0.5 \times 0.3^2) \times 1 = -0.025$$

$$sig1sdt = \sigma_1\sqrt{\Delta t} = 0.2\sqrt{1} = 0.2$$

$$sig2sdt = \sigma_2\sqrt{\Delta t} = 0.3\sqrt{1} = 0.3$$

$$srho = \sqrt{1-\rho^2} = \sqrt{1-0.5^2} = 0.8660$$

For each simulation $j = 1$ to $M (M = 100)$, S_1 and S_2 are simulated. For example, for $j = 1$ we have

$$\varepsilon_1 = -0.8265,\ \varepsilon_2 = -0.0833$$

$$z_1 = \varepsilon_1 = -0.8265$$

FIGURE 4.17 **Pseudo-code for Monte Carlo Valuation of a European Spread Option in a Black–Scholes World**

```
initialise_parameters
  { K, T, S1, S2, sig1, sig2, div1, div2, rho, r, N, M }

{ precompute constants }

N = 1 { no path dependency }

dt = T/N
nu1dt = (r-div1-0.5*sig1^2)*dt
nu2dt = (r-div2-0.5*sig2^2)*dt
sig1sdt = sig1*sqrt(dt)
sig2sdt = sig2*sqrt(dt)
srho = sqrt( 1 - rho^2 )

sum_CT = 0
sum_CT2 = 0

for j = 1 to M do { for each simulation }

  St1 = S1
  St2 = S2

  for i = 1 to N do { for each time step }
    ε1 = standard_normal_sample
    ε2 = standard_normal_sample
    z1 = ε1
    z2 = rho * ε1 + srho * ε2
    St1 = St1*exp( nu1dt + sig1sdt*z1 )
    St2 = St2*exp( nu2dt + sig2sdt*z2 )
  next i

  CT = max( 0 , St1 - St2 - K )
  sum_CT = sum_CT + CT
  sum_CT2 = sum_CT2 + CT*CT

next j

call_value = sum_CT/M*exp(-r*T)
SD = sqrt( ( sum_CT2 - sum_CT*sum_CT/M )*exp(-2*r*T)/(M-1) )
SE = SD/sqrt(M)
```

$$z_2 = \rho \times \varepsilon_1 + srho \times \varepsilon_2 = 0.5 \times (-0.8265) + 0.8660 \times (-0.0833) = -0.4854$$

$$S_{1,T} = S_1 \times \exp(nu1dt + sig1sdt \times z_1)$$

$$= 100 \times \exp(0.0100 + 0.2 \times (-0.8265)) = 85.615$$

$$S_{2,T} = S_2 \times \exp(nu2dt + sig2sdt \times z_2)$$

$$= 110 \times \exp(-0.0250 + 0.3 \times (-0.4854)) = 92.746$$

FIGURE 4.18 Monte Carlo Valuation of a European Spread Option in a Black–Scholes World

K	T	S1	S2	sig1	sig2	div1	div2	rho	r	N	M		
1	1	100	110	0.2	0.3	0.03	0.04	0.50	0.06	1	100		
dt	**nu1dt**	**nu2dt**	**sig1sdt**	**sig2sdt**	**srho**					**sum_CT**		**sum_CT2**	**SD**
1.0000	0.0100	−0.0250	0.2000	0.3000	0.8660					742.97		21844.2	12.09319
j	ε1	ε2	z1	z2	St1	St2	CT	CT*CT		**call_value**		**SE**	
1	−0.8265	−0.0833	−0.8265	-0.4854	85.62	92.75	0.0000	0.00		6.9970		1.2093	
2	−0.6445	0.8050	−0.6445	0.3748	88.79	120.05	0.0000	0.00					
3	−0.9527	−1.3859	−0.9527	−1.6766	83.48	64.88	17.6036	309.89					
4	−1.8013	0.9632	−1.8013	−0.0665	70.45	105.16	0.0000	0.00					
5	2.4056	−0.5148	2.4056	0.7569	163.41	134.63	27.7798	771.71					
95	2.3200	−0.4380	2.3200	0.7807	160.64	135.60	24.0443	578.13					
96	1.9226	−0.2514	1.9226	0.7436	148.37	134.10	13.2711	176.12					
97	−0.6575	−0.0533	−0.6575	−0.3748	88.56	95.87	0.0000	0.00					
98	−1.0324	0.2024	−1.0324	−0.3409	82.16	96.85	0.0000	0.00					
99	−0.3316	0.1838	−0.3316	−0.0066	94.52	107.07	0.0000	0.00					
100	−0.4677	0.5573	−0.4677	0.2488	91.99	115.60	0.0000	0.00					

$$\text{CT} = \max(0, S_{1,T} - S_{1,T} - K) = \max(0, 85.615 - 92.746 - 1) = 0.0$$

For $j = 3$ we have

$$\varepsilon_1 = -0.9527, \qquad \varepsilon_2 = -1.3859$$

$$z_1 = \varepsilon_1 = -0.9527$$

$$z_2 = \rho \times \varepsilon_1 + srho \times \varepsilon_2 = 0.5 \times (-0.9527) + 0.8660 \times (-1.3859) = -1.6766$$

$$\begin{aligned} S_{1,T} &= S_1 \times \exp(nu1dt + sig1sdt \times z_1) \\ &= 100 \times \exp(0.0100 + 0.2 \times (-0.9527)) = 83.482 \\ S_{2,T} &= S_2 \times \exp(nu2dt + sig2sdt \times z_2) \\ &= 110 \times \exp(-0.0250 + 0.3 \times (-1.6766)) = 64.878 \\ C_T &= \max(0, S_{1,T} - S_{2,T} - K) = \max(0, 83.482 - 64.878 - 1) = 17.604 \end{aligned}$$

The sum of the values of CT and the squares of the values of CT are accumulated in sum_CT and sum_CT2, giving sum_CT = 742.968 and sum_CT2 = 21844.2. The estimate of the option value is then given by

$$\text{call\_value} = \text{sum\_CT/M} \times \exp(-r \times T) = 742.968/100 \times \exp(-0.06 \times 1) = 6.9970$$

In the same way if we want to price an option under more general stochastic processes such as stochastic volatility and/or stochastic interest rates we simply simulate the required stochastic processes. For example, imagine we want to price the European spread option when the underlying asset prices, S_1 and S_2, follow GBM, but where the variance of returns, V_1 and V_2, of the assets follow mean reverting square root processes (see Hull and White, 1988). The SDE's for the asset prices and variances are given by equations (4.41)–(4.44) respectively

$$dS_1 = rS_1\,dt + \sigma_1 S_1\,dz_1 \tag{4.41}$$

$$dS_2 = rS_2\,dt + \sigma_2 S_2\,dz_2 \tag{4.42}$$

$$dV_1 = \alpha_1(\overline{V}_1 - V_1)\,dt + \xi_1\sqrt{V_1}\,dz_3 \tag{4.43}$$

$$dV_2 = \alpha_2(\overline{V}_2 - V_2)\,dt + \xi_2\sqrt{V_2}\,dz_4 \tag{4.44}$$

where $V_i = \sigma_i^2$, α_i is the rate of mean reversion on the variance, ξ_i is the volatility of the variance and the Wiener processes have the following correlation matrix:

$$\rho_z = \begin{vmatrix} 1 & \rho_{12} & \rho_{13} & \rho_{14} \\ \rho_{12} & 1 & \rho_{23} & \rho_{24} \\ \rho_{13} & \rho_{23} & 1 & \rho_{34} \\ \rho_{14} & \rho_{24} & \rho_{34} & 1 \end{vmatrix}$$

In this case we need to generate four correlated normal variates in order to simulate the four processes (4.41)–(4.44). Then, we simply add the simulation of the variances into the pseudo-code of Figure 4.17. The resulting pseudo-code is shown in Figure 4.19.[6] Figure 4.20 gives a numerical example, the calculations are similar to those for the previous example.

FIGURE 4.19 Pseudo-code for Monte Carlo Valuation of a European Spread Option with Stochastic Volatilities

```
initialise_parameters
  { K, T, S1, S2, sig1, sig2, div1, div2, alpha1, alpha2,
   Vbar1, Vbar2, xi1, xi2, rhoz, r, N, M }

{ precompute constants }

N = 1 { no path dependency }

dt = T/N
alpha1dt = alpha1*dt
alpha2dt = alpha2*dt
xi1sdt = xi1*sqrt(dt)
xi2sdt = xi2*sqrt(dt)
lnS1 = ln(S1)
lnS2 = ln(S2)

sum_CT = 0
sum_CT2 = 0

for j = 1 to M do { for each simulation }

  lnSt1 = lnS1
  lnSt2 = lnS2

  for i = 1 to N do { for each time step }

   generate_correlated_normals( rhoz, z[] )

   { simulate variances first }

   Vt1 = Vt1 + alpha1dt*(Vbar1-Vt1) + xi1sdt*sqrt(Vt1)*z[3]
   Vt2 = Vt2 + alpha2dt*(Vbar2-Vt2) + xi2sdt*sqrt(Vt2)*z[4]

   { simulate asset prices }

   lnSt1 = lnSt1 + (r-div1-0.5*Vt1)*dt + sqrt(Vt1)*sdt*z[1]
   lnSt2 = lnSt2 + (r-div2-0.5*vt2)*dt + sqrt(Vt2)*sdt*z[2]

 next i

 St1 = exp(lnSt1)
 St2 = exp(lnSt2)
 CT = max( 0 , St1 - St2 - K )
 sum_CT = sum_CT + CT
 sum_CT2 = sum_CT2 + CT*CT

next j

call_value = sum_CT/M*exp(-r*T)
SD = sqrt( ( sum_CT2 - sum_CT*sum_CT/M )*exp(-2*r*T)/(M-1) )
SE = SD/sqrt(M)
```

FIGURE 4.20 Numerical Example for Monte Carlo Valuation of a European Spread Option with Stochastic Volatilities

K	T	S1	S2	sig1	sig2	div1	div2	alpha1	alpha2	Vbar1	Vbar2				
1	1	100	110	0.2	0.3	0.03	0.04	1.0	2.0	0.04	0.09				
xi1	**xi2**	**rho12**	**rho13**	**rho14**	**rho23**	**rho24**	**rho34**	**r**	**N**	**M**		**sum_CT**		**sum_CT2**	**SD**
0.05	0.06	0.50	0.20	0.01	0.01	0.30	0.30	0.06	10	100		747.42		22810.0	12.4219
dt	**sdt**	**alpha1dt**	**alpha2dt**	**xi1sdt**	**xi2sdt**	**lnS1**	**lnS2**					**call_value**		**SE**	
0.1000	0.3162	0.1000	0.2000	0.0158	0.0190	4.6052	4.7005					7.0389		1.2422	
j = 100															
i	0	1	2	3	4	5	6	7	8	9	10				
t	0	0.1	0.2	0.3	0.4	0.5	0.6	0.7	0.8	0.9	1				
ε1	0	0.1834	−1.1942	0.0110	−1.3283	−1.6112	−1.1443	−0.6281	2.3196	−0.6359	1.3040				
ε2	0	−2.3608	0.8641	0.3365	−0.6725	−1.1617	0.5131	2.1820	0.8927	1.3425	0.7955				
ε3	0	0.8857	1.4512	0.5038	−0.3170	0.7995	−0.7687	0.3317	−0.8933	1.4908	1.3724				
ε4	0	0.5571	−1.8262	−1.3109	0.5054	0.5144	−1.4457	−0.9238	1.1758	0.3540	−0.9657				
z1	0	0.6911	−1.2425	0.0804	−0.6890	−1.1128	−0.2886	−1.2928	1.2354	−1.7865	0.3465				
z2	0	1.5421	−1.4429	−0.4211	−0.7095	−0.3732	−1.8632	−1.5528	1.6031	−0.4005	0.8264				
z3	0	−1.8217	−1.2013	−0.3317	−0.7780	−1.8556	−0.0723	0.7337	2.4169	−0.2034	0.1552				
z4	0	−0.9626	1.0477	0.7938	−1.4369	−1.3035	−0.3854	1.3337	1.0752	1.1226	2.1615				
Vt1	0.04	0.0112	0.0049	0.0032	0.0054	0.0204	0.0213	0.0347	0.0735	0.0669	0.0667				
Vt2	0.09	0.0717	0.0953	0.1093	0.0782	0.0558	0.0553	0.0876	0.1085	0.1261	0.1599	ST			
lnSt1	4.6052	4.6307	4.6059	4.6102	4.5969	4.5485	4.5372	4.4622	4.5675	4.4210	4.4489	85.53588	CT	CT*CT	
lnSt2	4.7005	4.8295	4.6859	4.6384	4.5738	4.5451	4.4058	4.2581	4.4216	4.3724	4.4709	87.43187	0.0000	0.00	

4.8 PATH-DEPENDENT OPTIONS

An important application of Monte Carlo simulation is in pricing complex or exotic path-dependent options.[7] Simple analytical formulae exist for certain types of exotic options, these options being classified by the property that the path-dependent condition applies to the continuous path. For example, a popular class of exotic option is the barrier option. These are standard European options except that the option either ceases to exist or only comes into existence if the underlying asset price crosses a predetermined barrier level. If we assume that the underlying asset price is checked continuously for the crossing of the barrier, then simple analytical formulae exist for the price of these options. In contrast, with actual barrier options the underlying asset price is checked (fixed) at most once a day and often much less frequently. This significantly affects the price of the option since the price is much less likely to be observed crossing the barrier if the fixings occur infrequently, and it also complicates the pricing formulae. However, these options can be priced very easily by Monte Carlo simulation.

Consider pricing a daily fixed down-and-out call option. This is a particular type of barrier option which is a normal call option unless the underlying asset price observed once per day crosses the predetermined barrier level H from above, in which case the option ceases to exist. For this option we must simulate the underlying asset price for each fixing date in order to check for the crossing of the barrier. Assuming the asset price follows GBM, the simulation of the asset price takes the usual form:

$$S_{t+\Delta t} = S_t \exp(\nu\Delta t + \sigma\sqrt{\Delta t}z) \tag{4.45}$$

where we assume Δt is one day and z is a standard normal random variate as usual. The Monte Carlo simulation proceeds in exactly the same way as for a standard option, except that at each time step we check whether the asset price has crossed the barrier level H. If so then we terminate the simulation of that path and the pay-off for that path is zero. The pseudo-code is given in Figure 4.21. We can use the analytical formulae for continuously fixed barrier options to construct hedge sensitivity-based control variates as we described in earlier sections.

Example : Pricing a European Down and Out Call Option by Monte Carlo Simulation

We price a one-year maturity, at-the-money European down and out call option with the current asset price at 100 and volatility of 20 per cent. The continuously compounded interest rate is assumed to be 6 per cent per annum, the asset pays a continuous dividend yield of 3 per cent per annum, and the barrier is at 99. The simulation has 10 time steps and 100 simulations; $K = 100$, $T = 1$ year, $S = 100$, $\sigma = 0.2$, $r = 0.06$, $\delta = 0.03$, $H = 99$, $N = 10$, $M = 100$. Figure 4.22 illustrates the numerical results for the simulation of the path for $j = 100$.

Firstly, the constants; Δt (dt), $\nu\Delta t$ ($nudt$), $\sigma\sqrt{\Delta t}$ ($sigsdt$) are precomputed:

$$\Delta t = \frac{T}{N} = \frac{1}{10} = 0.1$$

$$nudt = (r - \delta - \tfrac{1}{2}\sigma^2)\Delta t = (0.06 - 0.03 - 0.5 \times 0.2^2) \times 0.1 = 0.001$$

$$sigsdt = \sigma\sqrt{\Delta t} = 0.2\sqrt{0.1} = 0.0632$$

FIGURE 4.21 Pseudo-code for Monte Carlo Valuation of a European Down and Out Call Option in a Black–Scholes World

```
initialise_parameters { K, T, S, sig, r, div, H, N, M }
{ N is the number of days in the life of the option T }

{ precompute constants }

dt = T/N
nudt = (r-div-0.5*sig*sig)*dt
sigsdt = sig*sqrt(dt)

sum_CT = 0
sum_CT2 = 0

for j = 1 to M do { for each simulation }

 St = S
 BARRIER_CROSSED = FALSE
 for i = 1 to N do { for each time step }
   ε = standard_normal_sample
   St = St*exp( nudt + sigsdt*ε )
   if ( St <= H ) then
    BARRIER_CROSSED = TRUE
    exit_loop
 next i

 if BARRIER_CROSSED then CT = 0
 else CT = max( 0 , St - K )

 sum_CT = sum_CT + CT
 sum_CT2 = sum_CT2 + CT*CT

next j

call_value = sum_CT/M*exp(-r*T)
SD = sqrt( ( sum_CT2 - sum_CT*sum_CT/M )*exp(-2*r*T)/(M-1) )
SE = SD/sqrt(M)
```

Then for each simulation $j = 1$ to M where $M = 100$, S_t is initialised to $S = 100$ and BARRIER_CROSSED = FALSE which indicates that the barrier has not yet been crossed. Then for each time step $i = 1$ to N, where $N = 10$, S_t is simulated and the crossing of the barrier is checked. For example for $j = 100$ and $i = 1$ we have

$$S_t = S_t \times \exp(nudt + sigsdt \times \varepsilon)$$

$$= 100 \times \exp(0.001 + 0.0632 \times 0.5087) = 103.37$$

$S_t > H$, therefore BARRIER_CROSSED is FALSE and the loop continues. For $i = 4$ we have

FIGURE 4.22 Monte Carlo Valuation of a European Down and Out Call Option in a Black–Scholes World

K	T	S	sig	r	div	H	N	M		sum_CT		sum_CT2		SD
100	1	100	0.2	0.06	0.03	99	10	100		410.49		13057.7		10.09384
dt	**nudt**	**sigsdt**								**call_value**		**SE**		
0.1	0.0010	0.0632								3.8659		1.0094		
j = 100														
i	0	1	2	3	4	5	6	7	8	9	10			
t	0	0.1	0.2	0.3	0.4	0.5	0.6	0.7	0.8	0.9	1			
ε	0	0.5087	1.2242	–0.3409	–1.8043	–0.3742	1.6139	–0.7529	–0.1701	0.6688	–0.9505	**CT**	**CT*CT**	
St	100	103.37	111.81	109.53	97.82	95.62	106.01	101.18	100.20	104.63	98.62	0	0	
BARRIER_CROSSED		FALSE	FALSE	FALSE	TRUE	TRUE	TRUE	TRUE	TRUE	TRUE	TRUE			

$$\begin{aligned} S_t &= S_t \times \exp(nudt + sigsdt \times \varepsilon) \\ &= 109.531 \times \exp(0.001 + 0.0632 \times (-1.8043)) = 97.82 \end{aligned}$$

$S_t < H$, therefore BARRIER_CROSSED = TRUE and the loop terminates.

For $j = 100$ we have BARRIER_CROSSED = TRUE therefore:

$$C_T = 0$$

The sum of the values of C_T and the squares of the values of C_T are accumulated in sum_CT and sum_CT2, giving sum_CT = 410.493 and sum_CT2 = 13057.7. The estimate of the option value is then given by

$$\text{call\_value} = \text{sum\_CT/M} \times \exp(-r \times T) = 410.493/100 \times \exp(-0.06 \times 1) = 3.8659$$

4.9 AN ARITHMETIC ASIAN OPTION WITH A GEOMETRIC ASIAN OPTION CONTROL VARIATE

In this example we price a European arithmetic Asian (average price) call option.[8] This option pays the difference, if positive, between the arithmetic average of the asset price A_T and the strike price K at the maturity date T. The arithmetic average is taken on a set of observations (fixings) of the asset price S_{t_i} (which we assume follows GBM) at dates t_i; $i = 1, \ldots, N$

$$A_T = \frac{1}{N}\sum_{i=1}^{N} S_{t_i} \tag{4.46}$$

Thus the pay-off at the maturity date is

$$\max(0, A_T - K) \tag{4.47}$$

Figure 4.23 illustrates two typical asset price paths and the fixing dates.

There is no analytical solution for the price of an arithmetic Asian option; however, there is a simple analytical formula for the price of a geometric Asian option. A geometric Asian call option pays the difference if positive, between the geometric average of the asset price G_T and the strike price K at the maturity date T. The geometric average is defined as

$$G_T = \left(\prod_{i=1}^{N} S_{t_i}\right)^{1/N} \tag{4.48}$$

Since the geometric average is essentially the product of lognormally distributed variables then it is also lognormally distributed. Therefore the price of the geometric Asian call option is given by a modified Black–Scholes formula:

$$C_{\text{GEOMETRIC\_ASIAN}} = \exp(-rT)\left(\exp(a + \tfrac{1}{2}b)N(x) - KN(x - \sqrt{b})\right) \tag{4.49}$$

where

$$a = \ln(G_t) + \frac{N-m}{N}(\ln(S) + \nu(t_{m+1} - t) + \tfrac{1}{2}\nu(T - t_{m+1}))$$

FIGURE 4.23 Typical Asset Price Paths and Fixing Dates for an Asian Option

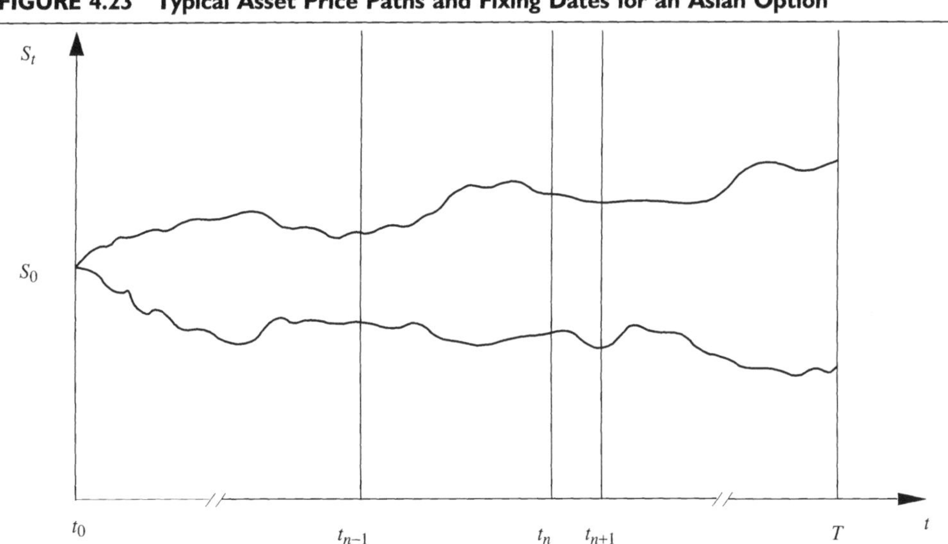

$$b = \frac{(N-m)^2}{N^2}\sigma^2(t_{m+1}-t) + \frac{\sigma^2(T-t_{m+1})}{6N^2}(N-m)(2(N-m)-1)$$

$$\nu = r - \delta - \tfrac{1}{2}\sigma^2, \qquad x = \frac{a - \ln(K) + b}{\sqrt{b}}$$

where G_t is the current geometric average and m is the last known fixing. The geometric Asian option makes a good static hedge style control variate for the arithmetic Asian option. Figure 4.24 shows a pseudo-code implementation of the Monte Carlo valuation of a European Asian call option with a geometric Asian call option control variate. We simulate the difference between the arithmetic and geometric Asian options or a hedged portfolio which is long one arithmetic Asian and short one geometric Asian option. This is much faster than using the delta of the geometric Asian option to generate a delta hedge control variate because we do not have to compute the delta at every time step and it is equivalent to a continuous delta hedge. Note the bold highlighted lines where we precompute the drift and volatility constant expressions required for the simulation of the asset price between the fixing dates. This increases the efficiency of the simulation significantly because these constants are used for every time step for every simulation.

Example : Pricing a European Asian Call Option by Monte Carlo Simulation with Geometric Asian Call Option Control Variate

We price a one-year maturity, European Asian call option with a strike price at 100, current asset price at 100 and volatility of 20 per cent. The continuously compounded interest rate is assumed to be 6 per cent per annum, the asset pays a continuous dividend yield of 3 per

FIGURE 4.24 Pseudo-code for Monte Carlo Valuation of a European Arithmetic Asian Call Option with a Geometric Asian call Option Control Variate

```
initialise_parameters { K, t[], S, sig, r, div, N, M }
{ t[] is an array containing the fixing times }

{ precompute constants }

for i = 1 to N do { for each fixing }
  nudt[i] = (r-div-0.5*sig*sig)*(t[i]-t[i-1])
  sigsdt[i] = sig*sqrt(t[i]-t[i-1])
next i

sum_CT = 0
sum_CT2 = 0
for j = 1 to M do { for each simulation }

  St = S
  sumSt = 0
  productSt = 1

  for i = 1 to N do { for each fixing }
    ε = standard_normal_sample
    St = St*exp( nudt[i] + sigsdt[i]*ε )
    sumSt = sumSt + St
    productSt = productSt * St
  next i

  A = sumSt/N
  G = productSt↑(1/N)
  CT = max( 0 , A - K )- max( 0 , G - K )
  sum_CT = sum_CT + CT
  sum_CT2 = sum_CT2 + CT*CT

next j

portfolio_value = sum_CT/M * exp(-r*T)
SD = sqrt( ( sum_CT2 - sum_CT*sum_CT/M )*exp(-2*r*T)/(M-1) )
SE = SD/sqrt(M)

{ add back in control variate value }

call_value = portfolio_value +
             geometric_Asian_call( K, t[], S, sig, r, div, N )
```

cent per annum, and their are 10 equally spaced fixing dates. The simulation has 10 time steps and 100 simulations; $K = 100$, $T = 1$ year, $S = 100$, $\sigma = 0.2$, $r = 0.06$, $\delta = 0.03$, $N = 10$, $M = 100$. Figure 4.25 illustrates the numerical results for the simulation of the path for $j = 100$.

FIGURE 4.25 Monte Carlo Valuation of a European Asian Call Option with a Geometric Asian Call Option Control Variate

K	T	S	sig	r	div	N	M	sum_CT	sum_CT2	SD
100	1	100	0.2	0.06	0.03	10	100	22.8411	17.9192	0.3373

dt	nudt	sigsdt	portfolio_value	SE
0.1	0.0010	0.063246	0.2151	0.0337

j=100

i	0	1	2	3	4	5	6	7	8	9	10
t	0	0.1	0.2	0.3	0.4	0.5	0.6	0.7	0.8	0.9	1
ε	0	2.1493	0.0430	0.3294	0.4444	–0.0765	–0.2008	1.6842	–0.0302	0.3285	0.0913
St	100	114.68	115.10	117.64	121.12	120.65	119.25	132.79	132.67	135.59	136.51
sumSt	0	114.68	229.78	347.42	468.54	589.19	708.44	841.23	973.90	1109.48	1245.99
productSt	1	1.1E+02	1.3E+04	1.6E+06	1.9E+08	2.3E+10	2.7E+12	3.6E+14	4.8E+16	6.5E+18	8.8E+20

CT	CT*CT
0.2730	0.0745
A	124.60
G	124.33

Geometric Asian Call Option

GA_a	GA_b	GA_nu	GA_x
4.6107	0.0154	0.0100	0.1684

call_value
5.5577

geometric_Asian_call
5.3426

Firstly, the constants; $\Delta t\ (dt)$, $\nu\Delta t\ (nudt)$, $\sigma\sqrt{\Delta t}\ (sigsdt)$ are precomputed:

$$\Delta t = \frac{T}{N} = \frac{1}{10} = 0.1$$

$$nudt = (r - \delta - \tfrac{1}{2}\sigma^2)\Delta t = (0.06 - 0.03 - 0.5 \times 0.2^2) \times 0.1 = 0.001$$

$$sigsdt = \sigma\sqrt{\Delta t} = 0.2\sqrt{0.1} = 0.0632$$

Then for each simulation $j = 1$ to M where M $= 100$, S_t is initialised to $S = 100$, *sumSt* $= 0$ and *productSt* $= 1$. Then for each time step $i = 1$ to N, where $N = 10$, S_t is simulated and the sum and product of the asset prices at the fixing times are accumulated. For example, for $j = 100$ we have, for $i = 1$,

$$\begin{aligned} S_t &= S_t \times \exp(nudt + sigsdt \times \varepsilon) \\ &= 100 \times \exp(0.0010 + 0.06325 \times 2.14929) = 114.675 \\ sumSt &= sumSt + S_t = 0 + 114.657 = 114.675 \\ productSt &= productSt \times S_t = 1 \times 114.675 = 114.675 \end{aligned}$$

For $i = 5$:

$$\begin{aligned} S_t &= S_t \times \exp(nudt + sigsdt \times e) \\ &= 121.118 \times \exp(0.0010 + 0.06325 \times (-0.0765)) = 120.654 \\ sumSt &= sumSt + S_t = 468.539 + 120.654 = 589.193 \\ productSt &= productSt \times S_t = 1.9\text{E}+08 \times 120.654 = 2.3\text{E}+10 \end{aligned}$$

After the i loop we have

$$\begin{aligned} A_T &= sumSt/N = 1245.99/10 = 124.599 \\ G_T &= productSt^{(1/N)} = (8.8\text{E}+20)^{(1/10)} = 124.326 \\ C_T &= \max(0, A - K) - \max(0, G - K) \\ &= \max(0, 124.599 - 100) - \max(0, 124.326 - 100) \\ &= 24.599 - 24.326 = 0.27303 \end{aligned}$$

The sum of the values of C_T and the squares of the values of CT are accumulated in sum_CT and sum_CT2 giving sum_CT = 22.8411 and sum_CT2 = 17.9192. The estimate of the portfolio value is then given by

$$\begin{aligned} \text{portfolio\_value} &= \text{sum\_CT/M} \times \exp(-r \times T) \\ &= 22.8411/100 \times \exp(-0.06 \times 1) = 0.21511 \end{aligned}$$

Finally the estimate of the option value is given by

$$\begin{aligned} \text{call\_value} &= \text{portfolio\_value} + \text{geometric\_Asian\_call}(K, \{t_1, \ldots, t_N\}, S, \sigma, r, \delta, N) \\ &= 0.21511 + 5.3426 = 5.5577 \end{aligned}$$

Table 4.2 gives the prices, standard errors and relative computation times with no variance reduction, an antithetic control variate, a geometric Asian control variate and

TABLE 4.2 Results from Pricing a European Arithmetic Asian Option by Monte Carlo Simulation

	Price	Standard error	Relative computation time
Simple Monte Carlo	5.038019	0.248236	1.00
Antithetic	5.156263	0.135463	1.23
Control variate	5.207977	0.010366	1.05
Antithetic and control variate	5.216232	0.006596	1.32

finally both an antithetic control variate and a geometric Asian control variate. The addition of the antithetic and geometric Asian control variate increase the computation time by approximately 30 per cent, but reduces the standard error by approximately 37 times. To achieve this reduction with the simple Monte Carlo would require increasing the number of simulations by $37 \times 37 = 1369$ times with a roughly equivalent increase in the computation time.

4.10 A LOOKBACK CALL OPTION UNDER STOCHASTIC VOLATILITY WITH DELTA, GAMMA AND VEGA CONTROL VARIATES

In this example we price a European fixed strike lookback call option. This option pays the difference, if positive, between the maximum of a set of observations (fixings) of the asset price S_{t_i} at dates t_i; $i = 1, \ldots, N$ and the strike price. Thus the pay-off at the maturity date is

$$\max(0, \max(S_{t_i}; i = 1, \ldots, N) - K) \tag{4.50}$$

We will also assume that the asset price and the variance of the asset price returns $V = \sigma^2$ are governed by the following stochastic differential equations:

$$dS = rS\,dt + \sigma S\,dz_1 \tag{4.51}$$

$$dV = \alpha(\overline{V} - V)\,dt + \xi\sqrt{V}\,dz_2 \tag{4.52}$$

and that the Wiener processes dz_1 and dz_2 are uncorrelated, but this is easily generalised as we saw in section 4.7. Figure 4.26 illustrates two typical asset price paths and the fixing dates.

There is no analytical solution for the price of European fixed strike lookback call option with discrete fixings and stochastic volatility. However, there is a simple analytical formula for the price of a continuous fixing fixed strike lookback call with constant volatility:[9]

$$\begin{aligned} C_{\text{FIXED\_STRIKE\_LOOKBACK\_CALL}} &= G + Se^{-\delta T}N(x + \sigma\sqrt{T}) - Ke^{-rT}N(x) \\ &\quad - \frac{S}{B}\left(e^{-rT}\left(\frac{E}{S}\right)^{B} N\left(x + (1-B)\sigma\sqrt{T}\right)\right. \\ &\quad \left. - e^{-\delta T}N\left(x + \sigma\sqrt{T}\right)\right) \end{aligned} \tag{4.53}$$

FIGURE 4.26 Typical Asset Price Paths and Fixing for a Lookback Option

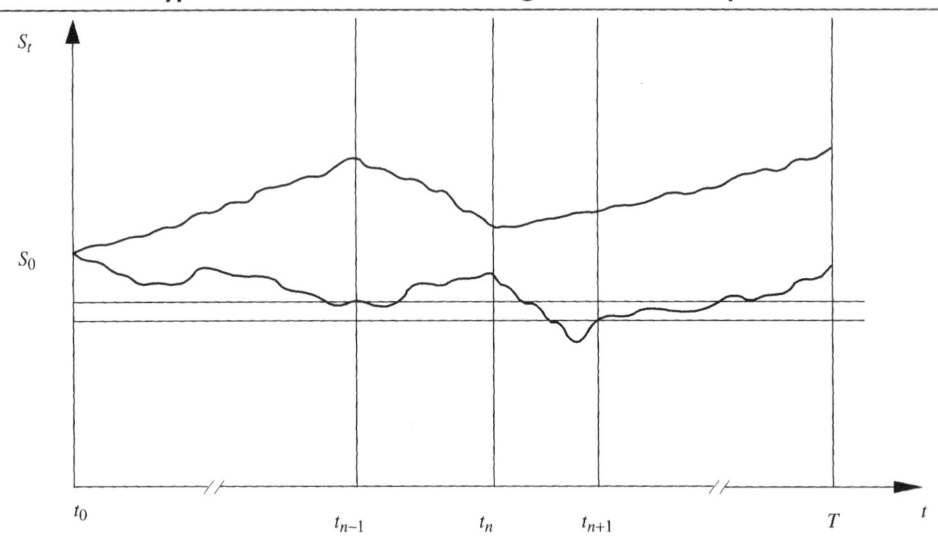

where

$$\left.\begin{matrix} E = K,\ G = 0 \\ E = M,\ G = e^{-rT}\ (\mathrm{M} - \mathrm{K}) \end{matrix}\right\} \left\{\begin{matrix} K \geq M \\ K < M \end{matrix}\right., B = \frac{2(r-\delta)}{\sigma^2}, x = \frac{\ln\left(\dfrac{S}{E}\right) + \left((r-\delta) - \dfrac{1}{2}\sigma^2\right)T}{\sigma\sqrt{T}}$$

and M is the current known maximum. We can therefore use the continuously fixed floating strike lookback call option formula to compute *delta, gamma* and *vega* hedge control variates. Rather than differentiate equation (4.52) with respect to the asset price twice and volatility once which would lead to extremely complex expressions it is more efficient to use finite difference approximations to the partial differentials for *gamma* and *vega*.

Figure 4.27 shows a pseudo-code implementation of the Monte Carlo valuation of a European fixed strike lookback call option with continuously fixed lookback call option *delta, gamma* and *vega* hedge control variates.[10]

As discussed in section 4.4, the values of β_1, β_2 and β_3 were obtained by linear regression. Table 4.3 gives typical standard errors and relative computation times for the example of the application of the Monte Carlo valuation of a European fixed strike lookback call option in a Black–Scholes world with stochastic volatility using antithetic and *delta-*, *gamma-* and *vega*-based control variates.

With the combined antithetic, *delta, gamma* and *vega* control variates the standard error is reduced by a factor of 12. To achieve this reduction with the simple Monte Carlo method would require 144 000 simulations with an execution time of roughly 3.5 hours. With careful choice of the most efficient control variates and optimisation of the code the execution time can typically be reduced by a factor of between two and five.

FIGURE 4.27 Pseudo-code for Monte Carlo Valuation of a European Fixed Strike Lookback Call Option with Stochastic Volatility and Continuously Fixed Lookback Call Option *Delta*, *Gamma* and *Vega* Hedge Control Variates

```
initialise_parameters
  { K, t[], S, sig, r, div, alpha, Vbar, xi, N, M }

{ precompute constants }

sig2 = sig^2
alphadt = alpha*dt
xisdt = xi*sqrt(*dt)
erddt = exp((r-div)*dt)
egam1 = exp(2*(r-div)*dt)
egam2 = -2*erddt+1
eveg1 = exp(-alpha*dt)
eveg2 = Vbar - Vbar*eveg1

sum_CT = 0
sum_CT2 = 0

beta1 = -0.88
beta2 = -0.42
beta3 = -0.0003

for j = 1 to M do { for each simulation }

 St1 = S ; St2 = S ; Vt = sig2
 maxSt1 = St ; maxSt2 = St
 cv1 = 0 ; cv2 = 0 ; cv3 = 0

 for i = 1 to N do { for each time step }

   { compute hedge sensitivities }
   t = (i-1)*dt
   delta1 = lookback_delta(St1,t,K,T,Vt,r,div,maxSt1)
   delta2 = lookback_delta(St2,t,K,T,Vt,r,div,maxSt2)
   gamma1 = lookback_gamma(St1,t,K,T,Vt,r,div,maxSt1)
   gamma2 = lookback_gamma(St2,t,K,T,Vt,r,div,maxSt2)
   vega1 = lookback_vegaV(St1,t,K,T,Vt,r,div,maxSt1)
   vega2 = lookback_vegaV(St2,t,K,T,Vt,r,div,maxSt2)

    { evolve variance }
    ε = standard_normal_sample
    Vtn = Vt + alphadt*(Vbar-Vt) + xisdt*sqrt(Vt)*ε

    { evolve asset price }
    ε = standard_normal_sample
    Stn1 = St1*exp( (r-div-0.5*Vt)*dt + sqrt(Vt)*sdt*(ε) )
    Stn2 = St2*exp( (r-div-0.5*Vt)*dt + sqrt(Vt)*sdt*(-ε) )

    { accumulate control variates }
    cv1 = cv1 + delta1*(Stn1-St1*erddt) +
                delta2*(Stn2-St2*erddt)
```

(*continues*)

FIGURE 4.27 ***(continued)***

```
      cv2 = cv2 +
        gamma1*((Stn1-St1)^2-St1^2*(egam1*exp(Vt*dt) + egam2)) +
        gamma2*((Stn2-St2)^2-St2^2*(egam1*exp(Vt*dt)+egam2))
      cv3 = cv3 + vega1*((Vtn-Vt)-(Vt*eveg1+eveg2-Vt)) +
                  vega2*((Vtn-Vt)-(Vt*eveg1+eveg2-Vt))

      Vt = Vtn
      St1 = Stn1
      St2 = Stn2

      if ( St1 > maxSt1 ) maxSt1 = St1
      if ( St2 > maxSt2 ) maxSt2 = St2

    next i

    CT = 0.5*( max( 0 , maxSt1 - K ) + max( 0 , maxSt2 - K ) +
               beta1*cv1 + beta2*cv2 + beta3*cv3 )
    sum_CT = sum_CT + CT
    sum_CT2 = sum_CT2 + CT*CT

next j

call_value = sum_CT/M*exp(-r*T)
SD = sqrt( ( sum_CT2 - sum_CT*sum_CT/M )*exp(-2*r*T)/(M-1) )
SE = SD/sqrt(M)
```

TABLE 4.3 Typical Standard Errors and Computation Times for the Monte Carlo Valuation of a European Fixed Strike Lookback Call Option in a Black–Scholes World with Stochastic Volatility Using Antithetic and Delta-, Gamma- and Vega-based Control Variates

Strike price		100
Time to maturity		1 year
Initial asset price		100
Volatility		20%
Riskless interest rate		6%
Continuous dividend yield		3%
Mean reversion rate (α)		5.0
Volatility of volatility (ξ)		0.02
Number of time steps		52
Number of simulations		1000
Continuous fixing fixed strike lookback call value		17.729
	Standard error	Relative computation time
Simple estimate	0.4803	1.00
With antithetic variate	0.2030	1.17
With control variates	0.0485	17.77
Combined variates	0.0378	29.23

4.11 GENERATING STANDARD NORMAL RANDOM NUMBERS

A critical part of Monte Carlo simulation is the simulation of the Brownian motions or the generation of the standard normal random variables. Most programming languages and spreadsheets provide a uniform pseudo-random number generator. This will usually generate a random integer between zero and a specified upper value, each integer in the range being generated with equal probability. Sometimes the generator produces the standard mathematical definition of a uniform random number, that is, a real number between zero and one. The integer version can be converted to the standard by specifying a large upper value and then dividing the generated random numbers by this value. The numbers generated by these routines are designed to appear random when subject to standard statistical tests for randomness. However, some routines are better than others and so the pseudo-random number generator you intend to use should always be subjected to the standard statistical tests (see Press *et al.*, 1992 and Ripley 1987, for excellent discussions of pseudo-random number generation and testing).

Armed with a standard uniform random number generator it is straightforward to convert these to standard normal random numbers. A common, but approximate, way to do this is to generate 12 standard uniform random numbers, add them together and subtract six from the total. The distribution of this combination has the correct zero mean and variance of one, and is a good approximation to a normal distributed random variable. However, if we consider the minimum and maximum possible values of z which are -6 and 6, this is a range of -6 to 6 standard deviations of true standard normal random variable. Thus a true standard normal random variable has a probability of approximately 0.000 000 001 of exceeding these minimum and maximum values. More importantly the kurtosis of z is only 0.15, which means that too many values close to the mean will be generated.

A simple alternative to this method is the Box–Muller transformation. This is an exact transformation of pairs of standard uniform random numbers to pairs of standard normal random variables. Let x_1 and x_2 be standard uniformly distributed random variables, then a pair of standard normally distributed variables z_1 and z_2 can be obtained via

$$z_1 = \sqrt{-2\ln(x_1)}\cos(2\pi x_2)$$

$$z_2 = \sqrt{-2\ln(x_1)}\sin(2\pi x_2)$$

A more efficient implementation is the polar rejection method which can be stated algorithmically as follows:

$$\begin{aligned}
&\text{repeat}\\
&\quad x_1 = \text{standard_uniform_random_number}\\
&\quad x_2 = \text{standard_uniform_random_number}\\
&\quad w = x_1^2 + x_2^2\\
&\text{until } w < 1\\
&\quad c = \sqrt{-2*\frac{\ln(w)}{w}}\\
&\quad z_1 = cx_1\\
&\quad z_2 = cx_2
\end{aligned} \tag{4.54}$$

TABLE 4.4 Relative Execution Speeds of Standard Normal Random Number Generator Methods

Method	Relative execution time
Adding twelve uniform random numbers	1.000
Box–Muller	0.500
Polar rejection	0.375

The only complication with the Box–Muller and polar rejection methods is that they generate two standard normal random variables at a time. Therefore, in order to obtain maximum efficiency the second random number must be saved for use the next time a standard normal random number is required, rather than generating two random numbers every time and throwing one away. If this is done the relative execution times of the 12 uniforms, Box–Muller and polar rejection methods are given in Table 4.4.

Since the polar rejection method is both faster and more accurate it is our preferred method of generating standard normal random numbers. The generation of the random numbers is generally about 30 per cent of the total execution time of a Monte Carlo simulation.

Another problem we encountered earlier is how to combine independent standard normal random variables to obtain correlated variables. The solution is the eigensystem representation of the covariance matrix of the correlated variables. The eigenvectors are the linear combinations of the correlated variables which give independent variables. Therefore, all we have to do is invert this relationship to obtain the linear combinations of independent variables which reproduce the required covariance matrix. In the case of a covariance matrix, which is real and symmetric the matrix of eigenvectors is orthogonal, i.e. the inverse of the matrix is equal to its transpose.

Consider n variables z_i, $i = 1, \ldots, n$ which are jointly normally distributed with mean zero, variance one and correlation/covariance matrix Σ so that they can be considered correlated Brownian motions with infinitesimal increments dz_i.

Principal components analysis (PCA) will give n eigenvectors $\underline{\nu}_i$ and n associated eigenvalues λ_i such that

$$\Sigma = \Gamma \Lambda \Gamma' \tag{4.55}$$

where

$$\Gamma = \begin{vmatrix} \nu_{11} & \nu_{12} & \cdots & \nu_{1n} \\ \nu_{21} & \nu_{22} & \cdots & \nu_{2n} \\ \cdots & \cdots & \cdots & \cdots \\ \nu_{n1} & \nu_{n2} & \cdots & \nu_{nn} \end{vmatrix} \quad \text{and} \quad \Lambda = \begin{vmatrix} \lambda_1 & 0 & 0 & 0 \\ 0 & \lambda_2 & 0 & 0 \\ 0 & 0 & \cdots & 0 \\ 0 & 0 & 0 & \lambda_n \end{vmatrix}$$

the columns of Γ are the eigenvectors.

Since the transpose of Γ is equal to its inverse, the rows of Γ represent the proportions of a set of n independent Brownian motions $dw_i; i = 1, \cdots, n$ which when linearly combined reproduce the original correlated Brownian motions. The eigenvalues represent the variances of the independent Brownian motions. Therefore, the correlated Brownian motions dz_i can be reproduced from linear combinations of the independent Brownian motions dw_i as follows:

$$dz_1 = \nu_{11}\sqrt{\lambda_1}\, dw_1 + \nu_{12}\sqrt{\lambda_2}\, dw_2 + \cdots + \nu_{1n}\sqrt{\lambda_n}\, dw_n$$

$$
\begin{aligned}
dz_2 &= \nu_{21}\sqrt{\lambda_1}\,dw_1 + \nu_{21}\sqrt{\lambda_2}\,dw_2 + \cdots + \nu_{2n}\sqrt{\lambda_n}\,dw_n \\
&\cdots \\
dz_n &= \nu_{n1}\sqrt{\lambda_1}\,dw_1 + \nu_{n2}\sqrt{\lambda_2}\,dw_2 + \cdots + \nu_{nn}\sqrt{\lambda_n}\,dw_n
\end{aligned}
\tag{4.56}
$$

where the dw_i are independent Brownian motions.[11] To use this in a Monte Carlo simulation we simply discretise equation (4.56) in the usual way.

4.12 QUASI-RANDOM NUMBERS

It turns out that pseudo random numbers, which are designed to be as random as possible, are poor choices for use in Monte Carlo simulation. To illustrate the reason for this consider two uniform independent random numbers between zero interpreted as the horizontal and vertical position on a graph. Figure 4.28 illustrates a graph with 500 points obtained in this way.

Since the numbers are uniform and independent then every point on the graph is equally likely to appear. However, every time we sample a point, all points are still equally likely and so we get "clumps" of points close together and empty spaces (see Figure 4.28). Eventually, as we sample more and more points we will obtain a distribution of points which appears smooth, the initial clumpiness will have been swamped by the large number

FIGURE 4.28 Plot of 500 Pairs of Uniform Random Numbers

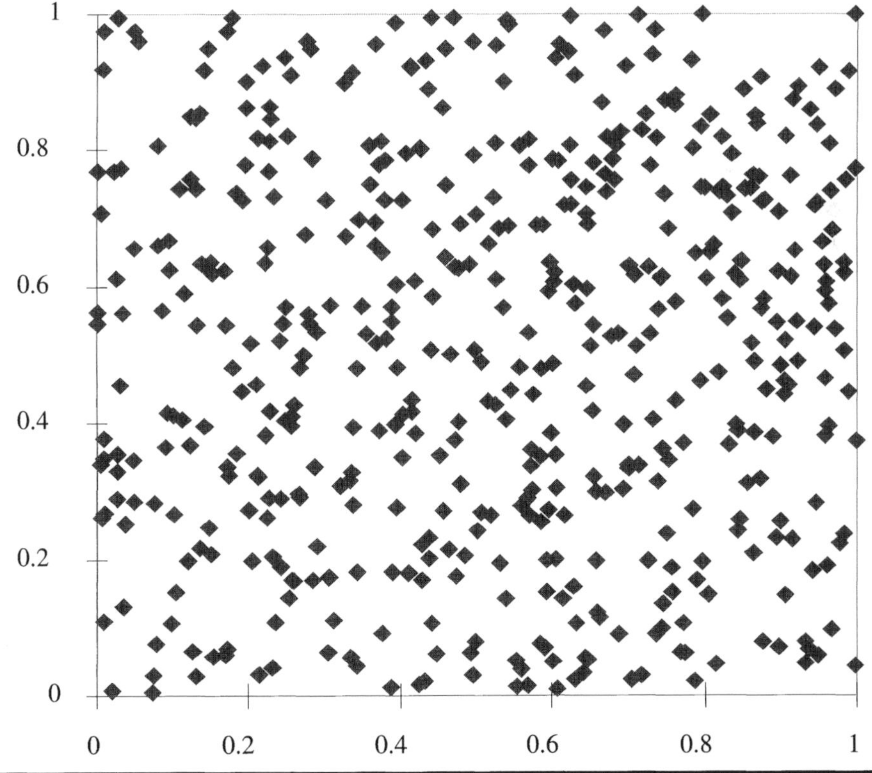

of points spread evenly across the graph. The problem with pseudo-random numbers for Monte Carlo simulation, is that for small samples, which has been the aim of the control variates, the clumpiness biases the results. A very large number of samples are needed to make the bias negligible.

Quasi-random numbers or low-discrepancy sequences are designed to appear random but not clumpy. In other words a quasi-random sample is not independent from the previous one, it "remembers" the previous samples and tries to position itself away from all the previous samples. There are many ways of producing quasi-random numbers (see Niederreiter, 1992, Niederreiter and Shiue, 1995), but we will just describe one, the Faure method, which we have found to work well for option valuation problems and which is reasonably efficient to compute. Figure 4.29 plots 500 pairs of Faure numbers, compare this with Figure 4.28 and notice how the Faure points are much more evenly distributed but still appear somewhat random. This behaviour is ideal for obtaining fast convergence in a Monte Carlo simulation and we illustrate this with an example shortly.

Consider generating the quasi-random numbers for the Monte Carlo simulation of the path of an asset price with N steps as usual. In the context of quasi-random numbers N is the dimension of the sequence, that is, the number of independent quasi-random numbers to be generated simultaneously. We must generate all the N random numbers simultaneously so that they are independent and the increments along the paths have the correct statistical properties. Let the N quasi-random numbers be $x_k; k = 1, \ldots, N$ then

FIGURE 4.29 Plot of 500 Pairs of Faure Quasi-random Numbers

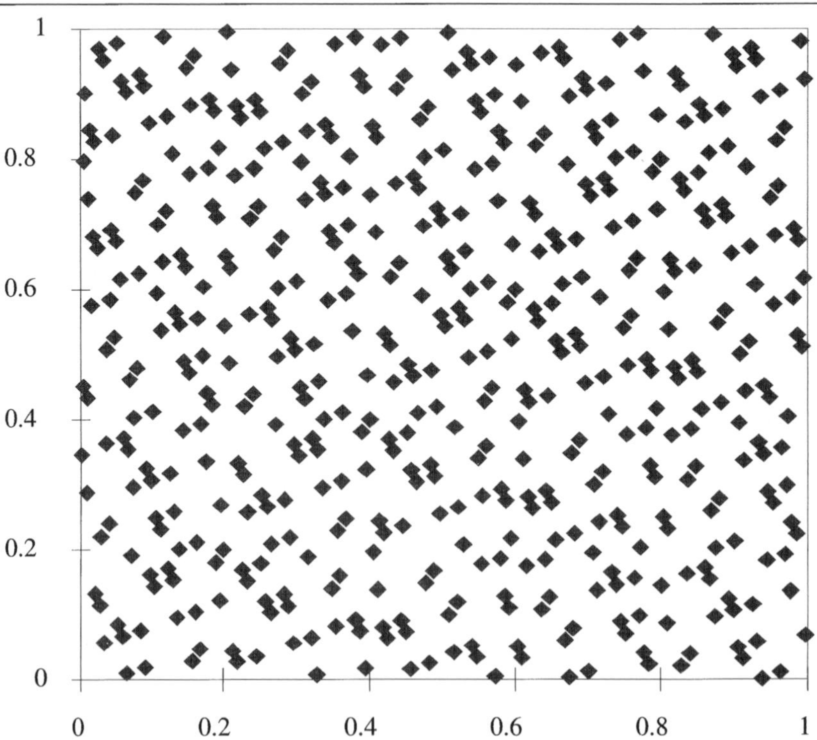

a Faure sequence of length M is defined by

$$x_k = \sum_{l=0}^{m} \frac{a_{k,l}}{p^{l+1}} \tag{4.57}$$

where m is the number of digits in the base p representation of M (m = integer part of $\ln(M)/\ln(p)$), $a_{0,l}$; $j = 0, \ldots, m(a_{0,l}$ = integer part of $(M\%p^{l+1}/p^1))$,[12]

$$a_{k,l} = \sum_{q=l}^{m} \frac{q!}{l!(q-l)!} a_{k-1,q} \% p \tag{4.58}$$

and p is the smallest prime number greater than or equal to N. Figure 4.30 gives the pseudo-code algorithm for the Monte Carlo valuation of a European call option using a Faure sequence.

The only difference between Figure 4.30 and Figure 4.2 are the two lines highlighted in bold where the Faure numbers for the current path are generated and standard normal random number is generated by Box–Muller from the appropriate Faure numbers (see section 4.11). Figure 4.31 illustrates the prices obtained from pricing a European call

FIGURE 4.30 Pseudo-code for Monte Carlo Valuation of a European Call Option in a Black–Scholes World using a Faure Sequence

```
initialise_parameters { K, T, S, sig, r, div, N, M }
{ precompute constants }

dt = T/N
nudt = (r-div-0.5*sig*sig)*dt
sigsdt = sig*sqrt(dt)
sum_CT = 0
sum_CT2 = 0
lnS = ln(S)

for j = 1 to M do { for each simulation }
 generate_Faure_sequence( x[], N, M )

 lnSt = lnS
 for i = 1 to N do { for each time step }
  ε = standard_normal_by_Box_Muller( x[i] )
  lnSt = lnSt + nudt + sigsdt*ε
 next i

 St = exp(lnSt)
 CT = max( 0 , St - K )
 sum_CT = sum_CT + CT
 sum_CT2 = sum_CT2 + CT*CT

next j

call_value = sum_CT/M*exp(-r*T)
SD = sqrt( sum_CT2/M*exp(-2*r*T) - call_value*call_value )
SE = SD/sqrt(M-1)
```

FIGURE 4.31 Relative Pricing Error for a European Call Option Using Pseudo-random Numbers and Faure Quasi-random Numbers

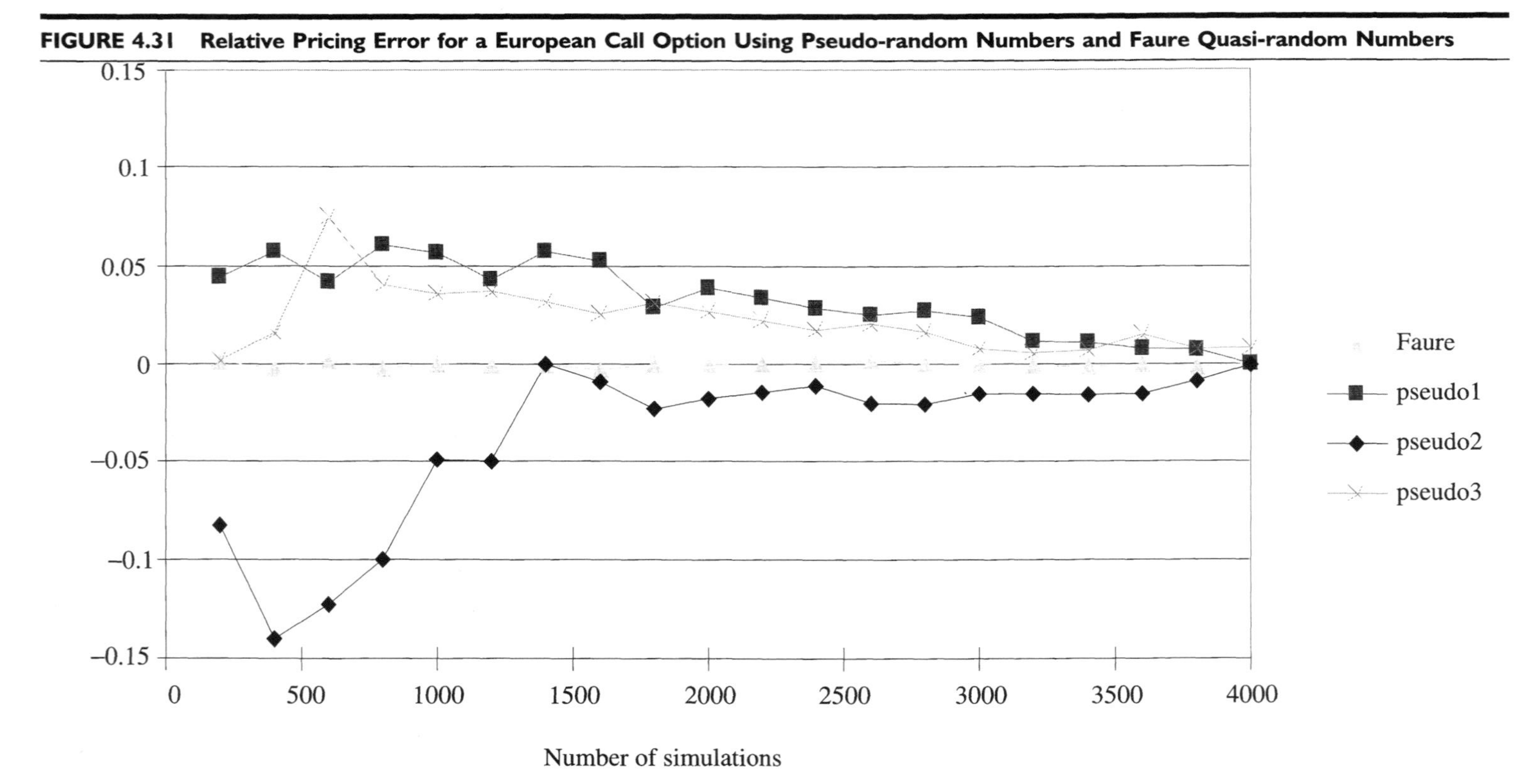

option using three different sets of pseudo-random numbers and a set of Faure quasi-random numbers.

It is clear that the prices using the Faure quasi-random numbers converge much faster as a function of the number of simulations than the prices using pseudo-random numbers. The Faure quasi-random numbers take approximately the same computation time to generate as pseudo random numbers.

4.13 SUMMARY

In this chapter we have described the use of Monte Carlo simulation for pricing and hedging derivatives. We discussed efficient implementation techniques using antithetic and control variates based on the concept of hedging and methods for computing hedge sensitivities. It was shown how the Monte Carlo method could be used to handle multiple stochastic variables and path-dependent options with detailed examples using Asian and lookback options. Finally, we discussed important aspects involved in the generation of the independent standard normal samples via pseudo-random and quasi-random methods.

ENDNOTES

1. In this section we explicitly show the time dependence of variables with a subscirpt because we will often need to refer to the time the variable is observed.
2. See Kloeden and Platen (1992,1994) for advanced methods of discretising stochastic differential equations.
3. We discuss the generation of standard normal random variates in section 4.11.
4. See also Hull and White (1988) on the use of control variates for tree or lattice methods.
5. It is more efficient to value this option by Gaussian quadrature (see Ravindran, 1993), but when we add path-dependent features or use more general stochastic processes, applying Gaussian quadrature becomes very difficult if not impossible.
6. Here we have applied a simple (Euler) discretisation to the SDE for the variance for clarity, see Kloeden and Platen (1992, 1994) for more advanced methods.
7. See Nelken (1996) and Clewlow and Strickland (1997) for more details on the specification of exotic options contracts, analytical pricing formulae and hedging techniques.
8. See Levy (1997) for a survey of Asian options and a review of published work on them.
9. see Heynen and Kat (1997b) for a survey of lookback options contracts, analytical results and a comparison of numerical methods.
10. Here we have applied a simple (Euler) discretisation to the SDE for the variance for clarity (see Kloeden and Platen, 1992, 1994 for more advanced methods). See Hull and White (1988) for details of the stochastic volatility process (in particular the expression for the expectation of the variance used in the vega-based control variate).
11. Standard libraries are available for performing PCA analysis, for example "Numerical recipes in C", Press *et al.* (1992).
12. % indicates the remainder after integer division,

5

Implied Trees and Exotic Options

5.1 INTRODUCTION

IMPLIED trees can be considered as generalisations of binomial and trinomial trees. The idea behind implied trees is to recognise that the market prices of standard European options contain important information about the markets expectation of the future. Since these (usually exchange traded) standard European options are used to hedge the more complex exotic options[1] then trees used to price and hedge the exotics should be built to be consistent with the market prices of the standard options. This can be done by generalising the trees of Chapters 2 and 3 by making previously constant parameters (such as the probabilities) time dependent and to imply these time-dependent parameters such that the tree returns the market prices of the standard options. In this way we are recognising that the real market is incomplete without the standard options and so the standard options should be treated as fundamental securities whose prices are observed in the market and which can be used to hedge the more complex derivatives.

Derman and Kani (1994) and Derman, Ergener and Kani (1995a) proposed binomial tree structures and Dupire (1994) worked with trinomial trees.[2] A trinomial tree structure is much more convenient, so we will work with trinomial trees. We first describe how an implied trinomial tree can be built to be consistent with prices of standard European calls and puts. We then go on to show how exotic options can be priced using a trinomial tree. Note that although we describe the pricing of exotics in a more general implied tree, the same techniques can be used for the binomial, trinomial and finite difference methods in Chapters 2 and 3.

The structure of the implied trinomial tree will be very similar to that of the constant coefficient trinomial tree in Chapter 3, Figure 5.1 illustrates the tree. As in Chapter 3, i is the time step and j is the level of the asset price relative to the initial asset price i.e. at node (i, j) we have $t = i\Delta t$ and $S_{i,j} = S\exp(j\Delta x)$. Note that we can allow the time steps Δt_i to be different without complicating the tree-building procedure. This will be convenient for ensuring that time steps fall on key dates required for the exotic options that we will be pricing. Furthermore, it is possible for the asset price levels to vary with the time step without complicating the procedure other than increasing the storage requirements slightly. This becomes important for the barrier options which we describe in section 5.4. At each node we have a state price $Q_{i,j}$, which was introduced in Chapter 1 and which we will define again in section 5.2, and instead of a single set of transition probabilities p_u, p_m and p_d we have a different set of transition probabilities $p_{u,i,j}$, $p_{m,i,j}$ and $p_{d,i,j}$

FIGURE 5.1 Implied Trinomial Tree Structure

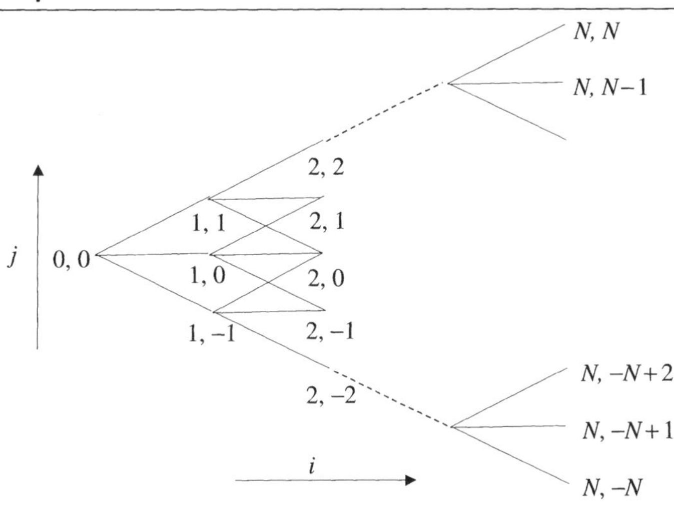

for every node (i, j). The value of an option at node (i, j) will be $C_{i,j}$ as before, and time step N will correspond to the maturity date of the longest maturity option in the market. In the following section we will use the market prices of standard European calls and puts to obtain implied state prices. In order to do this we will require the market prices of options with strike prices equal to every asset price level in the tree, and maturity dates equal to every time step in the tree. Clearly, there will not usually be this number of strikes and maturities trading in the market and so we must interpolate and extrapolate to obtain the strikes and maturities we need which are not traded from those that are traded. A reasonably robust way to do the interpolation is via Black–Scholes implied volatilities.

5.2 COMPUTING THE IMPLIED STATE PRICES

We introduced state prices (or Arrow–Debreu pure securities) in Chapter 1. They are the prices today of an instrument which pays one unit of cash (e.g. a dollar) if a single specific future state is reached and zero otherwise. They can be thought of as the building blocks of all securities. For example, consider the tree in Figure 5.1. and a security X which pays $X_{2,0}$, $X_{2,1}$ and $X_{2,2}$ if states (2,0), (2,1) and (2,2) are reached respectively and zero in every other state. A portfolio consisting of $X_{2,0}$ units of pure security $Q_{2,0}$, $X_{2,1}$ units of pure security $Q_{2,1}$ and $X_{2,2}$ units of pure security $Q_{2,2}$ will have exactly the same pay-off as X. So today's price of X must be

$$X_t = X_{2,0}Q_{2,0} + X_{2,1}Q_{2,1} + X_{2,2}Q_{2,2} \tag{5.1}$$

Generalising this argument, the price of a European call with strike price K and maturity date $N\Delta t$, in the tree is

$$c(K, N\Delta t) = \sum_{j=-N}^{N} \max(S_{N,j} - K, 0)Q_{N,j} \tag{5.2}$$

We want to compute the state prices for the nodes at time step N in the tree such that they are consistent with the market prices of standard European call and put options. Consider the highest node in the tree (N, N) at time step N. The price of a European call with strike price equal to the level of the asset price at the next node down $S_{N,N-1}$, and with a maturity date at time step N is

$$c(S_{N,N-1}, N\Delta t) = (S_{N,N} - S_{N,N-1})Q_{N,N} \tag{5.3}$$

because for all the nodes below (N, N) the pay-off of the call option is zero. Equation (5.3) can be rearranged to give the state price $Q_{N,N}$ at node (N, N) in terms of the known call price, asset price and strike price. Now consider a European option with a strike price equal to the asset price $S_{N,N-2}$ at node $(N, N-2)$, its price is given by

$$c(S_{N,N-2}, N\Delta t) = (S_{N,N-1} - S_{N,N-2})Q_{N,N-1} + (S_{N,N} - S_{N,N-2})Q_{N,N} \tag{5.4}$$

The only unknown in equation (5.4) is $Q_{N,N-1}$ since we have previously computed $Q_{N,N}$ using equation (5.3). In this way we can continue to work down the nodes at time step N to the middle of the tree computing the state prices. In general, for node (N, j), the option price is given by

$$c(S_{N,j-1}, N\Delta t) = (S_{N,j} - S_{N,j-1})Q_{N,j} + \sum_{k=j+1}^{N} (S_{N,k} - S_{N,j-1})Q_{N,k} \tag{5.5}$$

where everything is known except $Q_{N,j}$. Therefore, we can continue to work down the nodes computing the state prices. This procedure can be continued to the lowest node of the tree, however, because of the iterative nature of the calculations numerical errors can build up in the state prices. It is therefore better to stop this procedure when the central node of the tree is reached and begin a similar process, using put option prices, starting from the bottom node of the tree and working upwards. This method can be applied to every time step in the tree. Figure 5.2 gives a pseudo-code implementation of the procedure.

The functions `call(K, T)` and `put(K, T)` return the prices of European calls and puts with strike price K and time to maturity T by interpolating from the observed market prices.

Example : Computing Implied Trinomial Tree State Prices

We compute the state prices in a one year maturity, four time step tree with the current asset price at 100 and a space step of 0.2524 (chosen so that the stability and convergence condition will be satisified — see section 5.3). The continuously compounded interest rate is assumed to be 6 per cent per annum; $T = 1$ year, $S = 100$, $r = 0.06$, $N = 4$, $\Delta x = 0.2524$. Figure 5.3 shows the numerical results of the calculations where the interpolated market prices are given in the table above the tree.

Firstly the constants Δt (dt), edx and infl are precomputed

$$\Delta t = \frac{T}{N} = \frac{1}{4} = 0.25$$

$$\text{edx} = \exp(\Delta x) = \exp(0.2524) = 1.2871$$

$$\text{infl} = \exp(r \times \Delta t) = \exp(0.06 \times 0.25) = 1.0151$$

FIGURE 5.2 Pseudo-code for Implied Trinomial Tree State Prices

```
initialise_parameters { T, S, r, N, dx }

{ precompute constants }

dt = T/N
edx = exp(dx)

{ initialise asset prices }

St[-N] = S*exp(-N*dx)
for j = -N+1 to N do St[j] = St[j-1]*edx

{ for each time step }

for i = 1 to N do

  { for uppermost node down to centre of tree }

  for j = i downto 0 do

    sum = 0
    for k = i downto j+1 do
      sum = sum + Q[i,k]*( St[k] - St[j-1] )

    Q[i,j] = (call(St[j-1],i*dt) - sum )/( St[j] - St[j-1] )

   next j

   { for lowermost node up to centre of tree }

   for j = -i to -1 do

    sum = 0
    for k = -i to j-1 do
     sum = sum + Q[i,k]*( St[j+1] - St[k] )

    Q[i,j] = ( put(St[j+1],i*dt) - sum )/( St[j+1] - St[j] )

   next j
  next i
```

Then the asset prices are computed (these apply to every time step). The asset price at node (4, −4) is computed as

$$S_{4,-4} = S \times \exp(-N \times \Delta x) = 100 \times \exp(-4 \times 0.2524) = 36.44$$

The other asset prices are computed from this, for example the asset price at node (4, −3):

$$S_{4,-3} = S_{4,-4} \times \text{edx} = 36.44 \times 1.2871 = 46.90$$

FIGURE 5.3 Numerical Example of Implied Trinomial Tree State Prices

T	S	rate	N	dx
1	100	0.06	4	0.2524

dt	edx	infl
0.2500	1.2871	1.0151

Market Prices (each cell: call
put)

K , T	0	0.25	0.5	0.75	1
213.20	0.0000 113.2040	0.0000 110.0298	0.0001 106.9030	0.0011 103.8236	0.0055 100.7935
165.65	0.0000 65.6521	0.0000 63.1859	0.0050 60.7613	0.0412 58.4042	0.1399 56.1451
128.71	0.0000 28.7059	0.0403 26.8300	0.4195 25.3216	1.1159 24.1584	1.9965 23.2072
100.00	0.0000 0.0000	4.7469 3.2581	7.1559 4.2004	9.1754 4.7752	10.9895 5.1660
77.70	22.3035 0.0000	23.4719 0.0117	24.7110 0.1112	25.9912 0.2689	27.2682 0.4400
60.37	39.6325 0.0000	40.5313 0.0000	41.4170 0.0003	42.2922 0.0033	43.1598 0.0118
46.90	53.0966 0.0000	53.7949 0.0000	54.4828 0.0000	55.1604 0.0000	55.8281 0.0001

State Prices

j	i St , t	0 0	1 0.25	2 0.5	3 0.75	4 1
4	274.41					0.0001
3	213.20				0.0009	0.0027
2	165.65			0.0114	0.0282	0.0474
1	128.71		0.1654	0.2233	0.2517	0.2630
0	100.00	1.0000	0.6742	0.5524	0.4732	0.4166
–1	77.70		0.1461	0.1769	0.1867	0.1872
–2	60.37			0.0064	0.0151	0.0238
–3	46.90				0.0002	0.0009
–4	36.44					0.0000

Then for each time step the state prices are computed, firstly for the upper half of the tree and then for the lower half. For example for time step 3, for node (3, 3) we have:

$$Q_{3,3} = \text{call}(S_{3,2}, 3 \times \Delta t)/(S_{3,3} - S_{3,2}) = 0.0412/(213.20 - 165.65) = 0.0009$$

and for node (3, 2):

$$\begin{aligned} Q_{3,2} &= (\text{call}(S_{3,1}, 3 \times \Delta t) - Q_{3,3} \times (S_{3,3} - S_{3,1})/(S_{3,2} - S_{3,1}) \\ &= (1.1159 - 0.0009 \times (213.20 - 128.71))/(165.65 - 128.71) = 0.0282 \end{aligned}$$

and for node (3, −3) we have:

$$Q_{3,-3} = \text{put}(S_{3,-2}, 3 \times \Delta t)/(S_{3,-2} - S_{3,-3}) = 0.0033/(60.37 - 46.90) = 0.0002$$

5.3 COMPUTING THE IMPLIED TRANSITION PROBABILITIES

In order to obtain the transition probabilities given the state prices at every node in the tree, we specify the local no-arbitrage relationships which must hold at every node. Imagine we want to compute the transition probabilities for node (i, j) and we have computed the transition probabilities for all the nodes above node (i, j). The first no-arbitrage relationship is that the discounted expected value of a one-period pure discount bond must be equal to the discount factor over the next time step

$$e^{-r\Delta t}(p_{\text{d},i,j} + p_{\text{m},i,j} + p_{\text{u},i,j}) = e^{-r\Delta t} \tag{5.6}$$

which is equivalent to requiring that the transition probabilities sum to one:

$$p_{\text{d},i,j} + p_{\text{m},i.j} + p_{\text{u},i,j} = 1 \tag{5.7}$$

The second condition is that the asset price at node (i, j) must be equal to its local discounted expected value over the next time step[3]

$$S_{i,j} = e^{-r\Delta t}(p_{\text{d},i,j}S_{i+1,j-1} + p_{\text{m},i,j}S_{i+1,j} + p_{\text{u},i,j}S_{i+1,j+1}) \tag{5.8}$$

Finally, we have the forward evolution equation for the state price at node $(i+1, j+1)$:

$$Q_{i+1,j+1} = e^{-r\Delta t}(p_{\text{d},i,j+2}Q_{i,j+2} + p_{\text{m},i,j+1}Q_{i,j+1} + p_{\text{u},i,j}Q_{i,j}) \tag{5.9}$$

Given that we have computed the transition probabilities for all the nodes above (i, j) equation (5.9) can be rearranged to give $p_{\text{u},i,j}$ directly:

$$p_{\text{u},i,j} = \frac{e^{r\Delta t}Q_{i+1,j+1} - p_{\text{d},i,j+2}Q_{i,j+2} - p_{\text{m},i,j+1}Q_{i,j+1}}{Q_{i,j}} \tag{5.10}$$

Equations (5.7) and (5.8) can then be solved simultaneously for $p_{\text{m},i,j}$ and $p_{\text{d},i,j}$:

$$p_{\text{m},i,j} = \frac{e^{r\Delta t}S_{i,j} - S_{i+1,j-1} - p_{u,i,j}(S_{i+1,j+1} - S_{i+1,j-1})}{(S_{i+1,j} - S_{i+1,j-1})} \tag{5.11}$$

$$p_{\text{d},i,j} = 1 - p_{\text{m},i,j} - p_{\text{u},i,j} \tag{5.12}$$

Figure 5.4 shows the relationships between the state prices and transition probabilities in equations (5.8) and (5.9) diagramatically.

Now consider the highest node (i, i) at time step i, equation (5.10) reduces to

$$p_{u,i,i} = \frac{e^{r\Delta t} Q_{i+1,i+1}}{Q_{i,i}} \tag{5.13}$$

and then we can use equations (5.11) and (5.12) to obtain $p_{m,i,i}$ and $p_{d,i,i}$. Similarly, for node $(i, i-1)$ equation (5.10) reduces to

$$p_{u,i,i-1} = \frac{e^{r\Delta t} Q_{i+1,i} - p_{m,i,i} Q_{i,i}}{Q_{i,i-1}} \tag{5.14}$$

and then use equations (5.11) and (5.12) to obtain $p_{m,i,i-1}$ and $p_{d,i,i-1}$. Therefore, we can start at the top of the tree and work downwards solving for the transition probabilities in an iterative manner. This procedure is susceptible to numerical errors in the same way as for the state prices in the previous section. We therefore stop at the central node of the tree and start working up from the bottom node of the tree. For the lower half of the tree we first obtain $p_{d,i,j}$ directly from the forward evolution of the state prices, and then $p_{m,i,j}$ and $p_{u,i,j}$ are obtained from solving the remaining two equations simultaneously.

FIGURE 5.4 State Price and Transition Probabilities

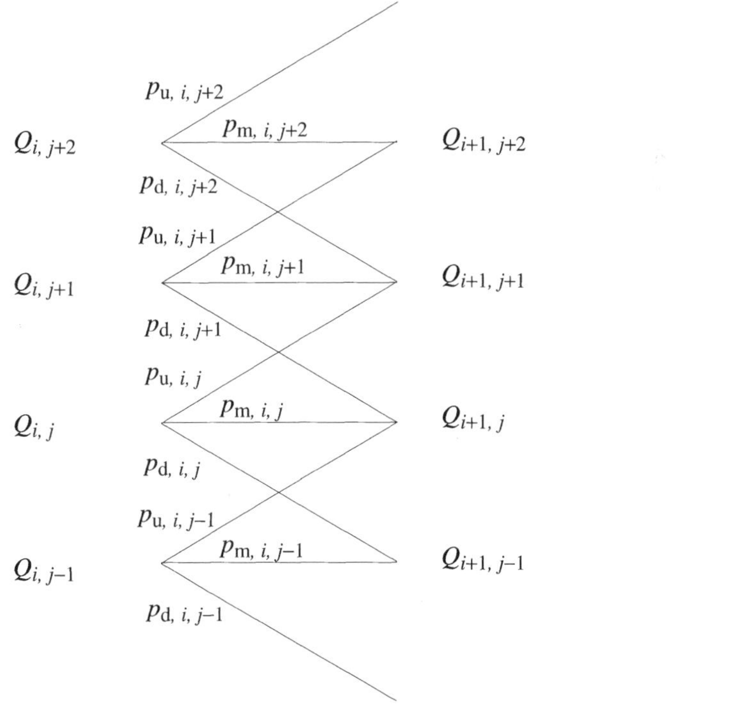

Therefore, equations (5.10)–(5.14) become

$$p_{d,i,j} = \frac{e^{r\Delta t}Q_{i+1,j-1} - p_{u,i,j-2}, Q_{i,j-2} - p_{m,i,j-1}Q_{i,j-1}}{Q_{i,j}} \tag{5.15}$$

$$p_{m,i,j} = \frac{e^{r\Delta t}S_{i,j} - S_{i+1,j+1} - p_{d,i,j}(S_{i+1,j-1} - S_{i+1,j+1})}{(S_{i+1,j} - S_{i+1,j+1})} \tag{5.16}$$

$$p_{u,i,j} = 1 - p_{m,i,j} - p_{d,i,j} \tag{5.17}$$

$$p_{d,i,-i} = \frac{e^{r\Delta t}Q_{i+1,-i-1}}{Q_{i,-i}} \tag{5.18}$$

$$p_{d,i,-i+1} = \frac{e^{r\Delta t}Q_{i+1,-i} - p_{m,i,-i}Q_{i,-i}}{Q_{i,-i+1}} \tag{5.19}$$

Again, we compute the tree in two halves because the transition probabilities we obtain depend on previously computed transition probabilities and so numerical errors can build up. Note that it is necessary to ensure that the transition probabilities remain positive and that the explicit finite difference method stability condition ($\Delta x \geq \sigma\sqrt{3\Delta t}$) is satisfied at every node (see section 3.5). This requires the calculation of the local volatility at each node which can be obtained by computing the local variance at each node:

$$\text{var}[\Delta x] = \sigma_{\text{local}}^2 \Delta t = E[\Delta x^2] - (E[\Delta x])^2 \tag{5.20}$$

A simple and robust way to ensure that the probabilities remain positive and the stability condition is met is to set the space step as follows:

$$\Delta x = \sigma_{\max}\sqrt{3\Delta t} \tag{5.21}$$

where $\sigma_{\max}$ is the maximum implied volatility from the standard options to which the tree is being fitted. Figure 5.5 gives the pseudo-code implementation for determining the implied trinomial tree transition probabilities, assuming the state prices have been computed.

FIGURE 5.5 Pseudo-code for Implied Trinomial Tree Transition Probabilities

```
initialise_parameters { T, S, r, N, dx }

{ precompute constants }

dt = T/N
edx = exp(dx)
infl = exp( r*dt )

{ initialise asset prices }

St[-N] = S*exp(-N*dx)
for j = -N+1 to N do St[j] = St[j-1]*edx

{ for each time step }
```

FIGURE 5.5 ***(continued)***

```
for i = 1 to N do

  { for uppermost node down to centre of tree }

  for j = i downto 0 do

    if j = i then
      pu[i,i] = infl*Q[i+1,i+1]/Q[i,i]
    else if j = i-1 then
      pu[i,i-1] = ( infl*Q[i+1,i] - pm[i,i]*Q[i,i] )/Q[i,i-1]
    else
    pu[i,j] = ( infl*Q[i+1,j+1] - pd[i,j+2]*Q[i,j+2] -
                pm[i,j+1]*Q[i,j+1] )/Q[i,j]

    pm[i,j] = ( infl*St[j]-St[j-1]-pu[i,j]*(St[j+1]-St[j-1]) )/
              ( St[j]-St[j-1] )

    pd[i,j] = 1 - pm[i,j] - pu[i,j]

  next j

  { for lowermost node up to centre of tree }

  for j = -i to -1 do

    if j = -i then
      pd[i,-i] = infl*Q[i+1,-i-1]/Q[i,-i]
    else if j = -i+1 then
      pd[i,-i+1] = ( infl*Q[i+1,-i] - pm[i,-i]*Q[i,-i] )/
                     Q[i,-i+1]
   else
   pd[i,j] = ( infl*Q[i+1,j-1] - pu[i,j-2]*Q[i,j-2] -
               pm[i,j-1]*Q[i,j-1] )/Q[i,j]

   pm[i,j] = ( infl*St[j]-St[j+1]-pd[i,j]*(St[j-1]-St[j+1]) )/
             ( St[j]-St[j+1] )

   pu[i,j] = 1 - pm[i,j] - pd[i,j]

   next j

  next i
```

Example : Computing Implied Trinomial Tree Transition Probabilities

We compute the transition probabilities for the example in section 5.2 with a one-year maturity, four time step tree, current asset price at 100 and a space step of 0.2524 (chosen so that the stability and convergence condition will be satisified — equation (5.21)). The continuously compounded interest rate is assumed to be 6 per cent per annum; $T = 1$ year, $S = 100$, $r = 0.06$, $N = 4$, $\Delta x = 0.2524$. Figure 5.6 shows the numerical results of the calculations.

FIGURE 5.6 Numerical Example for Implied Trinomial Tree Transition Probabilities

T	S	rate	N	dx
1	100	0.06	4	0.2524

dt	edx	infl
0.2500	1.2871	1.0151

Transition Probabilities

Tree node key:
stability <=1

Q[i,j]	pu[i,j]
stability	pm[i,j]
	pd[i,j]

j	i St , t	0 0	1 0.25	2 0.5	3 0.75	4 1
4	274.41					0.0001
3	213.20				0.0009 0.1056 0.7189 0.8263 0.0681	0.0027
2	165.65			0.0114 0.0775 0.5679 0.8904 0.0320	0.0282 0.0730 0.5394 0.9008 0.0262	0.0474
1	128.71		0.1654 0.0697 0.5178 0.9084 0.0219	0.2233 0.0830 0.6003 0.8779 0.0391	0.2517 0.0901 0.6398 0.8618 0.0481	0.2630
0	100.00	1.0000 0.1679 0.9733 0.6839 0.1483	0.6742 0.1134 0.7559 0.8083 0.0782	0.5524 0.1069 0.7254 0.8232 0.0698	0.4732 0.1043 0.7129 0.8291 0.0665	0.4166
−1	77.70		0.1461 0.0873 0.6247 0.8681 0.0446	0.1769 0.0951 0.6666 0.8502 0.0547	0.1867 0.0987 0.6850 0.8420 0.0593	0.1872
−2	60.37			0.0064 0.0830 0.6003 0.8780 0.0390	0.0151 0.0864 0.6195 0.8702 0.0434	0.0238
−3	46.90				0.0002 0.0808 0.5878 0.8829 0.0363	0.0009
−4	36.44					0.0000

Firstly the constants; Δt (dt), edx and infl are precomputed:

$$\Delta t = \frac{T}{N} = \frac{1}{4} = 0.25$$

$$\text{edx} = \exp(\Delta x) = \exp(0.2524) = 1.2871$$

$$\text{infl} = \exp(r \times \Delta t) = \exp(0.06 \times 0.25) = 1.0151$$

Next the asset prices are computed (see the example in section 5.2). Then for each time step the transition probabilities are computed, firstly for the upper half of the tree and then for the lower half. For example for node (3, 3) we have

$$p_{u,3,3} = \text{infl} \times Q_{4,4}/Q_{3,3} = 1.0151 \times 0.0001/0.0009 = 0.1056$$

$$\begin{aligned} p_{m,3,3} &= (\text{infl} \times S_{3,3} - S_{3,2} - p_{u,3,3}(S_{3,4} - S_{3,2}))/(S_{3,3} - S_{3,2}) \\ &= (1.01511 \times 213.20 - 165.65 - 0.1056 \\ &\quad \times (274.41 - 165.65))/(213.20 - 165.65) = 0.8263 \end{aligned}$$

$$p_{d,3,3} = 1 - p_{m,3,3} - p_{u,3,3} = 1 - 0.8263 - 0.1056 = 0.0681$$

and for node (3, −1):

$$\begin{aligned} p_{d,3,-1} &= (\text{ infl} \times Q_{4,-2} - p_{u,3,-3} \times Q_{3,-3} - p_{m,3,-2} \times Q_{3,-2})/Q_{3,-1} \\ &= (1.0151 \times 0.0238 - 0.0808 \times 0.0002 - 0.8702 \times 0.0151)/0.1867 \\ &= 0.0593 \end{aligned}$$

$$\begin{aligned} p_{m,3,-1} &= (\text{ infl} \times S_{3,-1} - S_{3,0} - p_{d,3,-1} \times (S_{3,-2} - S_{3,0}))/(S_{3,-1} - S_{3,0}) \\ &= (1.0151 \times 77.70 - 100.00 - 0.0593 \\ &\quad \times (60.37 - 100.00))/(77.70 - 100.00) = 0.8420 \end{aligned}$$

$$p_{u,3,-1} = 1 - p_{m,3,-1} - p_{d,3,-1} = 1 - 0.8420 - 0.0593 = 0.0987$$

The method we have described for computing both the state prices and transition probabilities is not the most stable or efficient since, as we have mentioned, the iterative procedure is susceptible to the build-up of numerical errors. Notice that in fact both the state prices and transition probabilities are uniquely determined by a system of linear equations. Therefore the best method of solving for both the state prices and the transition probabilities is by using a robust linear system solver (see, for example, Press *et al*, 1992).

5.4 PRICING BARRIER OPTIONS IN TRINOMIAL TREES

Barrier options (also called knock-in or knock-out or less commonly drop-in or drop-out options[4]) are standard calls or puts except that they disappear (knock-out) or only appear (knock-in) if the underlying asset price is found to have crossed a predetermined (barrier) level, H, on one of a predetermined set of fixing dates, $t_i; i = 1, \ldots, m$. They have a fairly standard naming convention which describes whether the barrier is below or above the current asset price ("down" or "up"), whether the option disappears or appears when the barrier is crossed ("out" or "in") and whether they have a standard call or put pay-off. With this convention there are $2 \times 2 \times 2 = 8$ possible combinations which are listed in

TABLE 5.1 The Barrier Option Family

Name	pay-off
Down and out call	$\max(0, S_T - K) 1_{\min(S_{t_1},\ldots,S_{tm})>H}$
Up and out call	$\max(0, S_T - K) 1_{\max(S_{t_1},\ldots,S_{tm})<H}$
Down and in call	$\max(0, S_T - K) 1_{\min(S_{t_1},\ldots,S_{tm})\leq H}$
Up and in call	$\max(0, S_T - K) 1_{\max(S_{t_1},\ldots,S_{tm})\geq H}$
Down and out put	$\max(0, K - S_T) 1_{\min(S_{t_1},\ldots,S_{tm})>H}$
Up and out put	$\max(0, K - S_T) 1_{\max(S_{t_1},\ldots,S_{tm})<H}$
Down and in put	$\max(0, K - S_T) 1_{\min(S_{t_1},\ldots,S_{tm})\leq H}$
Up and in put	$\max(0, K - S_T) 1_{\max(S_{t_1},\ldots,S_{tm})\geq H}$

where $1_{condition}$ is the indicator function which has value one if *condition* is true and zero otherwise

Table 5.1 together with a mathematical definition of their pay-off. For example, a down-and-out call option has the pay-off of a standard call option except if the asset price goes down below the level H then the option disappears (goes out) and pays nothing. We can express the pay-off of a down and out call as follows:

$$\text{down and out call payoff} = \max(0, S_T - K)1_{\min(S_{t_1},\ldots,S_{tm})>H}$$

Figure 5.7 illustrates two possible paths of the asset price for this example. Path 1 never falls below the barrier and therefore pays off $\max(0, S_T - K)$. Path 2 is above the barrier at fixing dates t_{i-1} and t_i, but at fixing date t_{i+1} it is below the barrier and the option therefore knocks out and the path will pay zero at date T, despite the fact that the asset price is above the strike price. A standard variation on the barrier family we

FIGURE 5.7 Down and Out Call Option Example Paths

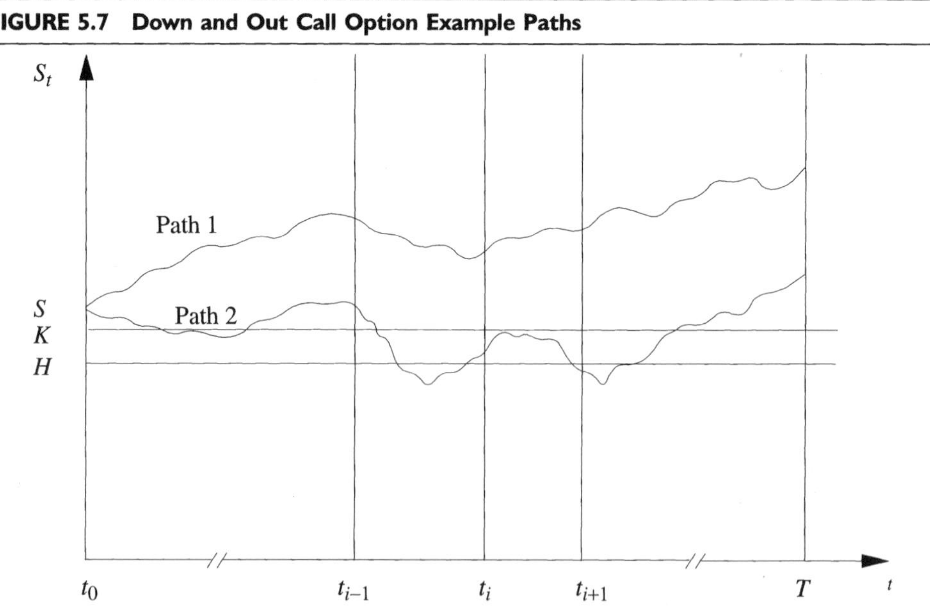

have just described are barrier options which pay a predetermined cash rebate (which we denote X_{rebate}) if an "out" option disappears or an "in" option never appears.

Barrier options are cheaper than standard options because of the possibility of the option disappearing or never appearing. For example a down-and-out call option will disappear if the asset price hits the barrier which is below the current asset price and usually the strike price. As the asset price becomes very low relative to the strike price the chances of it finishing in the money are very low. With a standard option the buyer still pays for this chance. The down-and-out option eliminates this, allowing the buyer to only pay for higher probability pay-offs. Analytical formulae can be derived for continuously fixed European style barrier options (see Heynen and Kat, 1997a). In reality these options are fixed at most on a daily basis and often less frequently. This substantially affects the price of the option since the probability of the price having crossed the barrier decreases as the price is observed (fixed) less frequently.

We illustrate the pricing of European and American barrier options in trees with the example of a up and out put option. The procedure is the same as for standard European and American options (see Chapter 3, section 3.2) except that we add the barrier boundary condition. In other words, we step back through the tree in the usual way except that the nodes which are on and above the barrier on fixing dates are set equal to the rebate amount (which may be zero).

Figure 5.8 gives the pseudo-code implementation of the trinomial tree valuation of an American up and out put option with fixing dates at the equally spaced time steps in the tree and assuming that an implied tree building routine exists. Notice that the indicator function becomes an "if" statement in the initialisation of the option values at maturity and the application of the barrier boundary condition. Also note that if the time step varied through the tree then the one-step discount factor would be different at each time step.

Example : Implied Trinomial Tree Valuation of an American Up-and-Out Put

We price a one-year maturity, at-the-money American up-and-out put option with the current asset price at 100. The barrier is set at 110 and is fixed at each time step, the rebate is 1, the continuously compounded interest rate is 6 per cent per annum and the implied trinomial tree is identical to the examples in sections 5.2 and 5.3 (four time steps, and a space step of 0.2524). That is, $K = 100$, $T = 1$, $S = 100$, $r = 0.06$, $H = 110$, $X_{\text{rebate}} = 1$, $N = 4$, $\Delta x = 0.2524$. Figure 5.9 illustrates the results of the calculations where the nodes of the tree are indicated by the boxes whose structure is defined by the tree node key.

Firstly the constants Δt (dt), $disc$ are precomputed:

$$\Delta t = \frac{T}{N} = \frac{1}{4} = 0.25$$

$$disc = \exp(-r \times \Delta t) = \exp(-0.06 \times 0.25) = 0.9851$$

Then the option values at maturity are computed. For node (4, −1) we have

$$S_{4,-1} < H, 77.70 < 110 \Rightarrow C_{4,-1} = \max(0, K - S_{4,-1}) = \max(0, 100 - 77.70) = 22.3035$$

For node (4, 1) we have

$$S_{4,1} > H, 128.71 > 110 \Rightarrow C_{4,1} = X_{\text{rebate}} = 1.0000$$

FIGURE 5.8 Pseudo-code for Trinomial Tree Valuation of an American Up and Out Put Option

```
initialise_parameters {K, T, S, r, H, X_rebate, N }

build_implied_trinomial_tree

{ precompute constants }

dt = T/N
disc = exp( -r*dt )

{ initialise option values at maturity }

for j = -N to N do
  if ( St[j] < H ) then
    C[N,j] = max( 0.0 , K - St[j] )
  else
    C[N,j] = 0.0
next j

{ step back through the tree applying the barrier and early
  exercise condition }

for i = N-1 downto 0 do

  for j = -i to i do

    if ( St[j] < H ) then

     C[i,j] =
       disc*(pu[i,j]*C[i+1,j+1] + pm[i,j]*C[i+1,j] +
             pd[i,j]*C[i+1,j-1])

     { apply the early exercise condition }

     C[i,j] = max(C[i,j], K - St[j])

   else

     C[i,j] = X_rebate

 next j

next i

American_Up_and_Out_Put = C[0,0]
```

FIGURE 5.9 Implied Trinomial Tree Valuation of an American Up and Out Put Option

K	T	S	rate	H	X_rebate	N	dx
100	1	100	0.06	110	1	4	0.2524

dt	disc
0.2500	0.9851

Tree node key:
stability<=1

Q[i,j]	pu[i,j]
stability	pm[i,j]
	pd[i,j]

j	i St , t	0 0	1 0.25	2 0.5	3 0.75	4 1
4	274.41					0.0001 1.0000
3	213.20				0.0009 0.1056 1.0000 0.8263 0.0681	0.0027 1.0000
2	165.65			0.0114 0.0775 1.0000 0.8904 0.0320	0.0282 0.0730 1.0000 0.9008 0.0262	0.0474 1.0000
1	128.71		0.1654 0.0697 1.0000 0.9084 0.0219	0.2233 0.0830 1.0000 0.8779 0.0391	0.2517 0.0901 1.0000 0.8618 0.0481	0.2630 1.0000
BARRIER						
0	100.00	1.0000 0.1679 6.2171 0.6839 0.1483	0.6742 0.1134 4.1470 0.8083 0.0782	0.5524 0.1069 2.9085 0.8232 0.0698	0.4732 0.1043 1.5644 0.8291 0.0665	0.4166 0.0000
−1	77.70		0.1461 0.0873 22.3035 0.8681 0.0446	0.1769 0.0951 22.3035 0.8502 0.0547	0.1867 0.0987 22.3035 0.8420 0.0593	0.1872 22.3035
−2	60.37			0.0064 0.0830 39.6325 0.8780 0.0390	0.0151 0.0864 39.6325 0.8702 0.0434	0.0238 39.6325
−3	46.90				0.0002 0.0808 53.0966 0.8829 0.0363	0.0009 53.0966
−4	36.44					0.0000 63.5577

Finally we perform discounted expectations back through the tree applying the barrier and early exercise conditions. For example, for node (3, −2) we have

$$S_{3,-2} < H, 60.37 < 110 \Rightarrow$$

$$C_{3,-2} = \max(disc \times (p_{u,3,-2} \times C_{4,-1} + p_{m,3,-2} \times C_{4,-2} + p_{d,3,-2} \times C_{4,-3}), K - S_{3,-2})$$

$$= \max(0.9851 \times (0.0864 \times 22.3035 + 0.8702 \times 39.6325 + 0.0434 \times 53.0966),$$

$$\times\ 100 - 60.37) = 39.6325$$

Therefore at node (3, −2) the up-and-out put option is exercised early. Figure 5.10 illustrates the value of a down-and-out call option as a function of the number of time steps in the tree and the level of the barrier computed by a standard trinomial tree with fixed space steps.

The values decrease with the number of time steps, particularly as the barrier gets closer to the current asset price. This is because the barrier is being fixed at every time step and therefore hitting the barrier becomes more likely with more time steps. More importantly, notice how the values jump at a certain number of time steps, and barrier options with different barrier levels are computed to have the same value by the tree. This is because the tree with a certain number of time steps and thus asset price levels cannot tell the difference between certain barrier levels which lie between rows of nodes. The tree therefore assigns an option price to the nodes nearest but not beyond the barrier which is too high. This problem can be handled in a number of ways. Boyle and Lau (1994) suggested choosing the number of time steps in a binomial tree such that there is a

FIGURE 5.10 Value of a European Down-and-Out Call Option as a Function of the Number of Time Steps and the Level of the Barrier

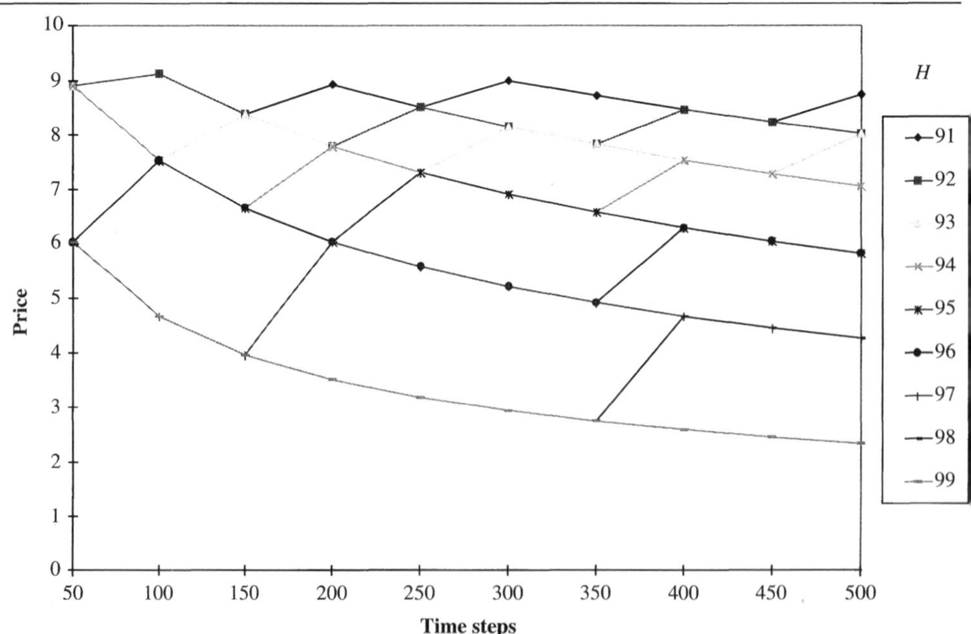

FIGURE 5.11 Pseudo-code for Trinomial Tree Valuation of an American Up-and-Out Put Option with Derman–Kani–Ergener Adjustment

```
initialise_parameters { K, T, S, r, H, X_rebate, N }

build_implied_trinomial_tree

{ precompute constants }

dt = T/N
disc = exp( -r*dt )

{ initialise option values at maturity }

for j = - N to N do
  if ( St[j] < H ) then
   C[N,j] = max( 0.0 , K - St[j] )
  else
   C[N,j] = 0.0
next j

{ step back through the tree applying the barrier and early
  exericise condition }

 for i = N-1 downto 0 do

   for j = -i to i do

     if ( St[j] < H ) then

      C[i,j] =
        disc*( pu[i,j]* C[i+1,j+1] + pm[i,j]*C[i+1,j] +
               pd[i,j]*C[i+1,j-1] )

        { apply the early exercise condition }

        C[i,j] = max(C[i,j], K - St[j])

      else

        C[i,j] = X_rebate

       if ( St[j] < H and St[j+1] >= H ) then
          C[i,j] = (X_rebate-C[i,j])/(St[j+1]-St[j])*(H-St[j])

 next j

next i

American_Up_and_Out_Put = C[0,0]
```

level of the asset price in the tree close to the barrier. With a trinomial tree we can always choose to have a level of the asset price equal to the barrier. Another way of dealing with the problem is by adjusting the option prices at the nodes nearest to the barrier to take into account the fact that the tree "thinks" the barrier is further away than it really is. Derman *et al.* (1995b) suggest that the option value at the nodes nearest but not beyond the barrier should be replaced by a value which is linearly interpolated from the values at the nodes either side of the barrier. This method works well for trinomial trees and is very simple to implement; the pseudo-code is given in Figure 5.11

5.5 PRICING LOOKBACK OPTIONS IN TRINOMIAL TREES

Lookback options are standard calls or puts, except that either the final asset price or the strike price is set equal to the minimum or maximum asset price observed on one of a set of predetermined fixing dates, t_i; $i = 1, \ldots, m$. If the final asset price is replaced they are called fixed strike lookbacks and if the strike price is replaced they are called floating strike lookbacks. Therefore, we have four variations which are listed in Table 5.2, together with a mathematical definition of their pay-offs.[5] For example, a fixed strike call option has the pay-off of a standard call option, except that the asset price at the maturity date is replaced by the maximum asset price that occurred over the set of fixings specified. Figure 5.12 illustrates two possible paths of the asset price for this example. The maximum level of the asset price at the fixing dates for path 1 occurs at fixing date t_1 this is below the strike price K and so the pay-off at T is zero. The maximum for path 2 occurs at fixing date t_3, just above the value at fixing date t_1. This is above the strike price and so the pay-off is $S_{t_3} - K$ even though the path finishes below the strike price.

Lookback options thus allow the holder to buy or sell the underlying asset for the best of the observed prices. For the floating strike lookbacks, if the maturity date is a fixing date then they are not really options since they will always be exercised. That is the worst pay-off that can occur is zero if the price at maturity is the maximum or minimum of the observed prices. Simple analytical formulae exist for European-style lookbacks which are fixed continuously. In reality these options are fixed at most on a daily basis and often much less frequently. This can substantially affect the value of the option since the more infrequently the price is observed the less extreme the maximum or minimum is likely to be.

The pricing of lookback options in trees is complicated by their path dependency. That is, the value of the lookback at any node in the tree depends on the current maximum or minimum asset price, which in turn depends on the path the asset price took to reach that node. Since there can be many different paths through a tree to a particular node (see Figure 5.13) then the lookback option can have many different values at a particular node.

TABLE 5.2 The Lookback Option Family

Fixed strike lookback call	$\max(0, \max(S_{t_1}, \ldots, S_{t_m}) - K)$
Fixed strike lookback put	$\max(0, K - \min(S_{t_1}, \ldots, S_{t_m}))$
Floating strike lookback call	$\max(0, S_T - \min(S_{t_1}, \ldots, S_{t_m}))$
Floating strike lookback put	$\max(0, \max(S_{t_1}, \ldots, S_{t_m}) - S_T)$

FIGURE 5.12 Fixed Strike Lookback Call Option Example Paths

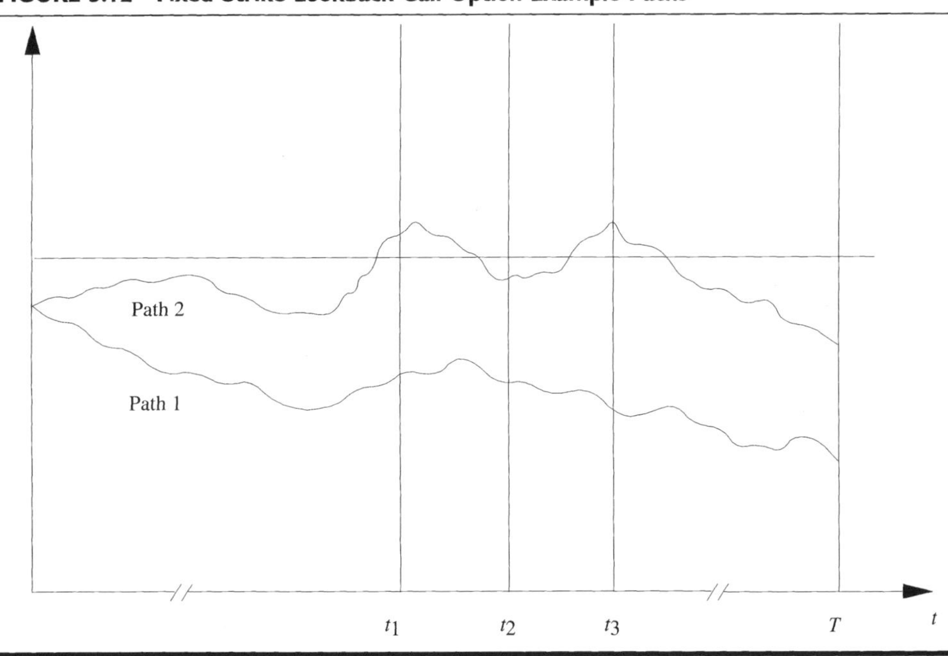

In order to compute the price of a lookback option in a tree we must consider all the possible values of the maximum or minimum at each node. Now the number of paths which reach a given node increases, in general, exponentially with the number of time steps to that node,[6] causing a serious computational problem for pricing some path-dependent options (for example Asians, see section 5.6). Fortunately the number of maximum or minimum asset prices only increases linearly with the number of time steps, but this still increases significantly the amount of computation required. To deal with this problem we describe in detail an approximation technique first introduced by Hull and White (1993).[7]

We illustrate the pricing of European and American lookback options in trees with the example of fixed strike lookback call option. The procedure is essentially the same as for standard European and American call options (see Chapter 3). We step back through the tree in the usual way except that at every node we have to deal with the possibility of more than one maximum asset price at the node. In order to do this we first determine the range (i.e. the minimum and maximum) of the possible maxima which can occur for every node in the tree. In other words we store, at every node, the minimum and maximum possible maximum asset prices which could have occurred for all paths which reach the node. We then choose an appropriate set of values of the maximum between the minimum and maximum possible for each node. In choosing this set of values, note that the nodes which lie on the upper and lower edges of the tree have only one path passing through them, and therefore there will be only one maximum. The largest range of values will occur in the central section of the tree. Therefore the number of values we consider should increase linearly with the number of time steps but also decrease linearly from the central nodes of the tree down to one at the edges of the tree. Let $n_{i,j}$ be the

FIGURE 5.13 Example of Different Paths Which Reach the Same Node in a Trinomial Tree

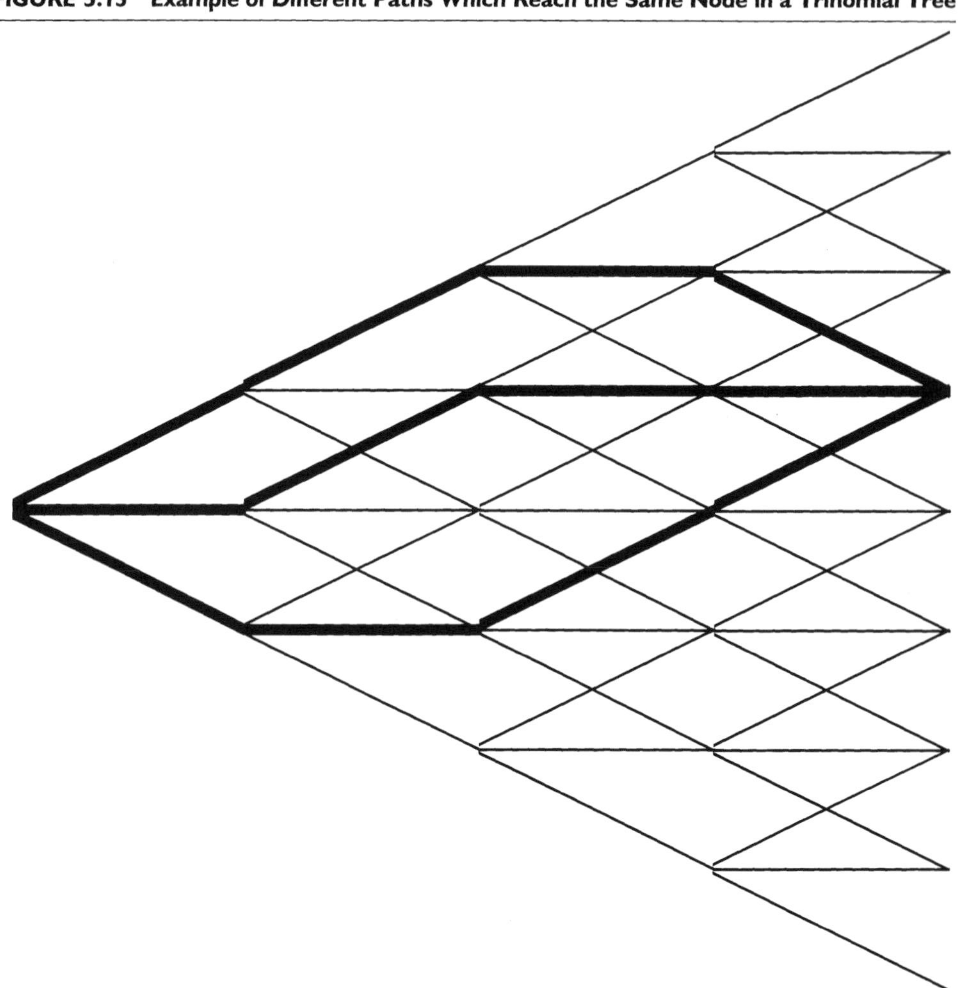

number of values we store at node (i, j) and $F_{i,j,k}$, $k = 1, \ldots, n_{i,j}$ be the values of the maximum, where $F_{i,j,1}$ is the minimum and $F_{i,j,n_{i,j}}$ is the maximum. We will in general drop the i, j subscripts on $n_{i,j}$ where it is clear to which node we are referring, as in $F_{i,j,n_{i,j}}$. Figure 5.14 illustrates the structure of the nodes.

We choose $n_{i,j}$ to be given by

$$n_{i,j} = 1 + \alpha(i - abs(j)) \tag{5.22}$$

where α is typically between one and five, so that $n_{i,j}$ will always be one at the edges of the tree ($j = i$ and $j = -i$) and $1 + \alpha i$ in the centre of the tree. In this way we can increase α to increase the accuracy of the approximation by considering more values of the maximum, whilst keeping the computational effort required under control. In order to find the range of values of the maximum we step forward through the tree from $i = 0$ to $i = N$. If we have found the range of maxima for all nodes up to time step $i - 1$, then for

FIGURE 5.14 Structure of Nodes for the Valuation of a Path-Dependent Option in a Trinomial Tree

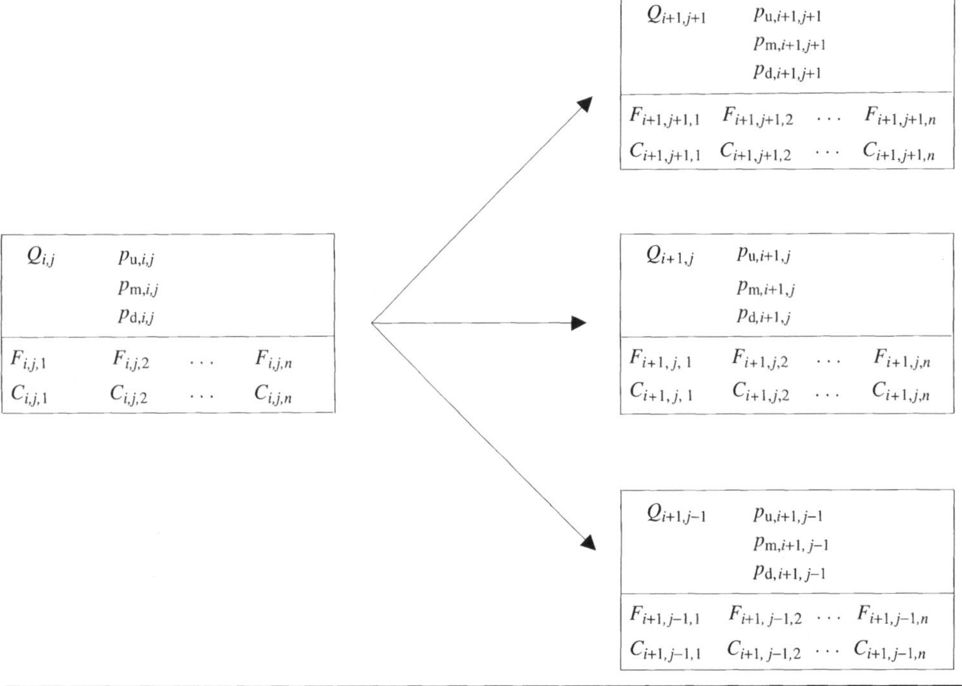

any node (i, j) the minimum maximum must be the greater of the minimum maximum of the lowest node at time step $i-1$ with a branch to the current node and the asset price at the current node:

$$F_{i,j,1} = \max(F_{i-1,j_l,1}, S_j) \tag{5.23}$$

where node $(i-1, j_l)$ is the lowest node with a branch to node (i, j). Similarly, the maximum maximum must be the greater of the maximum maximum of the highest node at time step $i-1$ with a branch to the current node and the asset price at the current node:

$$F_{i,j,n} = \max(F_{i-1,j_u,n}, S_j) \tag{5.24}$$

where node $(i-1, j_u)$ is the highest node with a branch to node (i, j). For clarity we choose a uniform spread for the set of $n_{i,j}$ values of the maximum over the range found at each node (i, j) which gives

$$F_{i,j,k} = F_{i,j,1} + \left(\frac{F_{i,j,n} - F_{i,j,1}}{n-1}\right)(k-1) \tag{5.25}$$

Once we have computed all the values of the maximum at every node we can set the value of the option at maturity at every node and for every value of the maximum

$$C_{N,j,k} = \max(0, F_{i,j,k} - K), \qquad j = -N, \ldots, N, k = 1, \ldots, n \tag{5.26}$$

Finally, we step back through the tree computing discounted expectations and applying the early exercise condition at every node and for every value of the maximum

$$C_{i,j,k} = e^{-r\Delta t_i}(p_{\mathrm{u},i,j}C_{i+1,j+1,\mathrm{u}} + p_{\mathrm{m},i,j}C_{i+1,j,\mathrm{m}} + p_{\mathrm{d},i.j}C_{i+1,j-1,\mathrm{d}}) \tag{5.27}$$

where $C_{i+1,j+1,\mathrm{u}}$, $C_{i+1,j,\mathrm{m}}$, $C_{i+1,j-1,\mathrm{d}}$, are the values of the option at time step $i+1$, given the current maximum, for upward, middle and downward branches of the asset. These are obtained by computing what the maximum would be, given the current maximum, after upward, middle and downward branches $F_{i+1,j+1,\mathrm{u}}$, $F_{i+1,j,\mathrm{m}}$, $F_{i+1,j-1,\mathrm{d}}$. For the middle and downward branches the maximum will remain the same, it cannot be changed by the asset price decreasing.

$$F_{i+1,j,\mathrm{m}} = F_{i,j,k}, \qquad F_{i+1,j-1,\mathrm{d}} = F_{i,j,k} \tag{5.28}$$

For the upward branch the maximum is the greater of the current maximum and the asset price at the upward branch node

$$F_{i+1,j+1,\mathrm{u}} = \max(F_{i,j,k}, S_{j+1}) \tag{5.29}$$

The maxima $F_{i+1,j+1,\mathrm{u}}$, $F_{i+1,j,\mathrm{m}}$, $F_{i+1,j-1,\mathrm{d}}$ and therefore also the option values $C_{i+1,j+1,\mathrm{u}}$, $C_{i+1,j,\mathrm{m}}$, $C_{i+1,j-1,\mathrm{d}}$ will not, in general, be stored at the upward, middle and downward nodes and therefore must be obtained by interpolation. For example using linear interpolation we have

$$C_{i+1,j+1,\mathrm{u}} = C_{i+1,j+1,k_i} + \left(\frac{C_{i+1,j+1,k_\mathrm{u}} - C_{i+1,j+1,k_i}}{F_{i+1,j+1,k_\mathrm{u}} - F_{i+1,j+1,k_i}}\right)(F_{i+1,j+1,\mathrm{u}} - F_{i+1,j+1,k_i}) \tag{5.30}$$

where k_i and k_u are such that

$$F_{i+1,j+1,k_i} \leq F_{i+1,j+1,\mathrm{u}} \leq F_{i+1,j+1,k_\mathrm{u}} \quad \text{and} \quad k_\mathrm{u} = k_i + 1.$$

That is, the two maxima which lie closest to either side of $F_{i+1,j+1,\mathrm{u}}$ are found and a linear interpolation between these is done to obtain an estimate for $C_{i+1,j+1,\mathrm{u}}$ and similarly for $C_{i+1,j,\mathrm{m}}$ and $C_{i+1,j-1,\mathrm{d}}$. This will always be possible because at every node the minimum and maximum possible values of the maximum are stored.

Figure 5.15 gives the pseudo-code implementation of the trinomial tree valuation of an American fixed strike lookback call option assuming that an implied tree-building routine exists and every time step is a fixing date. It is in fact possible to make the calculation of the minimum and maximum values of the maximum at each node more efficient; we have described the more general method for clarity.

Example : Implied Trinomial Tree Valuation of an American Fixed Strike Lookback Call

We price a one-year maturity, American lookback call option fixed at each time step, with a strike price of 100, and the current asset price at 100. The continuously compounded interest rate is 6 per cent per annum and the implied trinomial tree is identical to the examples in sections 5.2 and 5.3 (four time steps, and a space step of 0.2524). That is, $K = 100$, $T = 1$, $S = 100$, $r = 0.06$, $N = 4$, $\Delta x = 0.2524$. We set the number of values of the maximum we store at each node to be three except at the edges of the tree where

FIGURE 5.15 Pseudo-code for Trinomial Tree Valuation of an American Fixed Strike Lookback Call Option

```
initialise_parameters { K, T, S, r, N, alpha }

build_implied_trinomial_tree

{ find range of maximum values for each node and set number
  of values to store n[i,j] }

{ initialise root node }

n[0,0] = 1
F[0,0,1] = S

for i = 1 to N do

  for j = -i to i do

    { compute minimum maximum }

    if ( j < -i+1 ) then
      F[i,j,1] = max( F[i-1,j+1,1], St[j])
    else if ( j < -i+2 ) then
      F[i,j,1] = max( F[i-1,j,1], St[j])
    else
      F[i,j,1] = max( F[i-1,j-1,1], St[j])

    { compute maximum maximum }

    n[i,j] = 1 + alpha*(i-abs(j))

    if ( j > i-1 ) then
      F[i,j,n[i,j]] = max( F[i-1,j-1,n[i-1,j-1]] , St[j]
    else if ( j > i-2 ) then
      F[i,j,n[i,j]] = max( F[i-1,j,n[i-1,j]] , St[j] )
    else
      F[i,j,n[i,j]] = max( F[i-1,j+1,n[i-1,j+1]] , St[j] )

    { compute intermediate maxima values }

    ratio = ( F[i,j,n[i,j]] - F[i,j,1] )/(n[i,j]-1)
    for k = 2 to n[i,j]-1 do
      F[i,j,k] = F[i,j,1] + ratio*(k-1)
    next k

   next j

  next i

  { initialise option values at maturity }

  for j = -N to N do
```

(continues)

FIGURE 5.15 ***(continued)***

```
   for k = 1 to n[N,j] do
     C[N,j,k] = max( 0.0 , F[N,j,k] - K )
   next k
  next j

{ step back through the tree applying early exercise condition }

 for i = N-1 downto 0 do
   for j = -i to i do
    for k = 1 to n[i,j] do

      Fu = max( F[i,j,k] , S[j+1] )
      Fm = F[i,j,k]
      Fd = F[i,j,k]

      Cu = interpolate( i+1, j+1, Fu )
      Cm = interpolate( i+1,   j, Fm )
      Cd = interpolate( i+1, j-1, Fd )

      C[i,j,k] =
        disc*( pu[i,j]*Cu + pm[i,j]*Cm + pd[i,j]*Cd )

      { apply the early exercise condition }

      C[i,j,k] = max( C[i,j,k], F[i,j,k] - K )

    next k

   next j

 next i

 American_Fixed_Strike_Lookback_Call = C[0,0,1]
```

we store only one. Figure 5.16 illustrates the results of the calculations where the nodes of the tree are indicated by the boxes whose structure is defined by the tree node key.

Firstly the constants; Δt (dt), $disc$ are precomputed:

$$\Delta t = \frac{T}{N} = \frac{1}{4} = 0.25$$

$$disc = \exp(-r \times \Delta t) = \exp(-0.06 \times 0.25) = 0.9851$$

Then the minimum and maximum values of the maximum asset price at each node are computed by stepping forward through the tree. For node (3, 1):

$$F_{3,1,1} = \max(F_{2,0,1}, S_{3,1}) = \max(100.000, 128.71) = 128.71$$

$$F_{3,1,3} = \max(F_{2,2,1}, S_{3,1}) = \max(165.652, 128.71) = 165.652$$

FIGURE 5.16 Implied Trinomial Tree Valuation of an American Fixed Strike Lookback Call Option

K	T	S	rate	N	alpha	dx
100	1	100	0.06	4	3	0.2524

dt	disc
0.2500	0.9851

Tree node key:

Q[i,j]	pu[i,j]	
	pm[i,j]	
	pd[i,j]	
F[i,j,1]	F[i,j,2]	F[i,j,3]
C[i,j,1]	C[i,j,2]	C[i,j,3]

j	i St, t	0 0	1 0.25	2 0.5	3 0.75	4 1
4	274.41					0.0001 274.406 174.4062
3	213.20				0.0009 0.1056 0.8263 0.0681 213.204 117.8829	0.0027 213.204 213.204 213.204 113.2040 113.2040 113.204
2	165.65			0.0114 0.0775 0.8904 0.0320 165.652 63.6356	0.0282 0.0730 0.9008 0.0262 165.652 165.652 165.652 59.9543 59.9543 59.9543	0.0474 165.652 189.428 213.204 65.6521 89.4281 113.204
1	128.71		0.1654 0.0697 0.9084 0.0219 128.706 30.3744	0.2233 0.0830 0.8779 0.0391 128.706 128.706 128.706 28.3800 28.3800 28.3800	0.2517 0.0901 0.8618 0.0481 128.706 147.179 165.652 31.5562 48.1154 64.6747	0.2630 128.706 147.179 165.652 28.7059 47.1790 65.652
0	100.00	1.0000 0.1679 0.6839 0.1483 100.000 8.2098	0.6742 0.1134 0.8083 0.0782 100.000 4.5730	0.5524 0.1069 0.8232 0.0698 100.000 114.353 128.706 5.7163 16.9595 28.2027	0.4732 0.1043 0.8291 0.0665 100.000 114.353 128.706 2.9504 15.6145 28.2785	0.4166 100.000 132.826 165.652 0.0000 32.8260 65.652
−1	77.70		0.1461 0.0873 0.8681 0.0446 100.000 0.7280	0.1769 0.0951 0.8502 0.0547 100.000 100.000 100.000 0.2764 0.2764 0.2764	0.1867 0.0987 0.8420 0.0593 100.000 114.353 128.706 0.0000 14.1393 28.2785	0.1872 100.000 114.353 128.706 0.0000 14.3530 28.706
−2	60.37			0.0064 0.0830 0.8780 0.0390 100.000 0.0000	0.0151 0.0864 0.8702 0.0434 100.000 100.000 100.000 0.0000 0.0000 0.0000	0.0238 100.000 114.353 128.706 0.0000 14.3530 28.706
−3	46.90				0.0002 0.0808 0.8829 0.0363 100.000 0.0000	0.0009 100.000 100.000 100.000 0.0000 0.0000 0.000
−4	36.44					0.0000 100.000 0.0000

Then the option values at maturity are computed. For example at node (4, 0):

$$C_{4,0,1} = \max(0, F_{4,0,1} - K) = \max(0, 100.000 - 100) = 0.0000$$

$$C_{4,0,2} = \max(0, F_{4,0,2} - K) = \max(0, 132.826 - 100) = 32.826$$

$$C_{4,0,3} = \max(0, F_{4,0,3} - K) = \max(0, 165.652 - 100) = 65.652$$

Finally we perform discounted expectations back through the tree. For example at node (3,0) for $k = 2$ we have:

$$F_{4,1,\mathrm{u}} = \max(F_{3,0,2}, S_{4,1}) = \max(114.353, 128.706) = 128.706$$

$$F_{4,0,\mathrm{m}} = F_{3,0,2} = 114.353$$

$$F_{4,-1,\mathrm{d}} = F_{3,0,2} = 114.353$$

Therefore

$$\begin{aligned}
C_{4,1,\mathrm{u}} &= C_{4,1,1} = 28.7059 \\
C_{4,0,\mathrm{m}} &= C_{4,0,1} + (C_{4,0,2} - C_{4,0,1})/(F_{4,0,2} - F_{4,0,1})(F_{4,0,\mathrm{m}} - F_{4,0,1}) \\
&= 0.0000 + (32.8260 - 0.0000)/(132.826 - 100.00)(114.353 - 100.00) \\
&= 14.3530 \\
C_{4,-1,\mathrm{d}} &= C_{4,-1,2} = 14.3530
\end{aligned}$$

So finally

$$\begin{aligned}
C_{3,0,2} &= \max(disc \times (p_{\mathrm{u},3,0} \times C_{4,1,\mathrm{u}} + p_{\mathrm{m},3,0} \times C_{4,0,\mathrm{m}} + p_{\mathrm{d},3,0} \\
&\quad \times C_{4,-1,\mathrm{d}}), (F_{3,0,2} - K)) \\
&= \max(0.9851 \times (0.1043 \times 28.7059 + 0.8291 \times 14.3530 \\
&\quad + 0.0665 \times 14.3530), (114.353 - 100)) = 15.6145
\end{aligned}$$

Therefore there is no early exercise value at node (3, 0) for the $k = 2$ value of the maximum.

5.6 PRICING ASIAN OPTIONS IN TRINOMIAL TREES

Asian options are standard calls or puts, except that either the final asset price or the strike price is set equal to the arithmetic average of the asset prices observed on a set of predetermined fixing dates, t_i; $i = 1, \ldots, m$. If the final asset price is replaced they are called fixed strike and if the strike price is replaced they are called floating strike. Therefore we have four variations which are listed in Table 5.3 together with a mathematical definition of their pay-off.[8]

Asian options are path-dependent options in that the value of the option at any node in the tree depends on the current average asset price which is determined by the path the asset price took to reach that node. The approach described in the previous section for lookbacks can also be applied to Asian options. We illustrate the pricing of European and American Asian options in trees with the example of a fixed strike Asian call option.

TABLE 5.3 The Asian Option Family

Fixed strike Asian call	$\max\left(0, \dfrac{S_{t_1} + S_{t_2} + \cdots + S_{t_m}}{m} - K\right)$
Fixed strike Asian put	$\max\left(0, K - \dfrac{S_{t_1} + S_{t_2} + \cdots + S_{t_m}}{m}\right)$
Floating strike Asian call	$\max\left(0, S_T - \dfrac{S_{t_1} + S_{t_2} + \cdots + S_{t_m}}{m}\right)$
Floating strike Asian put	$\max\left(0, \dfrac{S_{t_1} + S_{t_2} + \cdots + S_{t_m}}{m} - S_T\right)$

We first determine the range (i.e. the minimum and maximum) of the possible averages which can occur for every node in the tree. In other words we store, at every node, the minimum and maximum possible average asset prices which could have occurred for all paths which reach the node. We then choose an appropriate set of values of the average between the minimum and maximum possible for each node. In choosing this set of values we note that the nodes which lie on the upper and lower edges of the tree have only one path which reaches them and therefore there will only be one value of the average. The largest range of values will occur in the central section of the tree. The number of averages increases exponentially with the number of time steps since there is a different average for each path. However, it is impractical to work with an exponentially increasing number of averages because the computational cost would be too high. Therefore we approximate with a number of values which increases linearly with the number of time steps, but also decreases linearly from the central nodes of the tree down to one at the edges of the tree.

Consistent with section 5.5 we let $n_{i,j}$ be the number of values we store at node (i, j) and $F_{i,j,k}, k = 1, \ldots, n_{i,j}$ the values of the average where $F_{i,j,1}$ is the minimum and $F_{i,j,n_{i,j}}$ is the maximum. We will, in general, drop the i, j subscripts on $n_{i,j}$, where it is clear to which node we are referring as in $F_{i,j,n_{i,j}}$ (see Figure 5.14 for an illustration of the node structure). We choose $n_{i,j}$ to be given by

$$n_{i,j} = 1 + \alpha(i - abs(j)) \tag{5.31}$$

so that $n_{i,j}$ will always be one at the edges of the tree ($j = i$ and $j = -i$) and $1 + \alpha i$ in the centre of the tree. In this way we can increase α to increase the accuracy of the approximation by considering more values of the average. In order to find the range of values of the average we step forward through the tree from $i = 0$ to $i = N$. If we have found the range for all nodes up to time step $i - 1$ then for any node (i, j) the minimum average is determined by the minimum average of the lowest node at time step $i - 1$ with a branch to the current node and the asset price at the current node. The minimum average is given by

$$F_{i,j,1} = \begin{cases} \dfrac{F_{i-1,j_l,1}m_{i-1} + S_j}{m_i} & \text{if } t_i = t_{m_i}\text{, i.e. a fixing date} \\ F_{i-1,j_l,1} & \text{otherwise} \end{cases} \tag{5.32}$$

where m_i is the number of fixing dates which have occurred up to time step i, and node $(i-1, j_l)$ is the lowest node with a branch to node (i, j). Similarly, the maximum average is determined by the maximum average of the highest node at time step $i-1$ with a branch to the current node and the asset price at the current node

$$F_{i,j,n} = \begin{cases} \dfrac{F_{i-1,j_{\mathrm{u}},n} m_{i-1} + S_j}{m_i} & \text{if } t_i = t_{m_i} \text{ i.e. a fixing date} \\ F_{i-1,j_u,n} & \text{otherwise} \end{cases} \tag{5.33}$$

where node $(i-1, j_{\mathrm{u}})$ is the highest node with a branch to node (i, j). Now since the arithmetic average is essentially a sum of lognormally distributed asset prices it will also be approximately lognormally distributed. We therefore choose a log-linear set for the $n_{i,j}$ values of the average at each node (i, j) which gives

$$F_{i,j,k} = F_{i,j,1} e^{(k-1)h} \tag{5.34}$$

where

$$h = \frac{\ln(F_{i,j,n}) - \ln(F_{i,j,1})}{n-1}$$

After we have computed all the values of the average at every node we can set the value of the option at maturity at every node and for every value of the average

$$C_{N,j,k} = \max(0, F_{i,j,k} - K), \quad j = -N, \ldots, N, k = 1, \ldots, n \tag{5.35}$$

Finally, we step back through the tree computing discounted expectations and applying the early exercise condition at every node and for every value of the average

$$C_{i,j,k} = e^{-r\Delta t_i}(p_{\mathrm{u},i,j} C_{i+1,j+1,\mathrm{u}} + p_{\mathrm{m},i,j} C_{i+1,j,\mathrm{m}} + p_{\mathrm{d},i,j} C_{i+1,j-1,\mathrm{d}}) \tag{5.36}$$

where $C_{i+1,j+1,\mathrm{u}}$, $C_{i+1,j,\mathrm{m}}$, $C_{i+1,j-1,\mathrm{d}}$ are the values of the option at time step $i+1$, given the current average, for upward, middle and downward branches of the asset. These are obtained by first computing what the average would be, given the current average, after upward, middle and downward branches $F_{i+1,j+1,\mathrm{u}}$, $F_{i+1,j,\mathrm{m}}$, $F_{i+1,j-1,\mathrm{d}}$

$$F_{i+1,j+1,\mathrm{u}} = \begin{cases} \dfrac{F_{i,j,k} m_i + S_{j+1}}{m_{i+1}} & \text{if } t_{i+1} = t_{m_{i+1}}, \text{ i.e. a fixing date} \\ F_{i,j,k} & \text{otherwise} \end{cases} \tag{5.37}$$

$$F_{i+1,j,\mathrm{m}} = \begin{cases} \dfrac{F_{i,j,k} m_i + S_j}{m_{i+1}} & \text{if } t_{i+1} = t_{m_{i+1}}, \text{ i.e. a fixing date} \\ F_{i,j,k} & \text{otherwise} \end{cases} \tag{5.38}$$

$$F_{i+1,j-1,\mathrm{d}} = \begin{cases} \dfrac{F_{i,j,k} m_i + S_{j-1}}{m_{i+1}} & \text{if } t_{i+1} = t_{m_{i+1}}, \text{ i.e. a fixing date} \\ F_{i,j,k} & \text{otherwise} \end{cases} \tag{5.39}$$

The averages $F_{i+1,j+1,\mathrm{u}}$, $F_{i+1,j,\mathrm{m}}$, $F_{i+1,j-1,\mathrm{d}}$ and therefore also the option values $C_{i+1,j+1,\mathrm{u}}$, $C_{i+1,j,\mathrm{m}}$, $C_{i+1,j-1,\mathrm{d}}$ will not in general be stored at the upward, middle and downward nodes and therefore must be obtained by interpolation. For example, using linear interpolation we have

$$C_{i+1,j+1,\mathrm{u}} = C_{i+1,j+1,k_l} + \left(\frac{C_{i+1,j+1,k_{\mathrm{u}}} - C_{i+1,j+1,k_i}}{F_{i+1,j+1,k_{\mathrm{u}}} - F_{i+1,j+1,k_i}} \right) (F_{i+1,j+1,\mathrm{u}} - F_{i+1,j+1,k_i}) \tag{5.40}$$

where k_i and k_{u} are such that

$$F_{i+1,j+1,k_i} \leq F_{i+1,j+1,\mathrm{u}} \leq F_{i+1,j+1,k_{\mathrm{u}}} \quad \text{and} \quad k_{\mathrm{u}} = k_i + 1.$$

That is, the two averages which lie closest to either side of $F_{i+1,j+1,\mathrm{u}}$ are found and a linear interpolation between these is done to obtain an estimate for $C_{i+1,j+1,\mathrm{u}}$ and similarly for $C_{i+1,j,\mathrm{m}}$ and $C_{i+1,j-1,\mathrm{d}}$.

Figure 5.17 gives the pseudo-code implementation of the trinomial tree valuation of an American fixed strike Asian call option, assuming that an implied tree building routine exists and every time step is a fixing date.

Example : Implied Trinomial Tree Valuation of an American Fixed Strike Asian Call

We price a one-year maturity, American Asian call option fixed at each time step, with a strike price of 100, and the current asset price at 100. The continuously compounded interest rate is 6 per cent per annum and the implied trinomial tree is identical to the examples in sections 5.2 and 5.3 (four time steps, and a space step of 0.2524). That is, $K = 100$, $T = 1$, $S = 100$, $r = 0.06$, $N = 4$, $\Delta x = 0.2524$. We set the number of values of the maximum we store at each node to be three, except at the edges of the tree where we store only one. Figure 5.18 illustrates the results of the calculations where the nodes of the tree are indicated by the boxes whose structure is defined by the tree node key.

Firstly the constants; Δt (dt), $disc$ are precomputed:

$$\Delta t = \frac{T}{N} = \frac{1}{4} = 0.25$$

$$disc = \exp(-r \times \Delta t) = \exp(-0.06 \times 0.25) = 0.9851$$

Then the minimum and maximum values of the average asset price at each node are computed by stepping forward through the tree. For node (3, 1):

$$F_{3,1,1} = (F_{2,0,1} \times 3 + S_{3,1})/4 = (92.566 \times 3 + 128.71)/4 = 101.601$$

$$F_{3,1,3} = (F_{2,2,1} \times 3 + S_{3,1})/4 = (131.453 \times 3 + 128.71)/4 = 130.766$$

Then the option values at maturity are computed. For example at node (4, 0):

$$C_{4,0,1} = \max(0, F_{4,0,1} - K) = \max(0, 83.152 - 100) = 0.0000$$

$$C_{4,0,2} = \max(0, F_{4,0,2} - K) = \max(0, 101.793 - 100) = 1.7930$$

$$C_{4,0,3} = \max(0, F_{4,0,3} - K) = \max(0, 124.613 - 100) = 24.613$$

Finally we perform discounted expectations back through the tree. For example at node (3, 0) for $k = 2$ we have

$$F_{4,1,\mathrm{u}} = (F_{3,0,2} \times 4 + S_{4,1})/5 = (114.353 \times 4 + 128.706)/5 = 117.224$$

$$F_{4,0,\mathrm{m}} = (F_{3,0,2} \times 4 + S_{4,0})/5 = (114.353 \times 4 + 100.00)/5 = 111.482$$

$$F_{4,-1,\mathrm{d}} = (F_{3,0,2} \times 4 + S_{4,-1})/5 = (114.353 \times 4 + 77.697)/5 = 107.022$$

Therefore

$$\begin{aligned} C_{4,1,\mathrm{u}} &= C_{4,1,2} + (C_{4,1,3} - C_{4,1,2})/(F_{4,1,3} - F_{4,1,2}) \times (F_{4,0,\mathrm{u}} - F_{4,1,2}) \\ &= 15.4828 + (37.743 - 15.4828)/(137.743 - 115.483) \times (117.224 - 115.483) \\ &= 17.224 \end{aligned}$$

$$C_{4,0,\mathrm{m}} = C_{4,0,2} + (C_{4,0,3} - C_{4,0,2})/(F_{4,0,3} - F_{4,0,2}) \times (F_{4,0,\mathrm{m}} - F_{4,0,2})$$
$$= 1.7930 + (24.613 - 1.7930)/(124.613 - 101.793) \times (111.482 - 101.793)$$
$$= 11.482$$
$$C_{4,-1,\mathrm{d}} = C_{4,-1,3} = 7.022$$

FIGURE 5.17 Pseudo-code for Trinomial Tree Valuation of an American Fixed Strike Asian Call Option

```
initialise_parameters {K, T, S, r, N, alpha}

build_implied_trinomial_tree

{ find range of average values for each node and set number of
  values to store n[i,j] }

{ initialise root node }

n[0,0] = 1
F[0,0,1] = S

for i = 1 to N do

  for j = -i to i do

    { compute minimum average }

     if ( j < -i+1 ) then
      F[i,j,1] = (F[i-1,j+1,1]*i + St[j])/(i+1)
     else if ( j < -i+2 ) then
      F[i,j,1] = (F[i-1,j,1]*i + St[j])/(i+1)
     else
      F[i,j,1] = (F[i-1,j-1,1]*i + St[j])/(i+1)

     { compute maximum average }

     n[i,j] = 1 + alpha*(i-abs(j))

     if ( j > i-1 ) then
      F[i,j,n[i,j]] = (F[i-1,j-1,n[i-1,j-1]]*i + St[j])/(i+1)
     else if ( j > i-2 ) then
      F[i,j,n[i,j]] = (F[i-1,j,n[i-1,j]]*i + St[j])/(i+1)
     else
      F[i,j,n[i,j]] = (F[i-1,j+1,n[i-1,j+1]]*i + St[j])/(i+1)

     { compute intermediate maxima values }

     h = ( ln(F[i,j,n[i,j]]) - ln(F[i,j,1]) )/(n[i,j]-1)
     for k = 2 to n[i,j]-1 do
       F[i,j,k] = F[i,j,1]*exp((k-1)*h)
```

FIGURE 5.17 ***(continued)***

```
      next k

    next j

  next i

   { initialise option values at maturity }

   for j = -N to N do
     for k = 1 to n[N,j] do
       C[N,j,k] = max( 0.0 , F[N,j,k] - K )
     next k
   next j

   { step back through the tree applying early exercise condition }

   for i = N-1 downto 0 do
     for j = -i to i do
       for k = 1 to n[i,j] do

         Fu = (F[i,j,k]*(i+1) + St[j+1])/(i+2)
         Fm = (F[i,j,k]*(i+1) + St[j])/(i+2)
         Fd = (F[i,j,k]*(i+1) + St[j-1])/(i+2)

         Cu = interpolate(i+1, j+1, Fu)
         Cm = interpolate(i+1, j, Fm)
         Cd = interpolate(i+1, j-1, Fd)

         C[i,j,k] =
           disc*(pu[i,j]*Cu + pm[i,j]*Cm + pd[i,j]*Cd)

         { apply the early exercise condition }

          Cv[i,j,k] = max( C[i,j,k] , F[i,j,k] - K)

        next k

      next j

   next i

     American_Fixed_Strike_Asian_Call = C[0,0,1]
```

So finally

$$
\begin{aligned}
C_{3,0,2} &= \max(disc \times (p_{\mathrm{u},3,0} \times C_{4,1,\mathrm{u}} + p_{\mathrm{m},3,0} \times C_{4,0,\mathrm{m}} + p_{\mathrm{d},3,0} \times C_{4,-1,\mathrm{d}}), (F_{3,0,2} - K)) \\
&= \max(0.9851 \times (0.1043 \times 17.224 + 0.8291 \times 11.482 + 0.0665 \times 7.022), \\
&\quad (114.353 - 100)) = 14.353
\end{aligned}
$$

Therefore at node (3, 0) for an average of 114.353 ($k = 2$) the Asian option should be exercised early.

FIGURE 5.18 Implied Trinomial Tree Valuation of an American Fixed Strike Asian Call Option

K	T	S	rate	N	dx
100	1	100	0.06	4	0.2524

dt	disc
0.2500	0.9851

Tree node key:

Q[i,j]	pu[i,j]	
	pm[i,j]	
	pd[i,j]	
F[i,j,1]	F[i,j,2]	F[i,j,3]
C[i,j,1]	C[i,j,2]	C[i,j,3]

j	i: St, t	0 0	1 0.25	2 0.5	3 0.75	4 1
4	274.41					0.0001 176.394 76.3936
3	213.20				0.0009 0.1056 0.8263 0.0681 151.891 63.8329	0.0027 141.512 152.413 164.153 41.5124 52.4130 64.153
2	165.65			0.0114 0.0775 0.8904 0.0320 131.453 45.2788	0.0282 0.0730 0.9008 0.0262 123.590 131.540 140.003 32.0188 38.285 44.954	0.0474 114.411 133.014 154.643 14.4109 33.0144 54.643
1	128.71		0.1654 0.0697 0.9084 0.0219 114.353 24.5214	0.2233 0.0830 0.8779 0.0391 109.569 114.253 119.137 18.0076 20.744 23.698	0.2517 0.0901 0.8618 0.0481 101.601 115.264 130.766 8.5464 18.069 30.766	0.2630 96.820 115.483 137.743 0.0000 15.4828 37.743
0	100.00	1.0000 0.1679 0.6839 0.1483 100.000 7.8699	0.6742 0.1134 0.8083 0.0782 100.000 5.1108	0.5524 0.1069 0.8232 0.0698 92.566 100.709 109.569 2.5086 3.681 9.569	0.4732 0.1043 0.8291 0.0665 88.848 100.797 114.353 0.9046 2.554 14.353	0.4166 83.152 101.793 124.613 0.0000 1.7930 24.613
−1	77.70		0.1461 0.0873 0.8681 0.0446 88.848 2.5464	0.1769 0.0951 0.8502 0.0547 85.131 88.770 92.566 2.7025 2.958 3.225	0.1867 0.0987 0.8420 0.0593 78.940 89.556 101.601 2.6910 3.710 4.866	0.1872 27.613 54.361 107.022 0.0000 0.0000 7.022
−2	60.37			0.0064 0.0830 0.8780 0.0390 79.355 0.4452	0.0151 0.0864 0.8702 0.0434 15.092 35.714 84.516 0.0000 0.000 0.327	0.0238 69.067 80.297 93.354 0.0000 0.0000 0.000
−3	46.90				0.0002 0.0808 0.8829 0.0363 71.242 0.0000	0.0009 9.381 26.875 76.993 0.0000 0.0000 0.000
−4	36.44					0.0000

5.7 PRICING GENERAL PATH-DEPENDENT OPTIONS IN TRINOMIAL TREES

The approach described in the previous sections for lookback and Asian options can be applied to a general path-dependent option whose pay-off depends on some function $F(.)$ of the path of the asset price. The procedure can be summarised as follows:

1. Step forward through tree computing the maximum and minimum values of the path dependent function $F(.)$ at each node.
2. Choose a functional approximation to represent the path-dependent function and the discrete set of values for which the option will be valued at each node.
3. Step back through the tree computing the option values in the usual way, but for each of the set of values of the function $F(.)$ at each node.

So firstly we determine the range (i.e. the minimum and maximum) of the possible values of $F(.)$ which can occur for every node in the tree. We do this by stepping forward through the tree from $i = 0$ to $i = N$ computing at each node what the minimum and maximum must be given the nodes at time step $i-1$ which have branches to the current node and the asset price at the current node.

We then choose an appropriate set of values of $F(.)$ between the minimum and maximum possible for each node. In choosing this set of values we note that the nodes which lie on the upper and lower edges of the tree have only one path which reaches them and therefore there can be only one value of $F(.)$. The largest range of values will typically occur in the central section of tree. The number of values we consider should in general increase only linearly with the number of time steps and also decrease linearly from the central nodes of the tree down to one at the edges of the tree in order to keep the computational requirements under control. Consistent with sections 5.5 and 5.6 we let $n_{i,j}$ be the number of values we store at node (i, j) and $F_{i,j,k}, k = 1, \ldots, n_{i,j}$ be the values of $F(.)$, where $F_{i,j,1}$ is the minimum and $F_{i,j,n_{i,j}}$ is the maximum (see Figure 5.14 for a diagram of the node structure). We will in general drop the i, j subscripts on $n_{i,j}$ where it is clear to which node we are referring as in $F_{i,j,n_{i,j}}$. We might choose $n_{i,j}$ to be given for example by

$$n_{i,j} = 1 + \alpha(i - abs(j)) \tag{5.41}$$

so that $n_{i,j}$ will always be one at the edges of the tree ($j = i$ and $j = -i$) and $1 + \alpha i$ in the centre of the tree. In this way we can increase α to increase the accuracy of the approximation by considering more values of $F(.)$.

In choosing the actual set of $n_{i,j}$ values for each node we should consider the distributional properties of the function $F(.)$. This will vary depending on the nature of $F(.)$ and therefore must be considered on a case-by-case basis (see section 5.6 on Asian options for an example).

Next we set the value of the option at maturity at every node and for every value of $F(.)$

$$C_{N,j,k} = \text{pay-off } (F_{i,j,k}), \qquad j = -N, \ldots, N, k = 1, \ldots, n \tag{5.42}$$

We now step back through the tree computing discounted expectations and applying the early exercise condition at every node and for every value of $F(.)$

$$C_{i,j,k} = e^{-r\Delta t_i}(p_{\text{u},i,j}C_{i+1,j+1,\text{u}} + p_{\text{m},i,j}C_{i+1,j,\text{m}} + p_{\text{d},i,j}C_{i+1,j-1,\text{d}}) \tag{5.43}$$

where $C_{i+1,j+1,\mathrm{u}}$, $C_{i+1,j,\mathrm{m}}$, $C_{i+1,j-1,\mathrm{d}}$ are the values of the option at time step $i+1$, given the current $F(.)$, for upward, middle and downward branches of the asset. These are obtained by computing what $F(.)$ would be, given the current $F(.)$, after upward, middle and downward branches $F_{i+1,j+1,\mathrm{u}}$, $F_{i+1,j,\mathrm{m}}$, $F_{i+1,j-1,\mathrm{d}}$.

The values $F_{i+1,j+1,\mathrm{u}}$, $F_{i+1,j,\mathrm{m}}$, $F_{i+1,j-1,\mathrm{d}}$ and therefore also the option values $C_{i+1,j+1,\mathrm{u}}$, $C_{i+1,j,\mathrm{m}}$, $C_{i+1,j-1,\mathrm{d}}$, will not in general be stored at the upward, middle and downward nodes and therefore must be obtained by interpolation. For example, using linear interpolation we have

$$C_{i+1,j+1,\mathrm{u}} = C_{i+1,j+1,k_l} + \left(\frac{C_{i+1,j+1,k_\mathrm{u}} - C_{i+1,j+1,k_l}}{F_{i+1,j+1,k_\mathrm{u}} - F_{i+1,j+1,k_l}}\right)(F_{i+1,j+1,\mathrm{u}} - F_{i+1,j+1,k_l}) \quad (5.44)$$

where k_l and k_u are such that $F_{i+1,j+1,k_l} \leq F_{i+1,j+1,\mathrm{u}} \leq F_{i+1,j+1,k_\mathrm{u}}$ and $k_\mathrm{u} = k_l + 1$. That is the two values of F which lie closest to either side of $F_{i+1,j+1,\mathrm{u}}$ are found and a linear interpolation between these is done to obtain an estimate for $C_{i+1,j+1,\mathrm{u}}$.

Figure 5.19 gives the pseudo-code implementation of the trinomial tree valuation of a general path-dependent American option assuming that an implied tree-building routine exists.

FIGURE 5.19 Pseudo-code for Trinomial Tree Valuation of a General Path-dependent American Option

```
initialise_parameters {K, T, S, r, N, alpha}

build_implied_trinomial_tree

{ find range of values of F for each node and set number of
    values to store n[i,j] }

{ initialise root node }

n[0,0] = 1
F[0,0,1] = initial_value_of_F

for i = 1 to N do

  for j = -i to i do

    F[i,j,1] = compute_minimum_F

    n[i,j] = 1 + alpha*(i-abs(j))

    F[i,j,n[i,j]] = compute_ maximum_F

    { compute intermediate F values }

    for k = 2 to n[i,j]-1 do
```

FIGURE 5.19 *(continued)*

```
      F[i,j,k] = functional_approximation_for_F

    next k

   next j

  next i

  { initialise option values at maturity }

  for j = -N to N do
    for k = 1 to n[N,j] do
      C[N,j,k] = payoff(F[N,j,k])
     next k
   next j

  { step back through the tree applying early exercise
    condition }

   for i = N-1 downto 0 do
     for j = -i to i do
       for k = 1 to n[i,j] do

         Fu = F_after_up_branch
         Fm = F_after_middle_branch
         Fd = F_after_down_branch

         Cu = interpolate(i+1, j+1, Fu)
         Cm = interpolate(i+1, j, Fm)
         Cd = interpolate(i+1, j-1, Fd)

         C[i,j,k] =
           disc*(pu[i,j]*Cu + pm[i,j]*Cm + pd[i,j]*Cd)

         { apply the early exercise condition }

      C[i,j,k] = max( C[i,j,k] , payoff( F[i,j,k] ) )

   next k

  next j

 next i

 General_Path_Dependent_American_Option = C[0,0,1]
```

5.8 STATIC REPLICATION OF EXOTIC OPTIONS

The implied tree we constructed in sections 5.2 and 5.3 is a discrete time and state approximation to the continuous time risk-neutral process represented by the following

SDE:

$$dS = rS\,dt + \sigma(S, t)\,dz \tag{5.45}$$

In sections 5.4–5.7 we saw how an implied tree could be used to price exotic options. We thus have a way of pricing exotic options consistent with the market prices of standard European options and therefore consistent with the implied volatility smile. Furthermore, we can use the implied tree to compute hedge sensitivities in order to dynamically hedge the exotics options with the standard options and underlying asset. However, note that if equation 5.45 is not a good representation of the behaviour of the asset, for example if the asset price behaviour involves jumps or stochastic volatility, then hedging strategies based on the implied tree may not perform very well. Furthermore, dynamic hedging with standard options is problematic because of the more complex structure of the instruments and their costs. A partial solution to both of these problems is the concept of static replication. The idea is to find a portfolio of standard options which can be acquired today which will replicate the exotic option in all possible future states of the world. The details of this approach are beyond the scope of this book and so we simply illustrate the technique with a simple example. We construct a static portfolio of standard European call options which replicates a European up-and-out call option in the implied tree constructed in sections 5.2 and 5.3.

Imagine that there exist exchange traded European call options on an index currently at 100 dollars with maturities every quarter of a year and strikes every 10 dollars above and below the current index level. We have written an up and out call option with a strike price (K_{UAOC}) at 60 and a barrier (H) at 140, and we wish to hedge this option by buying a portfolio of the European options such that we do not have to rebalance the hedge in the future.

First we construct an implied trinomial tree (see sections 5.2 and 5.3) with quarter-year time steps and levels of $\ln(S)$ separated by 0.2 ($\Delta x = 0.2$) (which satisifies the stability and convergence condition). Figure 5.20 illustrates the tree which is identical to the numerical example in sections 5.2 and 5.3. The next stage is to price the up-and-out call option using the tree (see section 5.4). Figure 5.21 illustrates the resulting up-and-out call values in the tree.

Now we have the values of the up-and-out call option at every node in the tree we can construct the static replicating portfolio of standard European options. The key observation is that if we construct a portfolio of standard options which matches the values of the up-and-out call option along its boundaries, that is, at the maturity date and barrier, then that portfolio will have the same values as the up-and-out call option at every node within the boundaries. Furthermore, at the barrier, where the up-and-out option has value zero so will the portfolio which means it can be liquidated (since the barrier option is extinguished) at zero cost. In fact in our numerical example we have chosen the barrier to be slightly below one of the asset levels in the tree for clarity. In this case we set the values of the nodes just above the barrier equal to zero.

We describe a simple step-by-step procedure for choosing standard European options to hedge the barrier option. Consider the maturity date of the up-and-out option, if the option has not been knocked out then it pays off like a standard call option, so a natural option to put in the replicating portfolio is the standard option with the same strike and maturity. Figure 5.22 illustrates the state of the tree after valuing a portfolio which is long one up-and-out call option and short one standard European option with the same strike and maturity.

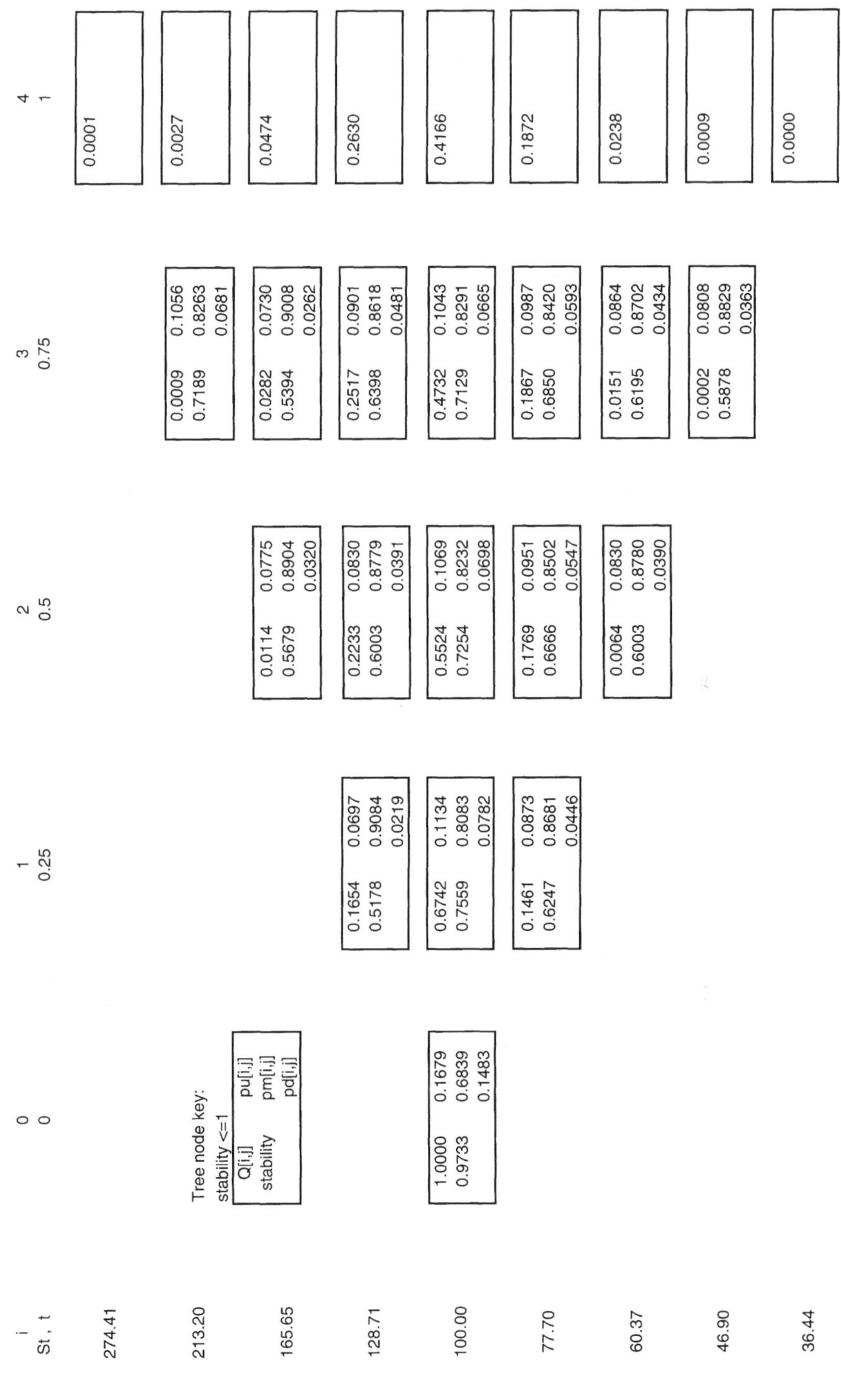

1	100	0.06	4	0.2524
dt	**edx**	**infl**		
0.2500	1.2871	1.0151		

Tree node key:
stability <=1

Q[i,j]	pu[i,j]
stability	pm[i,j]
	pd[i,j]

j	i St , t	0 0	1 0.25	2 0.5	3 0.75	4 1
4	274.41					0.0001
3	213.20				0.0009 0.1056 0.7189 0.8263 0.0681	0.0027
2	165.65			0.0114 0.0775 0.5679 0.8904 0.0320	0.0282 0.0730 0.5394 0.9008 0.0262	0.0474
1	128.71		0.1654 0.0697 0.5178 0.9084 0.0219	0.2233 0.0830 0.6003 0.8779 0.0391	0.2517 0.0901 0.6398 0.8618 0.0481	0.2630
0	100.00	1.0000 0.1679 0.9733 0.6839 0.1483	0.6742 0.1134 0.7559 0.8083 0.0782	0.5524 0.1069 0.7254 0.8232 0.0698	0.4732 0.1043 0.7129 0.8291 0.0665	0.4166
−1	77.70		0.1461 0.0873 0.6247 0.8681 0.0446	0.1769 0.0951 0.6666 0.8502 0.0547	0.1867 0.0987 0.6850 0.8420 0.0593	0.1872
−2	60.37			0.0064 0.0830 0.6003 0.8780 0.0390	0.0151 0.0864 0.6195 0.8702 0.0434	0.0238
−3	46.90				0.0002 0.0808 0.5878 0.8829 0.0363	0.0009
−4	36.44					0.0000

FIGURE 5.20 The Implied Trinomial Tree

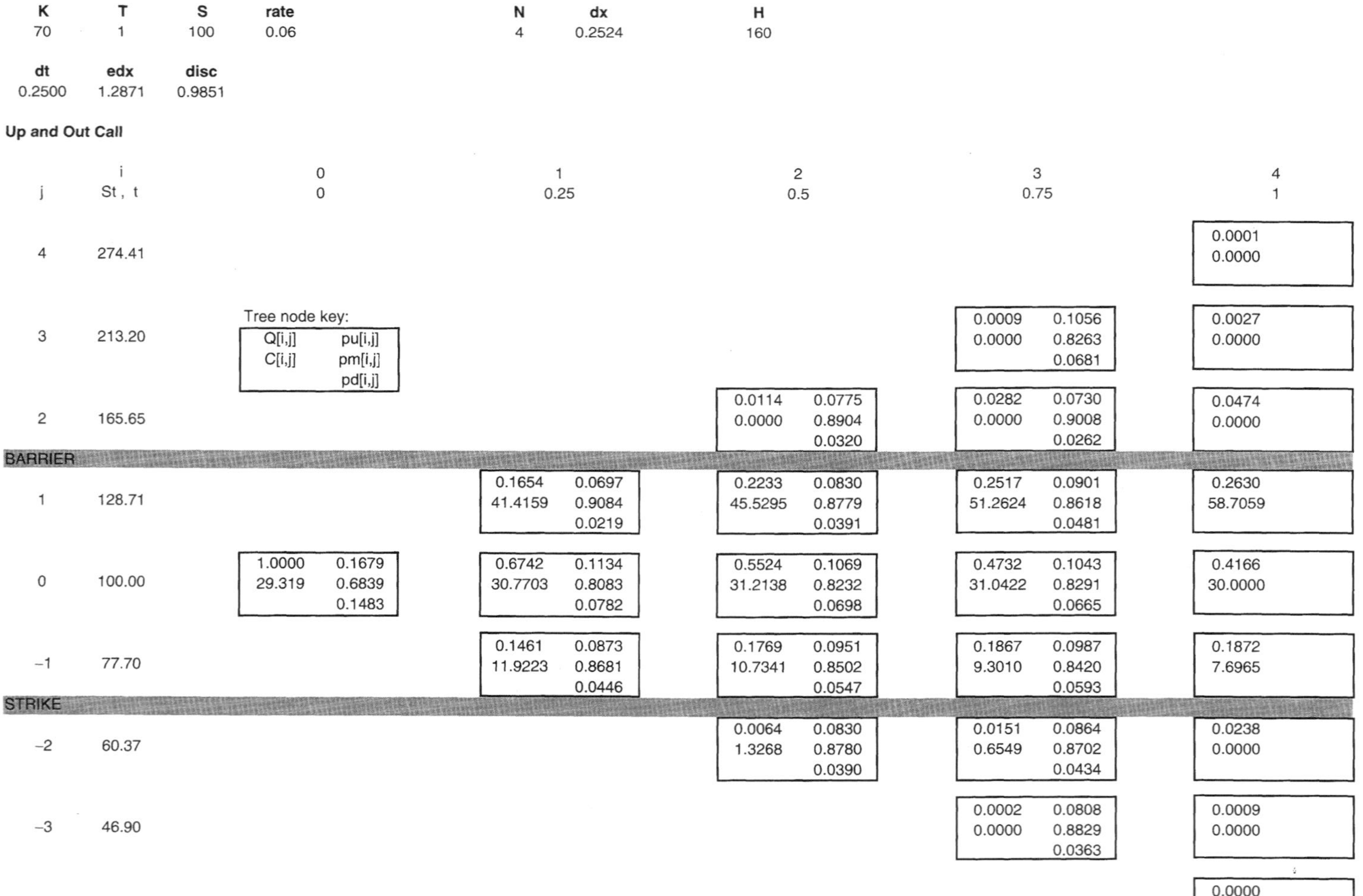

K	T	S	rate	N	dx	H
70	1	100	0.06	4	0.2524	160

dt	edx	disc
0.2500	1.2871	0.9851

Up and Out Call

Tree node key:

Q[i,j]	pu[i,j]
C[i,j]	pm[i,j]
	pd[i,j]

j	i St , t	0 0	1 0.25	2 0.5	3 0.75	4 1
4	274.41					0.0001 0.0000
3	213.20				0.0009 0.1056 0.0000 0.8263 0.0681	0.0027 0.0000
2	165.65			0.0114 0.0775 0.0000 0.8904 0.0320	0.0282 0.0730 0.0000 0.9008 0.0262	0.0474 0.0000
BARRIER						
1	128.71		0.1654 0.0697 41.4159 0.9084 0.0219	0.2233 0.0830 45.5295 0.8779 0.0391	0.2517 0.0901 51.2624 0.8618 0.0481	0.2630 58.7059
0	100.00	1.0000 0.1679 29.319 0.6839 0.1483	0.6742 0.1134 30.7703 0.8083 0.0782	0.5524 0.1069 31.2138 0.8232 0.0698	0.4732 0.1043 31.0422 0.8291 0.0665	0.4166 30.0000
–1	77.70		0.1461 0.0873 11.9223 0.8681 0.0446	0.1769 0.0951 10.7341 0.8502 0.0547	0.1867 0.0987 9.3010 0.8420 0.0593	0.1872 7.6965
STRIKE						
–2	60.37			0.0064 0.0830 1.3268 0.8780 0.0390	0.0151 0.0864 0.6549 0.8702 0.0434	0.0238 0.0000
–3	46.90				0.0002 0.0808 0.0000 0.8829 0.0363	0.0009 0.0000
–4	36.44					0.0000 0.0000

FIGURE 5.21 A European Up-and-out Call Option in an Implied Trinomial Tree

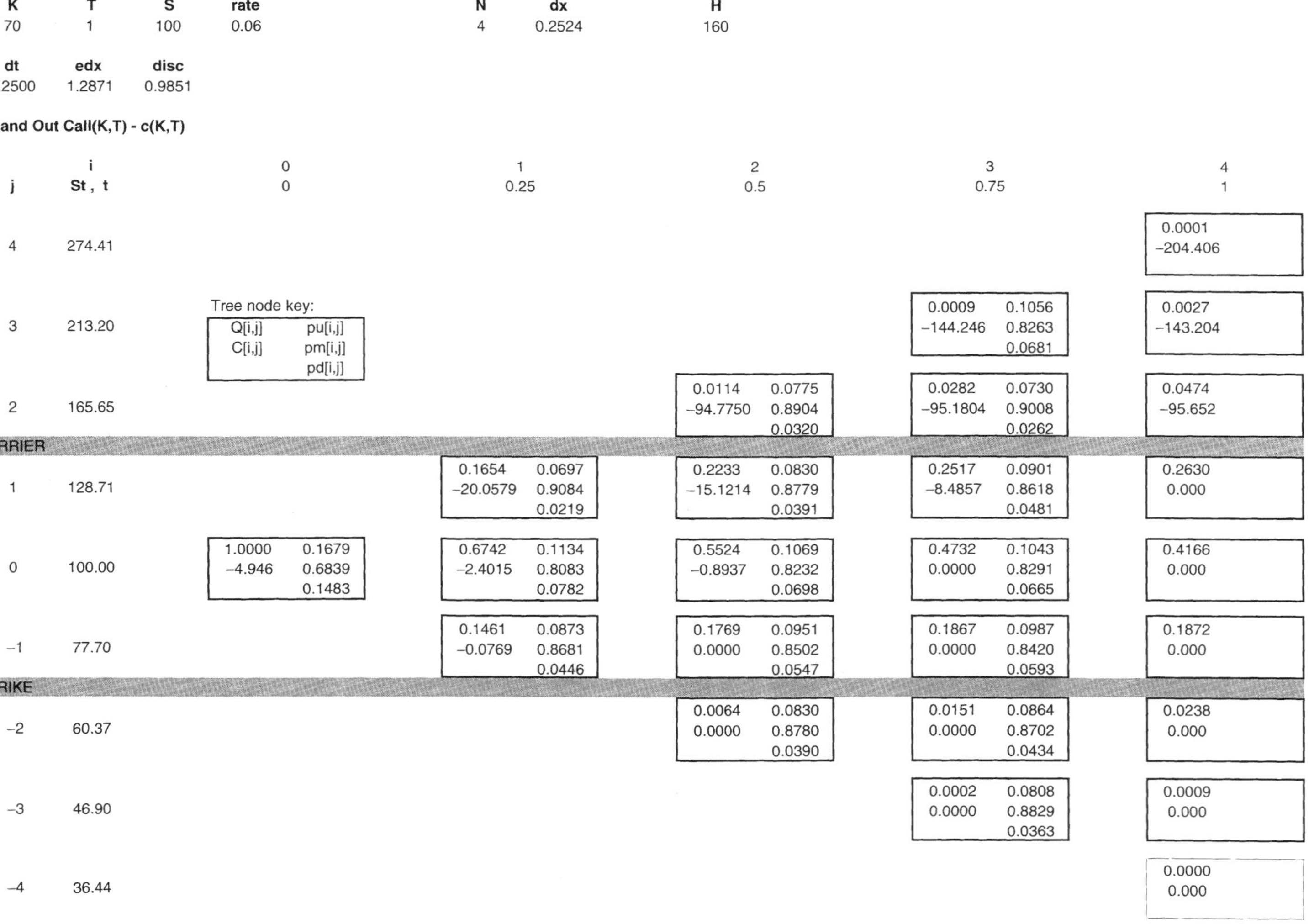

FIGURE 5.22 Portfolio of Long One European Up-and-out Call Option and Short One Standard European Call Option in an Implied Trinomial Tree

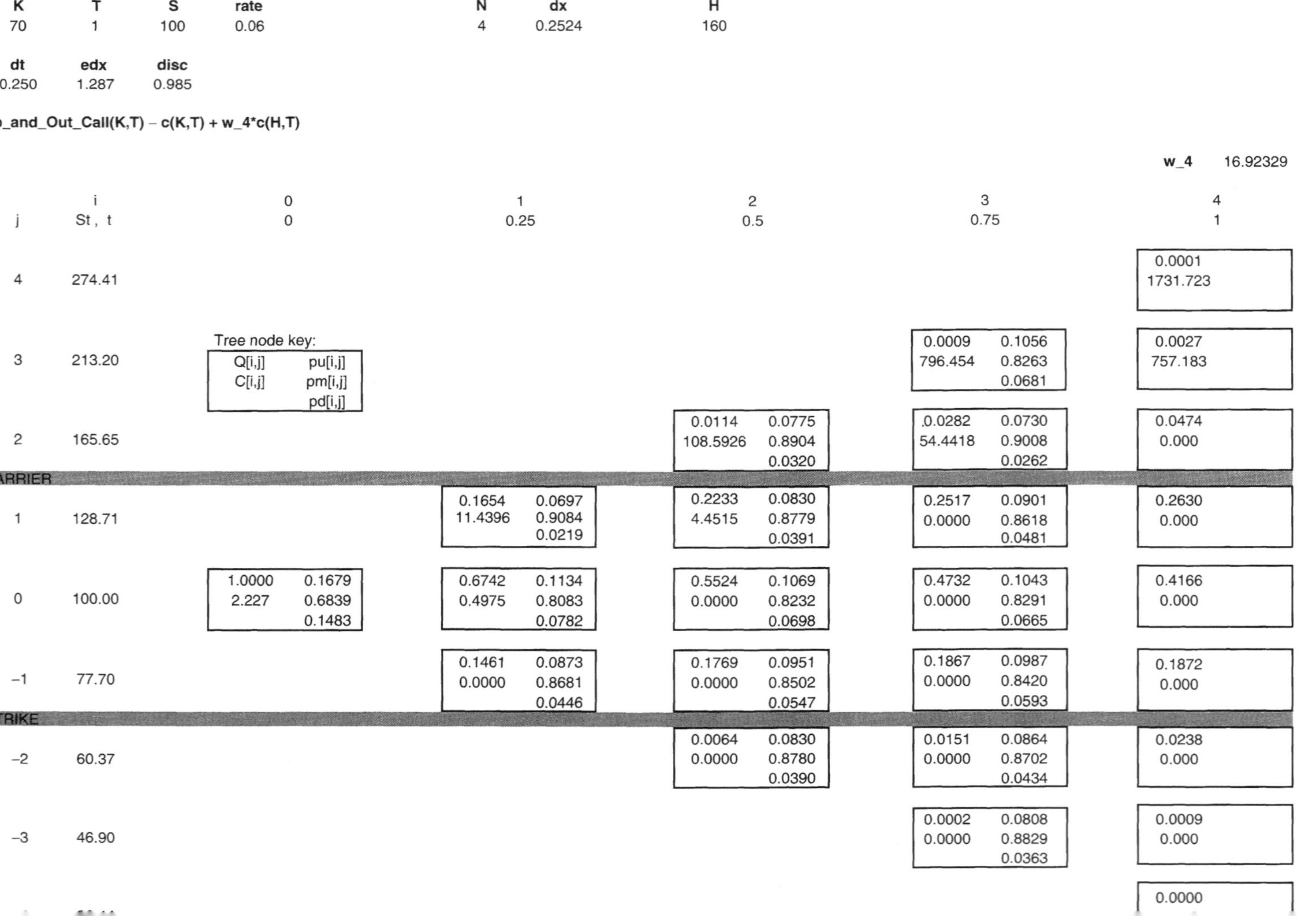

K	T	S	rate	N	dx	H
70	1	100	0.06	4	0.2524	160

dt	edx	disc
0.250	1.287	0.985

Up_and_Out_Call(K,T) – c(K,T) + w_4*c(H,T)

w_4 16.92329

Tree node key: Q[i,j] pu[i,j] / C[i,j] pm[i,j] / pd[i,j]

j	i St , t	0 0	1 0.25	2 0.5	3 0.75	4 1
4	274.41					0.0001 1731.723
3	213.20				0.0009 0.1056 796.454 0.8263 0.0681	0.0027 757.183
2	165.65			0.0114 0.0775 108.5926 0.8904 0.0320	0.0282 0.0730 54.4418 0.9008 0.0262	0.0474 0.000
BARRIER						
1	128.71		0.1654 0.0697 11.4396 0.9084 0.0219	0.2233 0.0830 4.4515 0.8779 0.0391	0.2517 0.0901 0.0000 0.8618 0.0481	0.2630 0.000
0	100.00	1.0000 0.1679 2.227 0.6839 0.1483	0.6742 0.1134 0.4975 0.8083 0.0782	0.5524 0.1069 0.0000 0.8232 0.0698	0.4732 0.1043 0.0000 0.8291 0.0665	0.4166 0.000
–1	77.70		0.1461 0.0873 0.0000 0.8681 0.0446	0.1769 0.0951 0.0000 0.8502 0.0547	0.1867 0.0987 0.0000 0.8420 0.0593	0.1872 0.000
STRIKE						
–2	60.37			0.0064 0.0830 0.0000 0.8780 0.0390	0.0151 0.0864 0.0000 0.8702 0.0434	0.0238 0.000
–3	46.90				0.0002 0.0808 0.0000 0.8829 0.0363	0.0009 0.000
	[illegible]					0.0000

FIGURE 5.23 Stage Two of a Static Hedge for a European Up-and-out Call in an Implied Trinomial Tree

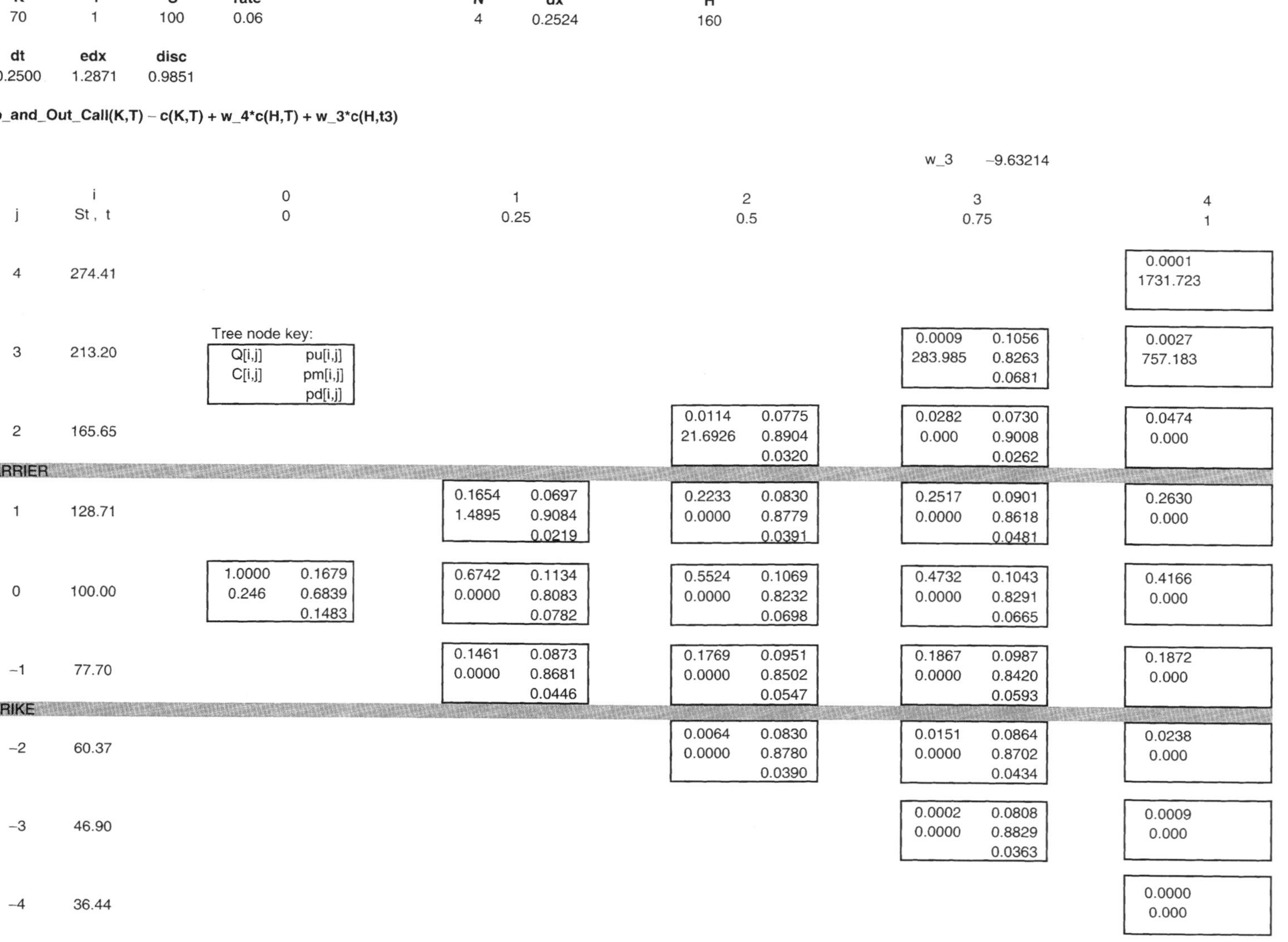

FIGURE 5.24 Stage Three of a Static Hedge for a European Up-and-out Call in an Implied Trinomial Tree

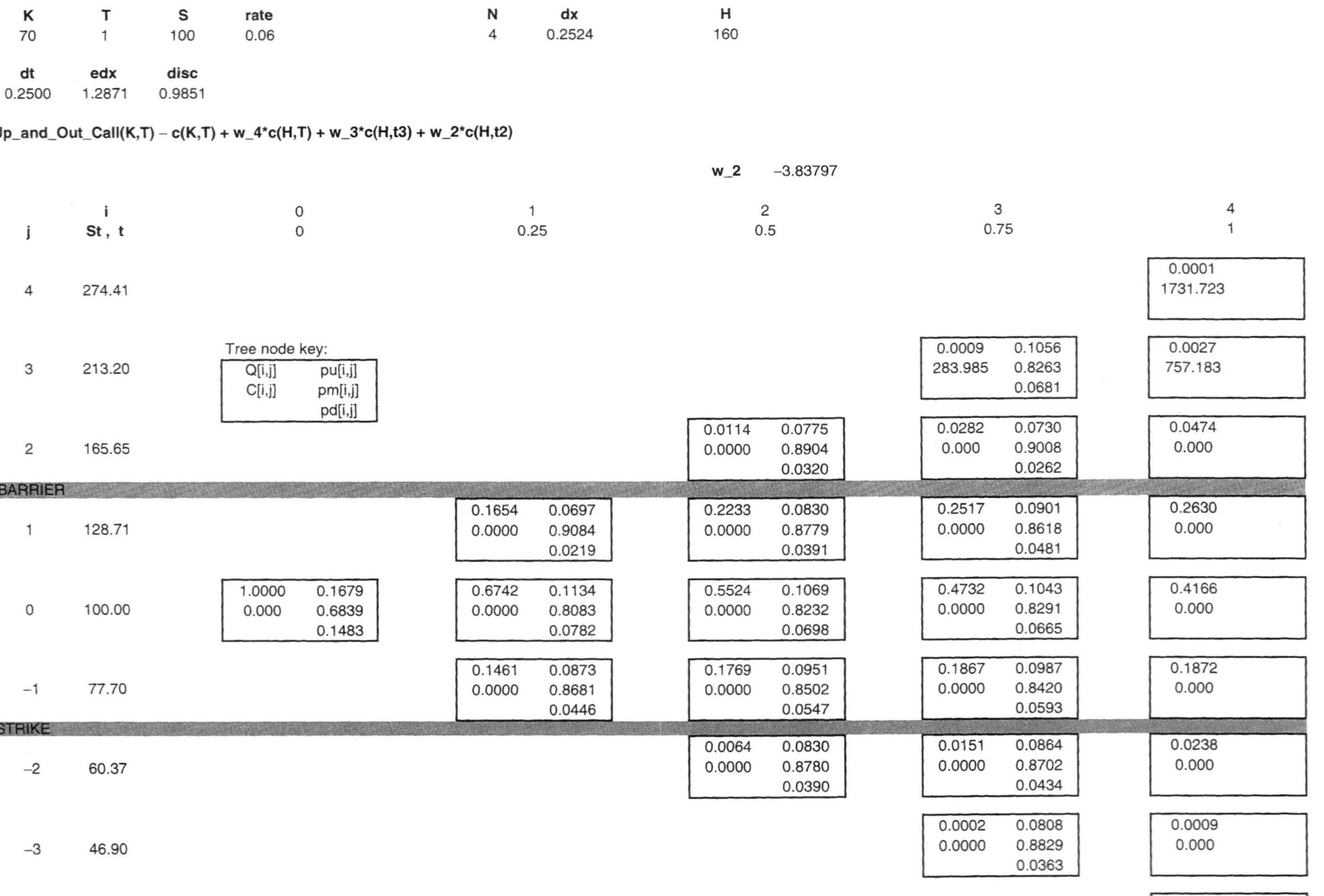

K	T	S	rate	N	dx	H
70	1	100	0.06	4	0.2524	160

dt	edx	disc
0.2500	1.2871	0.9851

Up_and_Out_Call(K,T) – c(K,T) + w_4*c(H,T) + w_3*c(H,t3) + w_2*c(H,t2)

w_2 –3.83797

Tree node key:

Q[i,j]	pu[i,j]
C[i,j]	pm[i,j]
	pd[i,j]

j	i **St , t**	0 0	1 0.25	2 0.5	3 0.75	4 1
4	274.41					0.0001 1731.723
3	213.20				0.0009 0.1056 283.985 0.8263 0.0681	0.0027 757.183
2	165.65			0.0114 0.0775 0.0000 0.8904 0.0320	0.0282 0.0730 0.000 0.9008 0.0262	0.0474 0.000
BARRIER						
1	128.71		0.1654 0.0697 0.0000 0.9084 0.0219	0.2233 0.0830 0.0000 0.8779 0.0391	0.2517 0.0901 0.0000 0.8618 0.0481	0.2630 0.000
0	100.00	1.0000 0.1679 0.000 0.6839 0.1483	0.6742 0.1134 0.0000 0.8083 0.0782	0.5524 0.1069 0.0000 0.8232 0.0698	0.4732 0.1043 0.0000 0.8291 0.0665	0.4166 0.000
–1	77.70		0.1461 0.0873 0.0000 0.8681 0.0446	0.1769 0.0951 0.0000 0.8502 0.0547	0.1867 0.0987 0.0000 0.8420 0.0593	0.1872 0.000
STRIKE						
–2	60.37			0.0064 0.0830 0.0000 0.8780 0.0390	0.0151 0.0864 0.0000 0.8702 0.0434	0.0238 0.000
–3	46.90				0.0002 0.0808 0.0000 0.8829 0.0363	0.0009 0.000

FIGURE 5.25 Static Hedge for a European Up-and-out Call in an Implied Trinomial Tree

This standard option pays off at and above the barrier where the up-and-out option pays nothing. The next task then is to create a zero pay-off at (or just above) the barrier. This can be achieved without interfering with the partial hedge already obtained by taking a position in a standard call option with the same maturity and a strike price equal to the barrier (140). The next nearest node to the barrier and above the barrier is (4, 2) so the position we need to take (w_4) in the 140 strike standard call option is minus the value at node (4, 2) before adding the new option divided by the value of the standard call option at that node:

$$w_4 = -\frac{C_{4,2}}{C_{4,2}(140, 1)} = 16.9233 \tag{5.46}$$

Figure 5.23 shows the tree after adding this option to the portfolio. The next step is to set the value of the portfolio at node (3, 2) equal to zero by taking a position in a standard call with strike 140 and maturity of 0.75. We choose the position in this option w_3 in the same way as before. This gives

$$w_3 = -\frac{C_{3,2}}{C_{3,2}(140, 0.75)} = -9.6321 \tag{5.47}$$

Figure 5.24 shows the tree after adding this further option to the portfolio.

Finally, we must set the value of the portfolio at node (2, 2) equal to zero by taking a position w_2 in a standard call with strike 140 and maturity of 0.5. Choosing the position to take in this option gives

$$w_2 = -\frac{C_{2,2}}{C_{2,2}(140, 0.5)} = -3.838 \tag{5.48}$$

Figure 5.25 shows the tree after adding this final option to the static portfolio. This shows that the up-and-out call option is now completely hedged, the value of the portfolio being zero at all nodes in the implied tree below the barrier.

5.9 SUMMARY

In this chapter we first described how trinomial trees can be constructed to be consistent with the market prices of standard European options. We then showed how trinomial trees can be used to price exotic path-dependent options such as barrier, lookback and Asian options. Finally we briefly discussed how implied trees can be used to construct static portfolios of standard European options to hedge exotic options using the example of an up-and-out call option.

ENDNOTES

1. We define exotic options as any option with a pay-off different from a standard European or American option.
2. Rubinstein (1994) also described implied binomial trees, but his approach is limited for practical applications.
3. We assume here for clarity that the dividend yield is zero. A non-zero dividend yield can be added using the methods in Chapters 2 and 3.
4. See Heynen and Kat (1997a) for a extensive classification of barrier options, their applications, and analytical formulae for the continuously fixed versions.

5. See Heynen and Kat (1997b) for a detailed account of lookback options, their applications and analytical formulae for the continuously fixed versions.
6. The number of paths reaching a given node can be obtained from the multinomial probabilities, see for example Feller (1968).
7. Babbs (1992) describes a method which allows the use of standard trees (Babbs uses a binomial tree) for floating strike lookback, but this method cannot be used for fixed strike lookbacks or other path-dependent options.
8. See Levy (1997) for a detailed account of the structure, uses, pricing and hedging of Asian options.

PART TWO

Implementing Interest Rate Models

6

Option Pricing and Hedging and Numerical Techniques for Pricing Interest Rate Derivatives

6.1 INTRODUCTION

IN the remainder of this book we concentrate on models for pricing interest rate derivatives. In recent years these securities have become very popular, with a wide variety of such instruments trading. In general, to value interest rate derivatives accurately and consistently we need to model the whole term structure of interest rates and the associated volatilities of these rates.

We begin by presenting a brief survey of the most important interest rate instruments. The list includes the most popular interest rate based derivatives as well as some institutional detail about their underlying instruments. We distinguish "government" debt instruments from "money market" debt instruments, the main distinction being in the default risk of the two types of instruments.

6.2 GOVERNMENT DEBT SECURITY INSTRUMENTS

These are securities issued by the government and it is usual to make the assumption that the probability of the issuers defaulting is zero where the issuer is a stable government. The basic government security is the government bond. These issues are known as "gilts" in the United Kingdom, and "treasury issues" in the United States and we can imply riskless interest rates from the prices of these bonds. A government bond with coupon c per cent will pay this proportion of the principal or face value of the bond, usually in the form of equal six-monthly payments of $c/2$, and at maturity it will pay this together with the principal.

In the UK, there are about 80 such bonds on issue with coupons ranging between 3 per cent and 15 per cent, and maturity dates which may be up to 30 years into the future. In addition, there are also index-linked bonds whose coupon payments are related to a measure of inflation. In the United States there are three types of treasury issues. US Treasury bills are issued with maturities to one year, and are discount instruments with the only cashflow occurring at the maturity of the bond. Treasury notes and treasury bonds pay interest semi-annually with notes being issued with maturities up to seven years, whilst treasury bonds may be issued with any maturity, but generally with an original maturity of over 10 years.

US Treasury STRIPS (Separate Trading of Registered Interest and Principal of Securities) have been available since February 1985 and are zero-coupon instruments derived from selected treasury bonds or notes of 10 or more years to maturity. The underlying treasury bonds and notes are separated on the books of the Federal Reserve into their component parts of principal and coupon payments. The resulting "zero-coupon" securities may be separately owned and only pay a cashflow at maturity.

Both futures and options are traded on government bonds. The LIFFE (London International Financial Futures and Options Exchange) long gilt futures contract (the right to buy or sell a notional 9 per cent coupon, 20-year maturity bond at a specified date) is the most popular government debt derivative contract in the UK.[1] Options exist on the long gilt futures contract and they are marked-to-market in the same way as the underlying contract. Options are also traded on specific gilts, which are themselves chosen to be representative gilts at various maturities.

6.3 MONEY MARKET INSTRUMENTS

In this category we include instruments which are not issued by the government, and as such are not considered to be default-free. The most basic money market reference rate is LIBOR (London interbank offer rate). It is a floating reference rate of interest determined by the trading of deposits between banks on the Eurocurrency market. At any one time it is possible to obtain LIBOR reference rates for maturities ranging between overnight and one year. The rates refer to borrowing in the spot market with the interest payment made at the end of the period.

Exchange traded futures contracts based on three-month LIBOR are called "short sterling" futures in the UK, and "eurodollar" futures in the US. Options are also traded with the underlying instrument being the futures contract. A forward rate agreement (FRA) is an agreement between two counterparties which guarantees the rate on borrowing a nominal sum over a certain time, beginning at a certain time in the future. There is no exchange of principal with an FRA, the only cashflow which occurs is a payment at maturity which represents the difference between the interest payment which would have occurred had no FRA been contracted (i.e. the market rate) and the interest that would have been paid at the FRA rate. The underlying reference rate for these agreements is usually based on one of the LIBOR rates.

Interest rate swaps are OTC agreements between two counterparties to swap interest rate cashflows on a nominal sum according to a prearranged formula. The simplest type of interest rate swap involves the exchange of fixed payments (say semi-annual) for floating payments (say six-month LIBOR). Swaps are quoted on bankers' screens for periods between two years and ten years. The quoted rate is the rate for fixed payments that can be swapped for LIBOR over the period. Also increasing in popularity are options on interest rate swaps. These instruments are called swaptions and give the holder the right, but not the obligation, to enter into a certain interest rate swap on or before a certain time in the future.

One of the most popular interest rate instruments is a cap rate agreement. These agreements are also made OTC, rather than via an exchange. An interest rate cap involves restricting the interest rate variations on floating rate loans, guaranteeing that the rate of interest on the loan will never go above a certain level. The rate charged will be the lesser of the prevailing rate and the cap rate. Caps are usually negotiated on three month, six month, and one year LIBOR rates.

Interest rate floors and interest rate collars can de defined analogously to caps. Floors place a lower limit on the interest rate that will be charged. If interest rates falls below the floor the borrower obtains financing at the floor rate. Collars specify both upper and lower limits for the rate of interest that will be charged.

For many derivatives on equity (including indices), foreign exchange, and commodities we can reasonably represent the level of the underlying asset and its volatility by a single variable and a single parameter. However, for many interest rate derivatives the "underlying asset" is the whole term structure of interest rates. The first stage to stochastic modelling is therefore to determine the term structure and the associated volatility structure.

6.4 THE TERM STRUCTURES OF INTEREST RATES AND INTEREST RATE VOLATILITIES

Investors can borrow or lend over different periods at different interest rates. If we plot out these interest rates they form the *term structure of interest rates* or *yield curve*. We can represent the yield curve in three different but equivalent ways. The first representation is by the prices of pure discount bonds that differ in their time to maturity. Pure discount bonds are bonds that give the holder a single unit cashflow (e.g. one dollar) at maturity with no intermediate cashflows. We define the function $P(t, s)$ to be the price, at time t, of a discount bond which matures at time s, with $t \leq s$ $(P(s, s) = 1)$. We can also represent the term structure by associating a continuously compounded interest rate $R(t, s)$ (sometimes called spot rate or par yield) with the pure discount bond price $P(t, s)$:

$$P(t, s) = e^{-R(t,s)(s-t)} \tag{6.1}$$

Inverting this equation we obtain:

$$R(t, s) = -\frac{1}{s-t} \ln P(t, s) \tag{6.2}$$

An important role in interest rate modelling is played by the yield on the instantaneously maturing bond, often called the short rate, which we denote by r. The third formulation is in terms of the forward rate curve, $f(t, s)$. This function represents at time t, the instantaneously maturing interest rate at time s and is derived from the discount bond function by applying the following transformation:

$$f(t, s) = -\frac{\partial}{\partial s} \ln P(t, s) \tag{6.3}$$

Combining equations (6.2) and (6.3) we can write the price of a pure discount bond as the final cashflow discounted by the instantaneous forward rates:

$$P(t, s) = \exp\left(-\int_t^s f(t, \tau) d\tau\right) \tag{6.4}$$

and the spot rate as the continuous average of forward rates:

$$R(t, s) = \frac{1}{s-t}\left(\int_t^s f(t, \tau)d\tau\right) \tag{6.5}$$

For each of these rates, or prices, we associate a volatility. The function that describes these volatilities we call the *term structure of interest rate volatilities*. In terms of spot rates, a typical volatility structure exhibits short-term interest rates that are more volatile than longer term interest rates — an empirical feature of most markets. This effect is illustrated in Figure 6.1.

We denote the volatility of the spot rate $R(t, s)$ as $\sigma_R(t, s)$. The front end of the curve is, by definition, the volatility of the short rate which we define by $\sigma(r) = \sigma_R(t, t)$.

6.4.1 Summary of Notation

$P(t, s)$	= price at time t of a pure discount bond that matures at time s
$R(t, s)$	= yield at time t on the s-maturity pure discount bond (spot rate)
r	= short-term interest rate
$f(t, s)$	= instantaneous forward rate at time t for time s
K	= strike price of the option
$c(t, T, s)$	= price at time t of a European call option with exercise date T on an s-maturity pure discount bond ($t \le T \le s$) and with strike price K
$p(t, T, s)$	= price at time t of a European put option with exercise date T on an s-maturity pure discount bond ($t \le T \le s$) and with strike price K
$\sigma(r)$	= volatility of the short rate
$\sigma_R(t, s)$	= volatility of yield $R(t, s)$

FIGURE 6.1 Spot Rate Volatility Structure

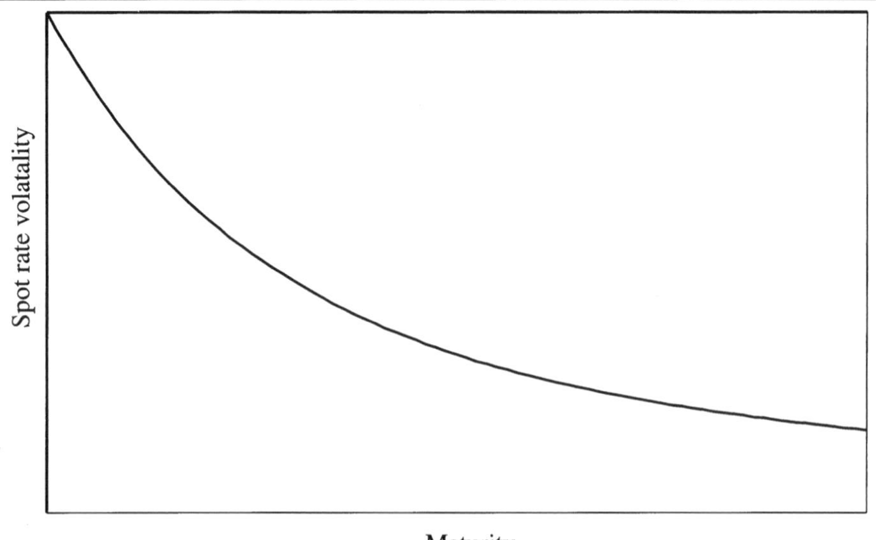

6.5 INTEREST RATE DERIVATIVES AS PORTFOLIOS OF DISCOUNT BOND OPTIONS

We show in this section that a number of complicated interest rate derivative instruments can, for valuation and hedging purposes, be viewed as portfolios of options contracts on discount bonds. The results from this section will be particularly useful for our calibration procedures later.

6.5.1 Coupon Bond Options

When there is only one factor of uncertainty, and an analytic relationship between the discount bond prices can be derived, Jamshidian (1989) has suggested a method of valuing options on coupon bearing bonds which views the instrument as a portfolio of options on discount bonds.

The price $c_{\text{CB}}(t, T, \{s_i\})$ of a European call option with exercise price K and maturity T on a coupon bearing bond which pays cash amounts c_i at time s_i, $s_i \geq T$, is given by the following sum of discount bond options:

$$c_{\text{CB}}(t, T, \{s_i\}) = \sum_{i=1}^{n} c_i c(t, T, s_i, K_i) \tag{6.6}$$

where n is the number of coupon payments of the bond occurring after the end of the life of the option, and where the extra argument denotes the strike price. The exercise price of the ith option is given by $K_i = P(r^*, T, s_i)$ i.e. the s_i-maturity discount bond price as seen from T when the level of the short rate is r^* such that the value of the coupon bond at time T is equal to the strike price K, i.e.

$$\sum_{i=1}^{n} c_i P(r^*, T, s_i) = K \tag{6.7}$$

Equation (6.6) expresses a call option on a coupon paying bond as equivalent to a portfolio of call options on the individual discount bonds with maturities equal to the coupon payment dates and adjusted exercise prices. A put option on a coupon bond, $p_{\text{CB}}(t, T, \{s_i\})$, is valued similarly as a portfolio of put options:

$$p_{\text{CB}}(t, T, \{s_i\}) = \sum_{i=1}^{n} c_i p(t, T, s_i, K_i) \tag{6.8}$$

6.5.2 Swaptions as Bond Options

Many practitioners calibrate their interest rate models to European swaption prices. Swaptions are options on interest rate swaps. The quoted swap rates are the fixed rates of interest that can be swapped for LIBOR-based floating payments. They represent fixed rates of interest in the money market once we realise that a fixed rate loan can be manufactured from a floating LIBOR loan and a swap. An interest rate swap can, therefore, be regarded as an exchange of a fixed rate (i.e. coupon) bond for a floating rate bond. At the start of the life of a swap, the value of the floating rate bond equals the principal amount of the swap. A European swaption can therefore be regarded as an option to exchange a coupon bond for the principal amount of the swap, i.e. its value is the same as an option on a coupon bond with the strike of the option set equal to the principal of the swap. We can therefore use the results for European options on coupon bonds to price European swaptions. In the following analysis we assume that the option exercises into a fixed term swap, i.e. if the investor exercises a one-year option into a three-year swap, the investor obtains a "new" three year swap.[2]

If the swaption gives the holder the right to pay fixed and receive floating (a "payer" swaption), it is a put on the fixed rate bond.

$$\text{payer swaption} = \sum_{i=1}^{n} \frac{R_{\text{swap}}}{2} p(t, T, s_i > T, K_i) \tag{6.9}$$

where R_{swap} is the swap rate at time t and the strike price of the option, K_i is calculated as in equation (6.6).

If the swaption gives the holder the right to pay floating and receive fixed (a "receiver" swaption), it is a call on the fixed rate bond.

$$\text{receiver swaption} = \sum_{i=1}^{n} \frac{R_{\text{swap}}}{2} c(t, T, s_i > T, K_i) \tag{6.10}$$

Note that in the above we have assumed that the principal of the swap has been normalised to be equal to 1. For non-unitary values, the price is scaled by the principal.

6.5.3 Caps, Floors and Collars as Pure Discount Bond Options

An interest rate cap places an upper, predetermined, limit on the borrower's floating interest rate to a fixed level, the cap rate, for a given period of time. An instrument of this kind can be interpreted as a series of put options on discount bonds, and therefore can be valued as such. Analogously an interest rate floor can be valued by summing the premiums on a portfolio of call options on discount bonds, and a collar as the sum of premiums of a portfolio consisting of both put and call options.

Consider an interest rate cap with cap level R_{cap} and reset dates $t_0, t_1, \ldots, t_n$. $t_i - t_{i-1} = \Delta\tau$ is the reset period.[3] The cap can be interpreted as a series of "caplets", covering each period $\Delta\tau$. We assume for our analysis that there is no caplet over the first $\Delta\tau$ period as the interest rate applicable to the period is known at time t_0. Figure 6.2 illustrates the individual caplets involved in the cap.

Consider an option that caps the interest rate on \$1 at the rate R_{cap} between times t_k and t_{k+1} (i.e. a single caplet of the cap). Let $R_k = R(t_k, t_{k+1})$ be the realised interest rate at time t_k for the period (t_k, t_{k+1}). The pay-off to the option at time t_{k+1} is

$$\Delta\tau \max(R_k - R_{\text{cap}}, 0)$$

At time t_k the discounted value of this pay-off is given by

$$\frac{\Delta\tau}{1 + R_k \Delta\tau} \max(R_k - R_{\text{cap}}, 0)$$

FIGURE 6.2 "Caplets" in an Interest Rate Cap

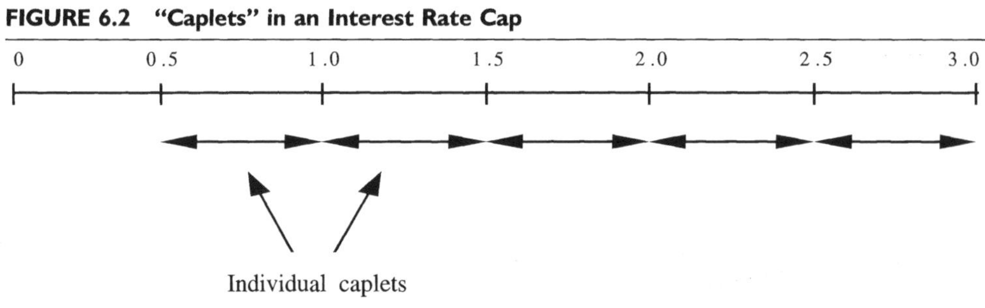

This expression is equivalent to

$$(1+R_{\text{cap}}\Delta\tau)\max\left(\frac{1}{1+R_{\text{cap}}\Delta\tau}-\frac{1}{1+R_k\Delta\tau},0\right)$$

Therefore, an option which caps the interest rate at R_{cap} between t_k and t_{k+1} is equivalent to $(1+R_{\text{cap}}\Delta\tau)$ European put options with exercise price

$$K_c=\frac{1}{1+R_{\text{cap}}\Delta\tau}$$

and expiration date t_k on a \$1 face value discount bond maturing at time t_{k+1}. More generally, an interest rate cap is a portfolio of European puts on a series of discount bonds.

$$\text{value cap}=(1+R_{\text{cap}}\Delta\tau)\sum_{i=1}^{n}p\left(t,T=i\Delta\tau,s=(i+1)\Delta\tau,K_c=\frac{1}{1+R_{\text{cap}}\Delta\tau}\right)\tag{6.11}$$

An interest rate floor agreement can be defined analogously. It places a lower limit on the interest rate that will be charged. An interest rate floor can be interpreted as a series of call options on discount bonds. Consider an option that provides a floor on the interest rate on \$1 at the rate R_{floor} between times t_k and t_{k+1}.

The pay-off to the option at time t_{k+1} is $\Delta\tau\max(R_{\text{floor}}-R_k,0)$. At time t_k the discounted value of this pay-off is given by

$$\frac{\Delta\tau}{1+R_k\Delta\tau}\max(R_{\text{floor}}-R_k,0)$$

This expression is equivalent to

$$(1+R_{\text{floor}}\Delta\tau)\max\left(\frac{1}{1+R_k\Delta\tau}-\frac{1}{1+R_{\text{floor}}\Delta\tau},0\right)$$

Therefore, an option which provides a floor on the interest rate between t_k and t_{k+1} is equivalent to $(1+R_{\text{floor}}\Delta\tau)$ European call options with exercise price

$$K_f=\frac{1}{1+R_{\text{floor}}\Delta\tau}$$

and expiration date t_k on a \$1 face value discount bond maturing at time t_{k+1}. More generally, an interest rate floor agreement is a portfolio of European calls on a series of discount bonds.

$$\text{value floor} = (1 + R_{\text{floor}}\Delta\tau)\sum_{i=1}^{n} c\left(t, T = i\Delta\tau, s = (i+1)\Delta\tau, K_f = \frac{1}{1 + R_{\text{floor}}\Delta\tau}\right) \tag{6.12}$$

A collar is just a long position on a cap and a short position on a floor with the same characteristics of settlement dates and reset intervals. This implies that the price of a collar is equal to the difference between the price of the portfolio of puts with strike price K_c, and the price of the portfolio of calls with strike K_f.

$$\begin{aligned}\text{Value collar} &= \text{long cap} - \text{short floor}\\ &= (1 + R_{\text{cap}}\Delta\tau)\sum_{i=1}^{n} p\left(t, T = i\Delta\tau, s = (i+1)\Delta\tau, K_c = \frac{1}{1 + R_{\text{cap}}\Delta\tau}\right)\\ &\quad - (1 + R_{\text{floor}}\Delta\tau)\sum_{i=1}^{n} c\left(t, T = i\Delta\tau, s = (i+1)\Delta\tau, K_f = \frac{1}{1 + R_{\text{floor}}\Delta\tau}\right)\end{aligned} \tag{6.13}$$

6.6 VALUATION OF INTEREST RATE DERIVATIVES

There are two main ways to value interest rate derivative securities, and these are shown by the first two branches in Figure 6.3. If we wanted to value bond options we could either model the bond price directly or model the equivalent representations in terms of spot rates or forward rates.

6.6.1 Adapting Black–Scholes for Pricing Interest Rate Derivatives

The most common way for practitioners to price basic interest rate derivatives (e.g. caps, floors and swaptions) is to adapt the Black–Scholes model and implement Black (1976). However, as we shall see, common practices involve making a number of different inconsistent assumptions for each instrument. We look here at three different adaptations that are currently employed by many practitioners to price bond options, caps and swaptions.

Black's Model For Bond Option Pricing

A popular way of handling the characteristics of the bond price volatility through time[4] is to take the forward price of the bond at the expiry date of the option and apply Black's (1976) formula. The option price therefore becomes

$$c(t, T, s) = P(t, T)[P_F(t, T, s)N(d_1) - KN(d_2)] \tag{6.14}$$

where

$$d_1 = \left(\ln\left(\frac{P_F(t, T, s)}{K}\right) + \frac{\sigma^2}{2}(T - t)\right) \Big/ \sigma\sqrt{T - t}$$

$$d_2 = d_1 - \sigma\sqrt{T - t}$$

FIGURE 6.3 Valuation of Interest Rate Derivatives

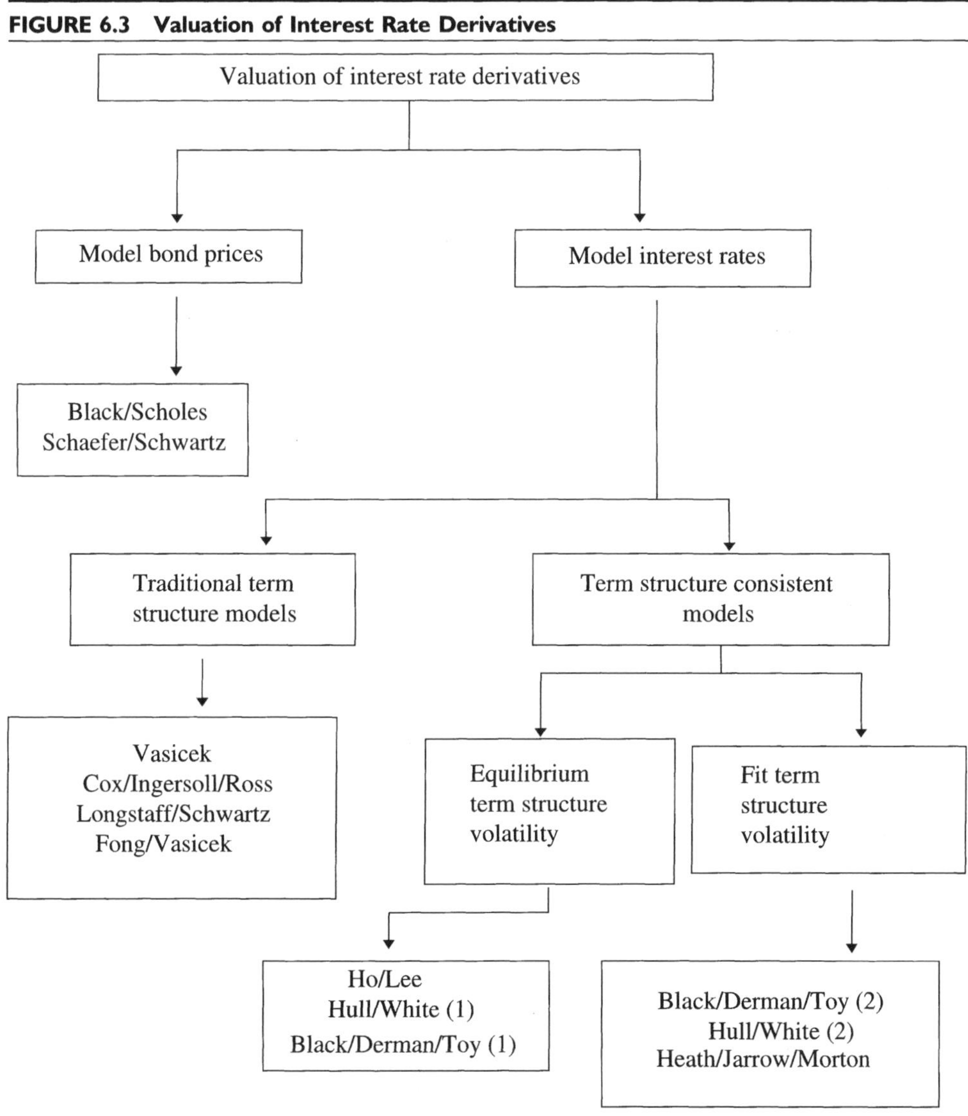

where $P_F(t, T, s)$ is the forward bond price between T and s, and σ the forward bond price volatility. This adaptation therefore implicitly assumes that forward bond prices are lognormal.

Example : The Black (1976) Model For Bond Option Pricing

Assume that the term structure is flat at 5 per cent with continuous compounding. We price a one-year year European call option on a five-year pure discount bond, assuming that the forward bond price volatility is 10 per cent. The strike price of the option is 0.80. Figure 6.4 illustrates the calculations.

FIGURE 6.4 Black (1976) for Pure Discount Bond Option Pricing

	Maturity	Rate	PDB price
Option	1	5.00%	0.9512
Bond	5	5.00%	0.7788
		K	0.8000
			10.00%
		PF(0,1,5)	0.8187
		d1	0.2814
		d2	0.1814
		c(0,1,5)	0.0404

The one- and five-year bond prices under the term structure assumption are given by

$$P(0,1) = e^{-0.05(1)} = 0.9512$$

$$P(0,5) = e^{-0.05(5)} = 0.7788$$

This implies that the forward bond price is

$$P_{\mathrm{F}}(0,1,5) = \frac{P(0,5)}{P(0,1)} = \frac{0.7788}{0.9512} = 0.8187$$

$$d_1 = \left(\ln\left(\frac{0.8187}{0.8}\right) + \frac{0.1^2}{2}(1)\right) \Big/ 0.1\sqrt{1} = 0.2814$$

$$d_2 = 0.2814 - 0.1\sqrt{1} = 0.1814$$

Therefore the call price is given by

$$c(0,1,5,0.8) = 0.9512(0.8187 \times N(0.2814) - 0.8 \times N(0.1814))$$
$$= 0.0404$$

Black's Model For Cap Pricing

A different assumption is made by many practitioners when using Black's model to price interest rate caps. Consider the caplet outlined earlier over the period between t_k and t_{k+1}. The market convention is to assume that the forward rate from t_k to t_{k+1} is lognormal and apply Black in the following way to obtain a cash price:

$$\text{caplet}(t, t_k, t_{k+1}) = P(t, t_k)[f(t, t_k, t_{k+1})N(d_1) - R_{\text{cap}}N(d_2)]\Delta\tau L \qquad (6.15)$$

where

$$d_1 = \left(\ln\left(\frac{f(t, t_k, t_{k+1})}{R_{\text{cap}}}\right) + \frac{\sigma^2}{2}(t_k - t)\right) \Big/ \sigma\sqrt{t_k - t}$$

$$d_2 = d_1 - \sigma\sqrt{t_k - t}$$

where L is the principal amount underlying the cap with $f(t, t_k, t_{k+1})$ the forward rate over the period.

Example : Black's Model For Cap Pricing

Assume a flat term structure at 5 per cent with continuous compounding. The cap rate is assumed to be 4.5 per cent. We normalise the principal underlying the cap to be $1m and assume a reset frequency of three months. We assume also that the volatility of the forward interest rate is 10 per cent and price the caplet from 9 to 12 months. Figure 6.5 illustrates the calculations.

In order to price the caplet, we implement equation (6.15) with $t_k = 0.75$ and $t_{k+1} = 1.0$. The relevant bond prices are determined from the yield curve as

$$P(0, 0.75) = e^{-0.05(0.75)} = 0.9632$$

$$P(0, 1) = e^{-0.05(1)} = 0.9512$$

implying that the forward rate from nine months until one year is 5 per cent:

$$f(0, 9, 12) = \frac{\ln\left(\dfrac{0.9632}{0.9512}\right)}{(1 - 0.75)} = 5.0 \text{ per cent}$$

$$d_1 = \frac{\ln\left(\dfrac{0.05}{0.045}\right) + \dfrac{0.10^2}{2}0.75}{0.1\sqrt{0.75}} = 1.2599$$

$$d_2 = 1.2599 - 0.1\sqrt{0.75} = 1.1733$$

FIGURE 6.5 Black (1976) for Pricing Interest Rate Caps

Capping the period from 0.75 to 1.0

Maturity	Rate		PDB price
0.75	5.00%		0.9632
1.00	5.00%		0.9512
		Rcap	4.50%
		L	1
		$\Delta\tau$	0.25
		σ	10.00%
		f(0, 0.75, 1.0)	5.00%
		d1	1.2599
		d2	1.1733
		Caplet(0, 0.75, 1.0)	0.0013

Therefore the value of the caplet is given by

$$\begin{aligned}\text{caplet } (0, 0.75, 1) &= 0.9632(0.05 \times N(1.2599) - 0.045 \times N(1.1733))0.25(1)\\ &= 0.0013\end{aligned}$$

Black's Model For Swaption Pricing

Finally, a third adaptation of the Black model is regularly used for pricing European swaptions. Consider a swaption with maturity date T where the swaption has a fixed tenure after this date.

$$\text{swaption}(t) = \Delta\tau \sum_{i=1}^{n} P(t, T_i)[R_{\text{fswap}} N(d_1) - KN(d_2)] \sum_{i=l}^{n} \frac{1}{(1 + R_{\text{fswap}})^n} \tag{6.16}$$

where R_{fswap} is the forward swap rate, n is the number of reset periods of the swap and $\Delta\tau$ is the reset period.

$$d_1 \left(\ln \left(\frac{R_{\text{fswap}}}{K} \right) + \frac{\sigma^2}{2}(T - t) \right) \Big/ \sigma\sqrt{T - t}$$

$$d_2 = d_1 - \sigma\sqrt{T - t}$$

where R_{fwap} is the forward swap rate with n the tenor of the swap (in years). Under this common usage the forward swap rate is the lognormal variable.

Example : Black's Model For Swaption Pricing

Assume a flat term structure at 5 per cent with continuous compounding. We price a two-year option which exercises into a new one-year semi-annual payer swap. The strike price of the option is 5 per cent and we assume a forward swap rate volatility of 20 per cent. Figure 6.6 illustrates the calculations.

Firstly, we have to calculate the forward swap rate. This is determined by equating the forward bond price (with coupon equal to the forward swap rate) and the price of the floating bond at the option maturity, i.e.

$$1 = \sum_{i=1}^{2} \frac{R_{\text{fswap}}}{2} P(T, t_i) + P(T, t_2)$$

where $T = 2.0$, with $t_1 = 2.5$ and $t_2 = 3.0$. Rearranging, we obtain

$$R_{\text{fswap}} = \left[\frac{1 - P(T, t_2)}{\sum_{i=1}^{2} P(T, t_i)} \right] \times 2$$

where

$$P(T, t_i) = \frac{P(t, t_i)}{P(t, T)}, t = 0$$

FIGURE 6.6 Black (1976) for Swaption Pricing

Two year option into a new 1 yr swap

Maturity	Rate	PDBprice	P(T,ti)
2.00	5.00%	0.9048	
2.50	5.00%	0.8825	0.9753
3.00	5.00%	0.8607	0.9512

K	5.00%
$\Delta\tau$	0.50
σ	20.00%
Rfswap	5.06%
d1	0.1857
d2	–0.0971
Swaption	0.0052

Under our term structure assumptions the relevant bond prices are given by

$$P(0,2) = e^{-0.05(2)} = 0.9048$$

$$P(0,2.5) = e^{-0.05(2.5)} = 0.8825$$

$$P(0,3) = e^{-0.05(3)} = 0.8607$$

In order to determine the forward swap rate, we need to calculate the relevant forward bond prices. These are determined to be:

$$P(2,2.5) = \frac{P(0,2.5)}{P(0,2)} = \frac{0.8825}{0.9048} = 0.9753$$

$$P(2,3) = \frac{P(0,3)}{P(0,2)} = \frac{0.8607}{0.9048} = 0.9512$$

So

$$R_{\text{fswap}} = \left[\frac{1 - P(2,3)}{P(2,2.5) + P(2,3)}\right] \times 2$$

$$= \frac{1 - 0.9512}{0.9753 + 0.9512} \times 2 = 0.0506 = 5.06 \text{ per cent}$$

Therefore, the swaption value is given as

$$\text{swaption} = 0.5 \times (0.8825 + 0.8607) \times [0.0506 \times N(0.1587) - 0.050 \times N(-0.0971)]$$

$$= 0.0052$$

where

$$d_1 = \left(\ln\left(\frac{0.0506}{0.050}\right) + \frac{0.2^2}{2}(2)\right) \Big/ 0.2\sqrt{2} = 0.1587$$

$$d_2 = 0.1587 - 0.2\sqrt{2} = -0.0971$$

In the above three subsections, we have presented three *ad hoc* adaptations of the Black formula, each based on a different, inconsistent, assumption made to handle the characteristics of the separate instruments. However, it does not lead to an integrated approach but to a "one model–one product" approach, each incompatible with the others where even the deltas cannot be aggregated.

6.6.2 Modelling Interest Rates

A more consistent way to price interest rate derivatives is by modelling the underlying source of uncertainty, e.g. interest rates, directly. One way of constructing a no-arbitrage model for interest rates is in terms of the process followed by the instantaneous short rate, r. It can be shown that the process for the short rate in a risk-neutral world determines the current term structure and how it can evolve. For example, arbitrage pricing theory tells us that s-maturity bond prices are given by

$$P(t, s) = \hat{E}_t\left[\exp\left(-\int_t^s r(\tau)\,d\tau\right)\right] \tag{6.17}$$

where $\hat{E}_t$ denotes expectations (with the information set at time t) in a risk-adjusted world, with $r(\tau)$ denoting the path of the short rate from t to s. Time t interest rate derivative prices, $C(t)$, are determined in the same way:

$$C(t) = \hat{E}_t\left[\exp\left(-\int_t^T r(\tau)\,d\tau\right) C(T)\right] \tag{6.18}$$

where $C(T)$ is the pay-off from a derivative at time T. For example, for the European discount bond call options described earlier we have

$$C(t) = \hat{E}_t\left[\exp\left(-\int_t^T r(\tau)\,d\tau\right) \max(P(T, s) - K, 0)\right] \tag{6.19}$$

In order to evaluate the expectation we need a process determining the evolution of the short rate.

The Traditional Term Structure Approach

During the late 1970s and early 1980s, models for interest rate derivatives were based on models developed to explain the term structure of interest rates. Perhaps the two best-known models are due to Vasicek (1977) and Cox, Ingersoll and Ross (CIR) (1985). They can be characterised by their assumptions about the short-term interest rate, which is assumed to be the single source of uncertainty.[5]

Vasicek. The stochastic differential equation representing the uncertainty of the short rate is given by

$$dr = \alpha(\bar{r} - r)\,dt + \sigma\,dz \tag{6.20}$$

where $r = r(t)$ is the level of the short rate, at time t, and dz is the increment in a Wiener process. The instantaneous drift represents the process as mean reverting towards some long-term level $\bar{r}$. The short rate is assumed to follow the Ornstein–Uhlenbeck diffusion process with the volatility of the process equal to a constant σ.

Both the term structure of rates and the associated volatility structure are determined by the model once we fix the constant parameters α, $\bar{r}$ and σ. In the Vasicek model, the prices of pure discount bonds and the equivalent continuously compounded yields are given by

$$P(t, s) = A(t, s)e^{-rB(t,s)} \tag{6.21}$$

$$R(t, s) = -\frac{\ln A(t, s)}{s - t} + \frac{B(t, s)}{s - t}r \tag{6.22}$$

where

$$B(t, s) = \frac{1}{\alpha}\left(1 - e^{-\alpha(s-t)}\right) \tag{6.23}$$

$$\ln A(t, s) = \frac{R_\infty}{\alpha}\left(1 - e^{-\alpha(s-t)}\right) - (s - t)R_\infty - \frac{\sigma^2}{4\alpha^3}\left(1 - e^{-\alpha(s-t)}\right)^2 \tag{6.24}$$

where

$$R_\infty = \lim_{\tau\to\infty} R(t, \tau) = \bar{r} - \frac{1}{2}\frac{\sigma^2}{\alpha^2}$$

The spot rate volatility structure is determined by the two parameters σ and α:

$$\sigma_R(t, s) = \frac{\sigma}{\alpha(s - t)}\left(1 - e^{-\alpha(s-t)}\right) \tag{6.25}$$

Equation (6.25) implies that the shape of the term structure of volatility is negative exponential; the general level of volatility is determined by the volatility of the short rate with the mean reversion parameter determining the attenuation of volatility with maturity — the higher the speed of mean reversion the greater the "dampening" of volatility. Figure 6.7 illustrates the effect of the volatility structure with α's of 0.01, 0.1 and 1.0 with $\sigma = 0.1$.

Jamshidian (1989) has shown that under the process (6.20), European discount bond call and put options are given by

$$c(t, T, s) = P(t, s)N(d_1) - KP(t, T)N(d_2) \tag{6.26}$$

$$p(t, T, s) = KP(t, T)N(-d_2) - P(t, s)N(-d_1) \tag{6.27}$$

with

$$d_1 = \frac{\ln\left(\dfrac{P(t, s)}{KP(t, T)}\right)}{\sigma_p} + \frac{\sigma_p}{2}$$

$$d_2 = d_1 - \sigma_p$$

$$\sigma_p = \frac{\nu(t, T)\left(1 - e^{-\alpha(s-T)}\right)}{\alpha}$$

$$\nu(t, T) = \sqrt{\frac{\sigma^2\left(1 - e^{-2\alpha(T-t)}\right)}{2\alpha}}$$

FIGURE 6.7 Spot Rate Volatility Structures in the Vasicek Model

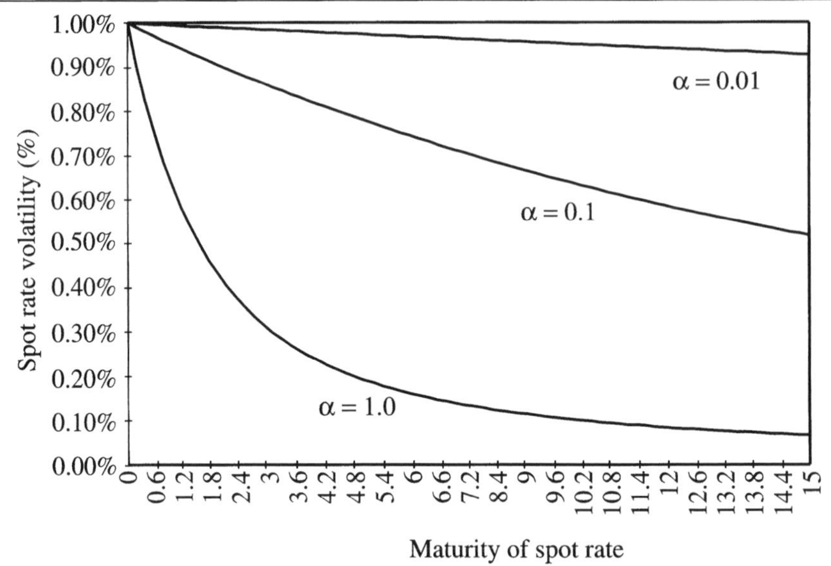

Example : Vasicek

We assume the level of the short rate is 5 per cent and that it is reverting to a long-term mean of 5 per cent with a speed of 15 per cent. The volatility of the short rate is assumed to be 1 per cent per annum. We price a one-year pure discount bond and a one-year European call option on a five-year pure discount bond with a strike of 0.67. Figure 6.8 illustrates the calculations.

$$r = \bar{r} = 0.05$$

$$\alpha = 0.15$$

$$\sigma = 0.01$$

$$K = 0.67$$

$$B(0, 1) = \frac{1}{0.15}\left(1 - e^{-0.15(1)}\right) = 0.9286$$

$$R_{\infty} = 0.05 - \frac{1}{2} \times \frac{0.01^2}{0.15^2} = 0.0478$$

$$\ln A(0, 1) = \frac{0.0478}{0.15}\left(1 - e^{-0.15(1)}\right) - 1(0.0478) - \frac{0.01^2}{4(0.15)^3}\left(1 - e^{-0.15(1)}\right)^2$$

$$= -0.0036$$

Therefore, the one-year pure discount bond price is given by

$$P(0, 1) = e^{-0.0036}e^{-0.05(0.9286)}$$

$$= 0.9512$$

FIGURE 6.8 Vasicek Calculations

process parameters		pure discount bond price		
α	15.00%	B(0,1)	0.9286	
r̄	5.00%	lnA(0,1)	−0.0036	
σ	1.00%			
r0	5.00%	R∞	0.0478	
T	1	P(0,1)	0.9512	5.00%
s	5	σR(0,1)	0.9286%	
K	0.6700	P(0,5)	0.7798	4.98%
		option price		
		v(0,1)	0.0093	
		σp	0.0280	
		d1	7.2281	
		d2	7.2002	
		c(0,1,5)	0.1424	

The one-year spot rate volatility is determined via equation (6.25).

$$\sigma_R(0,1) = \frac{0.01}{0.15(1)}\left(1 - e^{-0.15(1)}\right)$$
$$= 0.00928 = 0.9286 \text{ per cent}$$

In order to price the option, we first determine the five-year pure discount bond price as above:

$$P(0,5) = 0.7798$$

The price of the European call option is then determined via equation (6.26):

$$\nu(0,1) = \sqrt{\frac{0.01^2\left(1 - e^{-2(0.15)(1)}\right)}{2(0.15)}} = 0.0093$$

$$\sigma_p = \frac{0.0093\left(1 - e^{-0.15(5-1)}\right)}{0.15} = 0.0280$$

$$d_1 = \frac{\ln(0.7798/0.67(0.9512))}{0.0280} + \frac{0.0280}{2} = 7.2281$$

$$d_2 = 7.2281 - 0.0280 = 7.2002$$

Implying;

$$c(0,1,5) = 0.7798 \times N(7.2281) - 0.67 \times (0.9512) \times N(7.2002) = 0.1424$$

Cox–Ingersoll–Ross. The interest rate process of the Vasicek paper allows interest rates to go negative with a positive probability and ignores the empirical evidence of the positive relation between interest rates and the level of interest rate uncertainty.[6] CIR (1985) describe a model in which the volatility of the short rate increases with the square root of the level of the rate, precluding the existence of negative interest rates, and allowing more variability at times of high interest rates and less variability when rates are low. This dependence has led the model to be widely known as the "square-root" process:

$$dr = \alpha(\bar{r} - r)\,dt + \sigma\sqrt{r}\,dz \tag{6.28}$$

Pure discount bond prices, spot yields and the volatility structure of spot rates are given by respectively:

$$P(t, s) = A(t, s)e^{-B(t,s)r} \tag{6.29}$$

$$R(t, s) = -\frac{\ln A(t, s)}{s - t} + \frac{B(t, s)}{s - t}r \tag{6.30}$$

$$\sigma_R(t, s) = \frac{\sigma\sqrt{r}}{s - t}B(t, s) \tag{6.31}$$

where

$$A(t, s) = \left(\frac{\phi_1 e^{\phi_2(s-t)}}{\phi_2\left(e^{\phi_1(s-t)} - 1\right) + \phi_1}\right)^{\phi_3}, \qquad B(t, s) = \left(\frac{e^{\phi_1(s-t)} - 1}{\phi_2\left(e^{\phi_1(s-t)} - 1\right) + \phi_1}\right)$$

$$\phi_1 \equiv \sqrt{\alpha^2 + 2\sigma^2}, \qquad \phi_2 \equiv \frac{(\alpha + \phi_1)}{2}, \qquad \phi_3 \equiv \frac{2\alpha\bar{r}}{\sigma^2}$$

European pure discount bond option prices are given by the formula:

$$\begin{aligned} c(t, T, s) = {} & P(t, s)\chi^2\left(2r^*[\phi + \psi + B(T, s)]; \frac{4\alpha\bar{r}}{\sigma^2}, \frac{2\phi^2 r e^{\theta(T-t)}}{\phi + \psi + B(T, s)}\right) \\ & - KP(t, T)\chi^2\left(2r^*[\phi + \psi]; \frac{4\alpha\bar{r}}{\sigma^2}, \frac{2\phi^2 r e^{\theta(T-t)}}{\phi + \psi}\right) \end{aligned} \tag{6.32}$$

where

$$\theta \equiv \sqrt{(\alpha^2 + 2\sigma^2)}, \qquad \phi = \frac{2\theta}{\sigma^2(e^{-\theta(T-t)} - 1)},$$

$$\psi = \frac{\alpha + \theta}{\sigma^2}, \qquad r^* = \ln\left(\frac{A(T, s)}{K}\right) \Big/ B(T, s)$$

and where $\chi^2(.; p, q)$ is the non-central chi-squared density with p degrees of freedom and non-centrality parameter q. An algorithm to evaluate this density is presented in Schroder (1989).

Example : CIR

Assume the level of the short rate is 5 per cent and that it is reverting to a long-term mean of 5 per cent with a speed of 15 per cent. The volatility of the short rate is assumed to be 10 per cent per annum. We price a one-year pure discount bond and a one-year European call option on a five-year pure discount bond with a strike of 0.67. Figure 6.9 illustrates the calculations.

$$r = \bar{r} = 0.05$$
$$\alpha = 0.15$$
$$\sigma = 0.10$$
$$K = 0.67$$
$$\phi_1 = \sqrt{0.15^2 + 2(0.10)^2} = 0.2062$$
$$\phi_2 = \frac{0.15 + 0.2062}{2} = 0.1781$$
$$\phi_3 = \frac{2(0.15)(0.05)}{0.1^2} = 1.500$$
$$B(0.1) = \frac{e^{0.2062(1)} - 1}{0.1781(e^{0.2062(1)} - 1) + 0.2062} = 0.9272$$
$$A(0,1) = \left(\frac{0.2062e^{0.1781(1)}}{0.1781(e^{0.2062(1)} - 1) + 0.2062}\right)^{1.5} = 0.9964$$
$$P(0,1) = 0.9964e^{-0.9272(0.1)0.05} = 0.9513$$

Using equation (6.2) we obtain the yield:

$$R(0,1) = -\tfrac{1}{1}\ln P(0,1) = 0.0499$$

FIGURE 6.9 Cox–Ingersoll–Ross Calculations

process parameters		**pure discount bond price for matT**		
α	15.00%	φ1	0.2062	
r̄	5.00%	φ2	0.1781	
σ	10.00%	φ3	1.5000	
r	5.00%	B(0,1)	0.9272	
		A(0,1)	0.9964	
T	1			
S	5	P(0,1)	0.9513	4.99%
		vol rate	0.0207	
K	0.6700			
		P(0,5)	0.7835	4.88%
option price				
θ	0.4123	A(1,5)	0.9521	
φ	-244.06	B(0,5)	3.4199	
ψ	56.23	B(1,5)	2.9498	
		r*	0.1191	
		call(0,1,5)	0.1461	

The volatility of the one-year spot rate is determined by equation (6.31):

$$\sigma_R(0,1) = \left(\frac{0.1\sqrt{0.05}}{(1)}\right)0.9272 = 0.0207$$

In order to price the option we first determine the five-year pure discount bond price as above:

$$P(0,5) = 0.7835$$

The price of the European call option is then determined via equation (6.32):

$$\begin{aligned}
\theta &= \sqrt{0.15^2 + 2(0.1)^2} = 0.4123 \\
\phi &= \frac{2(0.4123)}{0.1^2\left(e^{-0.4123(1)} - 1\right)} = -244.06 \\
\psi &= \frac{0.15 + 0.4123}{0.1^2} = 56.23 \\
A(1,5) &= 0.9521 \\
r^* &= \ln\left(\frac{A(1,5)}{K}\right)\Big/B(1,5) = \ln\left(\frac{0.9521}{0.67}\right)\Big/2.9498 = 0.1191 \\
B(1,5) &= 2.9498
\end{aligned}$$

The arguments for the cumulative distribution function are determined as

$$\begin{aligned}
2r^*[\phi + \psi + B(1,5)] &= 2(0.1191)(-244.06 + 56.23 + 2.9498) = -44.0437 \\
\frac{4\alpha\bar{r}}{\sigma^2} &= \frac{4(0.15)(0.05)}{0.1^2} = 3 \\
\frac{2\phi^2 r e^{\theta(1)}}{\phi + \psi + B(1,5)} &= \frac{2(-244.06)^2(0.05)e^{0.4123(1)}}{-244.06 + 56.23 + 2.9498} = -48.6592 \\
2r^*[\phi + \psi] &= 2(0.1191)(-244.06 + 56.23) = -44.7464 \\
\frac{2\phi^2 r e^{\theta(1)}}{\phi + \psi} &= \frac{2(-244.06)^2(0.05)e^{0.4123(1)}}{-244.06 + 56.23} = -47.895
\end{aligned}$$

The value of the option is then given by

$$\begin{aligned}
c(0,1,5) &= 0.7835 \times \chi^2(-44.0437;3,-48.6592) - 0.67 \times 0.9513 \times \chi^2(-44.7464;3,-47.895) \\
&= 0.7835 \times 0.9971 - 0.67 \times 0.9513 \times 0.9964 \\
&= 0.1461
\end{aligned}$$

Two-factor Models

Although the two models that we have just looked at offer tractability, the yield curves that they are able to generate can only be monotonically increasing, monotonically decreasing or slightly humped. In order to generate more realistic term structures a number of authors have put forward models which involve more than a single source of uncertainty. Two of the more recent of these come from Longstaff and Schwartz (1992) and Fong and Vasicek (1992) who propose stochastic volatility models of the term structure (see also Richard,

1978, Brennan and Schwartz, 1979 and Schaefer and Schwartz 1984). Again, both the term structure of rates and of rate volatilities are determined once the parameters of the risk-adjusted process are obtained.

Fong and Vasicek. Fong and Vasicek (1992) (FV) present a two-factor model of the term structure of interest rates. The two driving factors are the short-term interest rate, r, and the variance of the short rate, ν. The risk-neutral processes are given by

$$\begin{aligned} dr &= [\alpha(\bar{r} - r)]\,dt + \sqrt{\nu}\,dz_1 \\ d\nu &= [\gamma(\bar{\nu} - \nu)]\,dt + \xi\sqrt{\nu}\,dz_2 \end{aligned} \tag{6.33}$$

with $dz_1\,dz_2 = \rho\,dt$.

Under the equilibrium condition of no arbitrage, FV show that prices of pure discount bonds have the form:

$$P(t, s) = \exp(-rD(t, s) + \nu F(t, s) + G(t, s)) \tag{6.34}$$

where

$$D(t, s) = \frac{1}{\alpha}\left(1 - e^{-\alpha(s-t)}\right) \tag{6.35}$$

The functions $F(t, s)$ and $G(t, s)$ are given in Appendix 6.1. The solutions proposed by the authors involve computation of the confluent hypergeometric function. However, Selby and Strickland (1995) propose a series solution for F and G which can be easily implemented on a spreadsheet. Figure 6.10 illustrates some of the possible term structures that can be obtained with this model.

The term structure of spot rate volatilities is given by the equation:

$$\sigma_R(t, s) = \frac{1}{s - t}\sqrt{\left(D(t, s)^2 - 2\rho\xi F(t, s)D(t, s) + \xi^2 F(t, s)^2\right)\nu} \tag{6.36}$$

FIGURE 6.10 Some Possible Shapes of the Term Structure under Fong and Vasicek

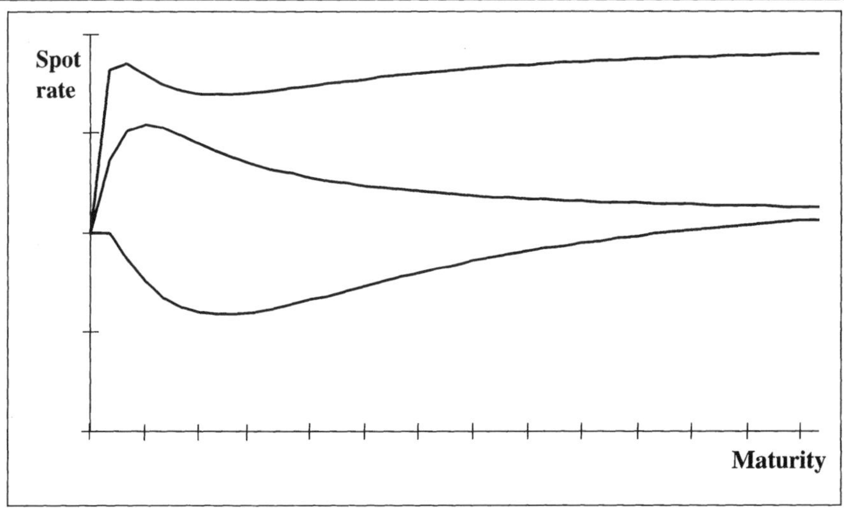

Example : Fong and Vasicek

We price a one-year pure discount bond under the assumptions that the short rate is currently at 8 per cent, and reverting to a level of 9.5 per cent at a rate of 200 per cent. The variance of the short rate is assumed to be at its mean level of 1.5 per cent, with mean reversion of 200 per cent. The correlation of the short rate and its volatility is assumed to be 0.6. Figure 6.11 illustrates the calculations.

$$\alpha = 2.0, \gamma = 2.0, \xi = 0.001, \lambda = 0.2, \eta = 0.1, \rho = 0.6$$

$$r = 0.08, \bar{r} = 0.0095$$

$$v = 0.015, \bar{v} = 0.015$$

$$D(0, 1) = \frac{1}{2.0}\left(1 - e^{-2.0(1)}\right) = 0.4323$$

The F and G functions are calculated using the Selby and Strickland algorithm.

$$F(0, 1) = -0.0022$$

$$G(0, 1) = -0.0540$$

$$P(0, 1) = e^{-0.08(0.4323)+0.015(-0.0022)+(-0.0540)}$$

$$= 0.9152$$

The volatility of the one-year spot rate is given by equation (6.36):

$$\sigma_R(0, 1) = \frac{1}{1}\sqrt{\left(0.4323^2 - 2(0.6)(0.001)(-0.0022)(0.4323) + 0.001^2(-0.0022)^2\right) 0.015}$$

$$= 0.0529$$

In order to be able to use this model, eight parameters in total need to be estimated; the parameters of the risk-adjusted process, the correlation between the state variables

FIGURE 6.11 Fong and Vasicek Pure Discount Bond Calculations

Inputs

α	2
γ	2
ξ	0.001
λ	0.2
η	0.1
ρ	0.6
r	0.08
r̄	0.095
v	0.015
v̄	0.015

Maturity	P(0,1)	R(0,1)	σR(0,1)	D(0,1)	From Selby and Strickland F(0,1)	From Selby and Strickland G(0,1)
1.0	0.9152	8.862%	5.29%	0.4323	−0.0022	−0.0540

and the coefficients of the factor risk premiums. FV do not discuss the issue of pricing derivatives within their framework. There is no known solution to pricing discount bond options and so numerical solutions must be employed. Clewlow and Strickland (1996) significantly extend the analysis of FV and show how Monte Carlo techniques can be efficiently employed to price discount bond options and a wide range of other term structure derivatives.

Longstaff and Schwartz (1992). Longstaff and Schwartz (1992) (LS) develop a two-factor, stochastic volatility interest rate model for the term structure. The model originates from a general equilibrium framework, but the short rate r is effectively defined by $r = \alpha x + \beta y$ with $\alpha \neq \beta; x$ and y follow the processes defined below. It follows that the short rate volatility v is given by $v = \alpha^2 x + \beta^2 y$. The state variables x and y follow the stochastic differential equations.

$$\begin{aligned} dx &= (\gamma - \delta x)\,dt + \sqrt{x}\,dz_1 \\ dy &= (\eta - \theta y)\,dt + \sqrt{y}\,dz_2 \end{aligned} \tag{6.37}$$

Combining equations (6.37) with the identity for r and v allows Longstaff and Schwartz to write down the processes for r and v (although they are not as intuitive as those for x and y). The resulting joint process for the dynamics of the short rate and the volatility of the short rate (or of the original state variables) allows the authors to arrive at closed-form solutions for the prices of pure discount bonds. Discount bond prices, when expressed in terms of r and v, take the form:

$$P(t, s) = \exp(G(t, s) + C(t, s)r + D(t, s)v) \tag{6.38}$$

where

$$\begin{aligned} \tau &= s - t \\ G(t, s) &= \kappa\tau + 2\gamma \ln A(t, s) + 2\eta \ln B(t, s) \\ A(t, s) &= \frac{2\phi}{(\delta + \phi)(e^{\phi\tau} - 1) + 2\phi} \\ B(t, s) &= \frac{2\psi}{(\theta + \psi)(e^{\psi\tau} - 1) + 2\psi} \\ C(t, s) &= \frac{\alpha\phi(e^{\psi\tau} - 1)B(t, s) - \beta\psi(e^{\phi\tau} - 1)A(t, s)}{\phi\psi(\beta - \alpha)} \\ D(t, s) &= \frac{\psi(e^{\phi\tau} - 1)A(\tau) - \phi(e^{\psi\tau} - 1)B(t, s)}{\phi\psi(\beta - \alpha)} \end{aligned}$$

and where

$$\begin{aligned} \phi &= \sqrt{2\alpha + \delta^2} \\ \psi &= \sqrt{2\beta + \theta^2} \\ \kappa &= \gamma(\delta + \phi) + \eta(\theta + \psi) \end{aligned}$$

The expression for the term structure of spot yield volatility implied by the model depends on the parameters of the two factors, allowing a greater variety of permissible volatility structures than single-factor models:

$$\sigma_R(t,s) = \frac{1}{\tau}\sqrt{\left(\frac{\alpha\beta\psi^2(e^{\phi\tau}-1)^2A^2(t,s)-\alpha\beta\phi^2(e^{\psi\tau}-1)^2B^2(t,s)}{\phi^2\psi^2(\beta-\alpha)}\right)r + \left(\frac{\beta\phi^2(e^{\psi\tau}-1)^2B^2(t,s)-\alpha\psi^2(e^{\phi\tau}-1)^2A^2(t,s)}{\phi^2\psi^2(\beta-\alpha)}\right)\nu} \tag{6.39}$$

Longstaff and Schwartz are also able to derive closed-form solutions for European discount bond options. The value of a call option is a complicated expression involving the solution of the bivariate non-central chi-square distribution function, Ψ:

$$c(t,T,s) = P(t,s)\Psi(\theta_1,\theta_2;4\gamma,4\eta,\omega_1,\omega_2) - KP(t,T)\Psi(\theta_3,\theta_4;4\gamma,4\eta,\omega_3,\omega_4) \tag{6.40}$$

where

$$\theta_1 = \frac{4\zeta\phi^2}{\alpha(e^{\phi(T-t)}-1)^2A(t,s)}, \qquad \theta_2 = \frac{4\zeta\psi^2}{\beta(e^{\psi(T-t)}-1)^2B(t,s)}$$

$$\theta_3 = \frac{4\zeta\phi^2}{\alpha(e^{\phi(T-t)}-1)^2A(t,T)}, \qquad \theta_4 = \frac{4\zeta\psi^2}{\beta(e^{\psi(T-t)}-1)^2B(t,T)}$$

$$\omega_1 = \frac{4\phi e^{\phi(T-t)}A(t,s)(\beta r-\nu)}{\alpha(\beta-\alpha)(e^{\phi(T-t)}-1)A(t,T-s)}, \qquad \omega_2 = \frac{4\psi e^{\psi(T-t)}B(t,s)(\nu-\alpha r)}{\beta(\beta-\alpha)(e^{\psi(T-t)}-1)B(t,T-s)}$$

$$\omega_3 = \frac{4\phi e^{\phi(T-t)}A(t,T)(\beta r-\nu)}{\alpha(\beta-\alpha)(e^{\phi(T-t)}-1)}, \qquad \omega_4 = \frac{4\psi e^{\psi(T-t)}B(t,T)(\nu-\alpha r)}{\beta(\beta-\alpha)(e^{\psi(T-t)}-1)}$$

$$\zeta = \kappa(s-T) + 2\gamma\ln A(t,s-T) + 2\eta\ln B(t,s-T) - \ln K$$

Example : Longstaff and Schwartz

We price a one-year pure discount bond with the following parameter values:

$$\alpha = 0.0024, \quad \beta = 0.0655, \quad \gamma = 1.0000, \quad \delta = 0.0164$$

$$\eta = 1.000, \quad \theta = 1.1457, \quad r = 0.0672, \quad \nu = 0.0008$$

Figure 6.12 illustrates the calculations:

$$\phi = \sqrt{2(0.0024) + 0.0164^2} = 0.0712$$

$$\psi = \sqrt{2(0.0655) + 1.1457^2} = 1.2015$$

$$\kappa = 1.0000(0.0164 + 0.0712) + 1.000(1.1457 + 1.2015) = 2.4348$$

$$A(0,1) = \frac{2(0.0712)}{(0.0164+0.0712)(e^{0.0712(1)}-1)+2(0.0712)} = 0.9566$$

$$B(0,1) = \frac{2(1.2015)}{(1.1457+1.2015)(e^{1.2015(1)}-1)+2(1.2015)} = 0.3057$$

$$C(0,1) = \frac{(0.0024)(0.0712)(e^{1.2015(1)}-1)(0.3057) - 0.0655(1.2015)(e^{0.0712(1)}-1)(0.9566)}{(0.0712)(1.2015)(0.0655-0.0024)}$$

$$= -1.0067$$

FIGURE 6.12 Longstaff and Schwartz Pure Discount Bond Calculations

Process Parameters		Maturities	
		T	1
		S	5
r	0.0672	A	0.9566
v	0.0008	B	0.3057
		C	–1.0067
α	0.0024	D	6.3369
β	0.0655	G	–0.0243
γ	1.0000		
δ	0.0164	P(0,1)	0.9168
η	1.0000	R(0,1)	8.683%
θ	1.1457		
			0.0016
φ	0.0712		0.3259
ψ	1.201511	σR(0,1)	1.91%
κ	2.434808		

$$D(0,1) = \frac{1.2015(e^{0.0712(1)} - 1)0.9566 - 0.712(e^{1.2015(1)} - 1)0.3057}{(0.0712)(1.2015)(0.0655 - 0.0024)} = 6.3369$$

$$G(0,1) = 2.4348(1) + 2(1)\ln(0.9566) + 2(1)\ln(0.3057) = -0.0243$$

$$P(0,1) = \exp(-0.0243 + (-1.0067)(0.0672) + 6.3369(0.0008)) = 0.9168$$

The one-year spot yield volatility is given by

$$\sigma_R(0,1) = \frac{1}{1}\sqrt{\left(\frac{\left\{\begin{array}{l}(0.0024)(0.0655)1.2015^2(e^{0.0712(1)} - 1)^2 0.9566^2\\ -(0.0024)(0.0655)0.0712^2(e^{1.2015(1)} - 1)^2 0.3057^2\end{array}\right\}}{(0.0712)^2(1.2015)^2(0.0655 - 0.0024)}\right)0.0672 + \left(\frac{\left\{\begin{array}{l}0.0655(0.0712)^2(e^{1.2015(1)} - 1)^2(0.3057)^2\\ -(0.0024)(1.2015)^2(e^{0.0712(1)} - 1)^2 0.9566^2\end{array}\right\}}{(0.0712)^2(1.2015)^2(0.0655 - 0.0024)}\right)0.0008}$$

$$= 0.0191$$

The Term Structure Consistent Approach

Although the approach just described to pricing interest rate derivatives has the important advantage that all interest rate derivatives are valued on a common basis, it has the severe disadvantage that the term structures provide a limited family which do not correctly price many traded bonds.

By valuing interest rate derivatives with reference to a theoretical yield curve rather than the actually observed curve, the traditional models produce contingent claims prices that disregard key market information affecting the valuation of any interest rate derivative security. Many models currently appearing in the literature are what we call "term structure consistent models", and an underlying motivation for the models has been to provide a unifying framework; unifying in both the sense of using as much market data as possible to build the models, and in trying to price and hedge the whole range of interest rate dependent securities consistently within the same set of model assumptions. These are the models that we now go on to study.

6.7 SUMMARY

In this chapter we have introduced models for pricing interest rate derivatives. We started by presenting a brief survey of the most common interest rate instruments, describing the composition of yield curves of rates and rate volatilities, and showing how a number of important interest rate derivatives can be viewed as portfolios of pure discount bond options. We have shown how the Black formula can be applied to interest rate options, but that it leads to an *ad hoc* pricing approach as different assumptions are made for different products. In the last part of the chapter we have presented a number of one- and two-factor traditional term structure models and described their use for pricing discount bond options.

ENDNOTES

1. See Strickland (1992b) for details and an empirical analysis of this contract.
2. In other types of swaptions an investor would exercise into an already existing swap, i.e. for the example just given, exercising the option after one year will result in obtaining a swap which now only has two years to go.
3. We are assuming that the reset dates are all equally spaced. The following analysis is easily generalised by defining $\Delta\tau_i = t_i - t_{i-1}$ instead of the fixed length $\Delta\tau$.
4. This is known as the "pull-to-par" effect and describes the fact that the uncertainty of the bond price declines as the bond approaches maturity. At the maturity date the bond equals its face value.
5. See Strickland (1996a,b) for an analysis of these models from the perspective of modelling the term structure and pricing interest rate derivatives. See also Courtadon (1982), Dothan (1977) and Merton (1973) for other one-factor term structure models.
6. See, for example, Chan *et al.* (1992).

APPENDIX 6.1 *F* AND *G* FUNCTIONS FOR FONG AND VASICEK MODEL

$$F(t,s) = -\frac{2i\alpha\kappa\delta}{\xi^2}e^{-\alpha\tau} + \frac{2\alpha\sum_{j=1}^{2}K_j e^{-\beta_j\alpha\tau}\left(\beta_j M(d_j, e_j, i\kappa e^{-\alpha\tau}) + i\kappa e^{-\alpha\tau}\frac{d_j}{e_j}M(d_j+1, e_j+1, i\kappa e^{-\alpha\tau})\right)}{\sum_{j=1}^{2}K_j e^{-\beta_j\alpha\tau}M(d_j, e_j, i\kappa e^{-\alpha\tau})}$$

where

$$\tau = s - t$$

$$\kappa = \frac{\xi}{\alpha^2}\sqrt{1-\rho^2}$$

$$\delta = \frac{1}{2} - \frac{i}{2}\frac{\rho}{\sqrt{1-\rho^2}}$$

$$d_j = \frac{1}{2}e_j - \frac{i}{2}\frac{\rho}{\sqrt{1-\rho^2}}\left(\frac{\xi}{\alpha^2}(1-\alpha\lambda) - \rho(\theta-1)\right) \quad \text{for } j = 1, 2$$

$$e_j = 2\beta_j - \theta + 1$$

$$\beta_1 = \beta$$

$$\beta_2 = \theta - \beta$$

$$i = \sqrt{-1}$$

and where

$$\beta = \frac{1}{2}\theta - \frac{1}{2}\sqrt{\theta^2 - \frac{\xi^2}{\alpha^4} + 2\lambda\frac{\xi^2}{\alpha^3}}$$

$$\theta = \frac{\gamma + \xi\eta}{\alpha} + \frac{\rho\xi}{\alpha^2}$$

The constants K_1 and K_2 are chosen to satisfy the boundary condition $F(0) = 0$. The function M is the confluent hypergeometric function with

$$M(d, e, z) = 1 + \sum_{n=1}^{\infty}\frac{d(d+1)\ldots(d+n)z^n}{e(e+1)\ldots(e+n)n!}$$

The expression for G is found as the solution to

$$G(\tau) = -\alpha\bar{r}\int_t^s D(u)du + \gamma\bar{v}\int_t^s F(u)du$$

7

Term Structure Consistent Models

7.1 INTRODUCTION

TERM structure consistent models set out to model the dynamics of the entire term structure in a way that is automatically consistent with the initial (observed) market data. We can further subdivide models in this approach into those that fit the term structure of interest rates only, and those that fit both the term structure of rates and the term structure of rate volatilities. Models that do not fit the volatility structure have them determined by the parameters of the model. There are two basic ways of achieving this goal. One is to specify a process for the short rate and then increase the parameterisation of the model by using time-dependent factors until all initial market data can be returned. The second starts by specifying the initial yield curve and its volatility structure and then to determine a drift structure that makes the model arbitrage free. The remainder of the book shows how to implement derivative pricing under both of these approaches. We will assume that the user has previously determined the term structure of interest rates and the volatility structure where appropriate.

Although the list of models that we look at in this chapter is by no means exhaustive, anecdotal evidence suggests that they are currently the most widely used models by practitioners and academics. We start our analysis of these models by looking at those models which have a degree of analytical tractability. These models are popular with the practitioner community because of their ease of calibration.

7.2 HO AND LEE (1986)

Ho and Lee (1986) (HL) were the first authors to develop a model consistent with the initial yield curve. Although originally developed in a discrete binomial framework starting from the observed structure of discount bond prices, the model has been shown to have plenty of analytical tractability, for example, the continuous time limit of the short rate is given by

$$dr = \theta(t)\,dt + \sigma\,dz \tag{7.1}$$

where $\theta(t)$ represents a time-dependent drift reflecting the slope of the initial forward rate curve and the volatility parameter of the short-rate process:

$$\theta(t) = \frac{\partial f(0,t)}{\partial t} + \sigma^2 t \tag{7.2}$$

where the partial derivative denotes the slope of the initial forward curve at maturity t. It is this time-dependent function that allows the model to return the observed bond prices. The model is single factor and similar to Merton (1973) and Ingersoll (1987); there is no mean reversion and interest rates can become negative with positive probability.

7.2.1 Term Structure of Volatility

As there is no dependence of the drift on the level of the short rate, the volatility structure for spot and forward rates is determined by the constant σ.

$$\sigma_R(t, s) = \sigma \tag{7.3}$$

7.2.2 Evaluating the Future Discount Function *P(T, s)*

Another analytical result relates future bond prices at time $T \geq t$ to the current term structure, $\{P(t, s) : s \geq T \geq t\}$ and the level of the short rate at time T:

$$P(T, s) = A(T, s)e^{-B(T,s)r(T)} \tag{7.4}$$

where

$$B(T, s) = (s - T)$$

$$\ln A(T, s) = \ln \frac{P(t, s)}{P(t, T)} - B(T, s)\frac{\partial \ln P(t, T)}{\partial T} - \frac{1}{2}\sigma^2(T - t)B(T, s)^2$$

and where $r(T)$ denotes the level of the short rate at time T. This result can be useful for performing Monte Carlo simulation or building trees for the short rate, as often we can terminate the simulation or the tree-building at the end of the life of the derivative rather than the instrument underlying the derivative — see Chapter 9.

Example : Calculation of *P(T, s)*

Assume that the term structure is flat at 5 per cent with continuous compounding and the short rate volatility $\sigma = 1$ per cent. We price a bond with four years remaining maturity in one year's time. We further assume that the short rate in one year, $r(1)$, is also 5 per cent. Figure 7.1 illustrates the calculations. $T = 1$, $s = 5$.

The market prices of the one- and five-year maturing discount bonds (assuming 5 per cent yields) are given by

$$P(0, 5) = e^{-0.05(5)} = 0.7788$$

$$P(0, 1) = e^{-0.05(1)} = 0.9512$$

The price of the bond in one year is therefore given by

$$P(1, 5) = A(1, 5)e^{-B(1,5)r(1)}$$

where

$$B(1, 5) = (5 - 1) = 4$$

$$\ln A(1, 5) = \ln \frac{P(0, 5)}{P(0, 1)} - B(1, 5)\frac{\partial \ln P(0, 1)}{\partial t} - \frac{1}{2}\sigma^2(1)B(1, 5)^2$$

FIGURE 7.1 Calculations for Ho and Lee Model

	maturity	rate	pdb price		
				B(1,5)	4.00
	0.00	5.00%	1.0000		
				slope	–0.05
	0.90	5.00%	0.9560	lnA(1,5)	–0.0008
T	1.00	5.00%	0.9512		
	1.10	5.00%	0.9465	**P(1,5)**	**0.8181**
s	5.00	5.00%	0.7788		
				c(0,1,5)	
	σ	1.00%			
				K	0.8187
				d1	0.0200
				d2	–0.0200
				σp	0.0400
				c(0,1,5)	**0.0124**

We approximate the slope

$$\frac{\partial \ln P(t,T)}{\partial T} \quad \text{by} \quad \frac{\ln P(t,T+\Delta t) - \ln P(t,T-\Delta t)}{2\Delta t}$$

choosing Δt to be 0.1 year.

$$\frac{\ln P(0,1.10) - \ln P(0,0.90)}{0.2} = \frac{\ln(0.9465) - \ln(0.9560)}{0.2} = -0.05$$

$$\ln A(1,5) = \ln\frac{0.7788}{0.9512} - 4(-0.05) - \frac{1}{2}(0.01)^2(1)4^2 = -0.0008$$

Therefore the bond price is

$$P(1,5) = e^{-0.0008}e^{-4(0.05)} = 0.8181$$

7.2.3 Pricing of European Call and Put Options on Pure Discount Bonds

Because the volatility of the short rate does not depend on its level the model is a normal model for interest rates and so bond prices are lognormally distributed. It should therefore not be surprising to find that prices of T-maturity European call and put options on a s-maturity pure discount bond are given by the modified Black and Scholes (1973) formulae:

$$c(t,T,s) = P(t,s)N(d_1) - KP(t,T)N(d_2) \tag{7.5}$$

$$p(t,T,s) = KP(t,T)N(-d_2) - P(t,s)N(-d_1) \tag{7.6}$$

where

$$d_1 = \frac{\ln(P(t,s)/KP(t,T))}{\sigma_P} + \frac{\sigma_P}{2}$$
$$d_2 = d_1 - \sigma_P$$
$$\sigma_P = \sigma(s-T)\sqrt{T-t}$$

Example : European Option Pricing Calculations

Assume that the term structure is flat at 5 per cent with continuous compounding and that the short rate volatility is 1 per cent per annum. We price a one-year European call option on a five-year pure discount bond struck at the forward bond price. The calculations are shown in Figure 7.1.

The market prices of the one- and five-year pure discount bonds are given by

$$P(0,1) = e^{-0.05(1)} = 0.9512$$
$$P(0,5) = e^{-0.05(5)} = 0.7788$$

The strike price of the option is the forward bond price:

$$K = \frac{P(0,5)}{P(0,1)} = \frac{0.7788}{0.9512} = 0.8187$$
$$\sigma_P = 0.01(5-1)\sqrt{1} = 0.01(4)\sqrt{1} = 0.04$$
$$d_1 = \frac{\ln\left(\frac{0.7788}{(0.8187)(0.9512)}\right)}{0.04} + \frac{0.04}{2}$$
$$= 0.02$$
$$d_2 = 0.02 - 0.04 = -0.02$$
$$c(0,1,5) = 0.7788 \times N(0.02) - 0.8187 \times 0.9512 \times N(-0.02)$$
$$= 0.0124$$

7.2.4 Calibrating Ho and Lee to Market Interest Rate Options Data

The simple structure of this model allows us to illustrate how models with closed form solutions can be calibrated to interest rate options data.

The HL model involves only one volatility parameter and, like Black–Scholes, it can be inferred from the market prices of actively traded interest rate options. Suppose, for example, that we have a set of M pure discount bond put options, the market price of which we denote by $market_i$ $(i = 1, \ldots M)$. One way to calibrate the model is to minimise the following function with respect to the parameter σ:

$$\underset{\sigma}{Minimise} \sqrt{\sum_{i=1}^{M} \left(\frac{model_i(\sigma) - market_i}{market_i}\right)^2} \tag{7.7}$$

where $model_i(\sigma)$ is the model price of the ith option, obtained by applying equation (7.6). The optimisation involves searching over all possible values of the parameter σ. The value which minimises this function is the parameter that best calibrates the model to the market for our choice of function to be minimised. Obviously if $M > 1$ then the model will not fit all of the option prices exactly for one choice of σ and we call calibration of this form "best fit". Recall from Chapter 6 that interest rate caps can be expressed as European put options on pure discount bonds. Therefore, if we know the prices of caps we can imply the HL volatility parameter by using equation (7.6).

Example : Calibrating Ho and Lee to an Individual Caplet

One problem with calibrating term structure consistent models with market caps data is that the quotes obtainable from brokers are not cash prices, but instead are Black volatilities. The first step in the calibration procedure, therefore, is to obtain cash prices from the quoted volatilities via equation (6.15). Table 7.1 contains quoted Black volatilities for US dollar caps on 21 January 1995. The data applies to caplets which mature on 21 March 1995, 21 June 1995, 21 September 1995, etc. Each caplet has a cap rate of 7 per cent, the resets are at quarterly intervals, and we have normalised the principal amount underlying each cap to be $L = 1$.

Figure 7.2 shows the cash prices calculated from these Black volatilities. The Black volatilities refer to the individual caplets. Recall from Chapter 6 that Black's model applied to the caplet covering the period from $k\Delta\tau$ to $(k+1)\Delta\tau$ is given by equation (6.15), therefore for a caplet covering the period from 21 March 1995 to 21 June 1995 (assuming the cap rate is 7 per cent) we have

$$\begin{aligned}
\sigma &= 0.1525 \\
T - t &= 0.16 \text{ years} \\
s - t &= 0.41 \text{ years} \\
P(0, T) &= 0.9898 \\
P(0, s) &= 0.9733 \\
R(0, T) &= -\frac{1}{T}\ln P(0, T) = \frac{-1}{0.16}\ln(0.9898) = 6.35 \text{ per cent}
\end{aligned}$$

Recall that the underlying variable in the Black model applied to a caplet is the forward rate applicable to the caplet.

$$f(0, T, s) = \frac{-1}{0.25}\ln\left(\frac{0.9733}{0.9898}\right) = 6.71 \text{ per cent}$$

We can now apply Black's formula with $K = 0.07$:

$$d_1 = \frac{\ln\left(\dfrac{0.0671}{0.07}\right) + \dfrac{0.1525^2}{2}(0.16)}{0.1525\sqrt{0.16}} = -0.6513$$

$$d_2 = -0.6513 - 0.1525\sqrt{0.16} = -0.7126$$

TABLE 7.1 US Dollar Cap Data for 21 January 1995

Caplet maturity	Cap vol. Black (1976)
	(%)
21 Jan 95	
21 Mar 95	15.25
21 Jun 95	17.25
21 Sep 95	17.25
21 Dec 95	17.50
21 Mar 96	18.00
21 Jun 96	18.00
21 Sep 96	18.00
21 Dec 96	18.00
21 Mar 97	17.75
21 Jun 97	17.50
21 Sep 97	17.50
21 Dec 97	17.50
21 Mar 98	17.25
21 Jun 98	17.25

FIGURE 7.2 Recovering Cash Prices from Black (1976) Volatilities

Date 21 Jan 95

Cap Rate 7.00%
Principal 1
Face Value Bond **1.0175**

Caplet Maturity	Maturity in Years	Cap Vol Black 76	PDB Price	Spot	Forward Price	Cap Price (Black 76) cash
21 Jan 95	0.00		1.0000			
21 Mar 95	0.16	15.25%	0.9898	0.0635	0.0671	0.0002
21 Jun 95	0.41	17.25%	0.9733	0.0654	0.0738	0.0015
21 Sep 95	0.67	17.25%	0.9555	0.0683	0.0781	0.0037
21 Dec 95	0.92	17.50%	0.9370	0.0711	0.0814	0.0067
21 Mar 96	1.16	18.00%	0.9182	0.0733	0.0816	0.0098
21 Jun 96	1.42	18.00%	0.8996	0.0747	0.0817	0.0129
21 Sep 96	1.67	18.00%	0.8815	0.0756	0.0816	0.0160
21 Dec 96	1.92	18.00%	0.8637	0.0764	0.0818	0.0192
21 Mar 97	2.16	17.75%	0.8462	0.0772	0.0810	0.0223
21 Jun 97	2.42	17.50%	0.8292	0.0775	0.0810	0.0254
21 Sep 97	2.67	17.50%	0.8126	0.0778	0.0810	0.0284
21 Dec 97	2.92	17.50%	0.7963	0.0781	0.0815	0.0316
21 Mar 98	3.16	17.25%	0.7803	0.0784	0.0809	0.0346
21 Jun 98	3.42		0.7647			

And so the caplet value is given by equation (6.15), i.e.:

$$\text{caplet}(0, 0.16, 0.41) = 0.9898[0.0671 \times N(-0.6513) - 0.07 \times N(-0.7126)]0.25$$
$$= 0.0002$$

The rest of the individual caplet prices are worked out in the same way, and are shown in Figure 7.2. We can now calibrate the HL model to these cash prices. Recall from Chapter 6 that the price of the caplet covering the period from $k\Delta\tau$ to $(k+1)\Delta\tau$ is equivalent to a put option with maturity $k\Delta\tau$ on a pure discount bond with maturity $(k+1)\Delta\tau$ when the face value of the bond is $L(1+R_{\text{cap}}\Delta\tau)$ and the strike price is L and so we can apply equation (7.6). Figure 7.3 illustrates the calculations.

In this example we have the face value of the bond underlying the option, $L(1+R_{\text{cap}}\Delta\tau)$, is equal to

$$1(1 + 0.07 \times 0.25) = 1.0175$$

For the first caplet we have $T = 0.16$ and $s = 0.41$, with

$$P(t, T) = 0.9898$$
$$P(t, s) = 0.9733$$

Therefore apply equation (7.6) with

$$T - t = 0.16$$
$$s - t = 0.41$$
$$P(t, s) = 0.9733 \times 1.0175$$

FIGURE 7.3 Results of Ho and Lee Calibration to Caps Data

Date	21 Jan 95							
					Ho and Lee Calibration			
Cap Rate		7.00%						
Principal		1						
Face Value Bond		**1.0175**			**Overall Volatility**			
Caplet Maturity	Maturity in Years	Cap Vol Black 76	PDB Price	Cap Price (Black 76) cash	HL vol **0.947%**	HL Price	Diff. (HL-B'76)
21 Jan 95	0.00		1.0000				
21 Mar 95	0.16	15.25%	0.9898	0.0002	0.95%	0.0002	0.0041
21 Jun 95	0.41	17.25%	0.9733	0.0015	0.95%	0.0014	0.0005
21 Sep 95	0.67	17.25%	0.9555	0.0037	0.95%	0.0036	0.0005
21 Dec 95	0.92	17.50%	0.9370	0.0067	0.95%	0.0065	0.0005
21 Mar 96	1.16	18.00%	0.9182	0.0098	0.95%	0.0095	0.0009
21 Jun 96	1.42	18.00%	0.8996	0.0129	0.95%	0.0124	0.0014
21 Sep 96	1.67	18.00%	0.8815	0.0160	0.95%	0.0153	0.0020
21 Dec 96	1.92	18.00%	0.8637	0.0192	0.95%	0.0182	0.0027
21 Mar 97	2.16	17.75%	0.8462	0.0223	0.95%	0.0210	0.0033
21 Jun 97	2.42	17.50%	0.8292	0.0254	0.95%	0.0238	0.0038
21 Sep 97	2.67	17.50%	0.8126	0.0284	0.95%	0.0265	0.0044
21 Dec 97	2.92	17.50%	0.7963	0.0316	0.95%	0.0294	0.0050
21 Mar 98	3.16	17.25%	0.7803	0.0346	0.95%	0.0321	0.0054
21 Jun 98	3.42		0.7647				
					Sum of squared errors		0.03458

$$P(t, T) = 0.9898$$

$$K = L = 1$$

The volatility that equates the HL price with the Black price is 0.917 per cent.

Figure 7.3 shows that the single volatility that "best-fits" all the caplets is 0.947 per cent. This figure is obtained by minimising the sum of squared percentage differences across all the individual caplets.

Although the HL model is analytically tractable for pricing discount bond options, we need to implement numerical procedures for pricing options with early exercise features or European options that involve complicated terminal pay-offs. We will present these procedures in Chapter 9.

7.3 HULL AND WHITE MODEL

Another model which has a great level of analytical tractability and is currently popular amongst practitioners is the Hull and White (1993) (HW) model. The defining stochastic differential equation for this model is given by

$$dr = [\theta(t) - \alpha r]\, dt + \sigma\, dz \tag{7.8}$$

This model also implies normally distributed interest rates and lognormal bond prices and, due to the similarity of equation (7.8) to equations (6.20) and (7.1) can be thought of as "Vasicek fitted to the term structure" or "HL with mean reversion" with the parameter α representing the speed of mean reversion. The single time-dependent parameter in the drift again allows the model to fit the observed term structure. This parameter is now given by

$$\theta(t) = \frac{\partial f(0, t)}{\partial t} + \alpha f(0, t) + \frac{\sigma^2}{2\alpha}(1 - e^{-2\alpha t}) \tag{7.9}$$

7.3.1 Term Structure of Volatility

Recall from Chapter 6 that the term structure of spot rate volatilities for the Vasicek model was determined by the short-rate volatility and mean reversion parameters. The HW model is the same model except that we have increased the parameterisation of the model by making the mean reversion level, scaled by its speed, $\theta(t)/\alpha$, time dependent. The volatility structure of spot rates is therefore again determined by both the volatility and rate of mean reversion of the short rate:

$$\sigma_R(t, s) = \frac{\sigma}{\alpha(s - t)}(1 - e^{-\alpha(s-t)}) \tag{7.10}$$

7.3.2 Evaluating the Future Discount Function *P(T, s)*

Future bond prices, at time T, dependent on the current term structure, the level of the short rate at time T, and the constant parameters of the short-rate process are given by

$$P(T, s) = A(T, s)e^{-B(T,s)r(T)} \tag{7.11}$$

where

$$B(T,s) = \frac{1}{\alpha}(1 - e^{-\alpha(s-T)})$$

$$\ln A(T,s) = \ln\frac{P(t,s)}{P(t,T)} - B(T,s)\frac{\partial \ln P(t,T)}{\partial T} - \frac{1}{4\alpha^3}\sigma^2(e^{-\alpha(s-t)} - e^{-\alpha(T-t)})^2(e^{2\alpha(T-t)} - 1)$$

and $r(T)$ the level of the short rate at time T.

Example : Calculation of *P(T, s)*

Assume that the term structure is flat at 5 per cent with continuous compounding. Assume further that the parameters describing the volatility structure are $\alpha = 10\%$ and $\sigma = 1\%$. We price a five-year maturity bond in one year's time, assuming that the short rate in one year's time is 5 per cent. Figure 7.4 presents the calculations:

$$T = 1, s = 5.$$

The market prices of the one- and five-year pure discount bonds are given by

$$P(0,1) = e^{-0.05(1)} = 0.9512$$

$$P(0,5) = e^{-0.05(5)} = 0.7788$$

$$P(1,5) = A(1,5)e^{-B(1,5)r(1)}$$

with $r(1) = 0.05$

$$B(1,5) = \frac{1}{0.1}(1 - e^{-0.1(5-1)}) = 3.30$$

FIGURE 7.4 Calculations for the Hull and White Model

	maturity	rate	pdb price		
				B(1,5)	3.30
	0.00	5.00%	1.0000	slope	−0.05
				lnA(1,5)	−0.03565
	0.90	5.00%	0.9560		
T	1.00	5.00%	0.9512	**P(1,5)**	**0.8183**
	1.10	5.00%	0.9465		
s	5.00	5.00%	0.7788	**c(0,1,5)**	
α		10.00%		K	0.8187
σ		1.00%			
				d1	0.0157
				d2	−0.0157
				σp	0.0314
				c(0,1,5)	**0.0098**

We approximate the slope

$$\frac{\partial \ln P(t,T)}{\partial T} \quad \text{by} \quad \frac{\ln P(t,T+\Delta t) - \ln P(t,T-\Delta t)}{2\Delta t}$$

choosing Δt to be 0.1 year.

$$\frac{\ln P(0,1.10) - \ln(0,0.90)}{0.2} = \frac{\ln(0.9465) - \ln(0.9560)}{0.2} = -0.05$$

$$\begin{aligned}\ln A(1,5) &= \ln\left(\frac{0.7788}{0.9512}\right) - 3.30(-0.05)\\ &\quad - \frac{1}{4(0.1)^3}0.01^2(e^{-0.1(5)} - e^{-0.1(1)})^2(e^{2(0.1)(1)} - 1)\\ &= -0.03565\end{aligned}$$

Therefore the bond price is given by

$$P(1,5) = e^{-0.03565}e^{-3.30(0.05)} = 0.8183$$

7.3.3 Pricing of European Call and Put Options on Pure Discount Bonds

The normally distributed interest rates implicit by the short rate process again lead to modified Black and Scholes (1973) formulas for prices of T-maturity European call and put options on a s-maturity pure discount bond, and are given by

$$c(t,T,s) = P(t,s)N(d_1) - KP(t,T)N(d_2) \tag{7.12}$$

$$p(t,T,s) = KP(t,T)N(-d_2) - P(t,s)N(-d_1) \tag{7.13}$$

where

$$d_1 = \frac{\ln(P(t,s)/KP(t,T))}{\sigma_P} + \frac{\sigma_P}{2}$$

$$d_2 = d_1 - \sigma_P$$

$$\sigma_P^2 = \frac{\sigma^2}{2\alpha^3}(1 - e^{-2\alpha(T-t)})(1 - e^{-\alpha(s-T)})^2$$

European options on coupon bonds can be valued using the decomposition of Jamshidian (1989).

Example : European Option Pricing Calculations

Assume a flat term structure of 5 per cent with continuous compounding, and with short rate parameters $\alpha = 10$ per cent and $\sigma = 1$ per cent. We price a one-year European call option on a five-year pure discount bond where the strike price of the option is the forward bond price. The calculations are shown in Figure 7.3. $T = 1$, $s = 5$.

The market prices of the one- and five-year pure discount bonds are given by

$$P(0,1) = e^{-0.05(1)} = 0.9512$$

$$P(0,5) = e^{-0.05(5)} = 0.7788$$

The strike price of the option is then

$$K = \frac{P(0,5)}{P(0,1)} = \frac{0.7788}{0.9512} = 0.8187$$

Equation (7.12) is applied resulting in

$$d_1 = \frac{\ln\left(\dfrac{0.7788}{(0.8187)(0.9512)}\right)}{0.0314} + \frac{0.0314}{2} = 0.0157$$
$$d_2 = 0.0157 - 0.0314 = -0.0157$$

where

$$\sigma_P = \sqrt{\frac{0.01^2}{2(0.1)^3}(1 - e^{-2(0.1)(1)})(1 - e^{-0.1(5-1)})^2} = 0.0314$$

which yields:

$$c(0,1,5) = 0.7788 \times N(0.0157) - 0.8187 \times 0.9512 \times N(-0.0157) = 0.0098$$

7.3.4 Calibrating Hull and White to Interest Rate Options Data

In contrast to the HL model, the HW spot rate volatility equation involves two parameters, α and σ: σ determines the overall volatility of the short rate, α determines the relative volatility of long and short rates. In order to calibrate the model to market prices we can follow the procedures outlined earlier for the HL model, but now best fit both α and σ simultaneously to market data. If we assume that we have the prices of M individual European pure discount bond put options we now minimise the following function:

$$\underset{\alpha,\sigma}{minimise} \sqrt{\sum_{i=1}^{M}\left(\frac{model_i(\alpha,\sigma) - market_i}{market_i}\right)^2} \tag{7.14}$$

where $model_i(\alpha, \sigma)$ is the option value derived from equation (7.13) with the parameter values α and σ.

Example : Calibrating Hull and White to an Individual Caplet

We calibrate the HW model to the caps data in Figure 7.2. For the first caplet we apply equation (7.13) with

$$T - t = 0.16$$
$$s - t = 0.41$$
$$P(t,T) = 0.9898$$
$$P(t,s) = 0.9733 \times 1.0175$$
$$K = L = 1$$
$$p(t,T,s) = 1 \times 0.9898 \times N(-d_2) - (0.9733 \times 1.0175) \times N(-d_1)$$

where

$$d_1 = \frac{\ln((0.9733 \times 1.0175)/(1 \times 0.9898))}{\sigma_P} + \frac{\sigma_P}{2}$$

$$d_2 = d_1 - \sigma_P$$

$$\sigma_P^2 = \frac{\sigma^2}{2\alpha^3}\left(1 - e^{-2\times 0.16\alpha}\right)\left(1 - e^{-\alpha(0.41-0.16)}\right)^2$$

with $\alpha = 0.10$ and $\sigma = 0.0116$ this implies a caplet value of 0.000227.

Figure 7.5 shows that the single volatility that "best-fits" all the caplets is $\alpha = -29.94$ and $\sigma = 0.0087$.

As with the HL model, numerical procedures are often required to price the majority of instruments which are traded in practice, and these procedures are presented in Chapter 9.

7.4 HULL AND WHITE — FITTING MARKET VOLATILITY DATA AND MORE GENERAL SPECIFICATIONS FOR THE SHORT-RATE VOLATILITY

The two models in the previous sections achieved consistency with the initial term structure by incorporating a time-dependent function in the drift and thus effectively increasing the parameterisation of the model until there are as many parameters as market bond prices. One extension to the HW model is to make the second drift parameter, the mean reversion rate, also time dependent, resulting in the following stochastic differential equation:

$$dr = [\theta(t) - \alpha(t)r]\,dt + \sigma\,dz \tag{7.15}$$

This extra time-dependent factor allows the model to also fit market volatility data. We assume that the market volatility function is known and we represent it in the familiar fashion, $\sigma_R(t, s)$, for the volatility of the s-maturity yield seen from date t. The model still results in normally distributed interest rates and we have the following analytical result.

7.4.1 Pricing of European Call and Put Options on Pure Discount Bonds

The price at time t of a T-maturity European call option on an s-maturity discount bond can be expressed by the modified Black–Scholes formula:

$$c(t, T, s) = P(t, s)N(d_1) - KP(t, T)N(d_2) \tag{7.16}$$

$$p(t, T, s) = KP(t, T)N(-d_2) - P(t, s)N(-d_1) \tag{7.17}$$

where

$$d_1 = \frac{\ln(P(t, s)/KP(t, T))}{\sigma_P} + \frac{\sigma_P}{2}$$

$$d_2 = d_1 - \sigma_P$$

$$\sigma_P^2 = [B(t, s) - B(t, T)]^2 \int_t^T \left[\frac{\sigma}{\partial B(t, \tau)/\partial \tau}\right]^2 d\tau$$

FIGURE 7.5 Results of Hull and White Calibration to Caps Data

Date	21 Jan 95						
			Calculations based on Δt=0.25			**Hull and White Calibration**	
Cap Rate		7.00%					
Principal		1				α	**–29.94%**
Face Value Bond		**1.0175**				σ	**0.87%**
Caplet Maturity	Maturity in Years	Cap Black Vol	PDB Price	Spot	Cap Price (Black 76) cash	HW Price	% Diff.
21 Jan 95	0.00		1.0000				
21 Mar 95	0.16	15.25%	0.9898	0.0635	0.000153	0.000155	0.000234
21 Jun 95	0.41	17.25%	0.9733	0.0654	0.001478	0.001444	0.000548
21 Sep 95	0.67	17.25%	0.9555	0.0683	0.003729	0.003668	0.000267
21 Dec 95	0.92	17.50%	0.9370	0.0711	0.006689	0.006597	0.000189
21 Mar 96	1.16	18.00%	0.9182	0.0733	0.009757	0.009598	0.000263
21 Jun 96	1.42	18.00%	0.8996	0.0747	0.012881	0.012657	0.000302
21 Sep 96	1.67	18.00%	0.8815	0.0756	0.016021	0.015738	0.000313
21 Dec 96	1.92	18.00%	0.8637	0.0764	0.019219	0.018893	0.000287
21 Mar 97	2.16	17.75%	0.8462	0.0772	0.022288	0.022017	0.000149
21 Jun 97	2.42	17.50%	0.8292	0.0775	0.025354	0.025220	0.000028
21 Sep 97	2.67	17.50%	0.8126	0.0778	0.028431	0.028492	0.000005
21 Dec 97	2.92	17.50%	0.7963	0.0781	0.031587	0.031901	0.000099
21 Mar 98	3.16	17.25%	0.7803	0.0784	0.034636	0.035371	0.000450
21 Jun 98	3.42		0.7647				
					Sum of squared errors		0.003133

The prices of the T and s maturity pure discount bonds are given by the market prices. The generalised duration measure can be recovered from observed market data via the formula:

$$B(t, s) = \frac{(s - t)R(t, s)\sigma_R(t, s)}{r\sigma} \tag{7.18}$$

The second extension to the basic model of equation (7.8) is to allow the volatility of the short rate to depend on the level of the rate. The general short-rate process can then be represented by an equation of the form:

$$dr = [\theta(t) - \alpha r]\, dt + \sigma r^{\beta}\, dz \tag{7.19}$$

for some β. Setting $\beta = \frac{1}{2}$ leads to a version of the Cox–Ingersoll–Ross (CIR) model which fits the initial term structure exactly. For $\beta \neq 0$ or $\frac{1}{2}$ the numerical procedures of Chapter 9 are needed to price all interest rate derivatives.

7.5 BLACK, DERMAN AND TOY

Black, Derman and Toy (1990) (BDT) developed a single-factor short-rate model to match the observed term structure of spot interest rate volatilities, as well as the term structure of interest rates, and which has proved popular with practitioners. As with the original HL, the model is developed algorithmically, describing the evolution of the entire term structure in a discrete-time binomial lattice framework. A binomial tree is constructed for the short rate in such a way that the tree automatically returns the observed yield function and the volatilities of different yields. In Chapter 8 we will show how to build these binomial trees.

Although this algorithmic construction means that the model is rather opaque with regard to its assumptions about the evolution of the short rate, several authors have shown that the implied continuous time limit of the BDT model, as we take the limit of the size of the time step to zero, is given by the following stochastic differential equation:

$$d \ln r(t) = \left[\theta(t) + \frac{\sigma'(t)}{\sigma(t)} \ln r(t)\right] dt + \sigma(t)\, dz \tag{7.20}$$

This representation of the model allows us to better understand the assumptions implicit in the model. The BDT model incorporates two independent functions of time, $\theta(t)$ and $\sigma(t)$, chosen so that the model fits the term structure of spot interest rates and the term structure of spot rate volatilities. In this model, changes in the short rate are lognormally distributed, with the resulting advantage that interest rates cannot become negative. Once $\theta(t)$ and $\sigma(t)$ are chosen, the future short-rate volatility, by definition, is entirely determined. An unfortunate consequence of the model is that for certain specifications of the volatility function $\sigma(t)$ the short rate can be mean-fleeing rather than mean-reverting. The model has the advantage that the volatility unit is a percentage, conforming with the market convention. Unfortunately, due to its lognormality, neither analytic solutions for the prices of bonds or the prices of bond options are available, and numerical procedures are required to derive the short-rate tree that correctly returns the market term structures — see Chapter 8.

Many practitioners choose to fit the rate structure only, holding the future short-rate volatility constant (see section 7.7 for a justification of this). The convergent limit therefore reduces to the following:

$$d \ln r = \theta(t)\, dt + \sigma\, dz \tag{7.21}$$

This process can be seen as a lognormal version of HL.

7.6 BLACK AND KARASINSKI

In the BDT model the mean reversion rate and the future volatility of the (log of the) short rate are intimately related and for certain specifications of the volatility curve we obtain mean-fleeing interest rates. Black and Karasinski (1991) (BK) propose a model with three independent functions of time which allows them to decouple the reversion rate and the short-rate volatility term which gives

$$d \ln r = [\theta(t) - \alpha(t) \ln r]\, dt + \sigma(t)\, dz \tag{7.22}$$

In their paper, they construct the three time-dependent functions to be consistent with the yield and volatility curves (as in HW) and the at-the-money differential cap curve. In order to construct a short-rate tree which is consistent with this extra data they need an extra degree of freedom in their tree over that of BDT. HW do this by using a trinomial tree, BK solve it by varying the spacing in the tree.

Again we can restrict the time-dependent functions α and σ to be constants, allowing a fit to only the term structure of rates.

$$d \ln r = [\theta(t) - \alpha \ln r]\, dt + \sigma\, dz \tag{7.23}$$

This short-rate specification can be seen as a lognormal version of the HW model. We will implement this model in Chapter 9.

7.7 A NOTE ON THE BEHAVIOUR OF THE VOLATILITY STRUCTURE FOR SINGLE-FACTOR MARKOVIAN SHORT-RATE MODELS

All of the models so far considered in this chapter are single-factor Markovian models of the short rate — the evolution of the short rate does not depend on its previous behaviour. These models have the unfortunate consequence that if they are fitted to the observed volatility structure then the volatility structure as well as the initial term structure is constrained to evolve through time. As an example, let us take the HW model fitted to both the observed yield and volatility curves (defined by equation (7.15)).

The s-maturity yield volatility is given by $\sigma_R(t, s)$. It can be shown that the spot rate yield volatilities at time $T(t \le T \le s)$, $\sigma_R(T, s)$, are constrained to be related to this initial level by the following relationship:[1]

$$\sigma_R(T, s) = \frac{\sigma}{(s-t)} \frac{[(s-t)\sigma_R(t, s) - (T-t)\sigma_R(t, T)]}{\left[(T-t)\dfrac{\partial \sigma_R(t, T)}{\partial T} + \sigma_R(t, T)\right]} \tag{7.24}$$

Therefore, the s-maturity yield volatility at time T is completely determined by the volatilities of the T-maturity and s-maturity yields at the initial time and the slope of the volatility curve at maturity T. Although we only have analytical results for this normal interest rate model, qualitatively this result holds for all one-factor Markovian models fitted exactly to the volatility structure by time-dependent parameters.

In order to illustrate the effect that this can have on derivative pricing, Figure 7.6 describes three initial volatility functions. The first, "Vasicek", has been generated by the Vasicek model (i.e. using equation (6.25)). The second, "flat" has the same initial slope as the first but "flattens" out a lot quicker, resulting in persistent volatility in the long end — which anecdotal evidence suggests is often seen in practice. The third is the "humped" volatility curve regularly reported in the caps market.

The equations describing all three volatility functions are then fed into equation (7.24). The Vasicek curve retains the same shape. However, the "flat" curve is constrained to evolve in a way which is described by Figure 7.7. Subsequent curves after the initial state — we plot every six months out to two years — are seen to lose the attenuation of the initial curve.

Figure 7.8 describes the evolution of the "humped" volatility curve. The initial hump is soon lost as we "ride down" the volatility curve.

For the reasons described in this section, many practitioners avoid fitting the initial volatility curve exactly when using the models so far described in this chapter, preferring to "best-fit" the volatility curve in some sense. For example, for the model used as the illustration of this section many practitioners find it better to restrict the model to the "one-time dependent" version of section (7.3) and chose α and σ so that the volatility structure is as close as possible to that implicit in market caps and swaption prices, without fitting it exactly. In this model, and all models where the volatility structure is described by constant parameters, the volatility structure remains stable through time.

FIGURE 7.6 Initial Volatility Curves

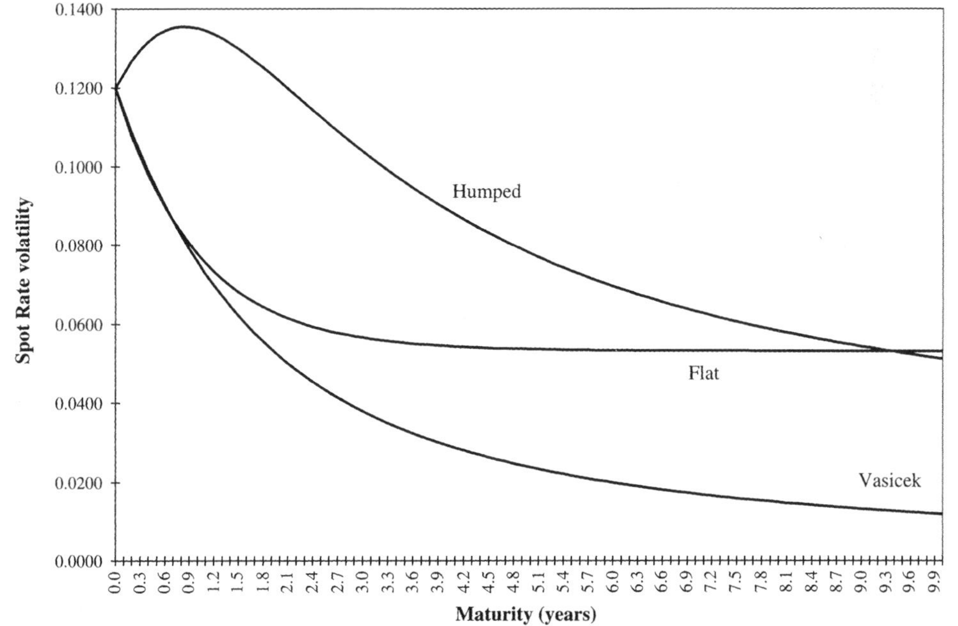

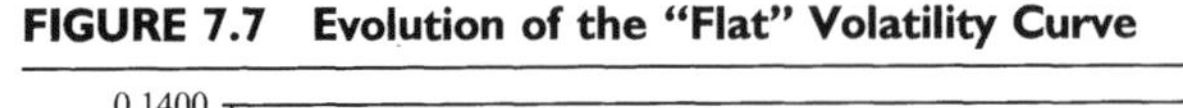

FIGURE 7.7 Evolution of the "Flat" Volatility Curve

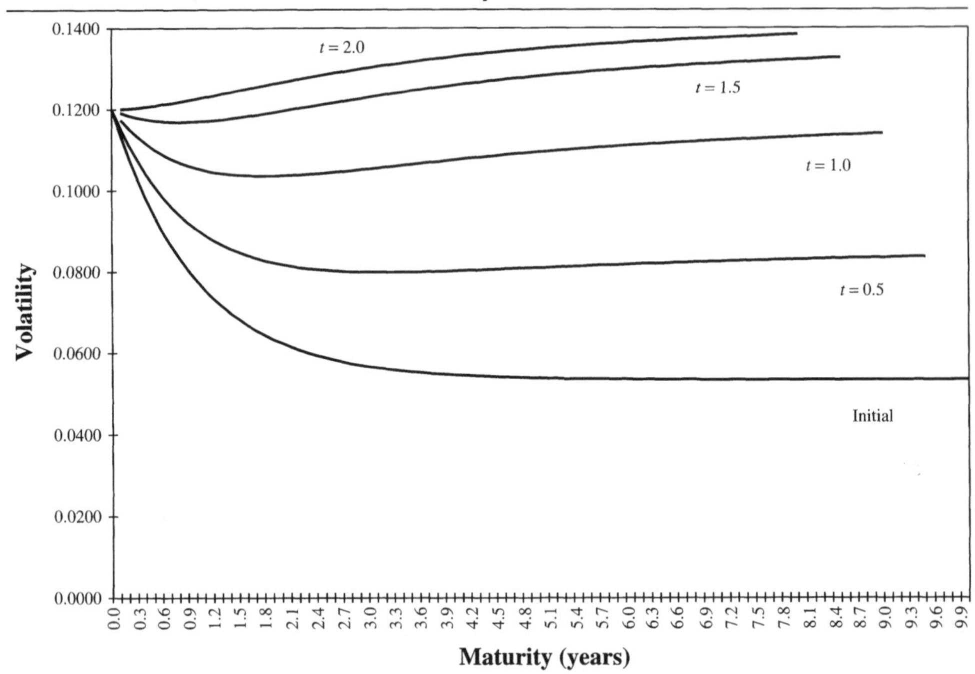

FIGURE 7.8 Evolution of the "Humped" Volatility Curve

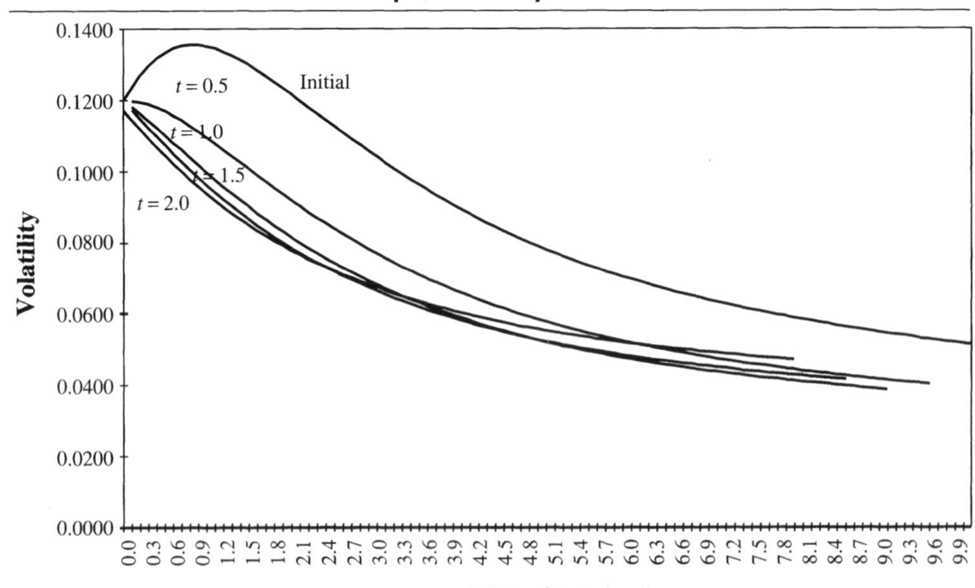

The single-factor models that we have analysed so far in this chapter have, as an underlying problem that they cannot generate a wide variety of term structures of volatility. The reason for this is that the stochastic structure of these models is quite simple. The following model is able to provide a richer volatility structure.

7.8 HULL AND WHITE — TWO-FACTOR MODEL

Recently, Hull and White (1994b) have developed a two-factor model which is partially analytically tractable. The defining stochastic differential equations are given by[2]

$$dr = [\theta(t) + u - \alpha r]\,dt + \sigma_1\,dz_1 \tag{7.25}$$

$$du = -bu\,dt + \sigma_2\,dz_2$$

where u can be interpreted as a random mean reversion level. The correlation between dz_1 and dz_2 is defined as ρ. The model is similar to the HW model discussed in section 7.3 with the time-dependent function, $\theta(t)$, allowing the model to fit the initially observed discount function. The extra flexibility in the drift term, introduced by the time-dependent parameter u, allows the model to provide a richer pattern of term structure movements and of possible volatility structures.

7.8.1 Term Structure of Volatility

The spot rate volatility structure for the Hull and White two-factor model is given by

$$\sigma_R(t, s) = \frac{1}{(s-t)}\sqrt{[(B(t, s)\sigma_1)^2 + (C(t, s)\sigma_2)^2 + 2\rho\sigma_1\sigma_2 B(t, s)C(t, s)]} \tag{7.26}$$

where

$$B(t, s) = \frac{1}{\alpha}(1 - e^{-\alpha(s-t)})$$

$$C(t, s) = \frac{1}{\alpha(\alpha - b)}e^{-\alpha(s-t)} - \frac{1}{b(\alpha - b)}e^{-b(s-t)} + \frac{1}{\alpha b}$$

Figure 7.9 shows a subset of possible volatility structures that can be obtained under this two-factor model. The model provides for a much greater variety of volatility structures than the one-factor models considered earlier, enabling us to fit both the "humped" volatility environments as well as the "persistent" environments.

7.8.2 Deriving the Future Discount Function *P(T, s)*

Under this formulation the future yield curve at time $T(t \leq T \leq s)$ can be calculated analytically from r, u and the constant parameters:

$$P(T, s) = A(T, s)e^{-r(T)B(T,s) - u(T)C(T,s)} \tag{7.27}$$

where

$$B(T, s) = \frac{1}{\alpha}(1 - e^{-\alpha(s-T)})$$

$$C(T, s) = \frac{1}{\alpha(\alpha - b)}e^{-\alpha(s-T)} - \frac{1}{b(\alpha - b)}e^{-b(s-T)} + \frac{1}{\alpha b}$$

FIGURE 7.9 Term Structures of Volatility in the Hull and White Two-factor Model

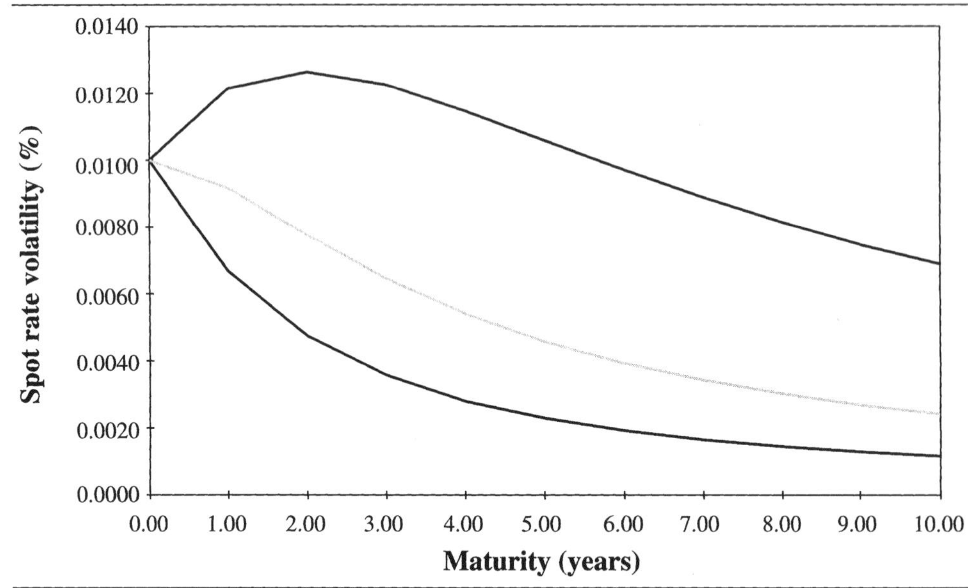

where $r(T)$ and $u(T)$ represent the level of the variables at time T. The function $A(T, s)$ is explicitly given in Appendix 7.1.

Example : Calculation of *P(T, s)*

We price a five-year pure discount bond after one year (i.e. four years remaining to maturity), with the following parameters for the processes $\alpha = 0.1$, $\sigma_1 = 0.01$, $u = 0.01$, $b = 1.40$, $\sigma_2 = 0.008$, and $\rho = 0.70$. The original term structure is flat at 5 per cent with continuous compounding. The levels for r and u after one year are assumed to remain at their initial levels. The calculations are shown in Figure 7.10.

$$T = 1$$

$$s = 5$$

$$r(1) = 0.05$$

$$u(1) = 0.01$$

$$B(1, 5) = \frac{1}{0.1}(1 - e^{-0.1(5-1)}) = 3.2968$$

$$B(0, 5) = \frac{1}{0.1}(1 - e^{-0.1(5)}) = 3.9347$$

$$B(0, 1) = \frac{1}{0.1}(1 - e^{-0.1(1)}) = 0.9516$$

FIGURE 7.10 Hull and White Two-factor Model Spreadsheet

Inputs									
				P(1,5)			**c(0,1,5)**	
α		10.00%						
σ1		1.00%		B(1,5)	3.2968		K	0.6442
u		0.0100		B(0,5)	3.9347			
b		1.40		B(0,1)	0.9516		U	2.2947
σ2		0.80%		C(1,5)	1.9886		V	0.1350
				C(0,5)	2.4777			
ρ		0.70		C(0,1)	0.3181		σp1	0.0010
				F(0,1)	0.0500		σp2	0.0003
maturity		rate	pdb price				σp3	0.0007
				γ1	0.3123			
	0.00	0.0500	1.0000	γ2	8.1266		σp	0.0449
				γ3	0.2988		d1	9.8150
T	**1.00**	0.0500	0.9512	γ4	0.0834		d2	9.7701
				γ5	5.0244			
	4.90	0.0500	0.7827	γ6	0.0235		**c(0,1,5)**	**0.0178**
s	**5.00**	0.0500	0.7788	η	0.0010			
	5.10	0.0500	0.7749					
				lnA(1,5)	−0.0362			
σR(0,5)		0.0110		**P(1,5)**	**0.8018**	**5.52%**		

$$C(1,5) = \frac{1}{0.1(0.1-1.40)}e^{-0.1(5-1)} - \frac{1}{1.40(0.1-1.40)}e^{-0.1(5-1)} + \frac{1}{0.1(1.40)} = 1.9886$$

$$C(0,5) = \frac{1}{0.1(0.1-1.40)}e^{-0.1(5)} - \frac{1}{1.40(0.1-1.40)}e^{-0.1(5)} + \frac{1}{0.1(1.40)} = 2.4777$$

$$C(0,1) = \frac{1}{0.1(0.1-1.40)}e^{-0.1(1)} - \frac{1}{1.40(0.1-1.40)}e^{-0.1(1)} + \frac{1}{0.1(1.40)} = 0.3181$$

$$\gamma_1 = \frac{e^{-(0.1+1.40)5}[e^{(0.1+1.40)(1)}-1]}{(0.1+1.40)(0.1-1.40)} - \frac{e^{-2(0.1)(5)}[e^{2(0.1)(1)}-1]}{2(0.1)(0.1-1.40)} = 0.3123$$

$$\gamma_2 = \frac{1}{0.1(1.40)}\left[0.3123 + 1.9886 - 2.4777 + \frac{1}{2}3.2968^2 - \frac{1}{2}3.9347^2 + \frac{1}{0.1} - \frac{e^{-0.1(5-1)} - e^{-0.1(5)}}{0.1^2}\right] = 8.1266$$

$$\gamma_3 = \frac{e^{-(0.1+1.40)(1)}-1}{(0.1-1.40)(0.1+1.40)} + \frac{e^{-2(0.1)(1)}-1}{2(0.1)(0.1-1.40)} = 0.2988$$

$$\gamma_4 = \frac{1}{0.1(1.40)}\left[0.2988 - 0.3181 - \frac{1}{2}(0.9516)^2 + \frac{1}{0.1} + \frac{e^{-0.1(1)}-1}{0.1^2}\right] = 0.0834$$

$$\gamma_5 = \frac{1}{1.40}\left[\frac{1}{2}(1.9886)^2 - \frac{1}{2}(2.4777)^2 + 8.1266\right] = 5.0244$$

$$\gamma_6 = \frac{1}{1.40}\left[0.0834 - \frac{1}{2}(0.3181)^2\right] = 0.0235$$

Therefore:

$$\begin{aligned}\eta &= \frac{(0.01)^2}{4(0.1)}(1 - e^{-2(0.1)(1)})(3.2968)^2 - 0.7(0.01)(0.008)\\ &\quad \times [(0.9516(0.3181)(3.2968) + 15.0306 - 7.9577]\\ &\quad - \tfrac{1}{2}(0.008)^2[(0.3181)^2(3.2968) + 9.6115 - 4.8733]\\ &= 0.0010\end{aligned}$$

$$\begin{aligned}P(0, 5) &= e^{-0.05(5)} = 0.7788\\ P(0, 1) &= e^{-0.05(1)} = 0.9512\\ F(0, 1) &= 0.05\end{aligned}$$

Implying

$$\ln A(1, 5) = \ln\left(\frac{0.7788}{0.9512}\right) + (3.2968)(0.05) - 0.0010 = -0.0362$$

Finally,

$$P(1, 5) = e^{-0.03621} e^{-0.05(3.2968)-(0.01)(1.9572)} = 0.8018$$

The volatility of a five-year yield is given by equation (7.26):

$$\begin{aligned}&\sigma_R(0, 5)\\ &= \tfrac{1}{5}\sqrt{((3.9347)(0.01))^2 + ((2.4777)(0.008))^2 + 2(0.7)(0.01)(0.008)(3.9347)(2.4777)}\\ &= 0.0110\end{aligned}$$

7.8.3 Pricing of European Call and Put Options on Pure Discount Bonds

European discount bond option prices are given by the modified Black–Scholes formulas of the one factor HW model, equations (7.12) and (7.13), with a more complicated expression for σ_P:

$$\begin{aligned}\sigma_P^2 &= \frac{\sigma_1^2}{2\alpha}B(T, s)^2(1 - e^{-2\alpha(T-t)}) + \sigma_2^2\left[\frac{U^2}{2\alpha}(e^{2\alpha(T-t)} - 1) + \frac{V^2}{2b}(e^{2b(T-t)} - 1)\right.\\ &\quad \left. - 2\frac{UV}{\alpha+b}(e^{(\alpha+b)(T-t)} - 1)\right] + \frac{2\rho\sigma_1\sigma_2}{\alpha}(e^{-\alpha(T-t)} - e^{-\alpha(s-t)})\left[\frac{U}{2\alpha}(e^{2\alpha(T-t)} - 1)\right.\\ &\quad \left. - \frac{V}{\alpha+b}(e^{(\alpha+b)(T-t)} - 1)\right] \qquad (7.28)\end{aligned}$$

where

$$U = \frac{1}{\alpha(\alpha - b)}[e^{-\alpha(s-t)} - e^{-\alpha(T-t)}]$$

$$V = \frac{1}{b(b - \alpha)}[e^{-b(s-t)} - e^{-b(T-t)}]$$

Example : European Option Calculation

We price a one-year option on a five-year pure discount bond with the following parameters for the processes; $\alpha = 0.1$, $\sigma_1 = 0.01$, $u = 0.01$, $b = 1.40$, $\sigma_2 = 0.008$, and $\rho = 0.70$. The original term structure is flat at 5 per cent with continuous compounding. The strike price of the option is $K = 0.6442$. The calculations are shown in Figure 7.10.

$$U = \frac{1}{0.1(0.1 - 1.40)}[e^{-0.1(5)} - e^{-0.1(1)}] = 2.2947$$

$$V = \frac{1}{1.40(1.40 - 0.1)}[e^{-1.40(5)} - e^{-1.40(1)}] = 0.1350$$

Intermediate calculations for σ_p:

$$\sigma_{P_1} = \frac{0.01^2}{2(0.1)}(3.2968)^2(1 - e^{-2(0.1)(1)}) = 0.0010$$

$$\begin{aligned}\sigma_{P_2} &= 0.008^2\left[\frac{(2.2947)^2}{2(0.1)}(e^{2(0.1)(1)} - 1) + \frac{(0.1350)^2}{2(1.40)}(e^{2(1.40)(1)} - 1)\right.\\ &\quad \left. - 2\frac{(2.2947)(0.1350)}{0.1 + 1.40}(e^{(0.1+1.40)(1)} - 1)\right]\\ &= 0.0003\end{aligned}$$

$$\begin{aligned}\sigma_{P_3} &= \frac{2(0.7)(0.01)(0.008)}{0.1}(e^{-0.1(1)} - e^{-0.1(5)})\left[\frac{2.2947}{2(0.1)}(e^{2(0.1)(1)} - 1)\right.\\ &\quad \left. - \frac{0.1350}{0.1 + 1.40}(e^{(0.1+1.40)(1)} - 1)\right]\\ &= 0.0007\end{aligned}$$

$$\sigma_p = \sqrt{0.0010 + 0.0003 + 0.0007} = 0.0449$$

$$d_1 = \frac{1}{0.0449}\ln\left(\frac{0.7788}{(0.6442)(0.9512)}\right) + \frac{0.0449}{2} = 5.3613$$

$$d_2 = 5.3613 - 0.0449 = 5.3164$$

$$c(0, 1, 5) = 0.7788 \times N(5.3613) - (0.6442)(0.9512) \times N(5.3164) = 0.0178$$

The models that we have seen so far in this chapter belong to a class of models that fit term structure data by modelling explicitly the short rate and making the process parameters time dependent. We finish this chapter by looking at a class of models that achieve the same objectives but by a different route. These models have been called "no arbitrage" models and were developed by Heath, Jarrow and Morton (1992) (HJM) and, like the original formulation of the HL model, they start from modelling the whole term structure simultaneously from its initial level. However, unlike HL, HJM work with instantaneous forward rates.

7.9 HEATH, JARROW AND MORTON (1992)

HJM extend the early term structure consistent framework of Ho and Lee (1986), proposing the following stochastic differential equation for the evolution of the instantaneous forward rate curve:

$$df(t,T) = \alpha(t,T)\,dt + \sum_{i=1}^{n} \sigma_i(t,T,f(t,T))\,dz_i(t) \tag{7.29}$$

where $f(0,t)$ is the initially observed forward rate curve and dz_i are independent Wiener processes. Equation (7.29) is the most general formulation of the HJM approach with n sources of randomness and with the volatilities of forward rates allowed to be dependent on the level of the forward rates. As shown by HJM, the drift rate $\alpha(t,T)$ is determined by no arbitrage and cannot be chosen independently of the volatility structure:

$$\alpha(t,T) = \sum_{i=1}^{n} \left\{ \sigma_i(t,T,f(t,T)) \left[\int_t^T \sigma_i(t,u,f(t,u))du \right] \right\} \tag{7.30}$$

The forward rate process is therefore completely specified by the volatility functions.

One way of thinking of HJM is as factor analysis of the forward curve. Assume that there is a single source of uncertainty and that the single forward rate volatility function, $\sigma(t,T)$, corresponds to Figure 7.11; short maturity instantaneous forward rates are more volatile than long forward rates, declining in a negative exponential manner.

Equation (7.29) determines that the new curve, after a period dt, is the old curve plus some deterministic drift function and a random component. Figure 7.12 shows how the random component determines the evolution of the curve. If the increment in the random process dz results in a positive shock to the curve, then the forward rates at the short end are most affected, with the shock having less of an effect as we move along the curve; the magnitude of the effect is determined by the size of the volatility for each maturity. The analogy with factor analysis comes about because we can use factor analysis to determine the factors that have historically driven the evolution of the curve and then model the curve forwards with the same factors constituting our volatility functions.

Although the original formulation of the HJM approach is in terms of forward rates, the model can be equivalently restated in terms of discount bond prices. Under this

FIGURE 7.11 Example of a Forward Rate Volatility Function in HJM

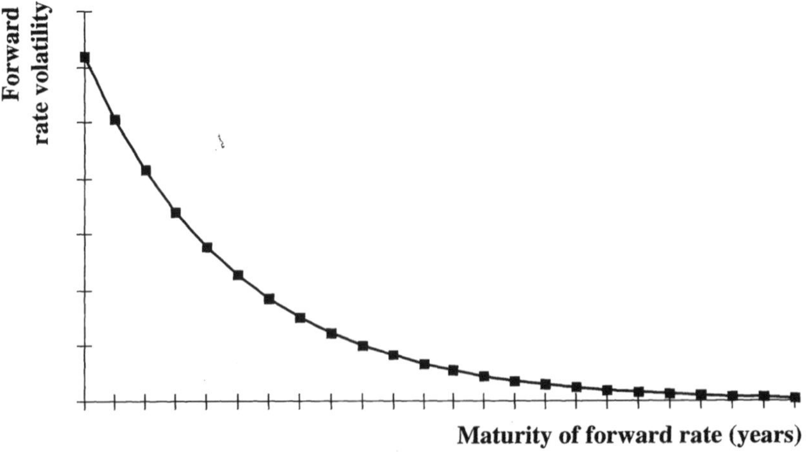

FIGURE 7.12 Increment of the Forward Curve in HJM

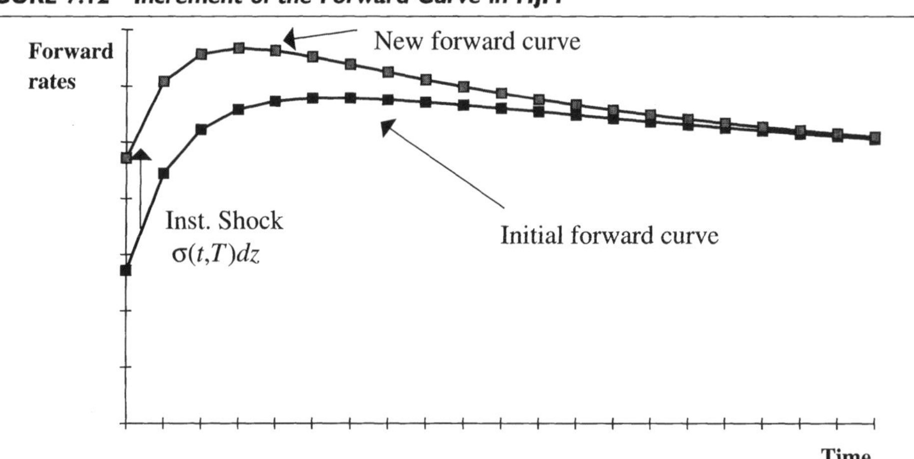

formulation (see for example Carverhill, 1995) the bond price returns satisfy the stochastic differential equation:

$$\frac{dP(t,T)}{P(t,T)} = r(t)\,dt + \sum_{i=1}^{n} v_i(t,T)\,dz_i(t) \tag{7.31}$$

where $P(0,T)$ is the initially observed pure discount bond price curve. The T-maturity bond price return volatility is related to the forward rate volatility function via

$$v_i(t,T) = -\int_t^T \sigma_i(t,u)\,du \tag{7.32}$$

The process for bond price returns is more intuitive than the forward rate process; because the bonds are traded assets the drift in a risk-neutral world is simply the short rate. For the rest of this chapter we will work with this formulation, as implementation is easier and more intuitive.

A description of the process for the stochastic evolution of the forward curve implies a process for the short rate as $r(t) = f(t,t)$ is the short rate at date t. This process is also entirely determined by the initial shape of the forward curve and the volatility structure and satisfies the following stochastic differential equation:

$$dr = \left[\frac{\partial f(0,t)}{\partial t} + \sum_{i=1}^{n}\left\{\int_0^t v_i(u,t)\frac{\partial^2 v_i(u,t)}{\partial t^2} + \frac{\partial v_i(u,t)^2}{\partial t}\,du + \int_0^t \frac{\partial^2 v_i(u,t)}{\partial t^2}\,dz_i(u)\right\}\right] dt$$
$$+ \sum_{i=1}^{n} \left.\frac{\partial v_i(u,t)}{\partial t}\right|_{u=t} dz_i(u) \tag{7.33}$$

The last component of the drift term shows that the short rate is non-Markovian in general as the evolution of the term structure could depend on the entire path taken by the term structure since it was initialised at time 0. This non-Markov property for the short rate can lead to a considerable increase in computation times when we implement the model, as we are forced to use Monte Carlo simulation or non-recombining trees to value derivative securities. The numerical techniques involved with this model are the subject of Chapter 10.

7.10 SUMMARY

In this chapter we have described the use of term structure consistent models — models built to be consistent with observed market term structure data — for pricing interest rate derivatives. We have introduced the short rate models of HL, HW, BDT, and BK, describing the assumptions made and presenting closed-form solutions of the term structure and for bond options, where they exist, and describing the calibration of the models to market caps data. Chapters 8 and 9 deal with numerical techniques for pricing options within the framework of these models. Finally, we introduce the term structure framework of HJM, which we return to in Chapter 10.

ENDNOTES

1. See for example Strickland (1992b). See also Hull and White (1995) and Carverhill (1995a) for a discussion of this issue.
2. The model can be defined in terms of continuous time changes for a function of r, e.g. $f(r) = \ln r$, but with greatly reduced tractability.

APPENDIX 7.1 *A(T, s)* FUNCTION FOR HULL AND WHITE (1994) TWO-FACTOR MODEL

$$\ln A(T,s) = \ln \frac{P(t,s)}{P(t,T)} + B(T,s)F(t,T) - \eta$$

where

$$\eta = \frac{\sigma_1^2}{4a}(1 - e^{-2a(T-t)})B(t,s)^2 - \rho\sigma_1\sigma_2[B(t,T)C(t,T)B(T,s) + \gamma_4 - \gamma_2]$$
$$- \frac{1}{2}\sigma_2^2[C(t,T)^2\ B(T,s) + \gamma_6 - \gamma_5]$$

$$\gamma_1 = \frac{e^{-(a+b)(s-t)}[e^{(a+b)(T-t)} - 1]}{(a+b)(a-b)} - \frac{e^{-2a(s-t)}[e^{2a(T-t)} - 1]}{2a(a-b)}$$

$$\gamma_2 = \frac{1}{ab}\left[\gamma_1 + C(T,s) - C(t,s) + \frac{1}{2}B(T,s)^2 - \frac{1}{2}B(t,s)^2 + \frac{(T-t)}{a} - \frac{e^{-a(s-T)} - e^{-a(s-t)}}{a^2}\right]$$

$$\gamma_3 = -\frac{e^{-(a+b)(T-t)} - 1}{(a-b)(a+b)} + \frac{e^{-2a(T-t)} - 1}{2a(a-b)}$$

$$\gamma_4 = \frac{1}{ab}\left[\gamma_3 - C(t,T) - \frac{1}{2}B(t,T)^2 + \frac{(T-t)}{a} + \frac{e^{-a(T-t)} - 1}{a^2}\right]$$

$$\gamma_5 = \frac{1}{b}\left[\frac{1}{2}C(T,s)^2 - \frac{1}{2}C(t,s)^2 + \gamma_2\right]$$

$$\gamma_6 = \frac{1}{b}\left[\gamma_4 - \frac{1}{2}C(t,T)^2\right]$$

8

Constructing Binomial Trees for the Short Rate

8.1 INTRODUCTION — INTEREST RATE TREES VS STOCK PRICE TREES

FOR most interest rate models the level of analytical tractability discussed in Chapter 7 is unobtainable. For these models, and for models which have some tractability but applied to pricing products which involve early exercise opportunities or complicated terminal pay-offs, the user must use numerical techniques similar to those outlined in the first section of this book. In this chapter we show how binomial trees can be constructed to represent a number of processes for the short rate, and how the resulting trees can then be used to price a wide range of interest rate derivatives. The idea behind constructing short-rate trees for term structure consistent models is the same as for binomial trees for the underlying asset price in the binomial framework of Chapter 2. A tree is constructed in such a way that it approximates the stochastic differential equation for the short rate (for example, one of the short rate processes discussed in Chapter 7) and automatically returns the observed prices of pure discount bonds and possibly the volatilities of these bonds. If the yield curve is broken into segments each of length Δt, then in a short-rate tree the variable at each node is the Δt period interest rate. For pricing derivatives, interest rate trees work similarly to stock price trees except that the discount rate used varies from node to node.

Initially, we divide the yield curve into, say, $i = 1, \ldots, N$ equal segments (each having length Δt) and define the following as those functions that describe the initial yield and volatility curves:[1]

$P(i)$: price at time 0 of a pure discount bond maturing at time $i\Delta t$.

$R(i)$: yield at time 0 on a pure discount bond maturing at time $i\Delta t$.

$\sigma_R(i)$: volatility at time 0 of yield $R(i)$.

As in Chapter 7 we will assume that $P(i)$, $R(i)$ and $\sigma_R(i)$ have been determined and are known.

Anecdotal evidence suggests that the most popular model that is implemented by building binomial trees is the BDT model that we introduced in Chapter 7. In order to illustrate the procedures we therefore concentrate on this model although the techniques are more generally applicable.

8.2 BUILDING BINOMIAL SHORT RATE TREES FOR BLACK, DERMAN AND TOY (1990)

As we discussed in Chapter 7, for the BDT model in particular, and for lognormal models in general, we lose the analytical tractability of the normal models. The consequence of this for pricing interest rate derivatives is that short-rate trees have to be built out until the end of the life of the instrument underlying the derivative. Suppose that the initial yield and volatility curves have been specified (i.e. we have determined the prices for discount bonds and their associated yield volatilities for each Δt). Figure 8.1 shows the first three steps in the tree. The risk-neutral probabilities of the binomial branches for this model are assumed to be equal to 1/2.

Before we describe the procedure in detail in the following sections, we first give a brief overview. The initial short rate r is, by definition, the yield on the bond which matures at the end of the first period Δt. The next stage is to choose the short rates r_U and r_D, at nodes which we denote by U and D, to match the initially specified curves. To match the initial yield curve we need the tree to correctly price a two-period bond (i.e. a bond which has value 1 in each of the three states at time 2 — r_{UU}, r_{UD} and r_{DD} — see Figure 8.1). To match the initial volatility curve at this time step we need to satisfy the following relationship:

$$\text{vol} = \frac{1}{2} \ln \left(\frac{yield_{\text{up}}}{yield_{\text{down}}} \right) \tag{8.1}$$

where $yield_{\text{up}}$ and $yield_{\text{down}}$ are determined from the tree as the yields on bonds maturing at time 2 as seen from the nodes U and D respectively. The rates r_U and r_D are chosen according to some "trial and error" procedure — or numerical search technique — to satisfy these two requirements.

The remainder of the tree is filled out analogously. The rates r_{UU}, r_{UD} and r_{DD} are chosen to match the price and yield volatility of a three-period bond. We can use the following relationship to limit our "search" to two short rates instead of three:

$$r_{UU}/r_{UD} = r_{UD}/r_{DD} \Rightarrow r_{UD}^2 = r_{UU} r_{DD}$$

We now go on to describe how the tree can be constructed efficiently, using the technique of forward induction developed by Jamshidian (1991). The procedure we describe

FIGURE 8.1 First three Steps in a Binomial Tree for the Short Rate

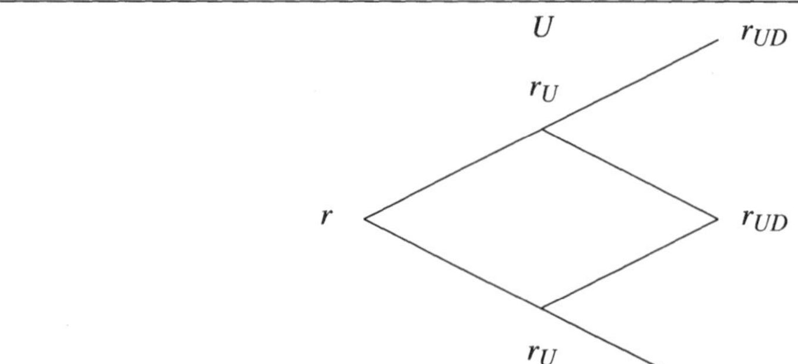

is applicable to models which Jamshidian describes as "Brownian path independent" and covers the models of HL (and the lognormal version) and BDT, but not the mean reverting models of HW and BK. For these later models we prefer to work with trinomial trees where this extra degree of freedom is better able to capture the mean reversion,[2] and these models are dealt with in the next chapter. Jamshidian (1991) shows that the level of the short rate at time t in the BDT model is given by

$$r(t) = U(t)\exp(\sigma(t)z(t)) \tag{8.2}$$

where $U(t)$ is the median of the (lognormal) distribution for r at time t, $\sigma(t)$ is the level of short-rate volatility and $z(t)$ is the level of the Brownian motion. In order to fit the model to both yield and volatility curves we have to determine both $U(t)$ and $\sigma(t)$ at each time step. If the model is implemented to fit just the yield curve, with $\sigma(t)$ set equal to a constant, we only have to determine the median $U(t)$ and the level of the short rate is then given by

$$r(t) = U(t)\exp(\sigma z(t)) \tag{8.3}$$

Figure 8.2 illustrates the nodes in the tree for the binomial discretisation of Brownian path-independent models.

At time $i = 0$ there is a single state which we index by j, $j = 0$. At time $i = 1$ there are two states $j = -1$ and $j = 1$. For general i there are $(i + 1)$ states $j = -i, -i+2, \ldots, i-2, i$. At time step N, j therefore has a centralised binomial distribution with mean 0 and variance N. Thus $j\sqrt{\Delta t}$ is distributed with mean 0 and variance t, which is the same as the random walk, implying that as $\Delta t \to 0$ the binomial process $j\sqrt{\Delta t}$ converges to the Wiener process $z(t)$.

FIGURE 8.2 Binomial Discretisation of Brownian Path-independent Models

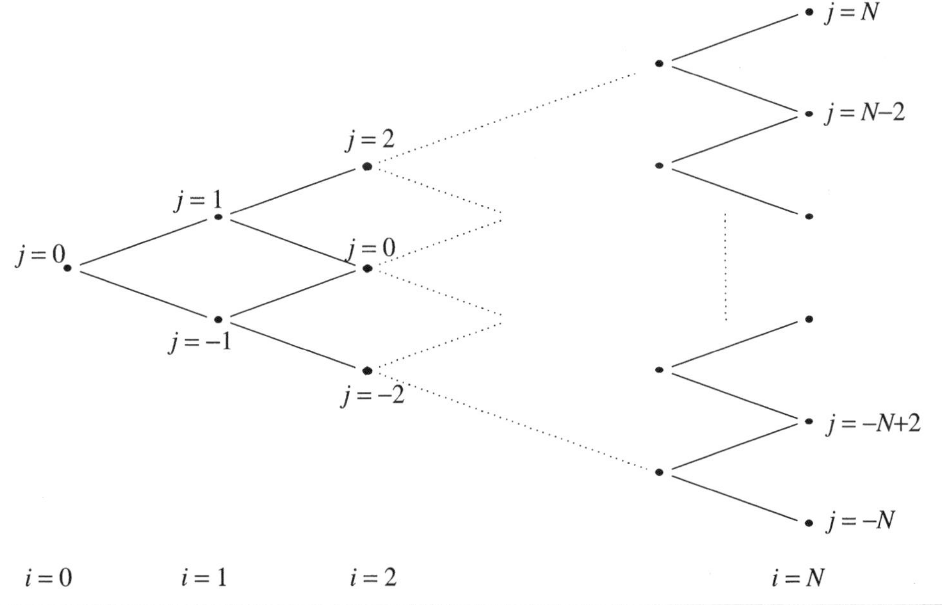

Using these results we can represent the level of the short rate (equation (8.2)) in the tree as

$$r_{i,j} = U(i)\exp(\sigma(i)j\sqrt{\Delta t}) \tag{8.4}$$

i.e. replace t by i and $z(t)$ by $j\sqrt{\Delta t}$. We refer to $r_{i,j}$ as the short (Δt-period) rate at the (i, j) node. To build a tree for the short rate (i.e. determining $r_{i,j}$ for all i and j) therefore requires us to determine $U(i)$ and $\sigma(i)$.

8.3 DETERMINING THE TIME-DEPENDENT FUNCTIONS $U(i)$ AND $\sigma(i)$

In order to determine these functions we use state prices. Recall that $Q_{i,j}$ is the value, at time 0, of a security that pays off the following:

$1 if node (i, j) is reached, and

$0 otherwise

By definition $Q_{0,0} = 1$ The $Q_{i,j}$'s can be thought of as discounted probabilities and are the building blocks of all securities. In particular the price of the pure discount bonds which mature at time $(i+1)\Delta t$ can be expressed in terms of the pure security prices and one-period discount factors at time $i\Delta t$:

$$P(i+1) = \sum_j Q_{i,j} d_{i,j} \tag{8.5}$$

where $d_{i,j}$ denotes the price at time $i\Delta t$ and state j of the zero-coupon bond maturing at time $(i+1)\Delta t$ (i.e. the one-period discount factor at node (i, j)) and where the summation takes place across all of the nodes j at time i. For simple compounding we have:[3]

$$d_{i,j} = \frac{1}{1 + r_{i,j}\Delta t} \tag{8.6}$$

The process of forward induction involves accumulating the state prices as we progress through the tree. Specifically, the pure security prices at time step i and node j are updated from the known values at time step $i-1$ according to the following equation:[4]

$$\begin{aligned} Q_{i,j} &= \tfrac{1}{2} Q_{i-1,j-1} d_{i-1,j-1} + \tfrac{1}{2} Q_{i-1,j+1} d_{i-1,j+1} \\ &= \frac{1}{2} Q_{i-1,j-1} \frac{1}{1 + r_{i-1,j-1}\Delta t} + \frac{1}{2} Q_{i-1,j+1} \frac{1}{1 + r_{i-1,j+1}\Delta t} \end{aligned} \tag{8.7}$$

i.e. for the two nodes that lead into node (i, j) we sum the product of their state prices, one-period discount factors and transitional probabilities. Equation (8.7) is valid for all nodes at time step i except the extreme nodes, (i, i) and $(i, -i)$, where there is a unique transitional path and we have

$$Q_{i,i} = \tfrac{1}{2} Q_{i-1,i-1} d_{i-1,i-1} \tag{8.8}$$

$$Q_{i,-i} = \tfrac{1}{2} Q_{i-1,-i+1} d_{i-1,-i+1} \tag{8.9}$$

Before showing how to implement the BDT model in its full generality, we begin by showing how a version of the model fitted only to the interest rate data can be constructed.

8.4 BLACK–DERMAN–TOY MODEL FITTED TO THE YIELD CURVE ONLY

Many practitioners when using the BDT model, set the short-rate volatility to be a constant and so only fit to the yield curve. The mean reversion parameter (the ratio of the slope of the function $\sigma(t)$ and its level — see equation (7.20)) therefore equates to zero, and the stochastic differential equation and the discrete representation for the level of the short rate at each node become respectively:

$$d \ln r = \theta(t)\, dt + \sigma\, dz \tag{8.10}$$

$$r_{i,j} = U(i) \exp(\sigma j \sqrt{\Delta t}) \tag{8.11}$$

Using equations (8.11) and (8.5) the time step $i+1$ pure discount bond prices can be constructed as

$$\begin{aligned} P(i+1) &= \sum_j Q_{i,j} \frac{1}{1 + r_{i,j}\Delta t} \\ &= \sum_j Q_{i,j} \frac{1}{1 + U(i)\exp(\sigma j \sqrt{\Delta t})\Delta t} \end{aligned} \tag{8.12}$$

As the discount function is known, the only unknown in equation (8.12) is $U(i)$. Unfortunately, for lognormal versions of the model, we cannot rearrange equation (8.12) to obtain $U(i)$ explicitly, and so we need to use a numerical search technique such as that of Newton–Raphson. Once $U(i)$ has been determined we can use equation (8.12) to determine the rates in the tree for that time step.

In summary the following are the steps that we take: Assume $i > 0$ and that $U(i-1)$, $Q_{i-1,j}$, $r_{i-1,j}$ and $d_{i-1,j}$ have been found for all j at time step $i-1$. (The values at the initial time, $i = 0$, are $U(0) = r_{0,0} = R(1)$, $Q_{0,0} = 1$, $d_{0,0} = 1/(1 + r_{0,0}\Delta t)$.)

Step 1: Generate $Q_{i,j}$

$$Q_{i,i} = \tfrac{1}{2} Q_{i-1,i-1} d_{i-1,i-1}$$

$$Q_{i,j} = \tfrac{1}{2} Q_{i-1,j-1} d_{i-1,j-1} + \tfrac{1}{2} Q_{i-1,j+1} d_{i-1,j+1} \qquad j = -i+1 \text{ to } i-1$$

$$Q_{i,-i} = \tfrac{1}{2} Q_{i-1,-i+1} d_{i-1,-i+1}$$

Step 2: Using $P(i+1)$ solve for $U(i)$

$$P(i+1) = \sum_j Q_{i,j} \frac{1}{1 + U(i)\exp(\sigma j \sqrt{\Delta t})\Delta t}$$

Step 3: From $U(i)$ calculate the short rate, and update the discount factors, for all nodes at time i:

$$r_{i,j} = U(i)\exp(\sigma j \sqrt{\Delta t})$$

$$d_{i,j} = \frac{1}{1 + r_{i,j}\Delta t}$$

Figure 8.3 gives a pseudo-code implementation of the procedure.

FIGURE 8.3 Pseudo-code for the BDT Model Fitted to Yield Curve Data

```
initialise_parameters { sig, N, T }

{ precompute constants }
dt = T/N

{ initialise yield curve }
for i = 1 to N do
  R[i] = initial_yield_curve[i]
  P[i] = 1/(1+R[i]*dt)^(i*dt)
next i

{ initialise first node }
   Q[0,0] = 1,
   U[0] = R[1]
   r[0,0] = R[1]
   d[0,0] = 1/(1+r[0,0]*dt)

{ evolve tree for the short rate }
for i = 1 to N do

  { update pure security prices at i }
  Q[i,-i] = 0.5*Q[i-1,-i+1]*d[i-1,-i+1]
  Q[i,i] = 0.5*Q[i-1,i-1]*d[i-1,i-1]
  for j = -i+2 to i-2 step 2 do
    Q[i,j] = 0.5*Q[i-1,j-1]*d[i-1,j-1]
             +0.5*Q[i-1,j+1]*d[i-1,j+1]

  { use numerical search to solve for U[i] }
  P[i+1]=Σj[Q[i,j]*1/[1+(U[i]*exp(sig*j*sqrt(dt))*dt)]

  { set r[.] and d[.] }

  for j = -i to i step 2 do
    r[i,j] = U[i]*exp(sig*j*sqrt(dt))
    d[i,j] = 1/(1+r[i,j]*dt)
  next j

next i
```

Example : The Black–Derman–Toy Model Fitted to Yield Curve Data

We build a short-rate tree consistent with a flat yield curve at 5 per cent. The size of the time step is one year and the short rate volatility is assumed to be 10 per cent. Figure 8.4. shows the calculations:

$$U(0) = r_{0,0} = R(0,1) = 0.05$$

$$d_{0,0} = 1/(1 + r_{0,0}\Delta t) = 0.9524$$

$$Q_{1,1} = Q_{0,0}(0.5)(0.9524) = 0.4762$$

FIGURE 8.4 The Black–Derman–Toy Model Fitted to Yield Curve Data

		Time	0	1	2	3	4
Δt	1	Yield		5.00%	5.00%	5.00%	5.00%
sqrt(Δt)	1	PDB	1.0000	0.9524	0.9070	0.8638	0.8227
σ	10.00%	ΣQ	1.0000	0.9524	0.9070	0.8638	
		U(i)	5.00%	4.98%	4.96%	4.94%	
		Σ		0.9070	0.8638	0.8227	
		diff		0.0000	0.0000	0.0000	

j	r(i,j)	0	1	2	3
3					6.67%
2				6.05%	
1			5.50%		5.46%
0		5.00%		4.96%	
−1			4.50%		4.47%
−2				4.06%	
−3					3.66%

j	d(i,j)	0	1	2	3
3					0.9375
2				0.9429	
1			0.9479		0.9482
0		0.9524		0.9528	
−1			0.9569		0.9572
−2				0.9610	
−3					0.9647

j	Q(i,j)	0	1	2	3
3					0.1064
2				0.2257	
1			0.4762		0.3224
0		1.0000		0.4535	
−1			0.4762		0.3255
−2				0.2278	
−3					0.1095

$U(1)$ is the solution to

$$P(2) = \sum_j Q_{1,j} \frac{1}{1 + U(1)\exp(\sigma j \sqrt{\Delta t})\Delta t} \qquad j = -1 \text{ to } 1 \text{ step } 2$$

$$= 0.4762 \frac{1}{1 + U(1)\exp(0.1 \times 1 \times \sqrt{1})1}$$

$$+ 0.4762 \frac{1}{1 + U(1)\exp(0.1 \times (-1) \times \sqrt{1})1}$$

$$= 0.9070$$

Therefore $U(1) = 0.0498 = 4.98$ per cent

$$Q_{3,1} = \tfrac{1}{2} Q_{2,2} d_{2,2} + \tfrac{1}{2} Q_{2,0} d_{2,0}$$

$$= \tfrac{1}{2}(0.2257)(0.9429) + \tfrac{1}{2}(0.4535)(0.9528)$$
$$= 0.3224$$

$U(3)$ is the solution to

$$P(4) = \sum_j Q_{3,j} \frac{1}{1 + U(3)\exp(\sigma j\sqrt{\Delta t})\Delta t} \qquad j = -3 \text{ to } 3 \text{ step } 2$$

$$= 0.1095\frac{1}{1 + U(3)\exp(\sigma(-3)\sqrt{1})1} + 0.3255\frac{1}{1 + U(3)\exp(\sigma(-1)\sqrt{1})1}$$
$$+ 0.3224\frac{1}{1 + U(3)\exp(\sigma(1)\sqrt{1})1} + 0.1064\frac{1}{1 + U(3)\exp(\sigma(3)\sqrt{1})1}$$
$$= 0.8227$$

Therefore $U(3) = 0.0494 = 4.94$ per cent

8.5 BLACK–DERMAN–TOY MODEL FITTED TO INTEREST RATE YIELD AND VOLATILITY DATA

The methodology of fitting the model to both the rate structure and the volatility structure has the same general form. In order to fit the term structure of volatilities, $\sigma(t)$ must now be made time dependent and so the level of the short rate at node (i, j) is given by

$$r_{i,j} = U(i)\exp(\sigma(i)j\sqrt{\Delta t}) \tag{8.13}$$

Let the up node from the first time step (node (1, 1) in Figure 8.2) be denoted by U and the down node (node $(1, -1)$) be denoted by D. Also, let $P_U(i)$ and $P_D(i)$ (for $i \geq 1$) be the discount function evaluated at nodes U and D respectively, with $R_U(i)$ and $R_D(i)$ the corresponding discount bond yields derived via equation (6.2). Specifying both the spot rate yield and volatility curves at the initial time $i = 0$, is equivalent to specifying at period $i = 1$ the two discount functions, $P_U(i)$ and $P_D(i)$, for all $i \geq 1$. In order that the short rate tree can be constructed to match both the initial yield and volatility curves $P_U(i)$ and $P_D(i)$ must be consistent with the known values of $P(i)$ and $\sigma_R(i)$.

The first step in the construction of the tree is to determine $P_U(i)$ and $P_D(i)$ for all $i \geq 2$. The known prices at the initial time, $P(i)$, and the newly defined functions $P_U(i)$ and $P_D(i)$ are related via discounted expectations:

$$\frac{1}{1 + r_{0,0}\Delta t}[0.5P_U(i) + 0.5P_D(i)] = P(i) \qquad i = 2, \ldots, N \tag{8.14}$$

The initial volatilities can be recovered by applying equation (8.1) which can be expressed in terms of $P_U(i)$ and $P_D(i)$ as

$$\sigma_R(i)\sqrt{\Delta t} = \frac{1}{2}\ln\frac{\ln P_U(i)}{\ln P_D(i)} \tag{8.15}$$

Equations (8.14) and (8.15) can be solved simultaneously to yield:

$$P_D(i) = P_U(i)^{\exp(-2\sigma_R(i)\sqrt{\Delta t})} \tag{8.16}$$

and where $P_U(i)$ is found as the solution to:[5]

$$P_U(i) + P_U(i)^{\exp(-2\sigma_R(i)\sqrt{\Delta t})} = 2P(i)(1 + r_{0,0}\Delta t) \tag{8.17}$$

Forward induction is again used to determine the time-dependent functions that ensure consistency with the initial yield curve data. However, state prices are now determined from the nodes U and D requiring the following notation:

$Q_{U,i,j}$: the value, as seen from node U, of a security that pays off \$1 if node (i, j) is reached and zero otherwise.

$Q_{D,i,j}$: the value, as seen from node D, of a security that pays off \$1 if node (i, j) is reached and zero otherwise.

By definition $Q_{U,1,1} = 1$ and $Q_{D,1,-1} = 1$. The tree is constructed from time Δt onward using a procedure similar to section 8.4. Now we have two equations similar to equation (8.12)

$$P_U(i+1) = \sum_j Q_{U,i,j} d_{i,j} \tag{8.18}$$

$$P_D(i+1) = \sum_j Q_{D,i,j} d_{i,j} \tag{8.19}$$

and where now:

$$d_{i,j} = \frac{1}{1 + r_{i,j}\Delta t} = \frac{1}{1 + U(i)\exp(\sigma(i) j \sqrt{\Delta t})\Delta t} \tag{8.20}$$

equations (8.18) and (8.19) define two equations with two unknowns, $U(i)$ and $\sigma(i)$. These can be solved by a two-dimensional Newton–Raphson technique.

The updating of the state prices is analogous to equation (8.7):

$$Q_{U,i,j} = \tfrac{1}{2} Q_{U,i-1,j-1} d_{i-1,j-1} + \tfrac{1}{2} Q_{U,i-1,j+1} d_{i-1,j+1} \tag{8.21}$$

$$Q_{D,i,j} = \tfrac{1}{2} Q_{D,i-1,j-1} d_{i-1,j-1} + \tfrac{1}{2} Q_{D,i-1,j+1} d_{i-1,j+1} \tag{8.22}$$

The full set of steps to building the tree are therefore the following. Assume $i > 0$ and that $U(i-1)$, $\sigma(i-1)$, $Q_{U,i-1,j}$, $Q_{D,i-1,j}$ and $r_{i-1,j}$ are known for all j at time step $i-1$. (The values at the initial time are $U_0 = r_{0,0} = R(1)$, $Q_{U,1,1} = 1$, $Q_{D,1,-1} = 1$, $\sigma(0) = \sigma_R(1)$, $d_{0,0} = 1/(1 + r_{0,0}\Delta t)$).

Step 1: Derive $P_U(i)$ and $P_D(i)$ for $i = 2$ to N.

$$P_D(i) = P_U(i)^{\exp(-2\sigma_R(i)\sqrt{\Delta t})}$$

$P_U(i)$ is found as the solution to

$$P_U(i) + P_U(i)^{\exp(-2\sigma_R(i)\sqrt{\Delta t})} = 2P(i)(1 + r_{0,0}\Delta t)$$

Step 2: Generate $Q_{U,i,j}$ and $Q_{D,i,j}$.

$$Q_{U,i,j} = \tfrac{1}{2} Q_{U,i-1,j-1} d_{i-1,j-1} + \tfrac{1}{2} Q_{U,i-1,j+1} d_{i-1,j+1}$$

$$Q_{D,i,j} = \tfrac{1}{2} Q_{D,i-1,j-1} d_{i-1,j-1} + \tfrac{1}{2} Q_{D,i-1,j+1} d_{i-1,j+1}$$

Step 3: Using the derived discount functions, $P_U(i+1)$ and $P_D(i+1)$, solve for $U(i)$ and $\sigma(i)$.

$$P_U(i+1) = \sum_j Q_{U,i,j} \frac{1}{1 + U(i)\exp(\sigma(i)j\sqrt{\Delta t})\Delta t}$$

$$P_D(i+1) = \sum_j Q_{D,i,j} \frac{1}{1 + U(i)\exp(\sigma(i)j\sqrt{\Delta t})\Delta t}$$

Step 4: From the calculated values of $U(i)$ and $\sigma(i)$ calculate the short rate, and one-period discount factors for all nodes j at time i:

$$r_{i,j} = U(i)\exp(\sigma(i)j\sqrt{\Delta t})$$

$$d_{i,j} = \frac{1}{1 + r_{i,j}\Delta t}$$

Figure 8.5 gives a pseudo-code implementation of the procedure.

FIGURE 8.5 Pseudo-code for the Black–Derman–Toy Model Fitted to Yield and Volatility Data

```
initialise_parameters { N,T }

{ pre-compute constants }

dt = T/N
sdt = sqrt(dt)

{ initiate yield curves }

for i = 1 to N do
  R[i] = initial_yield_curve[i]
  P[i] = 1/(1+R[i]*dt)^(i*dt)
  sigR[i] = initial_volatility_curve[i]
next i

{ compute Pu[.] and Pd[.] }

for i = 2 to N do

  { solve the following for Pu[i] }
  Pu[i] + Pu[i]^exp(-2*sigR[i]*sdt) = 2*P[i]*(1+r[0,0]*dt)

  Pd = Pu[i]^exp(-2*sigR[i]*sdt)

next i

{ initialise nodes }
U[0] = R[1]
r[0,0] = R[1]
```

FIGURE 8.5 ***(continued)***

```
d[0,0]  = 1/(1+r[0,0]*dt)
sig[0]  = sigR[1]
Qu[1,1]  = 1
Qd[1,-1]  = 1

{ evolve tree for the short rate }

for i = 1 to N do

  { update pure security prices at timestep i }
  for j = (-i-1) to (i+1) step 2 do
    Qu[i,j] = 0.5*(Qu[i-1,j-1]*d[i-1,j-1] + Qu[i-1,j+1]*d[i-1,j+1])
    Qd[i,j] = 0.5*(Qd[i-1,j-1]*d[i-1,j-1] + Qd[i-1,j+1]*d[i-1,j+1])
  next j

  { solve simultaneously for U[i] and sig[i] }
  Pu[i+1] = Σj[Qu[i,j] * 1/[1+U[i]*exp(sig[i]*j*sdt)*dt]
  Pd[i+1] = Σj[Qd[i,j] * 1/[1+U[i]*exp(sig[i]*j*sdt)*dt]

  { set r[.] and d[.] }
  for j = -i to i step 2 do
    r[i,j] = U[i]*exp(sig[i]*j*sdt)
    d[i,j] = 1/[1+ r[i,j]*dt]
  next j

next i
```

Example : The Black–Derman–Toy Model Fitted to Both Yield and Volatility Data

We build a short-rate tree consistent with a flat term structure of 5 per cent and with annual time increments. We also fit a declining volatility structure which declines from 10 per cent after one year to 7 per cent after four years. Figure 8.6 shows the tree construction.

$$U(0) = r_{0,0} = R(0,1) = 0.05$$

$$\sigma(0) = \sigma_R(0,\ 1) = 0.100$$

$$d_{0,0} = 1/(1 + r_{0,0}\Delta t) = 0.9524$$

$$Q_{U,1,1} = 1.000$$

$$Q_{D,1,1} = 1.000$$

Solve for P_U and P_D. $P_U(i)$ is found as the solution to

$$P_U(i) + P_U(i)^{\exp(-\sigma_R(i)2\sqrt{\Delta t})} = 2P(i)(1 + r_{0,0}\Delta t)$$

For $i = 2$:

$$P_U(2) + P_U(2)^{\exp(-(0.09)2\sqrt{1})} = 2(0.9070)(1 + 0.05(1))$$

FIGURE 8.6 Black–Derman–Toy Model Fitted to Both Yield and Volatility Data

		Time	**0**	**1**	**2**	**3**	**4**
Δt	1	Yield		5.00%	5.00%	5.00%	5.00%
sqrt(Δt)	1	σ		10.00%	9.00%	8.00%	7.00%
σ	10%	P	1.0000	0.9524	0.9070	0.8638	0.8227
		Pu			0.9482	0.9000	0.8550
		diff (slvr)			0.0000	0.0000	0.0000
		Pd			0.9566	0.9141	0.8727
		Rd			4.54%	4.59%	4.64%
		ΣQu			0.9482	0.9000	
		ΣQd			0.9566	0.9141	
		U(i)	5.00%	4.98%	4.98%	4.99%	
		σ(i)	10.00%	9.22%	7.18%	5.13%	
		ΣQuxd		0.9482	0.9000	0.8550	
		ΣQdxd		0.9566	0.9141	0.8727	
		diff (slvr)		0.0000	0.0000	0.0000	

j		0	1	2	3
3	**r(i,j)**				5.81%
2				5.75%	
1			5.46%		5.25%
0		5.00%		4.98%	
–1			4.54%		4.74%
–2				4.31%	
–3					4.27%
3	**d(i,j)**				0.9451
2				0.9457	
1			0.9482		0.9501
0		0.9524		0.9526	
–1			0.9566		0.9548
–2				0.9587	
–3					0.9590
3	**Qu(i,j)**				0.2242
2				0.4741	
1			1.0000		0.4500
0				0.4741	
–1					0.2258
–2					
–3					
3	**Qd(i,j)**				
2					
1					0.2278
0				0.4783	
–1			1.0000		0.4570
–2				0.4783	
–3					0.2293

which implies $P_U(2) = 0.9482$. For $i = 3$:

$$P_U(3) + P_U(3)^{\exp(-(0.08)2\sqrt{1})} = 2(0.8638)(1 + 0.05(1))$$

which implies $P_U(3) = 0.9000$.

By equation (8.16) we can calculate $P_D(i)$

$$\begin{aligned} P_D(2) &= P_U(2)^{\exp(-2\sigma_R(2)\sqrt{\Delta t})} \\ &= 0.9482^{\exp(-2(0.09)\sqrt{1})} \\ &= 0.9565 \\ P_D(3) &= 0.9000^{\exp(-2(0.08)\sqrt{1})} = 0.9141 \end{aligned}$$

$U(1)$ and $\sigma(1)$ are the solutions to

$$\begin{aligned} P_U(2) = 0.9482 &= Q_{U,1,1} \frac{1}{1 + U(1)\exp(\sigma(1)(1)\sqrt{1}(1)} \\ &= \frac{1}{1 + U(1)\exp(\sigma(1)(1)\sqrt{1})(1)} \\ P_D(2) = 0.9565 &= Q_{D,1,-1} \frac{1}{1 + U(1)\exp(\sigma(1)(-1)\sqrt{1})(1)} \\ &= \frac{1}{1 + U(1)\exp(\sigma(1)(-1)\sqrt{1})(1)} \end{aligned}$$

These can be solved to obtain $U(1) = 0.0498$, $\sigma(1) = 0.0922$.

Now we can obtain the short rate and discount factors.

$$\begin{aligned} r_{1,1} &= U(1)\exp(\sigma(1)(1)\sqrt{1})(1) \\ &= 0.0498\exp(0.0922(1)\sqrt{1})(1) \\ &= 0.0546 \\ r_{1,-1} &= 0.0498\exp(0.0922(-1)\sqrt{1})(1) \\ &= 0.0454 \\ d_{1,1} &= \frac{1}{1 + r_{1,1}(1)} = \frac{1}{1 + 0.0546(1)} = 0.9482 \\ d_{1,-1} &= \frac{1}{1 + 0.0454(1)} = 0.9566 \end{aligned}$$

The discount factors at time 1 are used to find the pure security prices $Q_{U,2,2}$, $Q_{U,2,0}$, $Q_{D,2,0}$ and $Q_{D,2,-2}$; $U(2)$ and $\sigma(2)$ are found as the solutions to

$$P_U(3) = 0.9000 = \sum_j Q_{U,2,j} \frac{1}{1 + U(2)\exp(\sigma(2)j\sqrt{1})(1)}$$

$$= 0.4741 \frac{1}{1 + U(2)\exp(\sigma(2)(0)\sqrt{1})(1)} + 0.4741 \frac{1}{1 + U(2)\exp(\sigma(2)(2)\sqrt{1})1}$$

$$P_D(3) = 0.9141 = \sum_j Q_{D,2,j} \frac{1}{1 + U(2)\exp(\sigma(2)j\sqrt{1})(1)}$$

$$= 0.4783 \frac{1}{1 + U(2)\exp(\sigma(2)(-2)\sqrt{1})(1)} + 0.4783 \frac{1}{1 + U(2)\exp(\sigma(2)(0)\sqrt{1})1}$$

which implies that $U(2) = 0.0498$ and $\sigma(2) = 0.0718$.

8.6 PRICING INTEREST RATE DERIVATIVES WITHIN A BINOMIAL TREE

Once the short-rate tree has been constructed we know the short rate at every time and every state of the world consistent with our original assumptions about the process, and we can use the tree to derive prices for a wide range of interest rate derivatives in the usual manner via backwards induction — see Chapter 2 for pricing options in a binomial tree constructed to approximate GBM. Let $C_{i,j}$ represent the value of a contingent claim at node (i, j). The value at this node is related to the two connecting nodes at time step $i + 1$ according to the usual discounted expectation adjusted for the state index j:

$$C_{i,j} = \tfrac{1}{2} d_{i,j} [C_{i+1,j+1} + C_{i+1,j-1}] \tag{8.23}$$

As an example of the procedure we begin by showing how to use the tree to price discount bond options.

8.6.1 Pricing Discount Bond Options

We price a T maturity call option on a s-maturity discount bond ($T \le s$) with a strike price of K. Let N_s and N_T represent the number of time steps until the maturity of the bond and option respectively ($s = N_s \Delta t$ and $T = N_T \Delta t$). We assume that the short-rate tree has been constructed out as far as time step N_s. Let $Ps_{i,j}$ represent the value of the s-maturity bond at node (i, j).

The first step to pricing the derivative is to set the maturity condition for the bond underlying the option, $Ps_{N_s,j} = 1$ for all j at time step N_s, and then perform backwards induction for the bond price, calculating the value of the s-maturity bond for every node in the tree, i.e.

$$Ps_{i,j} = \tfrac{1}{2} d_{i,j} [Ps_{i+1,j+1} + Ps_{i+1,j-1}] \quad \forall \text{ nodes } j \text{ at time step } i \tag{8.24}$$

For European discount bond options this second stage only has to be completed as far back as time step N_T when the maturity condition for the option is implemented. For American discount bond options, in order to be able to evaluate the early exercise condition when we perform backwards induction for the option price, we continue applying equation (8.24) back to the root of the tree, node (0, 0).

Next, evaluate the maturity condition for the option at all of the nodes for time step N_T:

$$C_{N_T,j} = \max\{0, Ps_{N_T,j} - K\} \quad \forall j \text{ at } N_T \tag{8.25}$$

For European options the call price can be obtained by repeatedly applying equation (8.23) back through to the origin of the tree ($i = N_T - 1$ to 0). For American options we need to allow for the possibility of early exercise in the normal way, by taking the maximum of the discounted expectation and the intrinsic value of the option at each node. The American option value at node (i, j) is given by

$$C_{i,j} = \max\{Ps_{i,j} - K, \tfrac{1}{2}d_{i,j}[C_{i+1,j+1} + C_{i+1,j-1}]\} \quad \forall j \text{ at time } i \tag{8.26}$$

A more efficient procedure for valuing European option prices utilises the fact that the state prices are equivalent to discounted probabilities. The value of any European option can be calculated directly from the tree as the sum of the product of the maturity condition

FIGURE 8.7 Pseudo-code for Pricing Discount Bond Options in a Binomial Tree

```
initialise_parameters { Ns, NT, K }

build_short_rate_tree { determines d[i,j] and Q[i,j] for all
                        i and j until time step Ns}

{ initialise maturity condition for pure discount bond
underlying the option }

for j = -Ns to Ns step 2 do Ps[Ns,j] = 1

{ backward induction for pure discount bond price }

for i = Ns-1 downto 0
  for j = -i to i step 2 do
   Ps[i,j] = d[i,j]*0.5*(Ps[i+1,j+1] + Ps[i+1,j-1])
next i

{ initialise maturity condition for option }

for j = -NT to NT step 2 do C[NT,j] = max{0, Ps[NT,j]-K}

{ evaluate European option price using state prices }

C[0,0] = 0
for j = -NT to NT step 2 do
   C[0,0] = C[0,0] + Q[NT,j]*C[NT,j]

European_call_price = C[0,0]

{ backward induction for American call option price }

for i = (NT-1) downto 0 do
  for j = -i to i step 2 do
    C[i,j] = d[i,j]*0.5*(C[i+1,j+1] + C[i+1,j-1])
    C[i,j] = max{C[i,j], Ps[i,j]-K}
  next j
next i

American_call_price = C[0,0]
```

of the option and the state price, for each node at the maturity time, i.e. for a call option:

$$C_{0,0} = \sum_{j} Q_{N_T,j} \max\{0, Ps_{N_T,j} - K\} \quad \forall j \text{ at } N_T \tag{8.27}$$

Figure 8.7 gives a pseudo-code implementation of the procedure.

Example : Pricing Pure Discount Bond Options in a Binomial Tree

Figure 8.8 shows a tree for the discount function and pure security prices, built to be consistent with the initial yield curve, out to 10 years with Δt = one year, and with the initial term structure flat at 5 per cent. The short rate volatility is assumed to be 10 per cent. We use the tree to price a six-year European put options on a pure discount bond with maturity 10 years and $K = 0.80$

In order to price the option we first construct a tree for the 10-year pure discount bond price by setting $Ps_{10,j} = 1$ for $j = -10$ to 10 and then apply equation (8.24) to obtain the upper part of Figure 8.9.

The price at the origin of the tree, 0.6139, is today's 10-year pure discount bond price. Secondly, we construct the tree for the option price, resulting in the lower tree of Figure 8.9. We begin by evaluating the maturity condition for the option. For example, at node (6, 6) we obtain

$$\begin{aligned} C_{6,6} &= \max\{K - Ps_{6,6}, 0\} \\ &= \max\{0.8 - 0.7094, 0\} \\ &= 0.0906 \end{aligned}$$

The other nodes are worked similarly. The European price is obtained by applying equation (8.27) applied to a put option:

$$\begin{aligned} C_{0,0} = {} & (0.0107 \times 0.0906) + (0.665 \times 0.0467) + (0.1708 \times 0.083) \\ & + (0.2335 \times 0) + (0.1791 \times 0) + (0.0731 \times 0) + (0.0124 \times 0) \\ = {} & 0.0055 \end{aligned}$$

For American options we apply equation (8.26), adapted for a put. For example node (5,5):

$$\begin{aligned} C_{5,5} &= \max\{0.8 - 0.6765, 0.5 \times 0.9251 \times (0.0906 + 0.0467)\} \\ &= \max\{0.0653, 0.1235\} \\ &= 0.1235 \end{aligned}$$

The American price is given by node $C_{0,0}$, i.e. 0.1681.

8.6.2 Pricing of European Swaptions

As a second example of pricing interest rate derivatives within trees, we price a European option to enter into a fixed life swap — specifically a one-year option that exercises into a three year swap with semi-annual reset dates. This instrument is illustrated in Figure 8.10.

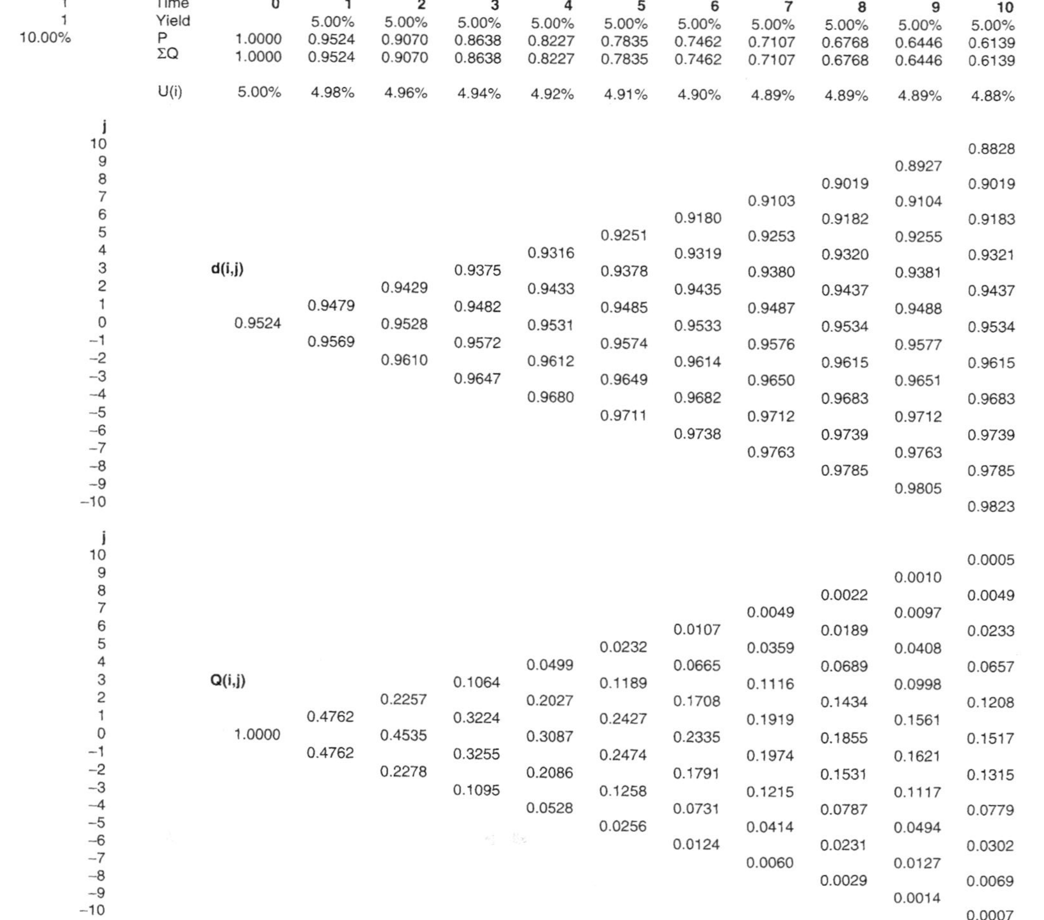

Δt	1
sqrt(Δt)	1
σ	10.00%

Strike 0.8

Time	0	1	2	3	4	5	6	7	8	9	10
Yield		5.00%	5.00%	5.00%	5.00%	5.00%	5.00%	5.00%	5.00%	5.00%	5.00%
P	1.0000	0.9524	0.9070	0.8638	0.8227	0.7835	0.7462	0.7107	0.6768	0.6446	0.6139
ΣQ	1.0000	0.9524	0.9070	0.8638	0.8227	0.7835	0.7462	0.7107	0.6768	0.6446	0.6139
U(i)	5.00%	4.98%	4.96%	4.94%	4.92%	4.91%	4.90%	4.89%	4.89%	4.89%	4.88%

d(i,j)

j	0	1	2	3	4	5	6	7	8	9	10
10											0.8828
9										0.8927	
8									0.9019		0.9019
7								0.9103		0.9104	
6							0.9180		0.9182		0.9183
5						0.9251		0.9253		0.9255	
4					0.9316		0.9319		0.9320		0.9321
3				0.9375		0.9378		0.9380		0.9381	
2			0.9429		0.9433		0.9435		0.9437		0.9437
1		0.9479		0.9482		0.9485		0.9487		0.9488	
0	0.9524		0.9528		0.9531		0.9533		0.9534		0.9534
−1		0.9569		0.9572		0.9574		0.9576		0.9577	
−2			0.9610		0.9612		0.9614		0.9615		0.9615
−3				0.9647		0.9649		0.9650		0.9651	
−4					0.9680		0.9682		0.9683		0.9683
−5						0.9711		0.9712		0.9712	
−6							0.9738		0.9739		0.9739
−7								0.9763		0.9763	
−8									0.9785		0.9785
−9										0.9805	
−10											0.9823

Q(i,j)

j	0	1	2	3	4	5	6	7	8	9	10
10											0.0005
9										0.0010	
8									0.0022		0.0049
7								0.0049		0.0097	
6							0.0107		0.0189		0.0233
5						0.0232		0.0359		0.0408	
4					0.0499		0.0665		0.0689		0.0657
3				0.1064		0.1189		0.1116		0.0998	
2			0.2257		0.2027		0.1708		0.1434		0.1208
1		0.4762		0.3224		0.2427		0.1919		0.1561	
0	1.0000		0.4535		0.3087		0.2335		0.1855		0.1517
−1		0.4762		0.3255		0.2474		0.1974		0.1621	
−2			0.2278		0.2086		0.1791		0.1531		0.1315
−3				0.1095		0.1258		0.1215		0.1117	
−4					0.0528		0.0731		0.0787		0.0779
−5						0.0256		0.0414		0.0494	
−6							0.0124		0.0231		0.0302
−7								0.0060		0.0127	
−8									0.0029		0.0069
−9										0.0014	
−10											0.0007

FIGURE 8.8 Black–Derman–Toy Discount Factors and Pure Security Prices

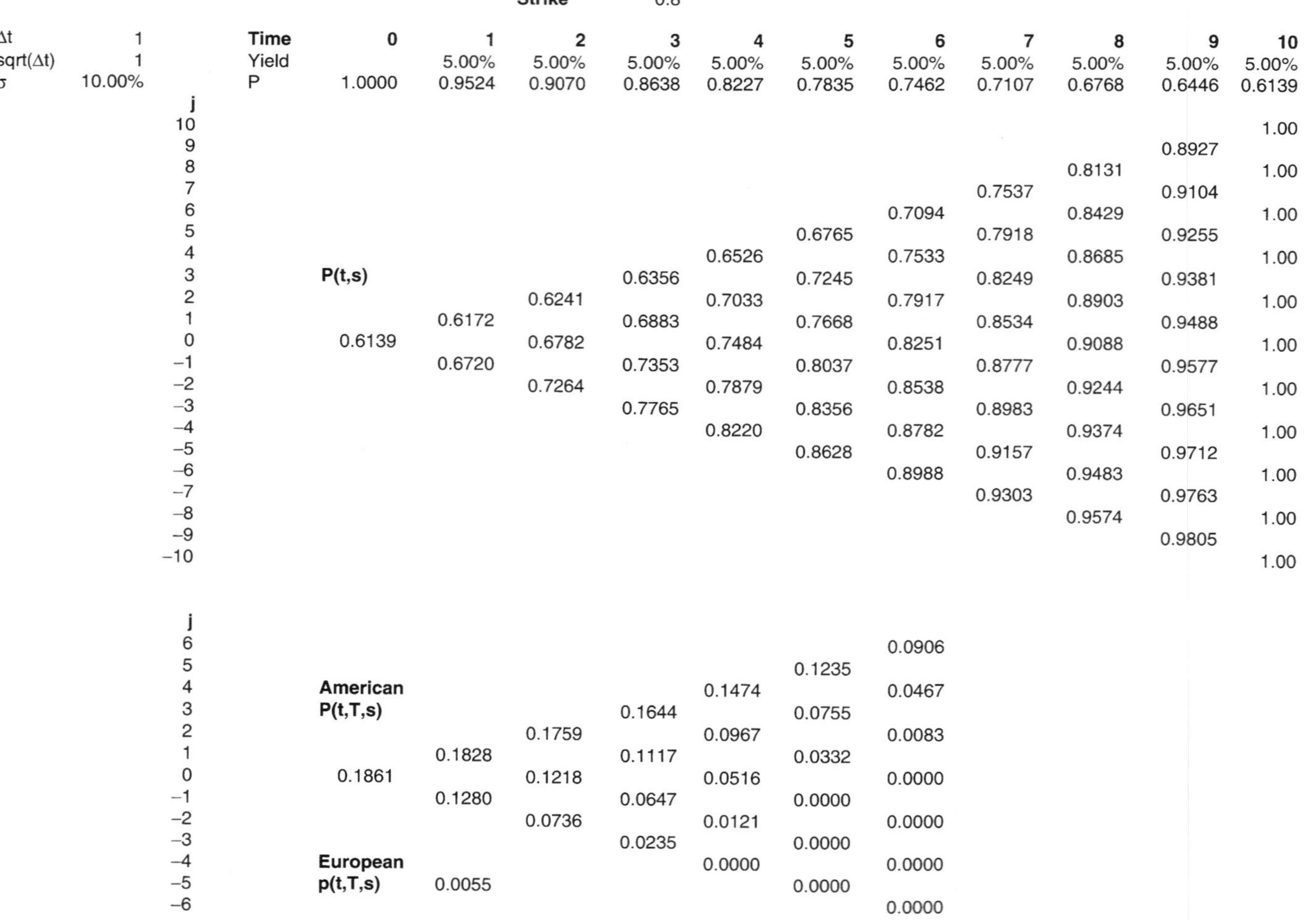

			Strike	0.8
Δt	1			
sqrt(Δt)	1			
σ	10.00%			

j		Time	0	1	2	3	4	5	6	7	8	9	10
		Yield		5.00%	5.00%	5.00%	5.00%	5.00%	5.00%	5.00%	5.00%	5.00%	5.00%
		P	1.0000	0.9524	0.9070	0.8638	0.8227	0.7835	0.7462	0.7107	0.6768	0.6446	0.6139
10													1.00
9												0.8927	
8											0.8131		1.00
7										0.7537		0.9104	
6									0.7094		0.8429		1.00
5								0.6765		0.7918		0.9255	
4							0.6526		0.7533		0.8685		1.00
3	P(t,s)					0.6356		0.7245		0.8249		0.9381	
2					0.6241		0.7033		0.7917		0.8903		1.00
1				0.6172		0.6883		0.7668		0.8534		0.9488	
0			0.6139		0.6782		0.7484		0.8251		0.9088		1.00
−1				0.6720		0.7353		0.8037		0.8777		0.9577	
−2					0.7264		0.7879		0.8538		0.9244		1.00
−3						0.7765		0.8356		0.8983		0.9651	
−4							0.8220		0.8782		0.9374		1.00
−5								0.8628		0.9157		0.9712	
−6									0.8988		0.9483		1.00
−7										0.9303		0.9763	
−8											0.9574		1.00
−9												0.9805	
−10													1.00

j		0	1	2	3	4	5	6
6								0.0906
5							0.1235	
4	**American**					0.1474		0.0467
3	**P(t,T,s)**				0.1644		0.0755	
2				0.1759		0.0967		0.0083
1			0.1828		0.1117		0.0332	
0		0.1861		0.1218		0.0516		0.0000
−1			0.1280		0.0647		0.0000	
−2				0.0736		0.0121		0.0000
−3					0.0235		0.0000	
−4	**European**					0.0000		0.0000
−5	**p(t,T,s)**		0.0055				0.0000	
−6								0.0000

FIGURE 8.9 Spreadsheet for Pure Discount Bond Price

FIGURE 8.10 Characteristics of a European Swaption

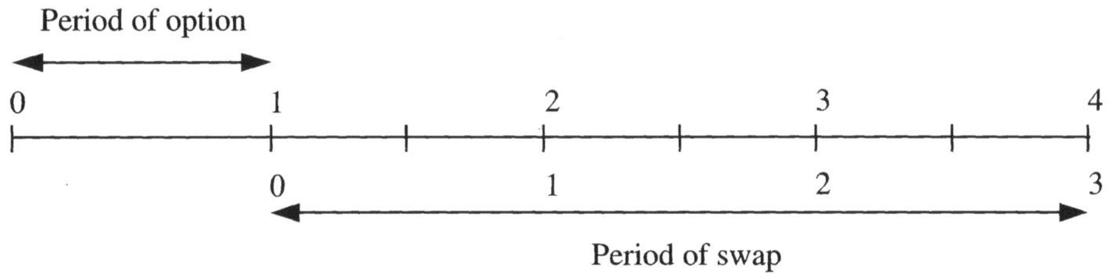

Recall from Chapter 6 that a swaption giving the holder the right to pay fixed and receive floating ("payer" swaption) is equivalent to a put on a fixed rate bond with strike price equal to the principal of the swap, and with the coupon payments equal to half the quoted swap rate if the reset dates are semi-annual. If the swaption gives the holder the right to pay floating and receive fixed ("receiver" swaption) it is equivalent to a call on a fixed rate bond. Let $B_{i,j}$ represent the value of the fixed rate bond at node (i, j) in the tree, and *coupon*/2 the cashflow at each coupon date.[6]

The first stage to pricing the derivative is to construct the short-rate tree out until the end of the life of the instrument underlying the option. In our example $N_T = 1$ and $N_s = 1 + 3 = 4$. We initialise the value of the fixed rate bond underlying the swap at each of the nodes at time step N_s, $B_{Ns,j}$:

$$B_{Ns,j} = 1 + \frac{coupon}{2} \tag{8.28}$$

We then apply backward induction for the coupon bond price, taking discounted expectations until time T:[7]

$$B_{i,j} = \tfrac{1}{2}d_{i,j}(B_{i+1,j+1} + B_{i+1,j-1}) \quad \forall \text{ nodes } j \text{ at time step } i \tag{8.29}$$

Using the state prices at all nodes at time step N_T the swaption price can be evaluated for payer swaptions and receiver swaptions, we have respectively:

$$\text{payer swaption} = \sum_j Q_{N_T,j} \max\{0, 1 - B_{N_T,j}\} \tag{8.30}$$

$$\text{receiver swaption} = \sum_j Q_{N_T,j} \max\{0, B_{N_T,j} - 1\} \tag{8.31}$$

Figure 8.11 gives a pseudo-code implementation of the procedure for pricing a European receiver swaption.

Example : Payer Swaption Valuation in a Binomial Tree

We price a two-year European payer swaption which exercises into a new three-year swap. The term structure is assumed to be flat at 5 per cent with annual compounding, and the short-rate volatility is assumed to be 10 per cent. The exercise price of the swaption is 4.5 per cent. We assume annual payments are made on the underlying swap. Figure 8.12 shows the calculations.

FIGURE 8.11 Pseudo-code for Pricing European Receiver Swaptions in a Binomial Tree

```
initialise_parameters { Ns, NT, coupon }

build_short_rate_tree { determines d[i,j] and Q[i,j] for all
                        i and j until time step Ns }

{ initialise coupon bond maturity condition for fixed side of swap }

for j = -Ns to Ns step 2 do B[Ns,j] = 1 + coupon/2

{ derive the coupon bond price in the tree via discounted expectations }

for i = (Ns-1) downto NT do

  for j = -i to i step 2 do
    if i = coupon_payment_date
     then B[i,j] = d[i,j]*0.5*(B[i+1,j+1]+B[i+1,j-1]+coupon/2)
     else B[i,j] = d[i,j]*0.5*(B[i+1,j+1]+B[i+1,j-1])
  next j

next i

{ for European swaption value utilise the pure security prices }
C[0,0] = 0
for j = -NT to NT step 2 do
  C[0,0] = C[0,0] + Q[NT,j]*max{0, B[NT,j] - 1}

European_receiver_swaption_price = C[0,0]
```

We have constructed trees for the one-period discount factor and the state prices as far as year 5 with $\Delta t = 1$ year. A receiver swaption is a put option on a coupon bond with the strike price equal to the principal of the swap (=1) and the coupon on the bond equal to the swap rate.

The first step is to recover the bond price and so we construct a tree for $B_{i,j}$. At the maturity time the pay-off to the bond $= 1 + 0.045 = 1.045$. The bond price tree is constructed via backwards induction in the usual manner, taking into account the annual coupon payments. For example:

$$\begin{aligned}B_{4,2} &= \tfrac{1}{2} \times 0.9433 \times (1.045 + 1.045 + 0.045)\\ &= 1.0069\\ B_{2,0} &= \tfrac{1}{2} \times 0.9528 \times (0.9811 + 0.9996 + 0.045)\\ &= 0.9650\end{aligned}$$

The pay-off to the option at node (i, j), $C_{i,j}$, is calculated as the pay-off to a put on the bond with strike price equal to 1, i.e.

$$\begin{aligned}C_{2,2} &= \max(0, 1 - 0.9360)\\ &= 0.0640\end{aligned}$$

FIGURE 8.12 Payer Swaption Valuation in a Binomial Tree

swap rate 4.50%

Assume annual payments

2 year option into a (new) 3 year swap

Δt	1	**Time**	**0**	**1**	**2**	**3**	**4**	**5**
sqrt(Δt)	1	Yield		5.00%	5.00%	5.00%	5.00%	5.00%
σ	10.00%	P	1.0000	0.9524	0.9070	0.8638	0.8227	0.7835
		ΣQ	1.0000	0.9524	0.9070	0.8638	0.8227	0.7835
		U(i)	5.00%	4.98%	4.96%	4.94%	4.92%	4.91%

d(i,j)

j	0	1	2	3	4	5
5						0.9251
4					0.9316	
3				0.9375		0.9378
2			0.9429		0.9433	
1		0.9479		0.9482		0.9485
0	0.9524		0.9528		0.9531	
−1		0.9569		0.9572		0.9574
−2			0.9610		0.9612	
−3				0.9647		0.9649
−4					0.9680	
−5						0.9711

Q(i,j)

j	0	1	2	3	4	5
5						0.0232
4					0.0499	
3				0.1064		0.1189
2			0.2257		0.2027	
1		0.4762		0.3224		0.2427
0	1.0000		0.4535		0.3087	
−1		0.4762		0.3255		0.2474
−2			0.2278		0.2086	
−3				0.1095		0.1258
−4					0.0528	
−5						0.0256

B(t,s)

j	0	1	2	3	4	5
5						1.0450
4					0.9944	
3				0.9592		1.0450
2			0.9360		1.0069	
1		–		0.9811		1.0450
0	–		0.9650		1.0174	
−1		–		0.9996		1.0450
−2			0.9897		1.0261	
−3				1.0151		1.0450
−4					1.0334	
−5						1.0450

Receiver Swaption

j	0	1	2
2			0.0640
1		0.0469	
0	**0.0327**		0.0350
−1		0.0217	
−2			0.0103

$$C_{2,0} = \max(0, 1 - 0.9650)$$
$$= 0.0350$$

The value of the option at (0, 0) is calculated using the pure security prices:

$$C_{0,0} = \sum_j Q_{2,j} C_{2,j} = 0.0640 \times 0.2257 + 0.0350 \times 0.4535 + 0.0103 \times 0.2278$$
$$= 0.0327$$

8.6.3 Pricing of Interest Rate Exotics

In a recent paper Clewlow, Pang and Strickland (1997) extend the numerical procedures of this chapter to the pricing of exotic (both American featured and path-dependent) interest rate derivatives. Examples that they consider are American swaptions into new and existing swaps, down and out barrier caps, lookback caps, average rate caps, and index amortising rate swaps.

8.7 SUMMARY

In this chapter we have shown how to construct binomial trees for the short rate — concentrating on the model of BDT, although the techniques are more generally applicable. We construct binomial trees for versions of the model fitted to market yield curve data only, as well as extensions to models fitted to both yield and volatility data. Using the constructed trees we have then shown how to price a number of interest rate derivatives.

ENDNOTES

1. We consider the yield curve out as far as the life of the instrument underlying the interest rate derivative.
2. It is possible to capture mean reversion in a binomial tree for the short rate, but this involves varying the time step.
3. See Sandmann and Sondermann (1994) for the unsuitability of using continuous compounding for lognormal models.
4. This is the discrete version of the Kolmogorov forward equation.
5. This must be solved using a numerical search technique such as that of Newton–Raphson.
6. We assume that the principal of the swap is 1.
7. At the time steps that coincide with coupon payment dates for the bond underlying the swap we have to add back the coupon payments.

9

Constructing Trinomial Trees for the Short Rate

9.1 INTRODUCTION

IN this chapter we extend the binomial procedures of Chapter 8 to building trinomial trees for the short rate. The extra degree of freedom which this extension allows, enables us to implement short-rate models that exhibit mean reversion, including the well-known models of HW and BK — see sections 7.3 and 7.6 of Chapter 7. We again look at both models that fit to yield curve data and models that fit to yield and volatility data. The material in this chapter is partially based on a series of papers by John Hull and Alan White (Hull and White, 1993, 1994a,b) and will be developed consistent with the notation of Chapter 8 unless otherwise stated.

9.2 BUILDING SHORT-RATE TREES

In the binomial framework of Chapter 8 the time step was fixed (at Δt) and the probabilities fixed (at 1/2) which left us with the freedom of adjusting the space step. For the trinomial trees of this chapter we will fix the time step (again at Δt) and also the space step (at Δr), leaving us with the probabilities to adjust in order that the change in r in the tree has the correct mean and standard deviation over each time interval Δt for the process that we are approximating. Thus the values of the short rate r at nodes other than the origin are equally spaced and have the form $r_{0,0} + j\Delta r$, where j is a positive or negative integer. The time values considered are the same as in Chapter 8 and have the form $i\Delta t$, where i is a non-negative integer. The node on the tree where $t = i\Delta t$ and $r_{0,0} + j\Delta r$ is referred to as the (i, j) node.

As we saw in Chapter 3 the trinomial technique is basically an explicit finite difference scheme, and stability and convergence conditions suggest a good relationship between Δr and the time step Δt to be (see Hull and White, 1993)

$$\Delta r = \sigma\sqrt{3\Delta t} \tag{9.1}$$

Figure 9.1 shows three possible alternative branching processes at each node in a trinomial tree.

Interpreting these branching processes in the context of a mean reverting short rate, then branching process (a) is a normal branching process where we can move up by Δr, stay the same and move down by Δr. Branching process (b) represents the situation when r is currently low and we can move up by $2\Delta r$, move up by Δr and stay the same, whilst

FIGURE 9.1 Alternative Branching at Nodes in a Trinomial Tree

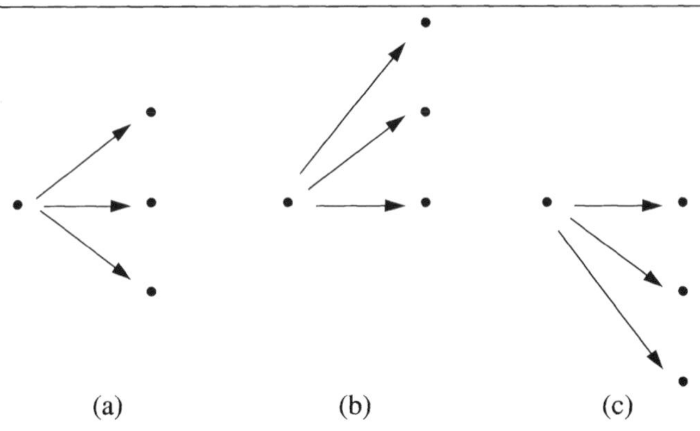

branching process (c) represents the situation when r is currently high and we can stay the same, move down by Δr and move down by $2\Delta r$. The branching processes (b) and (c) are therefore determined by mean reversion in the short rate to a long term mean, from below and above respectively. Figure 9.2 depicts a typical tree after three time steps.

Note that the state index j now runs from the lowermost node at time step i to the upper most node in steps of 1. Because of the effect of mean reversion we cannot determine the index value of the uppermost and lowermost nodes are at time $i\Delta t$ until we construct the tree. This is different from Chapter 8 when we knew that at the lower node $j = -i$ and the upper node $j = i$.

We begin in the following section by describing the general procedure applied to one of the simplest term structure consistent short-rate models that captures mean reversion. This model is the "normal" interest rate model of Chapter 7 commonly referred to as the "extended Vasicek" or "Hull and White" model — it fits the initial yield curve by

FIGURE 9.2 Typical Trinomial Tree After three Time Steps

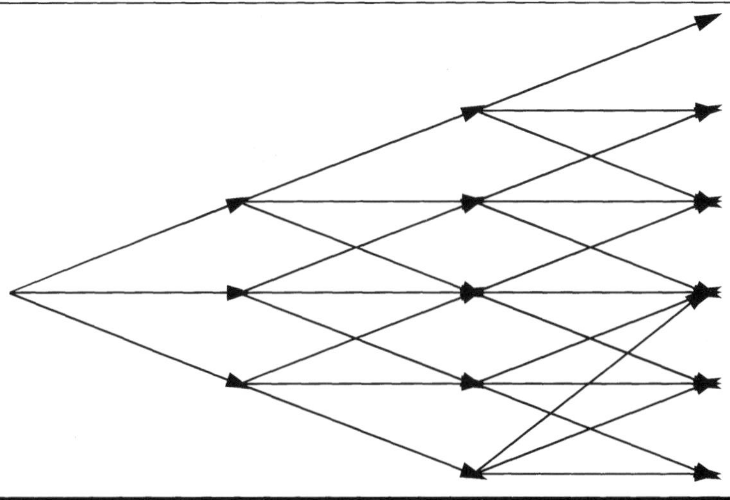

construction, and its defining stochastic differential equation is given by equation (7.8) which we repeat here:

$$dr = [\theta(t) - \alpha r]dt + \sigma\, dz \tag{9.2}$$

Although in some cases we can use the analytical solutions discussed in Chapter 7, we will need to build trees for the short rate for pricing American options, and for European options with more complicated pay-offs than simple puts or calls.

Later in this chapter we show how the methodology can be extended to the cases where the short-rate volatility can be dependent on the level of the rate, extended to processes that are functions of the short rate (for example, a popular implementation is in terms of the log of the short rate) and also to short-rate processes that are consistent with initial market volatility data.

9.3 BUILDING TRINOMIAL TREES CONSISTENT WITH THE PROCESS $dr = [\theta(t) - \alpha r]dt + \sigma\, dz$

For this process the drift function is known but contains the unknown function of time $\theta(t)$ that permits consistency with the initial yield curve. Recall that the volatility structure is determined by the constant parameters of the model and is given by equation (7.10). In order to be able to construct the tree, $\theta(t)$ must be determined so that all discount bonds are priced correctly. In order to aid our exposition, we define the following notation:

$\theta(i\Delta t)$: time-dependent θ at the ith time step.

$\mu_{i,j}$: drift rate of r at node (i, j).

$p_{\mathrm{u},i,j}$: probability associated with the upward branch emanating from node (i, j).

$p_{\mathrm{m},i,j}$: probability associated with the middle branch emanating from node (i, j).

$p_{\mathrm{d},i,j}$: probability associated with the downward branch emanating from node (i, j).

For the model considered in this section the drift term $\mu_{i,j}$ is given by $\mu_{i,j} = [\theta(i\Delta t) - \alpha r_{i,j}]\Delta t$. The short rate at the origin of the tree $r_{0,0}$ is by definition the yield on the shortest maturing bond $R(1)$. Many practitioners implement this model with continuously compounded interest rates which we adopt for this chapter. With this convention the one-period discount factors are given by

$$d_{i,j} = e^{-r_{i,j}\Delta t} \tag{9.3}$$

Suppose the tree has already been constructed up to time $n\Delta t$. The short rate at time $i\Delta t$ applies to the period between $i\Delta t$ and $(i+1)\Delta t$, and so a tree up to $i\Delta t$ reflects the values of $R(n)$ for $n \leq i+1$. In constructing the branches between $i\Delta t$ and $(i+1)\Delta t$ a value of $\theta(i\Delta t)$ must be chosen so that the tree is consistent with the yield on a bond maturing at time $i+2$ (i.e. $R(i+2)$). Once $\theta(i\Delta t)$ has been determined, the drift rates $\mu_{i,j}$ for r at nodes $i\Delta t$ can be calculated. The branches emanating from the nodes at time $i\Delta t$ and their associated probabilities are then chosen to be consistent with the drift term of the process and with the short-rate volatility, σ. The three nodes from node (i, j) are $(i+1, k+1)$ — the "upper" node, $(i+1, k)$ — the "middle" node and $(i+1, k-1)$ — the "lower" node with the (integer) value of k being chosen so that $r_{i+1,k}$ is as close as possible to the expected value of r, which by definition is given by $r_{ij} + \mu_{i,j}$. Note that for the normal branching process $k = j$ and for the branching processes (b) and (c) of Figure 9.1, $k = j + 1$ and $k = j - 1$ respectively.

The probabilities associated with node (i, j) can be shown to be

$$\begin{aligned} p_{\mathrm{u},i,j} &= \frac{\sigma^2 \Delta t + \eta^2}{2\Delta r^2} + \frac{\eta}{2\Delta r} \\ p_{\mathrm{m},i,j} &= 1 - \frac{\sigma^2 \Delta t + \eta^2}{\Delta r^2} \\ p_{\mathrm{d},i,j} &= 1 - p_{\mathrm{u},i,j} - p_{\mathrm{m},i,j} \end{aligned} \tag{9.4}$$

where $\eta = \mu_{i,j} + (j - k)\Delta r$.

To derive the function $\theta(.)$ we again use forward induction, deriving state prices as the tree is being constructed, from known values at the previous time step, via the relationship:

$$Q_{i,j} = \sum_{j'} Q_{i-1,j'} p_{j',j} d_{i-1,j'} \tag{9.5}$$

with $p_{j',j}$ the probability of moving from node $(i - 1, j')$ to node (i, j). For any given j', this is zero for most of the j's. Although this equation looks more complicated than the corresponding relationship for the binomial methodology (cf. equation (8.7)) it is in fact exactly the same, i.e. the summation over the nodes which lead to node (i, j) of the product of the state prices at time step $i-1$, the transition probabilities, and the one-period discount factors. Once determined, the state prices can be used to derive the function $\theta(.)$ which, for the short-rate model of this section, is given at the ith time step by[1]

$$\theta(i\Delta t) = \frac{1}{\Delta t}(i+2)R(i+2) + \frac{\sigma^2 \Delta t}{2} + \frac{1}{\Delta t^2} \ln \sum_j Q_{i,j} e^{-2r_{i,j}\Delta t + \alpha r_{i,j}\Delta t^2} \tag{9.6}$$

For the initial θ this simplifies to

$$\theta(0\Delta t) = \frac{2R(2)}{\Delta t} + \frac{\sigma^2 \Delta t}{2} + \frac{\alpha r_{0,0}\Delta t^2 - 2r_{0,0}\Delta t}{\Delta t^2} \tag{9.7}$$

The full procedure to construct the trees is the following. Assume $i > 0$ and that $\theta((i - 1)\Delta t)$, $Q_{i-1,j}$, $\mu_{i-1,j}$, $p_{i-1,j}$, $r_{i-1,j}$ and $d_{i-1,j}$ have been found for all j at time step $i - 1 (r_{0,0} = R(1), Q_{0,0} = 1)$.

Step 1: From $\mu_{i-1,j}$ and the implied branching process create the short-rate and discount factors at time i.

$$\begin{aligned} r_{i,j} &= r_{0,0} + j\Delta r \quad \forall j \text{ at } i \\ d_{i,j} &= e^{-r_{i,j}\Delta t} \end{aligned}$$

Step 2: Update the pure security prices for every node at time step i according to equation (9.5).

Step 3: Determine $\theta(i\Delta t)$ from equation (9.6).

Step 4: Using $\theta(i\Delta t)$ and $r_{i,j}$ determine $\mu_{i,j}$ for all j.

$$\mu_{i,j} = [\theta(i\Delta t) + \alpha r_{i,j}]\Delta t$$

Step 5: Decide on the branching process (determines k).
Step 6: Calculate the probabilities via equation (9.4).

Figure 9.3 gives a pseudo-code implementation of the procedure. The tree is constructed with N time steps.

FIGURE 9.3 Pseudo-code for Constructing a Trinomial Tree Consistent with the Process $dr = [\theta(t) - \alpha r]dt + \sigma dz$

```
initialise_parameters (alpha, sig, N, T)

{ pre-calculate constants }
dt = T/N
dr = sig*sqrt(3*dt)

{ initialise yield curve }
for i = 0 to N do
  R[i] = initial_yield_curve[i]
  P[i] = exp(-R[i]*i*dt)
next i

{ initialise first node }
r[0,0] = R[1]
Q[0,0] = 1
d[0,0] = exp(-r[0,0]*dt)

{ evolve tree for the short rate }

for i = 0 to (N-1) do

  if i > 0 do
   { using mu[i-1,j] create rate nodes at time step i }

    for j = low_node[i] to top_node[i] do
      r[i,j] = r[0,0]+j*dr
      d[i,j] = exp(-r[i,j]*dt)
    next j

    { update pure security prices at time step i }

    for j = low_node[i] to top_node[i] do
      Q[i,j] = Σj'Q[i-1,j']*p[j',j]*d[i-1,j']

    { find theta at time step i }
    Q1 = 0
    for j = low_node[i] to top_node[i] do
      Q1 = Q1 + Q[i,j]*exp(-2*r[i,j]*dt+alpha*r[i,j]*dt*dt)

  end if

theta[i]= 1/dt*(i+2)*R[i+2]+(sig*sig*dt)/2+1/(dt*dt)*ln(Q1)
```

(continues)

FIGURE 9.3 ***(continued)***

```
{ calculate drift and decide branch process }

for j = low_node[i] to top_node[i] do
  mu[i,j] = (theta[i]-alpha*r[i,j])*dt

  decide_branch_process { determines k }

  { calculate probabilities }
  eta = mu[i,j] + (j-k)*dr
  pu[i,j] = (sig*sig*dt+eta*eta)/(2*dr*dr)+eta/(2*dr)
  pm[i,j] = 1 - (sig*sig*dt+eta*eta)/(dr*dr)
  pd[i,j] = 1 - pu[i,j] - pm[i,j]
next j

next i
```

Example : Constructing a Trinomial Tree Consistent with the Process $dr = [\theta(t) - \alpha r]dt + \sigma dz$

Figure 9.4 shows a trinomial tree constructed for two time steps (Δt = one year) for the HW model consistent with the initial term structure of interest rates. The term structure is assumed to be increasing from 5 per cent after one year to 6.5 per cent at year 5. The parameters describing the volatility structure are assumed to be $\alpha = 0.10$ and $\sigma = 0.014$. The structure at each node (i, j) of the tree has the following form:

$r_{i,j}$	$p_{u,i,j}$
$Q_{i,j}$	$p_{m,i,j}$
$\mu_{i,j}$	$p_{d,i,j}$

$$r_{0,0} = R(1) = 0.05$$

$$\Delta r = \sigma\sqrt{3\Delta t} = 0.014\sqrt{3 \times 1} = 0.0242 = 2.42 \text{ per cent}$$

In order to show the calculations the following notation also holds:

$$\Sigma(i) = \sum_j Q_{i,j} e^{-2r_{i,j}\Delta t + \alpha r_{i,j}\Delta t^2}$$

for j across all the nodes at time i, with

$$\theta(i) = \frac{1}{\Delta t}(i+2)R(i+2) + \frac{\sigma^2 \Delta t}{2} + \frac{1}{\Delta t^2} \ln \Sigma(i)$$

We show how to construct the relevant formulation at node (2, 1). The first step is to determine the short rate:

$$\begin{aligned} r_{2,1} &= r_{0,0} + \Delta r \\ &= 0.05 + 0.0242 \\ &= 0.0742 = 7.42 \text{ per cent} \end{aligned}$$

FIGURE 9.4 Two-step Trinomial Tree for Hull–White Model

			Initial Yield Curve	
			Maturity	Yield
α	0.100		1.00	5.00%
σ	0.014		2.00	5.50%
			3.00	6.00%
Δt	1.000		4.00	6.25%
Δr	0.0242	1.212%	5.00	6.50%

i	0	1.00	2.00
Σ(i)	−0.0950	0.8489	0.7845
θ(i)	0.0151	0.0163	0.0074
R[i]		5.00%	5.50%
P[i]	1.0000	0.9512	0.8958
ΣQ		0.9512	**0.8958**

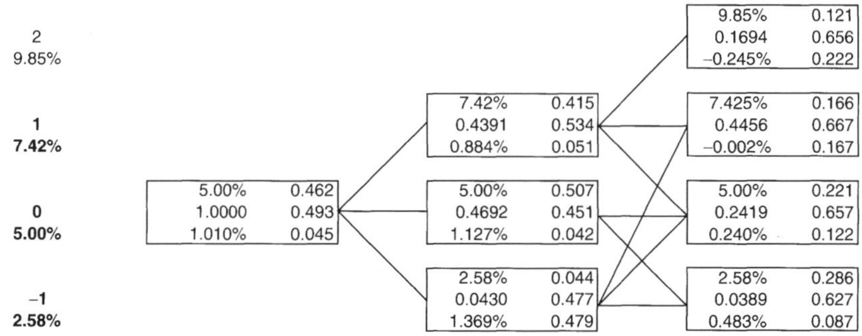

Node (j, rate)	Step 0		Step 1		Step 2	
2 9.85%					9.85% 0.1694 −0.245%	0.121 0.656 0.222
1 **7.42%**			7.42% 0.4391 0.884%	0.415 0.534 0.051	7.425% 0.4456 −0.002%	0.166 0.667 0.167
0 **5.00%**	5.00% 1.0000 1.010%	0.462 0.493 0.045	5.00% 0.4692 1.127%	0.507 0.451 0.042	5.00% 0.2419 0.240%	0.221 0.657 0.122
−1 **2.58%**			2.58% 0.0430 1.369%	0.044 0.477 0.479	2.58% 0.0389 0.483%	0.286 0.627 0.087

We then update the state prices

$$Q_{i,j} = \sum_{j'} Q_{i-1,j'} P_{j',j} e^{-r_{i-1,j'}\Delta t}$$

$$\begin{aligned} Q_{2,j} &= \sum_{j'} Q_{1,j'} P_{j',j} e^{-r_{1,j'}\Delta t} \\ &= 0.4391 \times 0.534 e^{-0.0742(1)} + 0.4692 \times 0.507 e^{-0.050(1)} \\ &\quad + 0.0430 \times 0.044 e^{-0.0258(1)} \\ &= 0.4456 \end{aligned}$$

Next determine $\Sigma(i) = \sum_j Q_{i,j} e^{-2r_{i,j}\Delta t + \alpha r_{i,j}\Delta t^2}$

$$\begin{aligned} &= 0.1694 e^{-2\times 0.0985(1) + 0.10 \times 0985(1)^2} \\ &\quad + 0.04456 e^{-2\times 0.0742(1) + 0.10\times 0.0742(1)^2} \\ &\quad + 0.2419 e^{-2\times 0.0500(1) + 0.10\times 0.0500(1)^2} \\ &\quad + 0.0389 e^{-2\times 0.0258(1) + 0.10\times 0.0258(1)^2} \\ &= 0.7845 \end{aligned}$$

which gives

$$\theta(i\Delta t) = \frac{1}{\Delta t}(i+2)R(i+2) + \frac{\sigma^2 \Delta t}{2} + \frac{1}{\Delta t^2} \ln \Sigma(i)$$

$$
\begin{aligned}
&= \frac{1}{1}(2+2)(0.0625) + \frac{0.014^2(1)}{2} + \frac{1}{1^2}\ln(0.7845) \\
&= 0.0074
\end{aligned}
$$

In order to check if the state prices are correct we can apply equation (8.27) to the bond price, i.e.

$$
\begin{aligned}
P_{0,n} &= \sum_j 1 \times Q_{n,j} \\
0.8958 &= 0.1694 + 0.4456 + 0.2419 + 0.0389 = P_{0,2}
\end{aligned}
$$

Now that $\theta(.)$ has been determined we can decide the branching process.

$$
\begin{aligned}
\mu_{i,j} &= [\theta(i) - \alpha r_{i,j}]\Delta t \\
&= [0.0074 - 0.1(0.0742)] \times 1 \\
&= -0.002 \text{ per cent}
\end{aligned}
$$

The expected value of the short rate at the end of the period is therefore

$$
7.425 \text{ per cent} - 0.002 \text{ per cent} = 7.423 \text{ per cent}
$$

and so we have a normal branching process, i.e. $k = 1$.

Now compute the probabilities according to equation (9.4).

$$
\begin{aligned}
\eta &= \mu_{2.1} + (1-k)\Delta t \\
&= -0.000021 + (1-1)1 \\
&= -0.000021 \\
p_{u,2,1} &= \frac{\sigma^2 \Delta t + \eta^2}{2\Delta r^2} + \frac{\eta}{2\Delta r} \\
&= \frac{0.014^2(1) + (-0.000021)^2}{2(0.024)^2} + \frac{(-0.000021)}{2(0.024)} \\
&= 0.166 \\
p_{m,2,1} &= 1 - \frac{\sigma^2 \Delta t + \eta^2}{\Delta r^2} \\
&= 1 - \left[\frac{0.014^2(1) + (-0.000021)^2}{0.024^2}\right] \\
&= 0.667
\end{aligned}
$$

$$
\begin{aligned}
p_{d,2,1} &= 1 - p_{u2,1} - p_{m,2,1} \\
&= 1 - 0.166 - 0.667 \\
&= 0.167
\end{aligned}
$$

9.4 BUILDING TREES CONSISTENT WITH THE PROCESS $dr = [\theta(t) - \alpha r]dt + \sigma r^{\beta} dz$

Although we have concentrated on the HW model, the approach we describe in section 9.3 is sufficiently general to cover a range of specifications for the drift term — to implement these models we simply adjust the drift term which may influence the branching process. We now go on to describe a generalisation of the tree which allows the user to build trees consistent with the short rate when there is a more general specification for the volatility term. We will concentrate on models with a mean-reverting drift term and the general volatility specification of Chapter 7:

$$dr = [\theta(t) - \alpha r]dt + \sigma r^{\beta} dz \tag{9.8}$$

If $\beta = 0$ we have the HW model, with $\beta = \frac{1}{2}$ giving us a model similar to Cox-Ingersoll-Ross (CIR) (see Chapter 6). In order to construct short-rate trees consistent with models specified by equation (9.8) we define a function of r, $x(t) = x(r(t))$, that has a constant instantaneous standard deviation. This can be achieved for the short-rate models of this section by setting:

$$x(t) = r(0)^{\beta} \int \frac{dr}{r(t)^{\beta}} \tag{9.9}$$

where $r(0)$ denotes the level of the short rate at the initial time. A tree is constructed in the same way as before, but now for $x(t)$, where the spacing between x-values, Δx, is constant and equal to $\sigma r(0)^{\beta}\sqrt{3\Delta t}$. Firstly, information at the initial node on the tree, (0, 0), is determined. For the short rate and pure security prices this is given as before by

$$r_{0,0} = R(1), \qquad Q_{0,0} = 1$$

For the equivalent x-tree $x_{0,0}$ is given by

$$x_{0,0} = r_{0,0} \ln(r_{0,0}) \quad \text{if } \beta = 1 \tag{9.10}$$

$$x_{0,0} = \frac{r_{0,0}}{1-\beta} \qquad \text{if } \beta \neq 1$$

We can now sweep through, creating the x-tree as described in section 9.3 for the short-rate tree. In order to determine the branching process for the x-tree we have to determine the drift term of the new process. For the models of this section the drift term is calculated as

$$\left[[\theta(t) - \alpha r] \left(\frac{r(0)}{r} \right)^{\beta} - \frac{\sigma^2 \beta r(0)^{\beta} r^{\beta-1}}{2} \right] \Delta t \tag{9.11}$$

Therefore the drift term at each node (i, j), $\mu(i, j)$ is given by

$$\left[[\theta(i) - \alpha r_{i,j}] \left(\frac{r(0)}{r_{i,j}} \right)^{\beta} - \frac{\sigma^2 \beta r(0)^{\beta} r_{i,j}^{\beta-1}}{2} \right] \Delta t \tag{9.12}$$

where the function θ is now given at the ith time step by

$$\theta(i) = \frac{\sum_j [Q_{i,j} e^{-2r_{i,j}\Delta t}(1 + \alpha r_{i,j}\Delta t^2)] - e^{(-(i+2)R(i+2)\Delta t)}}{\sum_j [Q_{i,j} e^{-2r_{i,j}\Delta t} \Delta t^2]} \tag{9.13}$$

For the initial θ this simplifies to

$$\theta(0\Delta t) = \frac{e^{-2r_{0,0}\Delta t}(1 + \alpha r_{0,0}\Delta t^2) - e^{(-2R(2)\Delta t)}}{e^{-2r_{0,0}\Delta t} \Delta t^2} \tag{9.14}$$

In order to recover the short rate from the x-tree, we can translate between $x(t)$ and $r(t)$ via the solution to equation (9.9) which is given by

$$r = \exp\left(\frac{x}{r(0)}\right) \qquad \text{if } \beta = 1 \tag{9.15}$$

$$r = \left((1-\beta)\frac{x}{r(0)^{\beta}}\right)^{\frac{1}{1-\beta}} \qquad \text{if } \beta \neq 1$$

The transition probabilities are given by equation (9.4) with σ replaced with σr^{β}.

$$p_{\mathrm{u},i,j} = \frac{(\sigma r_0^{\beta})^2 \Delta t + \eta^2}{2\Delta x^2} + \frac{\eta}{2\Delta x} \tag{9.16}$$

$$p_{\mathrm{m},i,j} = 1 - \frac{(\sigma r(0)^{\beta})^2 \Delta t + \eta^2}{\Delta x^2}$$

$$p_{\mathrm{d},i,j} = 1 - p_{\mathrm{u},i,j} - p_{\mathrm{m},i,j}$$

Figure 9.5 gives a pseudo-code implementation of the procedure with N time steps.

Figure 9.6 shows a trinomial tree constructed for two time steps ($\Delta t =$ one year) for the process in equation (9.8) with $\beta = \frac{1}{2}$. The term structure is assumed to be increasing from 5 per cent after one year to 5.6 per cent after 4 years. The constant short rate parameters are given by $\alpha = 0.10$ and $\sigma = 0.045$. The top tree is the tree for x-nodes and the bottom tree the tree for r. The structure for the x-nodes is as follows:

$x_{i,j}$	$p_{u,i,j}$
$Q_{i,j}$	$p_{m,i,j}$
$\mu_{i,j}$	$p_{d,i,j}$

FIGURE 9.5 Pseudo-code for General Short Rate Volatility ($\beta \neq 1$) Fitted to Yield Curve Data

```
initialise_parameters { alpha, r = R[1], sig, beta, N, T }

{ pre-calculate constants }
dt = T/N
dx = (sig*r^beta)*sqrt(3*dt)

{ initialise yield curve}
for i = 0 to N do
  R[i] = initial_yield_curve[i]
  P[i] = exp(-R[i]*i*dt)
next i

{ initialise first node }
r[0,0] = R[1]
x[0,0] = r[0,0]/(1-beta)
d[0,0] = exp(-r[0,0]*dt)
Q[0,0] = 1

{ evolve tree for the short rate }
```

FIGURE 9.5 ***(continued)***

```
for i = 0 to (N-1) do

  if i > 0
    { using mu[i-1,j] create x, r and d nodes at step i }

    for j = low_node[i] to top_node[i] do
      x[i,j] = x[0,0]+j*dx
      r[i,j] = (1-beta)*(x[i,j]/(r[0,0]^beta))^(1/(1-beta))
      d[i,j] = exp(-r[i,j]*dt)
    next j

    { update pure security prices at i }

    for j = low_node[i] to top_node[i] do
      Q[i,j]=Σj'Q[i-1,j']*p[j',j]*d[i-1,j']

  { find theta }
  Q1 = 0
  Q2 = 0
  for j = low_node[i] to top_node[i] do
    Q1 = Q1+Q[i,j]*exp(-2*r[i,j]*dt)*(1+alpha*r[i,j]*dt*dt)
    Q2 = Q2+Q[i,j]*exp(-2*r[i,j]*dt+alpha*r[i,j]*dt*dt)
  next j

  theta[i] = (Q1 - exp(-(i+2)*R[i+2]*dt)) / Q2

  { calculate drift and decide branch process }

  for j = low_node[i] to top_node[i] do
    mu[i,j] = ((theta[i]-alpha*r[i,j])*(r[0,0]/r[i,j])^beta
            - (sig^2*beta*r[0,0]^beta*r[i,j]^(beta-1))/2)*dt

    decide_branch_process {determines k}

    { calculate probabilities }
    eta = mu[i,j] + (j-k)*dx
    pu[i,j] = ((sig*r[0,0]^beta)^2+eta*eta)/(2*dx*dx)+eta/(2*dx)
    pm[i,j] = 1 - ((((sig*r[0,0]^beta)^2)*dt+eta*eta)/(dx*dx)
    pd[i,j] = 1 - pu[i,j] - pm[i,j]
  next j

next i
```

The structure for the r-nodes is:

$r_{i,j}$
$d_{i,j}$

$$\Delta x = 0.045 \times \sqrt{0.05} \times \sqrt{3 \times 1} = 0.017$$

$$x_{0,0} = \frac{0.05}{1 - 0.5} = 0.10$$

FIGURE 9.6 Building a Trinomial Tree for the Process $dr = [\theta(t) - \alpha r]dt + \sigma r^{\beta} dz$

α	0.100			
σ	0.045		r(0)	5.00%
β	0.5		x(0)	10.00%
Δt	1.000			
Δx	0.017	0.866%	σr^β	0.01

Initial Yield Curve

Maturity	Yield
1.00	5.00%
2.00	5.25%
3.00	5.50%
4.00	5.60%

i	0	1.00	2.00
Σu(i)		0.8569	
Σl(i)		0.8522	
θ(i)	0.0100	0.0105	
R[i]		5.00%	5.25%
P[i]	1.0000	0.9512	0.9003
ΣQ(i,j)		0.9512	0.9003

Tree for x

j / x	i = 0	i = 1	i = 2
2 **13.46%**			13.46% 0.0749
1 **11.73%**		11.73% 0.256 / 0.3137 0.643 / 0.267% 0.101	11.73% 0.3827
0 **10.00%**	10.00% 0.330 / 1.0000 0.600 / 0.449% 0.071	10.00% 0.353 / 0.5703 0.583 / 0.502% 0.064	10.00% 0.3703
−1 **8.27%**		8.27% 0.042 / 0.0672 0.376 / 0.798% 0.582	8.27% 0.0724

Tree for r

i = 0	i = 1	i = 2
		9.06% 0.9133
	6.88% 0.9335	6.88% 0.9335
5.00% 0.9512	5.00% 0.9512	5.00% 0.9512
	3.42% 0.9664	3.42% 0.9664

$$x_{i,j} = x_{0,0} + j \times \Delta x$$

i.e.

$$x_{1,1} = 0.10 + (1 \times 0.0173) = 0.1173$$

$$r_{1,1} = 1 - 0.5\frac{0.1173}{\sqrt{0.05}} = 0.0688$$

From equation (9.13)

$$\theta(1) = \frac{\Sigma u(1) - e^{-(1+2)\times 0.055\times 1}}{\Sigma l(1)} = 0.0105$$

where

$$\begin{aligned}\Sigma u(1) &= 0.3137e^{-2\times 0.0688\times 1} \times (1 + 0.10 \times 0.0688 \times 1^2)\\ &\quad + 0.5703e^{-2\times 0.0500\times 1} \times (1 + 0.10 \times 0.0500 \times 1^2)\\ &\quad + 0.0672e^{-2\times 0.0342\times 1} \times (1 + 0.10 \times 0.0342 \times 1^2)\\ &= 0.8569\end{aligned}$$

$$\begin{aligned}\Sigma l(1) &= 0.3137e^{-2\times 0.0688\times 1} \times 1^2\\ &\quad + 0.5703e^{-2\times 0.0500\times 1} \times 1^2\\ &\quad + 0.0672e^{-2\times 0.0342\times 1} \times 1^2\\ &= 0.8522\end{aligned}$$

9.5 A MORE EFFICIENT PROCEDURE FOR THE PROCESS $dr = [\theta(t) - \alpha r]dt + \sigma\, dz$

Recently, Hull and White (1994a, 1994b) have proposed another methodology for computing short-rate trees which is computationally more efficient than the general method that we have outlined and has better accuracy. However, the methodology is only valid for models where the short rate (or some function of the rate — see the next section) follows a mean-reverting, arithmetic process.[2] The computational savings and increased accuracy arise because, instead of restricting the interest rate at each time step to be of the form: $r_{0,0} + j\Delta r$, the geometry of the tree is arranged so that it is symmetrical about a central node which corresponds exactly to the expected value of r. The following exposition is based on building a tree for the HW model.

First we build a tree for r, as before, assuming that $\theta(t) = 0$ and the initial value of r is zero:

$$dr = -\alpha r\, dt + \sigma\, dz \tag{9.17}$$

The values of r, in this simplified tree, at time $i\Delta t$ are just $j\Delta r$, where $-m_i \leq j \leq m_i$, for some m_i as the tree is symmetrical about the central node. Figure 9.7 illustrates the geometry of a typical tree after three time steps.

As before, to build the tree we must determine the branching process at each node. The choice of which branching process to take depends on the sign of α and the magnitude of j, and is chosen to ensure that the probabilities, which are themselves chosen to match the expected change and variance of the change in the simplified process for r, are positive.[3] When α is strictly positive, HW suggest switching from a normal branching process ((a) of Figure 9.1) to a downward branching process ((c) of Figure 9.1) when j equals the smallest integer greater than $-0.184/M$, where M is the expected value of the change in r

FIGURE 9.7 Typical Simplified Tree After Three Time Steps

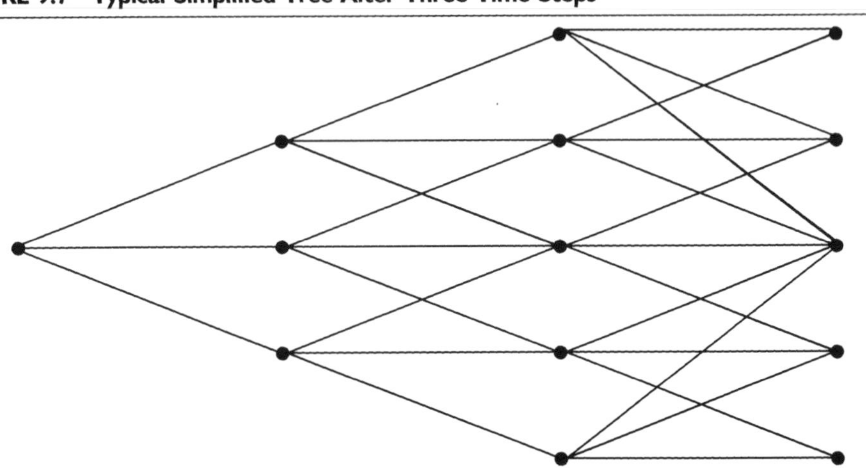

(i.e. $M = -\alpha\Delta t$), and to maintain symmetry we switch from the normal branching process to an upward branching process ((b) of Figure 9.1) at node j equal to the negative of this.

Hull and White (1994a) show that the probabilities corresponding to the branching process (a), (b), and (c) of Figure 9.1 are given by

(a)

$$p_{\mathrm{u}} = \frac{1}{6} + \frac{j^2M^2 + jM}{2}$$

$$p_{\mathrm{m}} = \frac{2}{3} - j^2M^2$$

$$p_{\mathrm{d}} = \frac{1}{6} + \frac{j^2M^2 - jM}{2}$$

(b)

$$p_{\mathrm{u}} = \frac{1}{6} + \frac{j^2M^2 - jM}{2}$$

$$p_{\mathrm{m}} = -\frac{1}{3} - j^2M^2 + 2jM$$

$$p_{\mathrm{d}} = \frac{7}{6} + \frac{j^2M^2 - 3jM}{2}$$

(c)

$$p_{\mathrm{u}} = \frac{7}{6} + \frac{j^2M^2 + 3jM}{2}$$

$$p_{\mathrm{m}} = -\frac{1}{3} - j^2M^2 - 2jM$$

$$p_{\mathrm{d}} = \frac{1}{6} + \frac{j^2M^2 + jM}{2}$$

The simplified tree at this stage is obviously not consistent with the observed term structure. We now introduce the time varying drift component into the short-rate process by displacing the nodes at time $i\Delta t$ by an amount a_i. The a_i are chosen to ensure that the tree correctly returns the observed discount function. The value of r at node (i, j) in the new tree equals the value of r at the corresponding node in the old "simple" tree plus a_i; the probabilities remain unchanged. The new tree represents the familiar HW process $dr = [\theta(t) - \alpha r]dt + \sigma\, dz$. Figure 9.8 illustrates the geometry of the resulting tree after the simplified tree has been adjusted by the displacements.

To describe how these displacement coefficients are constructed, suppose that the $Q_{i,j}$'s have been determined as far as time step i. In order to choose a_i so that the tree correctly prices an $(i+1)\Delta t$ discount bond the displacement term must take the form (see Hull and White, 1994a for a proof).

$$a_i = \frac{\ln \sum_j Q_{i,j} e^{-j\Delta r \Delta t} - \ln P(i+1)}{\Delta t} \tag{9.18}$$

At the origin of the tree a_0 reduces to the simpler form:

$$a_0 = \frac{-\ln P(1)}{\Delta t} \tag{9.19}$$

Hedge parameters can be quickly and easily calculated within this framework. If we calculate hedge parameters with respect to some "shift" in the term structure, then this shift only affects the displacement coefficients — it does not affect the position of the branches relative to the central branch or the probabilities associated with the branches.

Figure 9.9 gives a pseudo-code implementation of the procedure.

FIGURE 9.8 Simplified Tree with Displacements After Three Time Steps

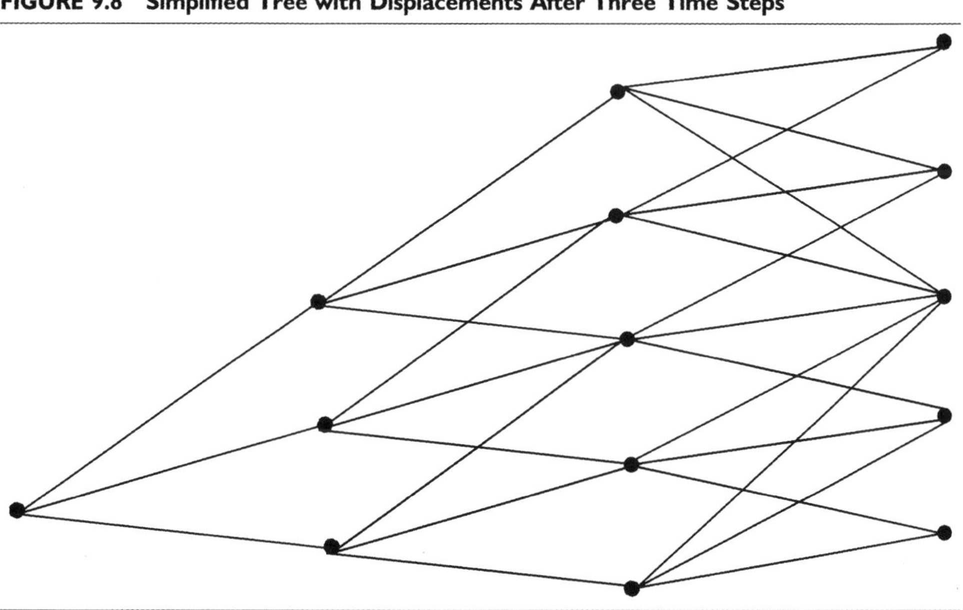

FIGURE 9.9 Pseudo Code for Constructing a Trinomial Tree Consistent with the Process $dr = [\theta(t) - \alpha r]dt + \sigma\, dz$ Using the New Procedure

```
initialise_parameters { alpha, sig, N, T }

{ precalculate constants }
dt = T/N
dr = sig*sqrt(3*dt)
M = -alpha*dt
jmax = smallest_integer > -1.835/M

{ initialise yield curve }
for i = 1 to N do
    R[i] = initial_yield_curve[i]
    P[i] = exp(-R[i]*i*dt)
next i

{ initialise first node for simplified process }
r[0,0] = 0
Q[0,0] = 1

{ calculate tree for simplified process }

for i = 0 to (N-1) do

  if i < jmax then top_node[i] = i else top_node[i] = jmax
  { create rate nodes at time step i }
  for j = -top_node[i] to top_node[i] do r[i,j] = j*dr

  { calculate probabilities - first central to top nodes }
  for j = 0 to top_node[i] do
    if j = jmax
      then
        pu[i,j] = 7/6+(j*j*M*M-3*j*M)/2
        pm[i,j] = -1/3-(j*j*M*M-2*j*M)
        pd[i,j] = 1 - pu[i,j] - pm[i,j]
      else
        pu[i,j] = 1/6+(j*j*M*M+j*M)/2
        pm[i,j] = 2/3-(j*j*M*M)
        pd[i,j] = 1 - pu[i,j] - pm[i,j]
  next j

  { calculate other probabilities by reflection }
  for j = -1 down to -top_node[i] do
    pu[i,j] = pd[i,-j]
    pm[i,j] = pm[i,-j]
    pd[i,j] = pu[i,-j]
  next j

{ update state prices, find time-varying drift and displace nodes }

for i = 0 to (N-1) do
```

FIGURE 9.9 (*continued*)

```
if i > 0 do
  { update pure security prices }
  for j = -low_node[i] to top_node[i] do
     Q[i,j] = Σj'Q[i-1,j']*p[j',j]*d[i-1,j']

  { find a[i]'s}
  sum = 0
  for j = -low_node[i] to top_node[i] do
    sum = sum + Q[i,j]*exp(-j*dt*dr)
  a[i] = (ln(sum)-lnP[i+1])/dt

  { displace nodes to obtain r[.] and d[.] }
  for j = -low_node[i] to top_node[i] do
    r[i,j] = r[i,j] + a[i]
    d[i,j] = exp(-r[i,j]*dt)
  next j

next i
```

Example : Constructing a Trinomial Tree Consistent with the Process $dr = [\theta(t) - \alpha r]dt + \sigma\, dz$ Using the New Procedure

We construct a tree to match an upward-sloping term structure from 5 per cent at one year to 6.75 per cent at four years with continuous compounding. The constant short-rate parameters are assumed to be $\alpha = 0.10$ and $\sigma = 0.01$. The time step for the tree is further assumed to be one year. Figure 9.10 shows the calculations. The top tree is the tree for x-nodes, which here represents the short rate in the simplified tree, and the bottom tree the tree for r. The structure for the x-nodes is as follows:

$x_{i,j}$	$p_{u,i,j}$
$Q_{i,j}$	$p_{m,i,j}$
	$p_{d,i,j}$

The structure for the r-nodes is

$r_{i,j}$
$d_{i,j}$

$$\Delta t = 1.0$$

$$x_{0,0} = 0.0$$

$$r_{0,0} = R(1) = 0.05$$

$$Q_{0,0} = 1$$

$$d_{0,0} = e^{-0.05\times 1} = 0.9512$$

$$\Delta x = \Delta r = \sigma\sqrt{3\Delta t} = 0.01 \times \sqrt{3 \times 1} = 0.017$$

$$M = -0.1 \times 1 = -0.1$$

FIGURE 9.10 Trinomial Tree Consistent with the Process $dr = [\theta(t) - \alpha r]dt + \sigma dz$ Using the New Procedure

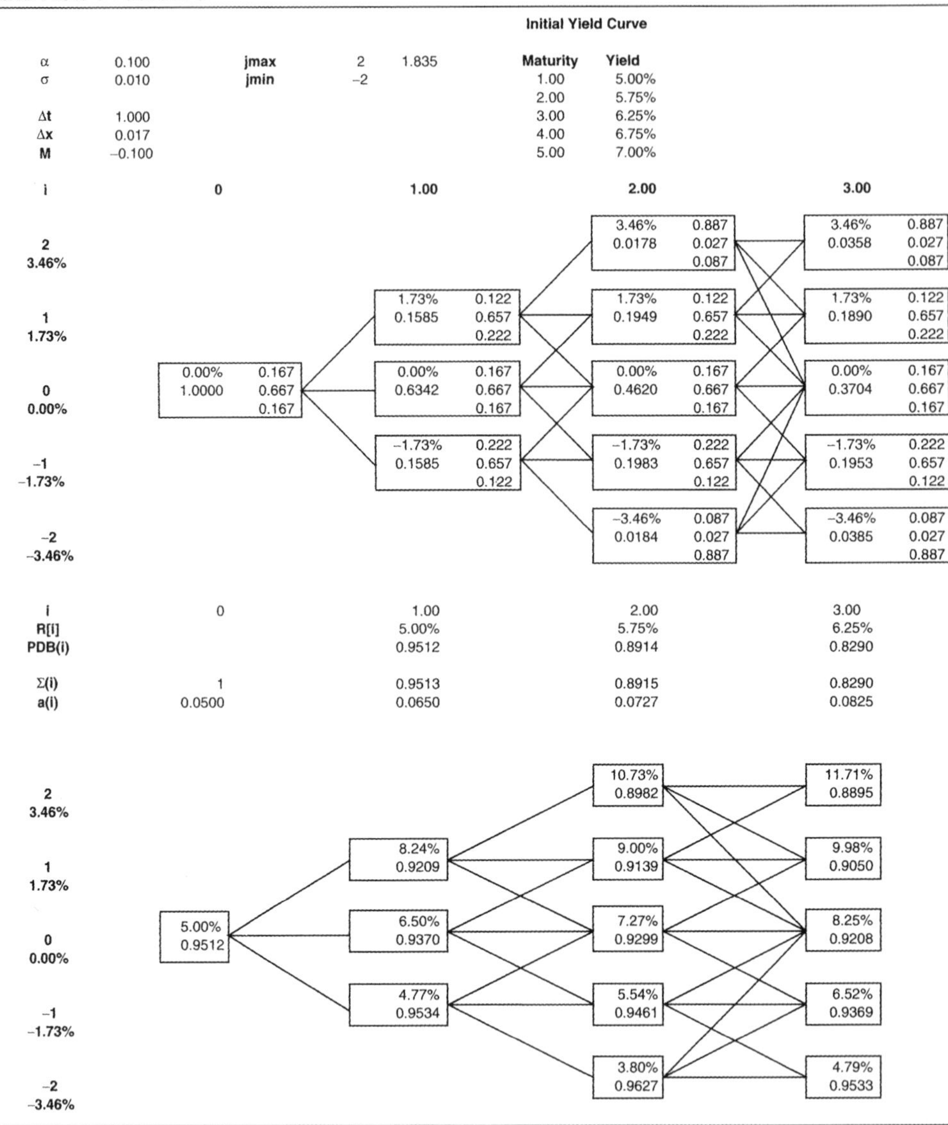

The branching process switches from normal to downward at $j = 2 = jmax$ (the smallest integer $> 1.835 = -0.1835/(-0.1)$).

At time step $i = 1$, the x-nodes are equally spaced at Δx, with the pure securities constructed in the usual way.

$$a(1) = \frac{\ln \sum_j - \ln P(2)}{\Delta t}$$

where

$$\sum_j = \sum_j Q_{i,j} e^{-j\Delta r\Delta t}$$
$$= 0.1585e^{-(-1)(0.017)(1)} + 0.6343e^{-(0)(0.017)(1)} + 0.1585e^{-(1)(0.017)(1)}$$
$$= 0.9513$$

Implying

$$a(1) = \frac{\ln(0.9513) - \ln(0.8914)}{1}$$
$$= 0.0650$$

The tree gets 'truncated' at $jmax = 2$.

The branching process at node (1,1) is normal ($j = 1 < jmax$) and so the probabilities are determined as follows:

$$p_{u,1,1} = \tfrac{1}{6} + \frac{1^2 \times (-0.1)^2 + 1 \times (-0.1)}{2} = 0.122$$
$$p_{m,1,1} = \tfrac{2}{3} - 1^2 \times (-0.1)^2 = 0.657$$
$$p_{d,1,1} = 1 - 0.122 - 0.657 = 0.222$$

The branching probabilities at node $(1, -1)$ are obtained by "reflecting" those at node (1, 1), i.e.

$$p_{u,1,-1} = p_{d,1,1} = 0.222$$
$$p_{m,1,-1} = p_{m,1,1} = 0.657$$
$$p_{d,1,-1} = p_{u,1,1} = 0.122$$
$$x_{1,-1} = x_{0,0} - \Delta x = 0.0 - 0.0173 = -0.0173$$
$$r_{1,-1} = x_{1,-1} + a(1) = -0.0173 + 0.0650 = 0.0477$$

9.6 BUILDING A TREE FOR THE PROCESS $d \ln r = [\theta(t) - \alpha \ln r]dt + \sigma\, dz$

Many practitioners dislike models which allow negative interest rates and so prefer to work with a lognormal process for the short rate. One process that is currently popular can be represented by the stochastic differential equation:

$$d \ln r = [\theta(t) - \alpha \ln r]dt + \sigma\, dz \tag{9.20}$$

By comparison with equations (7.8) and (7.22) we can view this model as a lognormal version of the HW model or as a restriction of the Black and Karasinski (1991) model to one time-dependent drift function. As with all the models so far in this chapter, the time-dependent term in the drift allows the model to return the observed discount function with the constant parameters α and σ determining the term structure of volatility.[4] The procedures for the model outlined in the previous section can be adapted to the model of

(9.20). We begin by setting $x = \ln r$, obtaining the process:

$$dx = [\theta(t) - \alpha x]dt + \sigma\, dz \tag{9.21}$$

We can now use the procedures of section 9.5 to build a tree for x, setting $\theta(t) = 0$ and starting with $x = 0$. The equations to calculate the functions a_j and $Q_{i,j}$ are modified. Recall that a_i is chosen so that the model prices an $(i+1)\Delta t$ bond correctly. The Δt-period interest rate at the jth node at time $i\Delta t$ is given by

$$r_{i,j} = \exp(a_i + j\Delta x) \tag{9.22}$$

Combining equation (8.5) and (9.22), a_i is found as the solution to the following equation:

$$P(i+1) = \sum_{j=-m_i}^{m_i} Q_{i,j} \exp[-\exp(a_i + j\Delta x)\Delta t] \tag{9.23}$$

where m_i denotes the uppermost node at time step i. When $i = 0$ equation (9.23) can be inverted to give $a_0 = \ln(r_{0,0})$.

Once we have constructed the tree for x the one-period short rate is given at each node as

$$r_{i,j} = e^{x_{i,j}} \tag{9.24}$$

Figure 9.11 gives a pseudo-code implementation of the procedure.

FIGURE 9.11 Pseudo-Code for Constructing a Trinomial Tree Consistent with the Process $d \ln r = [\theta(t) - d \ln r]dt + \sigma\, dz$

```
initialise_parameters { alpha,sig,N,T }

{ precalculate constants }
dt = T/N
dx = sig*sqrt(3*dt)
M = -alpha*dt
jmax = smallest_integer > -1.835/M

{ initialise yield curve }
for i = 1 to N do
    R[i] = initial_yield_curve[i]
    P[i] = exp(-R[i]*i*dt)
next i

{ initialise first node for simplified process for x }
x[0,0] = 0
Q[0,0] = 1

{ calculate tree for simplified process for x }

for i = 0 to (N-1) do
  if i < jmax then top_node[i] = i else top_node[i] = jmax
  { create rate nodes at time step i }
```

FIGURE 9.11 ***(continued)***

```
  for j = -low_node[i] to top_node[i] do x[i,j] = j*dx

  { calculate probabilities - first central to top nodes }
  for j = 0 to top_node[i] do
    if j = jmax
      then
        pu[i,j] = 7/6+(j*j*M*M-3*j*M)/2
        pm[i,j] = -1/3-(j*j*M*M-2*j*M)
        pd[i,j] = 1 - pu[i,j] - pm[i,j]
      else
        pu[i,j] = 1/6+(j*j*M*M+j*M)/2
        pm[i,j] = 2/3-(j*j*M*M)
        pd[i,j] = 1 - pu[i,j] - pm[i,j]
  next j

  { calculate other probabilities by reflection }
  for j = -1 down to -top_node[i] do
    pu[i,j] = pd[i,-j]
    pm[i,j] = pm[i,-j]
    pd[i,j] = pu[i,-j]
  next j

{ update state prices, find time-varying drift and displace
nodes for x }

for i = 0 to (N-1) do

  if i > 0
    { update pure security price's }
    for j = -low_node[i] to top_node[i] do
      Q[i,j] = Σj'Q[i-1,j']*p[j',j]*d[i-1,j']

  { solve for a[i] via a numerical search technique }
  { j runs from -low_node[i] to top_node[i] }
  P[i+1] = ΣjQ[i,j]*exp(-exp((a[i]+j*dr)*dt)

  { displace nodes in simplified tree to obtain updated x,
   calculate r[.] and d[.] }

  for j = -low_node[i] to top_node[i] do
    x[i,j] = x[i,j] + a[i]
    r[i,j] = exp(x[i,j])
    d[i,j] = exp(-r[i,j]*dt)
  next j

next i
```

Example : Constructing a Trinomial Tree Consistent with the Process $d \ln r = [\theta(t) - \alpha \ln r]dt + \sigma\, dz$

We construct a tree to match an upward-sloping term structure from 5 per cent at one year to 6.75 per cent at four years with continuous compounding. The constant short-rate parameters are assumed to be $\alpha = 0.15$ and $\sigma = 0.10$. The time step for the tree is further assumed to be one year. Figure 9.12 shows the calculations. The top tree is the tree for x-nodes and the bottom tree the tree for r. The structure for the x-nodes is as follows:

$x_{i,j}$	$p_{u,i,j}$
$Q_{i,j}$	$p_{m,i,j}$
$a_i + x_{i,j}$	$p_{d,i,j}$

The structure for the r-nodes is

$r_{i,j}$
$d_{i,j}$

$$\Delta t = 1.0$$

$$x_{0,0} = 0.0$$

$$r_{0,0} = R(1) = 0.05$$

$$d_{0,0} = e^{-0.05\times 1} = 0.9512$$

$$\Delta x = \sigma\sqrt{3\Delta t} = 0.1 \times \sqrt{3 \times 1} = 0.173$$

$$M = -\alpha\Delta t = -0.15 \times 1 = -0.15$$

The branching process switches from normal to downward at $j = 2$ (the smallest integer $> 1.223 = -0.1835/(-0.15)$).

At time step $i = 1$, the x-nodes are equally spaced at Δx, with the pure securities constructed in the usual way; a_1 is formed as the solution to equation (9.23):

$$P(2) = \sum_{j=-1}^{1} Q_{1,j} e^{[-\exp(a_1 + j\Delta x)\Delta t]}$$

$$0.8914 = 0.1585 e^{[-\exp(a_1+(-1)\times 0.173)\times 1]} + 0.6343 e^{[-\exp(a_1+(0)\times 0.173)\times 1]} + 0.1585 e^{[-\exp(a_1+(1)\times 0.173)\times 1]}$$

The solution to this equation is given by $a_1 = -2.7380$; a_1 is used to update the x-nodes at time 1:

$$x_{1,1} = 0.1732 + (-2.7380) = -2.5648$$

$$x_{0,0} = 0.0000 + (-2.7380) = -2.7380$$

$$x_{1,-1} = -0.1732 + (-2.7380) = -2.9112$$

The short rates and one-period discount factors can now be updated according to equation (9.24):

$$r_{1,1} = e^{x_{1,1}} = e^{-2.5648} = 0.0769$$

FIGURE 9.12 Trinomial Tree Consistent with the Process $d \ln r = [\theta(t) - \alpha \ln r]dt + \sigma dz$

α	0.150	jmax	2	1.223356
σ	0.100	jmin	−2	
Δt	1.000			
Δx	0.173			
M	−0.150			

Initial Yield Curve

Maturity	Yield
1.00	5.00%
2.00	5.75%
3.00	6.25%
4.00	6.75%
5.00	7.00%

Tree for x=lnr when θ(t) = 0

j				
2 0.3464			0.3464 0.762 0.0151 0.177 −2.2852 0.062	0.3464 0.0287 −2.0776
1 0.1732		0.1732 0.103 0.1585 0.644 −2.5648 0.253	0.1732 0.103 0.1936 0.644 −2.4584 0.253	0.1732 0.1900 −2.2508
0 0.0000	0.0000 0.167 1.0000 0.667 −2.9957 0.167	0.0000 0.167 0.6342 0.667 −2.7380 0.167	0.0000 0.167 0.4714 0.667 −2.6316 0.167	0.0000 0.3857 −2.4240
−1 −0.1732		−0.1732 0.253 0.1585 0.644 −2.9112 0.103	−0.1732 0.253 0.1958 0.644 −2.8048 0.103	−0.1732 0.1944 −2.5972
−2 −0.3464			−0.3464 0.062 0.0155 0.177 −2.9780 0.762	−0.3464 0.0302 −2.7704

i	0	1.00	2.00	3.00
t		1.00	2.00	3.00
R[i]		5.00%	5.75%	6.25%
PDB(i)		0.9512	0.8914	*0.8290*
Σ(i)		0.8914	0.8290	0.7582
a(i)	−2.9957	−2.7380	−2.6316	−2.4240
Solver		0.0000	0.0000	0.0000
ΣQ(i, j)		**0.9512**	**0.8914**	***0.8290***

j				
2			10.18% 0.9033	12.52% 0.8823
1		7.69% 0.9260	8.56% 0.9180	10.53% 0.9000
0	5.00% 0.9512	6.47% 0.9374	7.20% 0.9306	8.86% 0.9152
−1		5.44% 0.9470	6.05% 0.9413	7.45% 0.9282
−2			5.09% 0.9504	6.26% 0.9393

$$d_{1,1} = e^{-r_{1,1}\Delta t} = e^{-0.0769\times 1} = 0.9260$$

$$r_{1,0} = e^{-2.7380} = 0.0647$$
$$d_{1,0} = e^{-0.0647\times 1} = 0.9374$$

$$r_{1,-1} = e^{-2.9112} = 0.0544$$
$$d_{1,-1} = e^{-0.0544} = 0.9470$$

9.7 BUILDING TREES CONSISTENT WITH YIELD AND VOLATILITY DATA

The extension to fitting trinomial trees to pre-specified yield and volatility data is analogous to the binomial case and requires a change to the geometry of the trinomial tree so that it is binomial in the first time step, with equal probabilities of up and down movements, reverting to trinomial thereafter. This binomial first step allows us to determine the functions $P_U(i)$ and $P_D(i)$, identified in Chapter 8 as the yield curves from the first up step (U) and the first down step (D) respectively, consistent with the initial yield and volatility functions $P(i)$ and $\sigma_R(i)$. The idea of tree construction is then to sweep through the tree from the perspective of U and D determining the pure securities prices — exactly as in the binomial case. Because we are using continuously compounded interest rates, rather than the discrete rates of Chapter 8 we must replace equation (8.14) with the following:

$$\tfrac{1}{2}e^{-r_{0,0}\Delta t}[P_U(i) + P_D(i)] = P(i) \tag{9.25}$$

In the following section we show how the HW model of section 7.4 (defined by equation 7.15) can be implemented in a trinomial tree.[5]

9.8 BUILDING TREES CONSISTENT WITH THE PROCESS $dr = [\theta(t) - \alpha(t)r]dt + \sigma\, dz$

As in section 8.5 the first step in the tree construction is to determine $P_U(i)$ and $P_D(i)$ for all $i \geq 2$, consistent with equations (9.25) and (8.15). Which can be solved simultaneously to yield:

$$P_D(i) = P_U(i)^{\exp(-2\sigma_R(i)\sqrt{\Delta t})} \tag{9.26}$$

and where $P_U(i)$ is found as the solution to

$$P_U(i) + P_U(i)^{\exp(-2\sigma_R(i)\sqrt{\Delta t})} = 2P(i)e^{r_{0,0}\Delta t} \tag{9.27}$$

Once $P_U(i)$ and $P_D(i)$, have been determined we have determined the short rate at the two nodes at time Δt:

$$r_U = r_{1,1} = R_U(2) = -\frac{1}{\Delta t}\ln P_U(2) \tag{9.28}$$

$$r_D = r_{1,-1} = R_D(2) = -\frac{1}{\Delta t}\ln P_D(2)$$

At time $i \geq 2$ the nodes are equally spaced at $r_{0,0} + j\Delta r$ for some integer j. Figure 9.13 illustrates a typical tree after three time steps.

The tree is constructed from time Δt onward, using a procedure similar to that described in section 8.5. The two functions of time $\theta(t)$ and $\alpha(t)$ are chosen to be consistent with the identified $P_U(i)$ and $P_D(i)$.

The updating of the pure security prices, Q_U and Q_D, is analogous to equation (9.4):

$$Q_{U,i,j} = \sum_{j'} Q_{U,i-1,j'}\, p_{j',j}\, d_{i-1,j'} \tag{9.29}$$

$$Q_{D,i,j} = \sum_{j'} Q_{D,i-1,j'}\, p_{j',j}\, d_{i-1,j'} \tag{9.30}$$

FIGURE 9.13 Trinomial Tree for the Short Rate Consistent with Both Yield and Volatility Data

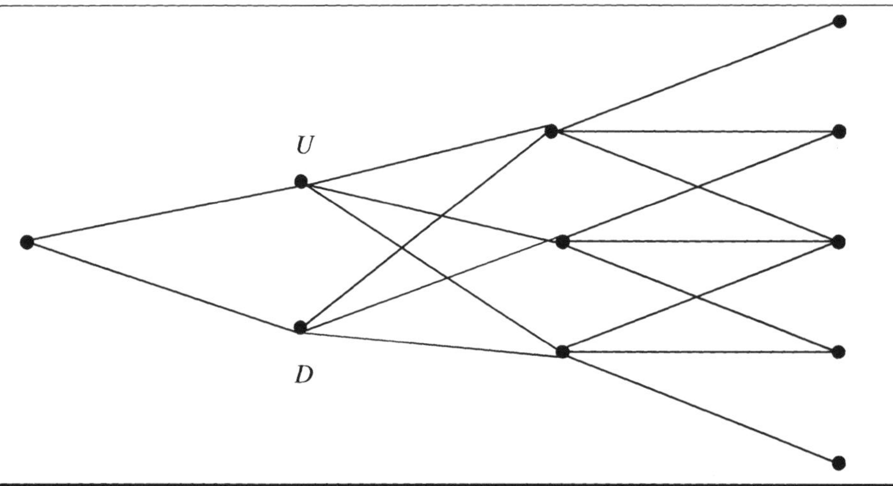

where $Q_{U,1,1} = 1$ and $Q_{D,1,-1} = 1$. Suppose that the tree has been constructed up to time $i\Delta t (i \geq 1)$. In order to determine the branching process for the next time step we need to determine the expected change, in the short-rate process, $[\theta(t) - \alpha(t)r]\Delta t$. Therefore, we need to identify $\theta(i\Delta t)$ and $\alpha(i\Delta t)$ and these need to be consistent with $P_U(i)$ and $P_D(i)$. It can be shown that:

$$\theta(i\Delta t) = \frac{de - bf}{ad - bc} \qquad \alpha(i\Delta t) = \frac{af - ce}{ad - bc} \tag{9.31}$$

where

$$a = \sum_j Q_{U,i,j} e^{-2r_{i,j}\Delta t} \Delta t^2 \qquad b = -\sum_j Q_{U,i,j} e^{-2r_{i,j}\Delta t} r_{i,j} \Delta t^2$$

$$c = \sum_j Q_{D,i,j} e^{-2r_{i,j}\Delta t} \Delta t^2 \qquad d = -\sum_j Q_{D,i,j} e^{-2r_{i,j}\Delta t} r_{i,j} \Delta t^2$$

$$e = \sum_j Q_{U,i,j} e^{-2r_{i,j}\Delta t} - P_U(i+2) \qquad f = \sum_j Q_{D,i,j} e^{-2r_{i,j}\Delta t} - P_D(i+2)$$

Once $\theta(i\Delta t)$ and $\alpha(i\Delta t)$ have been determined, the drift rates $\mu_{i,j}$ for r at nodes $i\Delta t$ are calculated as

$$\mu_{i,j} = \left[\theta(i\Delta t) - \alpha(i\Delta t) r_{i,j}\right] \Delta t \tag{9.32}$$

Consistent with our previous analysis, the drift determines the nodes where we can go to, enabling us to create the nodes $r_{i+1,j}$ for all j. The transition probabilities from nodes at time $i\Delta t$ to nodes at time $(i+1)\Delta t$ are calculated as equation (9.4), with the small difference that at $i = 1$, $\eta = r_{1,j} + \mu_{1,j} - (r_{0,0} + k\Delta r)$. Figure 9.14 gives a pseudo-code implementation of the procedure.

FIGURE 9.14 Pseudo-code for Building Short Rate Trees Consistent with Two Term Structures

```
initialise_parameters { N,T }

{ initialise yield curves }
for i = 1 to N do
    R[i] = initial_yield_curve[i]
    P[i] = exp(-R[i]*i*dt)
    sigR[i] = initial_volatility_curve[i]
next i

{ pre-compute constants }
dt = T/N
sdt = sqrt(dt)
sig = sigR[1]
dr = sig*sqrt(3*dt)
r[0,0] = R[1]

{ compute Pu[.] and Pd[.] }

for i = 2 to N do
  { using numerical search solve the following for Pu[i] }
  Pu[i] + Pu[i]^exp(-2*sigR[i]*sdt) = 2*P[i]*exp(r[0,0]*dt)
  Pd[i] = Pu[i]^exp(-2*sigR[i]*sdt)
next i

{ initialise first node }
pu = 0.5
pd = 0.5
d[0,0] = exp(-r[0,0]*dt)

{ initialise up (U) and down (D) nodes }
r[1,1] = -1/dt*ln(Pu[2])
r[1,-1] = -1/dt*ln(Pd[2])
d[1,1] = exp(-r[1,1]*dt)
d[1,-1] = exp(-r[1,-1]*dt)
Qu[1,1] = 1.0
Qd[1,-1] = 1.0

{ find theta and alpha for first time step }

a = exp(-2*r[1,1]*dt)*dt^2
b = -exp(-2*r[1,1]*dt)*r[1,1]*dt^2
c = exp(-2*r[1,-1]*dt)*dt^2
d = -exp(-2*r[1,-1]*dt)*r[1,-1]*dt^2
e = exp(-2*r[1,1]*dt)-Pu[3]
f = exp(-2*r[1,-1]*dt)-Pd[3]

theta[1] = ((d*e) - (b*f))/((a*d) - (b*c))
alpha[1] = ((a*f) - (c*e))/((a*d) - (b*c))
```

FIGURE 9.14 ***(continued)***

```
for j= -1 to 1 step 2 do

  mu[1,j] = (theta[1] - alpha[1]*r[1,j])*dt

  decide_branch_process { determines k }

  eta = r[1,j] + mu[1,j] - (r[0,0] + k*dr)

  { calculate probabilities }

  pu[1,j] = (sig*sig*dt+eta*eta)/(2*dr*dr)+eta/(2*dr)
  pm[1,j] = 1 - (sig*sig*dt+eta*eta)/(dr*dr)
  pd[1,j] = 1 - pu[i,j] - pm[i,j]
next j

{ grow tree for the short rate }

for i = 2 to (N-1) do

  { using mu[i-1,j] create nodes at time step i }

  for j = low_node[i] to top_node[i] do
    r[i,j] = r[0,0] + j*dr
    d[i,j] = exp(-r[i,j]*dt)
  next j

  { update pure security prices at time step i }

  for j = low_node[i] to top_node[i] do
    Qu[i,j] = ∑j'Qu[i-1,j']*p[j',j]*d[i-1,j']
    Qd[i,j] = ∑j'Qd[i-1,j,]*p[j',j]*d[i-1,j']
  next j

  { find theta and alpha }
  a = b = c = d = e = f = 0
  for j = low_node[i] to top_node[i] do

    a = a + Qu[i,j]*exp(-2*r[i,j]*dt)*dt^2
    b = b - Qu[i,j]*exp(-2*r[i,j]*dt)*r[i,j]*dt^2
    c = c + Qd[i,j]*exp(-2*r[i,j]*dt)*dt^2
    d = d - Qd[i,j]*exp(-2*r[i,j]*dt)*r[i,j]*dt^2
    e = e + Qu[i,j]*exp(-2*r[i,j]*dt) - Pu[i+2]
    f = f + Qd[i,j]*exp(-2*r[i,j]*dt) - Pd[i+2]

  next j

  theta[i] = ((d*e) - (b*f))/((a*d) - (b*c))
  alpha[i] = ((a*f) - (c*e))/((a*d) - (b*c))

  { compute drift and decide branch process }
```

FIGURE 9.14 ***(continued)***

```
   for j = low_node[i] to top_node[i] do

      mu[i,j] = (theta[i]-alpha[i]*r[i,j])*dt

      decide_branch_process { determines k }

      eta = mu[i,j] + (j-k)*dr
      { calculate probabilities }
      pu[i,j] = (sig*sig*dt+eta*eta)/(2*dr*dr)+eta/(2*dr)
      pm[i,j] = 1 - (sig*sig*dt+eta*eta)/(dr*dr)
      pd[i,j] = 1 - pu[i,j] - pm[i,j]

   next j

 next i
```

Example : Building a Short-rate Tree for HW Fitted to Both Yield and Volatility Data

We build a tree for the short rate with annual time steps to fit the initial yield and volatility curves given by:

Maturity	Yield (%)	Volatility (absolute)
1.0	5.0	0.0100
2.0	4.8	0.0095
3.0	4.7	0.0090
4.0	4.6	0.0085

Figure 9.15 shows the tree calculation.

The format for each node (i, j) in the tree is given by

$r_{i,j}$	$p_{u,i,j}$
$Q_{U,i,j}$	$p_{m,i,j}$
$Q_{D,i,j}$	$p_{d,i,j}$
$d_{i,j}$	η
	$\mu_{i,j}$

The volatilities given in the example are absolute volatilities and so we need to convert them to percentage volatilities by dividing them by the relevant yield. For example:

$$\sigma_R(2) = 0.0095/0.048 = 0.1979$$

The initial short rate and its volatility are given by the shortest dated yield and its volatility, i.e.

$$\sigma = \sigma_R(1) = 0.01$$

FIGURE 9.15 Hull–White Fitted to Both Yield and Volatility Data

σ	1.00%	r0	5.00%
Δt	1.000		
Δr	0.017		
sqrt(Δt)	1.000		

Initial Yield and Volatility Curves

Maturity	Yield	Vol
1.00	5.00%	1.000%
2.00	4.80%	0.950%
3.00	4.70%	0.900%
4.00	4.60%	0.850%
5.00	4.50%	0.800%

i	0	1.00	2.00	3.00
R[i]		5.00%	4.80%	4.70%
P[i]	1.0000	0.9512	0.9085	0.8685
V[i](%)			19.79%	19.15%
Pu[i]			0.9465	0.8973
Ru[i]			0.0550	0.0542
Pd[i]			0.9636	0.9288
diff(slvr)			0.0000	0.0000
a		0.8958	0.8508	
b		−0.0493	−0.0452	
c		0.9286	0.8953	
d		−0.0344	−0.0328	
e		−0.0015	−0.0023	
f		−0.0002	−0.0007	
θ(i)		0.0029	0.0034	
α(i)		0.0830	0.1156	
ΣQu			0.9465	0.8973
ΣQd			0.9636	0.9288

j / rate	Time 0	Time 1	Time 2	Time 3
2 8.46%				8.46% 0.0181 0.0049
1 6.73%		5.50% 0.282 1.0000 0.629 0.089 0.9465 0.003 −0.17%	6.73% 0.073 0.2672 0.604 0.0724 0.324 0.9349 −0.004 −0.43%	6.73% 0.2120 0.0499
0 5.00%	5.00% 0.9512		5.00% 0.108 0.5954 0.648 0.0878 0.244 0.9512 −0.002 −0.23%	5.00% 0.4608 0.1981
−1 3.27%		3.70% 0.075 0.091 1.0000 0.834 0.9636 −0.013 −0.02%	3.27% 0.157 0.0838 0.666 0.8035 0.177 0.9678 0.000 −0.03%	3.27% 0.1920 0.5385
−2 1.54%				1.54% 0.0143 0.1375

$$r = r_{0,0} = R(1) = 0.05$$

$$\Delta t = 1.0$$

$$\Delta r = \sigma\sqrt{3\Delta t} = 0.01\sqrt{3(1)} = 0.017$$

The first stage of the procedure is to determine $P_D(i)$ and $P_U(i)$ for $i \geq 2$. For example $P_U(i)$ is found as the solution to equation (9.27):

$$P_U(2) + P_U(2)^{\exp(-2\times 0.1979\times\sqrt{1})} = 2 \times 0.9085e^{0.05\times 1}$$

where $P(2) = e^{R(2)\times 2} = 0.9085$, implying that $P_U(2) = 0.9465$. Therefore from equation (9.26)

$$P_D(2) = 0.9465^{\exp(-2\times 0.1979\times\sqrt{1})} = 0.9636$$

$P_U(2)$ and $P_D(2)$ are the one-period discount factors at nodes (1, 1) and (1, −1) respectively, implying that $r_{1,1} = 0.0550$ and $r_{1,-1} = 0.0370$.

To illustrate the calculation of the drift term and probabilities, we look at time step $i = 2$. In order to calculate $\theta(2\Delta t)$ and $\alpha(2\Delta t)$ from equation (9.31) we first need to calculate a, b, c, d, e and f:

$$\begin{aligned}
a &= 0.2672e^{-2(0.0673)(1)}(1)^2 + 0.5954e^{-2(0.050)(1)}(1)^2 + 0.0838e^{-2(0.0327)(1)}(1)^2 \\
&= 0.8508 \\
b &= -0.2672e^{-2(0.0673)(1)}0.0673(1)^2 - 0.5954e^{-2(0.050)(1)}0.050(1)^2 \\
&\quad - 0.0838e^{-2(0.0327)(1)}0.0327(1)^2 \\
&= -0.0452 \\
c &= 0.0724e^{-2(0.0673)(1)}(1)^2 + 0.0878e^{-2(0.050)(1)}(1)^2 + 0.8035e^{-2(0.0327)(1)}(1)^2 \\
&= 0.8953 \\
d &= -0.0724e^{-2(0.0673)(1)}0.0673(1)^2 - 0.0878e^{-2(0.050)(1)}0.050(1)^2 \\
&\quad - 0.8035e^{-2(0.0327)(1)}0.0327(1)^2 \\
&= -0.0328 \\
e &= 0.2672e^{-2(0.0673)(1)} + 0.5954e^{-2(0.050)(1)} + 0.0838e^{-2(0.0327)(1)} - 0.8531 \\
&= -0.0023 \\
f &= 0.0724e^{-2(0.0673)(1)} + 0.0878e^{-2(0.050)(1)} + 0.8035e^{-2(0.0327)} - 0.8960 \\
&= -0.0007
\end{aligned}$$

Therefore, from equation (9.31)

$$\theta(2\Delta t) = \frac{(-0.0328)(-0.0023) - (-0.0452)(-0.0007)}{(0.8508)(-0.0328) - (-0.0452)(0.8953)} = 0.0034$$

$$\alpha(2\Delta t) = \frac{(0.8508)(-0.0007) - (0.8953)(-0.0023)}{(0.8508)(-0.0328) - (-0.0452)(0.8953)} = 0.1156$$

These functions can now be used to calculate the drift term at each of the nodes according to equation (9.32), i.e. for node (2, 0)

$$\begin{aligned}
\mu_{2,0} &= [\theta(2\Delta t) - \alpha(2\Delta t)r_{2,0}]\Delta t \\
&= (0.0034 - 0.1156(0.050))1 \\
&= -0.0023
\end{aligned}$$

The branching process at this node is therefore normal ((a) of Figure 9.1), and so $k = j = 0$, and we can determine the transition probabilities according to equation (9.4):

$$\eta = \mu_{2,0} + (0-0)\Delta r = -0.0023$$

$$P_{\mathrm{u},2,0} = \frac{0.01^2(1) + (-0.0023)^2}{2(0.017)^2} + \frac{(-0.0023)}{2(0.017)} = 0.108$$

$$P_{\mathrm{m},2,0} = 1 - \frac{0.01^2(1) + (-0.0023)^2}{(0.017)^2} = 0.648$$

$$P_{\mathrm{d},2,0} = 1 - 0.108 - 0.648 = 0.244$$

In order to illustrate the updating of the state price equations (9.29) and (9.30) we concentrate on node (3, 1):

$$Q_{U,3,0} = (0.2672)(0.604)(0.9349) + (0.5954)(0.108)(0.9512) = 0.2120$$

$$Q_{D,3,0} = (0.0724)(0.604)(0.9349) + (0.0878)(0.108)(0.9512) = 0.0499$$

9.9 PRICING INTEREST RATE DERIVATIVES IN A TRINOMIAL TREE

Pricing interest rate derivatives in a trinomial tree is analogous to that of binomial trees (see section 8.6) once we take into account that there are three branches from each node and that the probabilities are not fixed. Recall from Chapter 8 that $C_{i,j}$ denotes the value of a contingent claim at node (i, j). The discounted expectation formula of (8.23) in the trinomial framework becomes

$$C_{i,j} = d_{i,j} \times [p_{\mathrm{u},i,j}C_{i+1,\mathrm{u}} + p_{\mathrm{m},i,j}C_{i+1,\mathrm{m}} + p_{\mathrm{d},i,j}C_{i+1,\mathrm{d}}] \tag{9.33}$$

where $C_{i+1,\mathrm{u}}$, $C_{i+1,\mathrm{m}}$ and $C_{i+1,\mathrm{d}}$ are the contingent claim values at time step $(i + 1)$ of the three branches ("up", "middle" and "down" respectively) originating from the node (i, j) with $p_{\mathrm{u},i,j}$, $p_{\mathrm{m},i,j}$ and $p_{\mathrm{d},i,j}$ the associated transition probabilities. To illustrate the procedure we return to the T-maturity European call option on an s-maturity bond example of section 8.6.1. The price of the bond in the tree is determined via the discounted expectation:

$$P_{S_{i,j}} = d_{i,j} \times [p_{\mathrm{u},i,j}P_{S_{i+1,\mathrm{u}}} + p_{\mathrm{m},i,j}P_{S_{i+1,\mathrm{m}}} + p_{\mathrm{d},i,j}P_{S_{i+1,\mathrm{d}}}] \tag{9.34}$$

where $P_{N_s,j} = 1$ for all nodes j at time step N_s which equates to the maturity of the bond underlying the option. Figure 9.16 presents the pseudo-code for discount bond option pricing in a trinomial tree. The maturity condition and European price of the call option are given by equations (8.25) and (8.27) respectively, with the early exercise condition for American options determined by the following:

$$C_{i,j} = \max \left\{ \begin{array}{l} P_{S_{i,j}} - K \\ d_{i,j} \times [p_{u,i,j}C_{i+1,\mathrm{u}} + p_{\mathrm{m},i,j}C_{i+1,\mathrm{m}} + p_{\mathrm{d},i,j}C_{i+1,\mathrm{d}}] \end{array} \right\} \tag{9.35}$$

For the HL and HW models we can take advantage of the analytical tractability of these models. For example, for the HW model equation (7.11) determines analytically $P(T, s)$. We can use this by growing the tree only until time step N_T, evaluating $P(N_T, j)$ directly and then implementing the maturity condition of the option.

FIGURE 9.16 Pseudo-code for Pricing a Discount Bond Option in a Trinomial Tree

```
initiate_parameters { Ns, NT, K }

build_short_rate_tree { determines d[i,j] and Q[i,j] for all
      i and j until time step Ns }

{ initialise maturity condition for pure discount bond
underlying the option }

for j = low_node[Ns] to top_node[Ns] do Ps[Ns,j] = 1

{ backward induction for pure discount bond price }

for i = Ns-1 downto 0 do
  for j = low_node[i] to top_node[i] do
     Ps[i,j] = d[i,j]*(pu[i,j]*Ps[i+1,u]+pm[i,j]*Ps[i+1,m]
                      +pd[i,j]*Ps[i+1,d])
next i

{ initialise maturity condition for option }

for j = low_node[NT] to top_node[NT] do
   C[NT,j] = max {0, Ps[NT,j] - K}

{ European price determined via the state prices }

C[0,0] = 0
for j = low_node[NT] to top_node[NT] do
  C[0,0] = C[0,0] + Q[NT,j]*C[NT,j]

European_call_price = C[0,0]

{ backward induction for American option price }

for i = (NT-1) downto 0 do
  for j = low_node[i] to top_node[i] do
    C[i,j] = d[i,j]
       *(pu[i,j]*C[i+1,u]+pm[i,j]*C[i+1,m]+pd[i,j]*C[i+1,d])
    C[i,j] = max {C[i,j], Ps[i,j] - K}
  next j
next i

American_call_price = C[0,0]
```

Example : Pricing a Discount Bond Option in a Trinomial Tree

We price three-year put options with state price 0.85 on a five-year discount bond using a short-rate tree with yearly time steps built consistent with the HW model fitted to an upward-sloping term structure and with volatility parameters $\alpha = 0.10$ and $\sigma = 0.01$. Figure 9.17 shows the calculations.

GURE 9.17 Pricing Put Options on a Discount Bond Using Trinomial Trees

α	0.100	jmax	2	1.835034
σ	0.010	jmin	−2	
Δt	1.000			
Δr	0.017			
M	−0.100			

Initial Yield Curve

Maturity	Yield
1.00	5.00%
2.00	5.75%
3.00	6.25%
4.00	6.75%
5.00	7.00%
6.00	7.25%

i	0	1.00	2.00	3.00	4.00	5.00
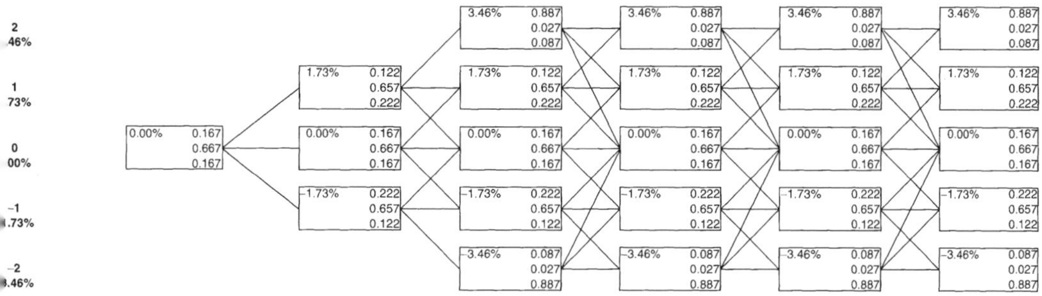 2 46%			3.46% 0.887 0.027 0.087	3.46% 0.887 0.027 0.087	3.46% 0.887 0.027 0.087	3.46% 0.887 0.027 0.087
1 73%		1.73% 0.122 0.657 0.222	1.73% 0.122 0.657 0.222	1.73% 0.122 0.657 0.222	1.73% 0.122 0.657 0.222	1.73% 0.122 0.657 0.222
0 00%	0.00% 0.167 0.667 0.167	0.00% 0.167 0.667 0.167	0.00% 0.167 0.667 0.167	0.00% 0.167 0.667 0.167	0.00% 0.167 0.667 0.167	0.00% 0.167 0.667 0.167
−1 .73%		−1.73% 0.222 0.657 0.122	−1.73% 0.222 0.657 0.122	−1.73% 0.222 0.657 0.122	−1.73% 0.222 0.657 0.122	−1.73% 0.222 0.657 0.122
−2 .46%			−3.46% 0.087 0.027 0.887	−3.46% 0.087 0.027 0.887	−3.46% 0.087 0.027 0.887	−3.46% 0.087 0.027 0.887

i	0	1.00	2.00	3.00	4.00	5.00
R[i]		5.00%	5.75%	6.25%	6.75%	7.00%
DB(i)		0.9512	0.8914	0.8290	0.7634	0.7047
Σ(i)	1	0.9513	0.8915	0.8293	0.7638	0.7053
a(i)	0.0500	0.0650	0.0727	0.0829	0.0806	0.0858
		0.9512	**0.8914**	**0.8290**	**0.7634**	**0.7047**

	0	1	2	3	4	5
2 46%			10.73% 0.0178 0.8982 | 0.887 0.027 0.087	11.75% 0.0358 0.8891 | 0.887 0.027 0.087	11.52% 0.0490 0.8912 | 0.887 0.027 0.087	12.05% 0.0575 0.8865 | 0.887 0.027 0.087
1 73%		8.24% 0.1585 0.9209 | 0.122 0.657 0.222	9.00% 0.1949 0.9139 | 0.122 0.657 0.222	10.02% 0.1890 0.9047 | 0.122 0.657 0.222	9.79% 0.1700 0.9067 | 0.122 0.657 0.222	10.32% 0.1503 0.9020 | 0.122 0.657 0.222
0 00%	5.00% 1.0000 0.9512 | 0.167 0.667 0.167	6.50% 0.6342 0.9370 | 0.167 0.667 0.167	7.27% 0.4620 0.9299 | 0.167 0.667 0.167	8.29% 0.3704 0.9205 | 0.167 0.667 0.167	8.06% 0.3117 0.9226 | 0.167 0.667 0.167	8.58% 0.2712 0.9177 | 0.167 0.667 0.167
−1 .73%		4.77% 0.1585 0.9534 | 0.222 0.657 0.122	5.54% 0.1983 0.9461 | 0.222 0.657 0.122	6.55% 0.1953 0.9366 | 0.222 0.657 0.122	6.33% 0.1779 0.9387 | 0.222 0.657 0.122	6.85% 0.1590 0.9338 | 0.222 0.657 0.122
−2 .46%			3.80% 0.0184 0.9627 | 0.087 0.027 0.887	4.82% 0.0385 0.9529 | 0.087 0.027 0.887	4.60% 0.0548 0.9551 | 0.087 0.027 0.887	5.12% 0.0667 0.9501 | 0.087 0.027 0.887

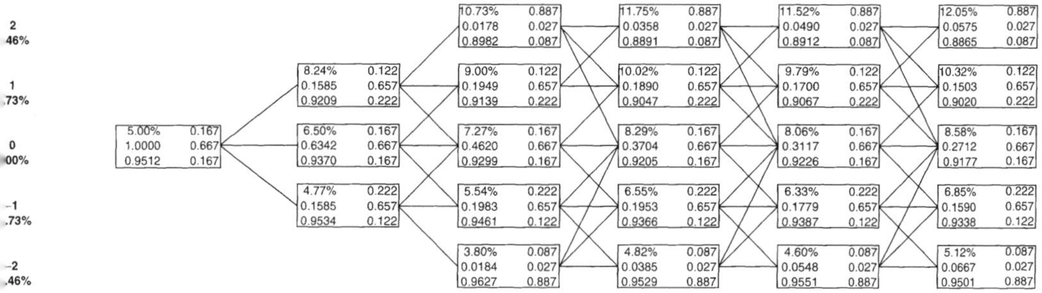

Discount Bond

0	1	2	3	4	5
		0.7191	0.7951	0.8912	1
	0.6976	0.7536	0.8218	0.9067	1
0.7047	0.7404	0.7899	0.8492	0.9226	1
	0.7858	0.8278	0.8777	0.9387	1
		0.8676	0.9070	0.9551	1

Strike **0.85**

European Put **0.0076**

American Put

0	1	2	3
		0.1309	0.0549
	0.1524	0.0964	0.0282
0.1453	0.1096	0.0601	0.0008
	0.0642	0.0222	0.0000
		0.0001	0.0000

The tree is built using the methodology of section 9.5. The structure of the nodes in the main tree is as follows:

$r_{i,j}$	$p_{u,i,j}$
$Q_{i,j}$	$p_{m,i,j}$
$d_{i,j}$	$p_{d,i,j}$

The two smaller trees at the base of Figure 9.16 represent the price of the five year bond and the American call option value. The discount bond price tree is calculated via equation (9.34). For example at node (2, 0):

$$\begin{aligned} Ps_{2,0} &= d_{2,0} \times [p_{u,2,0}Ps_{3,1} + p_{m,2,0}Ps_{3,0} + p_{d,2,0}Ps_{3,-1}] \\ &= 0.9299 \times [0.167 \times 0.8219 + 0.667 \times 0.8492 + 0.167 \times 0.8777 \\ &= 0.7899 \end{aligned}$$

The maturity condition for the option is determined via equation (8.25), i.e. for node (3, 1)

$$\begin{aligned} C_{3,1} &= \max\{0, K - Ps_{3,1}\} \\ &= \max\{0, 0.8500 - 0.8218\} \\ &= 0.0282 \end{aligned}$$

The European put price is calculated using the pure security prices, equation (8.27)

$$\begin{aligned} C_{0,0} &= \sum_j Q_{3,j} \max\{0, K - Ps_{3,j}\} \\ &= 0.0385 \times 0 + 0.1953 \times 0 + 0.3704 \times 0.0008 \\ &\quad + 0.1890 \times 0.0282 + 0.0358 \times 0.0549 \\ &= 0.0076 \end{aligned}$$

The American put price is calculated by the maximum of the intrinsic value and the discounted expectation, equation (9.35), adjusted for a put option, i.e. for node (2, 0)

$$\begin{aligned} C_{2,0} &= \max\{K - Ps_{2,0}, d_{2,0} \times (p_{u,2,0}C_{3,1} + p_{m,2,0}C_{3,0} + p_{d,2,0}C_{3,-1})\} \\ &= \max\{0.8500 - 0.7899, 0.9299 \times (0.1670 \times 0.0282 \\ &\quad + 0.6670 \times 0.0008 + 0.1670 \times 0)\} \\ &= 0.0601 \end{aligned}$$

The American put price is given by node $C_{0,0}$, i.e. 0.1453.

9.10 SUMMARY

In this chapter we have extended the binomial short-rate tree framework of Chapter 8 to trinomial trees — concentrating on the models of HW and a version of Black–Karasinski, although, again, the techniques are more generally applicable. As for binomial trees, we construct trees for models fitted to market yield curve data only, as well as extensions to models fitted to both yield and volatility data. Using the trees, we construct we have then shown how to price a number of interest rate derivatives.

ENDNOTES

1. See Hull and White (1993). By setting $\alpha = 0$ this expression also determines θ for the HL model (and hence the drift term).
2. This methodology is therefore valid for HL, HW and for their lognormal counterparts. For more general specifications of the short-rate process we have to use the methodologies outlined earlier in this chapter.
3. Because of the symmetrical nature of the tree we only have to determine the nodes for one half of the tree and then "reflect" them for the other half, thus saving considerable computation time.
4. However, due to the lognormal nature of the model discussed in this section we cannot represent this structure analytically.
5. The behaviour of the fitted volatility structure which we identified in section 7.7 still holds.

10

The Heath, Jarrow and Morton Model

10.1 INTRODUCTION

In this final chapter we briefly introduce some procedures for the efficient implementation of interest rate models in the Heath, Jarrow and Morton (1992) (HJM) framework. Many of the details of the efficient implementation of these models are beyond the present scope of this book. This chapter should therefore be viewed as an introduction to the techniques which can be used and the interested reader is referred to the cited papers. The HJM model was introduced in section 7.9, where the stochastic differential equation governing the evolution of forward rates was presented and we repeat it here:

$$df(t, T) = \alpha(t, T)\,dt + \sum_{i=1}^{n} \sigma_i(t, T, f(t, T))\,dz_i(t) \tag{10.1}$$

where the drift term is determined by no-arbitrage conditions to be

$$\alpha(t, T) = \sum_{i=1}^{n} \left\{ \sigma_i(t, T, f(t, T)) \left[\int_t^T \sigma_i(t, u, f(t, u))\,du \right] \right\} \tag{10.2}$$

The HJM model is extremely general, allowing the volatility functions, $\sigma_i(.)$, to depend on the entire forward rate curve. The initial forward rate curve is specified and then rates which differ in maturity evolve randomly through time with volatilities and correlations which are determined by the volatility functions. The main advantage of the model is the ability to easily specify the initial forward rate (or yield) curves and their volatilities and correlations.

An alternative formulation introduced in Chapter 7 is in terms of pure discount bond price returns:

$$\frac{dP(t, T)}{P(t, T)} = r(t)\,dt + \sum_{i=1}^{n} \nu_i(t, T)\,dz_i(t) \tag{10.3}$$

where the volatilities of forward rates and bond price are related via:

$$\nu_i(t, T) = -\int_t^T \sigma_i(t, u)\,du \tag{10.4}$$

In order to compute interest rate derivative prices it is necessary to specify explicitly the volatility functions. Before we describe the implementation of the HJM model with general volatility functions, it is informative to discuss some common restrictions of the volatility functions that result in simpler models discussed in earlier chapters with higher degrees of analytical tractability.

Two of the simplest specifications of the volatility function consist of firstly a single source of uncertainty across all maturities set equal to a constant σ, and secondly, a negative exponential volatility function of the form $\sigma(t, T) = \sigma e^{\alpha(T-t)}$. It can be shown that these specifications lead to short-rate equations of the form:

$$dr = \theta(t)\,dt + \sigma\,dz \tag{10.5}$$

$$dr = [\theta(t) - \alpha r]\,dt + \sigma\,dz \tag{10.6}$$

These can be seen as the defining stochastic differential equations of the HL and HW models respectively cf. equations (7.1) and (7.8). When authors talk about single-factor HJM models with constant and negative exponential volatilities of the above form they are therefore talking about the same model as HL and HW, which we analysed in Chapter 7. To value derivatives under these restricted versions of HJM we can use the analytical properties of the models described in Chapter 7 or the recombining tree methodologies for the short rate described in Chapters 8 and 9.[1]

The real advantage of the HJM framework is its ability to handle very general functions for the volatility structure. However, as we described in section 7.9 of Chapter 7, this generally leads to the evolution of the term structure being path dependent, making even numerical valuations complicated. In the remainder of this chapter we outline procedures for computing HJM derivative values under very general volatility functions both within a Monte Carlo simulation and multinomial tree framework. In both procedures our underlying variable is the current term structure, and the methods that we describe can be viewed as analogous to the tree and Monte Carlo procedures of Chapters 2, 3 and 4. The discussion in section 7.9 emphasised the equivalence between the formulations represented by equations (10.1) and (10.3). The mechanics for pricing a T-maturity option on a s-maturity bond, using the forward rate formulation, would be to firstly choose discrete points on the forward rate curve (obtained from the market), evolve these points through time until the maturity date of the option and then, in order to evaluate the maturity condition of the option, recover the s-maturity bond price from the forward curve via the equation:

$$P(T, s) = \exp\left(-\int_T^s f(T, u)\,du\right) \tag{10.7}$$

Accurate evaluation of this integral would require a very large number of discrete points on the forward rate curve to be evolved. Furthermore, computing the drift of the forward rates (see equation (10.2)) accurately is difficult. It is therefore more efficient to work with the pure discount bond prices directly. In the following sections we outline both Monte Carlo simulation and multinomial tree approaches in terms of the pure discount bond price formulations.

The date t value of a European claim, C_t having a terminal payout at date T, C_T, which is fully determined by the yield curve at that time, is given by the risk-neutral expectation formula:

$$C(t) = \tilde{E}_t\left[\exp\left\{-\int_t^T r(\tau)\,d\tau\right\} C(T)\right] \tag{10.8}$$

We begin by describing a general Monte Carlo simulation framework for pricing discount and coupon bond options and then show that, under the assumption of a Gaussian volatility structure we can obtain analytical solutions for cap and floor prices, and very efficient procedures for coupon bond option prices

10.2 MONTE CARLO SIMULATION FOR PURE DISCOUNT BOND OPTIONS IN GENERAL HJM

From equation (10.8) we have that a T-maturity European call option on a s-maturity pure discount bond, with strike price K is given by

$$c(t, T, s) = \tilde{E}_t \left[\exp\left\{ -\int_t^T r_\tau \, d\tau \right\} \max(0, P(T, s) - K) \right] \tag{10.9}$$

Similarly, American options are given by

$$C(t, T, s) = \max_{\theta \in \Psi[t,T]} \tilde{E}_t \left[\exp\left(-\int_t^\theta r_\tau \, d\tau \right) \max(0, P(\theta, s) - K) \right] \tag{10.10}$$

where $\max(0, P(\theta, s) - K)$ is the pay-off of the option when it is exercised at date θ and $\Psi[t, T]$ is the class of all early exercise strategies (stopping times) in $[t, T]$.

The price of a European call option on a pure discount bond (equation (10.9)) can be rewritten as (see Carverhill and Pang, 1995)

$$c(t, T, s) = \tilde{E}_t[\max(0, P(t, s)Y(t, T, s) - KP(t, T)Y(t, T, T))] \tag{10.11}$$

where

$$Y(t, T, \tau) = \exp\left[\int_t^T \nu(u, \tau) \, dz(u) - \frac{1}{2}\nu(u, \tau)^2 \, du \right]$$

We can implement this equation via Monte Carlo simulation with $j = 1, \ldots, M$ simulations:

$$c(t, T, s) = \frac{1}{M} \sum_{j=1}^{M} [\max\left(0, P(t, s)Y_j(t, T, s) - KP(t, T)Y_j(t, T, T)\right)] \tag{10.12}$$

where

$$Y_j(t, T, \tau) = \exp\left[\sum_{i=1}^{N} \nu(u_i, \tau)\varepsilon(u_i)\sqrt{\Delta t} - \frac{1}{2}\nu(u_i, \tau)^2 \Delta t \right]$$

Small simulation time steps (or advanced methods of simulating stochastic differential equations (see Kloeden and Paten, 1992, 1994)) must be used to accurately represent the stochastic behaviour of the term structure and the volatility functions must also be evaluated to the resolution of the simulation time step.

10.3 MONTE CARLO SIMULATION FOR COUPON BOND OPTIONS IN GENERAL HJM

Recall that the price of a European call option on a coupon bond, $c_{\mathrm{CB}}(t, T, \{s_k\})$, paying coupons c_k at dates s_k, $k = 1, \ldots, m$ $(T \leq s_1 \leq \ldots . \leq s_m)$ is given by

$$c_{\mathrm{CB}}(t, T, \{s_k\}) = \tilde{E}_t \left[\exp\left(-\int_t^T r_\tau \, d\tau \right) \max\left(0, \sum_{k=1}^{m} c_k P(T, s_k) - K \right) \right] \tag{10.13}$$

This can be rewritten as

$$c_{\mathrm{CB}}(t, T, \{s_k\}) = \tilde{E}_t\left[\max\left(0, \sum_{k=1}^{m} c_k P(t, s_k) Y(t, T, s_k) - K P(t, T) Y(t, T, T)\right)\right] \quad (10.14)$$

where

$$Y(t, T, s) = \exp\left[\int_t^T \nu(u, s)\, dz(u) - \frac{1}{2}\nu(u, s)^2\, du\right]$$

Monte Carlo valuation of the option price is given by

$$c_{\mathrm{CB}}(t, T, \{s_k\}) = \frac{1}{M}\sum_{j=1}^{M}\left[\max\left(0, \sum_{k=1}^{m} c_k P(t, s_k) Y_j(t, T, s_k) - K P(t, T) Y_j(t, T, T)\right)\right] \quad (10.15)$$

where

$$Y_j(t, T, s) = \exp\left[\sum_{i=1}^{N} \nu(u_i, s)\varepsilon(u_i)\sqrt{\Delta t} - \frac{1}{2}\nu(u_i, s)^2 \Delta t\right]$$

As with Monte Carlo simulation for the pure discount bond option in the previous section, accurate simulation of PDBs is important.

The control variate techniques described in Chapter 4 can be applied to improve the efficiency of the implementation in this and the previous section. However, practical implementation of this general formulation of HJM remains an open problem.

10.4 PURE DISCOUNT BOND OPTIONS IN GAUSSIAN HJM

In this section[2] we return to pricing of pure discount bond options, showing that under the assumption of Gaussian volatility structures pricing PDB options can be done analytically. In the first stage of our implementation we change the numeraire to the savings account

$$\beta(T) = \beta(t)\exp\left(\int_t^T r_\tau\, d\tau\right) \quad (10.16)$$

where we can assume $\beta(t) = 1$, and we obtain the following stochastic differential equation representing bond price returns under this new measure (cf. equation (10.3)):

$$\frac{dP(t, T)}{P(t, T)} = +\sum_{i=1}^{n} \nu_i(t, T)\, d\tilde{z}_i(t) \quad (10.17)$$

The effect of the change in measure, which can be thought of as discounting all prices back to today, is to eliminate the drift of the pure discount bond price return process, making it a martingale. If we think in terms of implementing equation (10.17) via Monte Carlo simulation, elimination of the drift avoids us having to inflate the pure discount bond prices at the short-rate and then discount the terminal pay-off of the derivative by the short-rate path. This saving can be considerable given the complex non-Markovian short-rate process given by equation (7.33).

Next we change the numeraire to $P(t, T)$ (the forward measure to the maturity date of the option) and so equation (10.9) becomes:

$$c(t, T, s) = P(t, T)E_t^T \left[\max\left(0, \frac{P(T, s)}{P(T, T)} - K\right)\right] \tag{10.18}$$

where $E_t^T[]$ indicates expectation with respect to the $P(t, T)$-numeraire. It can be shown that the solution to this equation is straightforward and analogous to the Black–Scholes equation (see e.g. Brace and Musiela, 1994, or Clewlow, Pang and Strickland, 1997):

$$c(t, T, s) = P(t, s)N(h) - KP(t, T)N(h - w) \tag{10.19}$$

where

$$h = \frac{\ln\left(\dfrac{P(t, s)}{P(t, T)K}\right) + \dfrac{1}{2}w}{\sqrt{w}}, \qquad w = \sum_{i=1}^{n} \left\{ \int_t^T (v_i(u, s) - v_i(u, T))^2 \, du \right\}$$

and w is the variance of the log relative discount bond prices.

The implication of equation (10.19) is that for multi-factor Gaussian versions of the HJM model, evaluating European options on pure discount bonds is as straightforward as using the Black–Scholes equation. The calculation requires only univariate integrations involving the volatilities of the discount bonds maturing at the time of the option and the bond underlying the option. This integration will usually be analytical, and if not standard numerical subroutines can be used to efficiently perform the numerical integration (see for example Press *et al.*, 1992).

In Chapter 6 we showed that interest rate caps (floors) can be priced as portfolios of European put (call) options on pure discount bonds and therefore we can use the results above for pricing these instruments. Pricing of interest rate caps can therefore be performed extremely efficiently, enabling us to calibrate the model to this set of market data.

10.5 MONTE CARLO SIMULATION FOR EUROPEAN SWAPTIONS IN GAUSSIAN HJM

We now turn our attention to pricing European options on interest rate swaps, or European swaptions.[3] In Chapter 6 we showed that European payer (receiver) swaptions can be priced as put (call) options on coupon bonds where the strike price of the option is set equal to the principal underlying the swap. We also showed that in a single factor world an option on a coupon bond can be valued as a portfolio of options on pure discount bonds. However, in a multi-factor world this simple decomposition no longer works in general (see El Karoui and Rochet (1995)). In this section we show how coupon bond option values can be efficiently calculated. The nature of our methodology implies that adding extra factors comes at the expense of only fractional increases in computation times. Under the forward measure of section 10.4 the discounted expectation of the option pay-off is given by

$$c_{\mathrm{CB}}(t, T, \{s_k\}) = P(t, T)E_t^T \left[\max\left(0, \sum_{k=1}^{m} c_k \frac{P(T, s_k)}{P(T, T)} - K\right)\right] \tag{10.20}$$

The expectation is taken over the m-dimensional normal distribution of the correlated log-relative discount bond prices,

$$\ln\left(\frac{P(T,s_k)}{P(T,T)}\right)$$

where m is the number of cashflows accruing to the coupon bond after the maturity of the option. In order to perform Monte Carlo simulation to evaluate (10.20) we must therefore compute the $m \times m$ covariance matrix Σ:

$$\begin{aligned}\Sigma_{kj} &= \text{cov}\left[\ln\left(\frac{P(T,s_k)}{P(T,T)}\right), \ln\left(\frac{P(T,s_j)}{P(T,T)}\right)\right] \\ &= \sum_{i=1}^{n}\left\{\int_t^T (v_i(u,s_k) - v_i(u,T))(v_i(u,s_j) - v_i(u,T))\,du\right\} \qquad (10.21)\end{aligned}$$

In order to efficiently sample from this covariance matrix we compute an orthogonal representation of the covariance matrix giving m eigenvectors $\mathbf{w}_i$ and m associated eigenvalues λ_i such that

$$\Sigma = \Gamma\Lambda\Gamma' \qquad (10.22)$$

where

$$\Gamma = \begin{vmatrix} w_{11} & w_{21} & \dots & w_{m1} \\ w_{12} & w_{22} & \dots & w_{m2} \\ \dots & \dots & \dots & \dots \\ w_{1m} & w_{2m} & \dots & w_{mm} \end{vmatrix} \quad \text{and} \quad \Lambda = \begin{vmatrix} \lambda_1 & 0 & 0 & 0 \\ 0 & \lambda_2 & 0 & 0 \\ 0 & 0 & \dots & 0 \\ 0 & 0 & 0 & \lambda_m \end{vmatrix}$$

The columns of Γ are the eigenvectors. Let M be the number of samples or simulations and ε_i, $i = 1, \dots, m$ be independent standard normal random numbers. Therefore, we have

$$c_{\text{CB}}(t,T,\{s_k\}) = P(t,T)\frac{1}{M}\sum_{j=1}^{M}\left[\max\left(0, \sum_{k=1}^{m} c_k \frac{P(t,s_k)}{P(t,T)} Y_j(t,T,s_k) - K\right)\right] \qquad (10.23)$$

where

$$Y_j(t,T,s_k) = \exp\left[-\frac{1}{2}\sum_{i=1}^{m}\{w_{ik}^2\lambda_i\} + \sum_{i=1}^{m}\left\{w_{ik}\sqrt{\lambda_i}\varepsilon_i\right\}\right]$$

and

$$\tilde{w}(t,T,s_k) = \sum_{i=1}^{m}\{w_{ik}^2\lambda_i\} = \sum_{i=1}^{m}\left\{\int_t^T (v_i(u,s_k) - v_i(u,T))^2\,du\right\}$$

Notice that because of the Gaussian nature of our framework we can effectively jump straight to the end of the life of the option under each simulation, rather than the more usual practice of simulating at a large number of small discrete time steps until maturity.

Although we have an efficient procedure for simulation of coupon bond option prices (we only have to simulate the bond prices corresponding to coupon cashflows and can jump straight to the end of each simulation) convergence is still slow.

The antithetic control variance technique (see Chapter 4) can be applied by computing the terminal coupon bond value based upon the negative of the standard normal increments. We now describe the application of a control variate based on an analytical approximation for coupon bonds described by Pang (1996) (see Clewlow, Pang and Strickland, 1997).

The coupon bond underlying the option is a weighted sum of the lognormally distributed pure discount bonds corresponding to the cashflows, and as such will not itself be lognormally distributed. However, since the final cashflow is much larger than the others then the coupon bond price will be highly correlated with the price of this pure discount bond. This implies that we can hedge it with an appropriate position in an option on a discount bond with a maturity corresponding to the final cashflow, s_m.

In our formulation we can compute the mean and variance of the coupon bond at the maturity date of the option analytically, as well as the value of the hedge discount bond option (via equation (10.19)). Our variance reduction technique consists of valuing a hedged portfolio — long the coupon bond option and short the discount bond option which matches the mean and variance.[4] This hedged portfolio has much smaller variance than the coupon bond option and so we obtain a much more accurate estimate of the option value.

The value of the coupon bond at the maturity of the option, $CB(T)$, is given as

$$CB(T) = \sum_{k=1}^{m} c_k \frac{P(T, s_k)}{P(T, T)} \tag{10.24}$$

Therefore, the expected value of the pay-off to the coupon bond is given by

$$E_t^T[CB(T)] = \sum_{k=1}^{m} c_k \frac{P(t, s_k)}{P(t, T)} \tag{10.25}$$

In order to compute the variance of the coupon bond we need the expectation of the squared pay-off to the bond:

$$E_t^T[CB(T)^2] = \sum_{j=1}^{m}\sum_{k=1}^{m} c_j c_k \frac{P(t, s_j)}{P(t, T)} \frac{P(t, s_k)}{P(t, T)} \exp\left(\operatorname{cov}\left[\ln\left(\frac{P(T, s_k)}{P(T, T)}\right), \ln\left(\frac{P(T, s_j)}{P(T, T)}\right)\right]\right) \tag{10.26}$$

Now we can equate the variance of the coupon bond with the variance of the discount bond with maturity s_m and with principal L.

$$\operatorname{var}[CB(T)] = L^2 \frac{P(t, s_m)^2}{P(t, T)^2} \left\{\operatorname{var}\left(\ln\left(\frac{P(T, s_m)}{P(T, T)}\right)\right) - 1\right\} \tag{10.27}$$

Equation (10.5.8) can then be inverted to determine L:

$$L = \sqrt{\frac{\operatorname{var}[CB(T)]}{\frac{P(t, S_m)^2}{P(t, T)^2}} \left\{\operatorname{var}\left(\ln\left(\frac{P(T, S_m)}{P(T, T)}\right)\right) - 1\right\}} \tag{10.28}$$

Finally, we want the mean of our hedging instrument to match the mean of the target instrument and so we adjust the strike of the coupon bond option by the difference between the means to obtain the strike for the discount bond option, K':[5]

$$K' = K - \left(E_t^T[CB(T)] - L\frac{P(t, S_m)}{P(t, T)}\right) \tag{10.29}$$

10.6 BINOMIAL TREES FOR SINGLE-FACTOR HJM

American options can be evaluated if we discretise equations (10.1) or (10.3) under the risk-neutral measure by building a binomial-type model. The binomial framework first proposed by Cox, Ross and Rubinstein (1979) assumes that asset price movements are binomial in a short period of time, moving to an "upstate" or a "downstate" with certain probabilities. The size of the movements, and their associated probabilities, are chosen at each step to give the correct mean and variance of the asset price during a short time interval (see Chapter 2).

The method that we propose for single factor ($\nu(.)$) HJM is to construct a binomial tree for the pure discount bond prices under the savings account numeraire (equation (10.17)). Using this numeraire means that we do not need to maintain the short rate at every node in the tree for discounting purposes.

Consider the binomial process for the pure discount bond prices illustrated in Figure 10.1. The s-maturity discount bond price $\tilde{P}(t,s)$,[6] in the next binomial time step can either move to $\tilde{P}_{\mathrm{u}}(t+\Delta t,s)$ in the upstate or $\tilde{P}_{\mathrm{d}}(t+\Delta t,s)$, with equal probability $p=0.5$.

For Gaussian versions of the model the up and down states can be written with general drift and volatility terms as the following:

$$\tilde{P}_{\mathrm{u}}(t+\Delta t,s)=\tilde{P}(t,s)\exp(\alpha_P(t,s)\Delta t+\nu(t,s)\sqrt{\Delta t}) \tag{10.30}$$

$$\tilde{P}_{d}(t+\Delta t,s)=\tilde{P}(t,s)\exp(\alpha_P(t,s)\Delta t-\nu(t,s)\sqrt{\Delta t}) \tag{10.31}$$

In order to satisfy the no-arbitrage condition the pure discount bond prices must be martingales, and so the expected value of the s-maturity bond after time Δt must be its value at time t, i.e.

$$E[\tilde{P}(t+\Delta t,s)]=\tilde{P}(t,s) \tag{10.32}$$

Therefore, we must choose the drift term, $\alpha_P(t,T)$, to satisfy this condition. Deriving the expected value of the bond from the tree and substituting into the no-arbitrage condition, equation (10.32) gives:

$$\tilde{P}_{\mathrm{u}}(t+\Delta t,s)=\tilde{P}(t,s)\frac{2}{1+\exp(-2\nu(t,s)\sqrt{\Delta t})} \tag{10.33}$$

$$\tilde{P}_{d}(t+\Delta t,s)=\tilde{P}(t,s)\frac{2}{1+\exp(+2\nu(t,s)\sqrt{\Delta t})} \tag{10.34}$$

FIGURE 10.1 Binomial Process for Pure Discount Bond Price

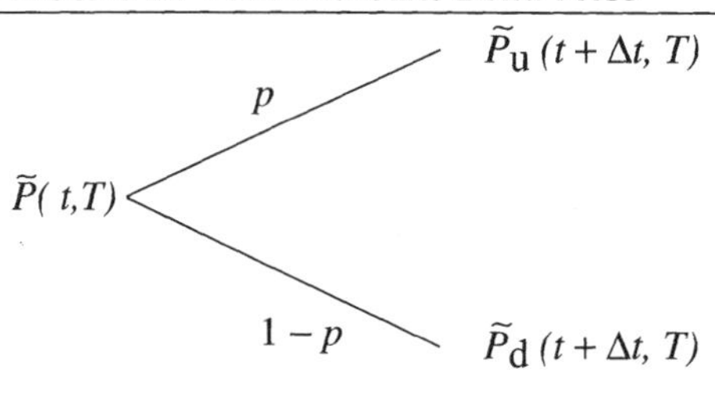

The pure discount bond price curve is discretised and evolved until the maturity of the derivative, T, by extending the binomial tree using equations (10.33) and (10.34). At each node we now have a discrete curve of pure discount bond prices, $\tilde{P}(T, s)\,(T \leq s)$, and so can evaluate the pay-off to options which depend on pure discount bond prices or the yield curve. For example, a coupon bond options pay-off is

$$\max\left(0, \sum_{k=1}^{m} c_k \tilde{P}(T, s_k) - K\right) \tag{10.35}$$

The discounting has been incorporated into the binomial evolution of the pure discount bond price and so we do not need to apply it as we step backwards through the tree in the normal way.

Note that the binomial tree is non-recombining in general, i.e. an upward move followed by a downward move does not result in the same pure discount bond price curve as a downward move followed by an upward move. Therefore the number of nodes in the tree after N time steps is 2^N, for example after 20 time steps there are more than 1 million nodes, and so the storage requirements and computational cost are very high for HJM trees.

10.7 TRINOMIAL TREES FOR TWO-FACTOR HJM

We now show how to extend the binomial tree methodology in the previous section to a trinomial tree for two-factor HJM with volatility functions $\nu_1(.)$ and $\nu_2(.)$. The extension to higher numbers of factors works in the same way although the computational cost becomes impractical unless advanced parallel computation systems are available. Consider a trinomial process for the pure discount bond prices illustrated by Figure 10.2. The s-maturity discounted discount bond price $\tilde{P}(t, s)$, in the next trinomial time step can either move to $\tilde{P}_{\mathrm{u}}(t + \Delta t, s)$ with probability of $p_{\mathrm{u}} = 0.5$ or to $\tilde{P}_{\mathrm{m}}(t + \Delta t, s)$ or $\tilde{P}_{\mathrm{d}}(t + \Delta t, s)$, with probability $p_{\mathrm{m}} = p_{\mathrm{d}} = 0.25$.

For Gaussian versions of the model the three possible states can be written with general drift and volatility terms as the following:

$$\tilde{P}_{\mathrm{u}}(t + \Delta t, s) = \tilde{P}(t, s)\exp(\alpha_P(t, s)\Delta t + \nu_1(t, s)\sqrt{\Delta t}) \tag{10.36}$$

$$\tilde{P}_{\mathrm{m}}(t + \Delta t, s) = \tilde{P}(t, s)\exp(\alpha_P(t, s)\Delta t - \nu_1(t, s)\sqrt{\Delta t} + \sqrt{2}\nu_2(t, s)\sqrt{\Delta t}) \tag{10.37}$$

$$\tilde{P}_{\mathrm{d}}(t + \Delta t, s) = \tilde{P}(t, s)\exp(\alpha_P(t, s)\Delta t - \nu_1(t, s)\sqrt{\Delta t} - \sqrt{2}\nu_2(t, s)\sqrt{\Delta t}) \tag{10.38}$$

FIGURE 10.2 Trinomial Process For Pure Discount Bond Price

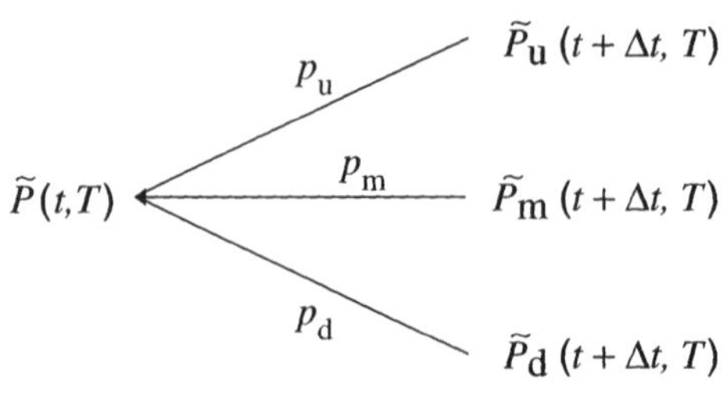

Now for no arbitrage the pure discount bond prices must be martingales and so $\alpha_P(t,s)$ now has to satisfy

$$e^{\alpha_P(t,s)\Delta t} = \frac{2}{e^{\nu_1(t,s)\sqrt{\Delta t}} + \frac{1}{2}e^{-\nu_1(t,s)\sqrt{\Delta t}+\sqrt{2}\nu_2(t,s)\sqrt{\Delta t}}} + \frac{1}{2}e^{-\nu_1(t,s)\sqrt{\Delta t}-\sqrt{2}\nu_2(t,s)\sqrt{\Delta t}} \tag{10.39}$$

The pure discount bond price curve is discretised and evolved until the maturity of the derivative, T, by extending the trinomial tree using equations (10.36), (10.37) and (10.38). At each node we now have a discrete curve of pure discount bond prices, $\tilde{P}(T,s)\ (T \leq s)$, and so can evaluate the pay-off to options which depend on pure discount bond prices or the yield curve. The discounting has been incorporated into the trinomial evolution so we do not need to apply it as we step backwards through the tree in the normal way. As in the previous section, this trinomial tree is non-recombining in, and therefore the number of nodes in the tree after N time steps is 3^N, leading to very high storage and computational requirements.

10.8 SUMMARY

In this chapter we introduced the techniques needed to efficiently implement models in the HJM framework. Firstly we showed that reformulating the model in terms of pure discount bond prices and applying appropriate changes of numeraire can greatly simplify the implementation. We then described how the general HJM model could be implemented via Monte Carlo simulation to price pure discount bond options and coupon bond options. The special case of Gaussian volatility structures was shown to lead to analytical prices for pure discount bond options and very efficient Monte Carlo valuation of coupon bond options. Finally, we described how multinomial trees should be implemented for the pricing of American-style options in the HJM framework. At the time of writing much research remains to be done to identify appropriate forms for the HJM volatility functions and efficient pricing methods for American and exotic interest rate derivatives.

ENDNOTES

1. Carverhill (1994) shows that to obtain a Markovian short rate with time homogeneous volatility functions, they must have the Vasicek form, i.e. $\sigma_i(t,T) = \sigma_i \exp(-\alpha_i(s-T))$.
2. This section is based on Clewlow, Pang and Strickland (1997).
3. This section is based on recent work by Clewlow, Pang and Strickland (1997).
4. The principle behind this variance reduction technique is similar to that used by Clewlow and Strickland (1996). In that paper the authors simulated a "delta-hedged" portfolio for the two-factor stochastic interest rate model of Fong and Vasicek (1992).
5. Note that alternatively we could have chosen the principal and maturity of the discount bond to match the mean and variance of the coupon bond, but this would then require the simulation of an extra pure discount bond.
6. The tilde over the pure discount bond price indicates it is under the savings account numeraire.

References

Babbs, S., 1992, "Binomial Valuation of Lookback Options", *Working Paper*, Midland Global Markets.

Black, F., 1976, "The Pricing of Commodity Contracts", *Journal of Financial Economics*, **3**, Jan–Mar, 167–179.

Black, F. and P. Karasinski, 1991 "Bond and Option Pricing When Short Rates are Lognormal", *Financial Analysts Journal*, July–August, 52–59.

Black, F., E. Derman and W. Toy, 1990, "A One-Factor Model of Interest Rates and Its Application to Treasury Bond Options", *Financial Analysts Journal*, Jan–Feb, 33–39.

Black, F. and M. Scholes, 1973, "The Pricing of Options and Corporate Liabilities", *Journal of Political Economy*, **81**, 637–659.

Boyle, P.P., 1977, "Options: A Monte Carlo Approach", *Journal of Financial Economics*, **4**, 323–338.

Boyle, P.P., 1988, "A Lattice Framework for Option Pricing with Two State Variables", *Journal of Financial and Quantitative Analysis*, **23**, 1–26.

Boyle, P.P. and S.H. Lau, 1994, "Bumping up against the Barrier with the Binomial Method", *The Journal of Derivatives*, **1**, 6–14.

Boyle, P.P., J. Evnine and S. Gibbs, 1989, "Numerical Evaluation of Multivariate Contingent Claims", *Review of Financial Studies*, **2**, 241–250.

Brennan, M.J. and E.S. Schwartz, 1978, "Finite Difference Methods and Jump Processes Arising in the Pricing of Contingent Claims: A Synthesis", *Journal of Financial and Quantitative Analysis*, **13**, 462–474.

Brennan, M.J. and E.S. Schwartz, 1979, "A Continuous Time Approach to the Pricing of Bonds", *Journal of Banking and Finance*, **3**, 133–155.

Carverhill, A.P., 1994, "When is the Short Rate Markovian?", *Mathematical Finance*, **4**, October, 305–312.

Carverhill, A.P., 1995a, "A Note on the Models of Hull and White for Pricing Options on the Term Structure", *Journal of Fixed Income*, **5**, 89–96.

Carverhill, A.P., 1995b, "A Simplified Exposition of the Health–Jarrow–Morton Model", *Stochastics and Stochastic Reports*, **53**, 227–240.

Carverhill, A.P., and K. Pang, 1995, "Efficient and Flexible Bond Option Valuation in the Heath, Jarrow, and Morton Framework", *Journal of Fixed Income*, **5**, 70–77.

Chan, K.C., G.A. Karolyi, F.A. Longstaff and A.B. Sanders, 1992, "The Volatility of Short Term Interest Rates: An Empirical Comparison of Alternative Models of the Term Structure of Interest Rates", *Journal of Finance*, **47**, 1209–1227.

Cheuk, T.H.F. and T.C.F. Vorst, 1994, "Lookback Options and the Observation Frequency", *Working Paper*, Erasmus University, Rotterdam.

Clewlow, L.J. and A. Carverhill, 1994, "On the Simulation of Contingent Claims", *Journal of Derivatives*, **2**, 66–74.

Clewlow, L.J. and C.R. Strickland, 1996, "Monte Carlo Valuation of Interest Rate Derivatives Under Stochastic Volatility", *Financial Options Research Centre Preprint 96/97*, University of Warwick.

Clewlow, L.J. and C.R. Strickland (eds), 1997, *Exotic Options: The State of The Art*, International Thomson Publishing, London.

Clewlow, L.J., K. Pang and C.R. Strickland, 1997, "Numerical Procedures for Pricing Interest Rate Exotics Using Markovian Models of the Short Rate", *Financial Options Research Centre Preprint 97/78*, University of Warwick.

Courtadon, G., 1982a, "The Pricing of Options on Default Free Bonds", *Journal of Financial and Quantitative Analysis*, **17**, 75–100.

Courtadon, G., 1982b, "A More Accurate Finite Difference Approximation for the Valuation of Options", *Journal of Financial and Quantitative Analysis*, **17**, 697–703.

Cox, J.C., S.A. Ross and M. Rubinstein, 1979, "Option Pricing: a Simplified Approach", *Journal of Financial Economics*, **7**, 229–263.

Cox, J.C. and S.A. Ross, 1976, "The Valuation of Options for Alternative Stochastic Processes", *Journal of Financial Economics*, **3**, 145–166.

Cox, J.C., J.E. Ingersoll and S.A. Ross, 1985a, "A Theory of the Term Structure of Interest Rates", *Econometrica*, **53**, 363–384.

Cox, J.C., J.E. Ingersoll and S.A. Ross, 1985b, "An Intertemporal General Equilibrium Model of Asset Prices", *Econometrica*, **53**, 363–384.

Derman, E. and I. Kani, 1994, "Riding on a Smile", *Risk*, **7**, 32–39.

Derman, E., D. Ergener and I. Kani, 1995a, "Static Options Replication", *Journal of Derivatives*, Summer, 78–95.

Derman, E., I. Kani, D. Ergener and I. Bardhan, 1995b, "Enhanced Numerical Methods for Options with Barriers", *Quantitative Strategies Research Notes*, Goldman Sachs.

Dothan, L.U., 1977, "On the Term Structure of Interest Rates", *Journal of Financial Economics*, **6**, 385–407, 1978.

Dupire, B., 1994, "Pricing with a Smile", *Risk* **7**, 18–20.

El Karoui, N. and J-C, Rochet, 1995, *A Pricing Formula for Options on Coupon Bonds*, SEEDS Discussion Series, Instituto de Economica Publica, Spain.

Feller, W., 1968, *An introduction to Probability Theory and its Applications*, 3rd edn, John Wiley & Sons, Chichester.

Fong, H.G. and O.A. Vasicek, 1992, "Interest Rate Volatility as a Stochastic Factor", *Gifford Fong Associates Working Paper*.

Heath, D., R. Jarrow and A. Morton. 1992, "Bond Pricing and the Term Structure of Interest Rates: A New Methodology for Contingent Claim Valuation", *Econometrica*, **60**, 77–105.

Heynen, R.C. and H.M. Kat, 1997a, "The Wonderful World of Barrier Options", in *Exotic Options: The State of the Art*, edited by L. Clewlow and C. Strickland, International Thomson Publishing, London.

Heynen, R.C. and H.M. Kat, 1997b, "Lookback Options: Pricing and Applications", in *Exotic Options: The State of the Art*, edited by L. Clewlow and C. Strickland, International Thomson Publishing, London.

Hines, W.W. and D.C. Montgomery, 1980, *Probability and Statistics in Engineering and Management Science*, 2nd edn Wiley, New York.

Ho, T.S.Y. and S-B. Lee, 1986, "Term Structure Movements and Pricing Interest Rate Contingent Claims", *Journal of Finance*, **41**, 1011–1029.

Hull, J., 1996, *Options, Futures, and Other Derivative Securities*, Prentice-Hall, Englewood Cliffs, New Jersey.

Hull, J. and A. White, 1988a, "An Analysis of the Bias in Option Pricing Caused by a Stochastic Volatility", *Advances in Futures and Options Research*, **3**, 29–61.

Hull, J. and White A., 1988b, "The Use of the Control Variate Technique in Option Pricing", *Journal of Financial and Quantitative Analysis*, **23**, 237–251.

Hull, J. and White A., 1993a, "One Factor Interest Rate Models and the Valuation of Interest Rate Derivative Securities", *Journal of Financial and Quantitative Analysis*, **28**, 235–254.

Hull, J. and A. White, 1993b, "Efficient Procedures for Valuing European and American Path Dependent Options", *Journal of Derivatives*, **1**, 21–32.

Hull, J. and A. White, 1994a, "Numerical Procedures for Implementing Term Structure Models I: Single-factor Models", *The Journal of Derivatives*, Fall, 7–16.

Hull, J. and A. White, 1994b, "Numerical Procedures for Implementing Term Structure Models II: Two-factor Models", *The Journal of Derivatives*, Winter, 37–48.

Hull, J. and White A., 1995, "A Note on the Models of Hull and White for Pricing Options on the Term Structure: Response", *Journal of Fixed Income*, **5**, 97–102.

Ingersoll, J.E. Jr., 1987, *Theory of Financial Decision Making*, Rowman & Littlefield.

Jamshidian, F., 1989, "An Exact Bond Option Formula", *The Journal of Finance*, **XLIV** March, 205–209.

Jamshidian, F., 1991, "Forward Induction and Construction of Yield Curve Diffusion Models", *Journal of Fixed Income*, **1**, 62–74.

Jarrow, R. and A. Rudd, 1983, *Option Pricing*, Dow Jones-Irwin, Homewood, Illinois.

Jarrow, R. and A. Rudd, 1991, "Option Pricing", Dow Jones-Irwin, Homewood, Illinois.

Kamrad, B., and P. Ritchken, 1991, "Multinomial Approximating Models for Options with k State Variables", *Management Science*, **37**, 1640–1652.

Kloeden, P.E. and E. Platen, 1992, *Numerical Solution of Stochastic Differential Equations*, Springer-Verlag, New York.

Kloeden, P.E. and E. Platen, 1994, *Numerical Solution of Stochastic Differential Equations Through Computer Experiments*, Springer-Verlag, New York.

Levy, E., 1997, "Asian Options", in *Exotic Options: The State of the Art*, edited by L. Clewlow and C. Strickland, International Thomson Publishing, London.

Longstaff, F.A. and E.S. Schwartz, 1992, "Interest Rate Volatility and the Term Structure: A Two-factor General Equilibrium Model", *The Journal of Finance*, **XLVII**, 1259–1282.

Merton, R.C., 1973, "Theory of Rational Option Pricing", *Bell Journal of Economics and Management Science*, **4**, 141–183.

Nelken, I., 1996, *The Handbook of Exotic Options — Instruments, Analysis and Applications*, Irwin Professional Publishing, Chicago.

Niederreiter, H., 1992, *Random Number Generation and Quasi-Monte Carlo Methods*, CBMS–NSF Regional Conference Series in Applied Maths, Vol. 63, Society of Industrial Applied Maths, Philadelphia.

Niederreiter, H. and P.J. Shiue, 1995, *Monte Carlo and Quasi-Monte Carlo Methods in Scientific Computing*, Springer-Verlag, New York.

Øksendal, 1995, *Stochastic Differential Equations*, Springer-Verlag, Berlin.

Pang, K., 1996, "Multi-Factor Gaussian HJM Approximation to Kennedy and Calibration to Caps and Swaptions", *Financial Options Research Centre Preprint 96/71*, University of Warwick.

Press, W.H., S.A. Teukolsky, W.T. Vetterling and B.P. Flannery, 1992, *Numerical Recipes in C: The Art of Scientific Computing*, 2nd edn, Cambridge University Press, Cambridge, UK.

Ravindran, K., 1993, "Low Fat Spreads", *Risk*, **6**, 66–67.

Richard, S., 1978, "An Arbitrage Model of the Term Structure of Interest Rates", *Journal of Financial Economics*, **6**, 33–57.

Ripley, B.D., 1987, *Stochastic Simulation*, Wiley, New York.

Ritchken, P., 1995, "On Pricing Barrier Options", The *Journal of Derivatives*, Winter, 19–28.

Rubinstein, M., 1994, "Implied Binomial Trees", *Journal of Finance*, **69**, 771–818.

Sandmann, K. and D. Sondermann, 1994, *On the Stability of Lognormal Interest Rate Models*, University of Bonn, Discussion Paper No. B-263.

Schaefer, S. and Schwartz, E., 1984, "A Two Factor Model of the Term Structure: An Approximate Analytical Solution", *Journal of Financial and Quantitative Analysis*, **19**, 413–424.

Schroder, M., 1989, "Computing the Constant Elasticity of Variance Option Pricing Formula", *The Journal of Finance*, **XLIV**, 221–229.

Schwartz, E.S., 1977, "The Valuation of Warrants: Implementing a New Approach", *Journal of Financial Economics*, **4**, 79–94.

Selby, M.J.P. and C.R. Strickland, 1995, "Computing the Fong and Vasicek Pure Discount Bond Price Formula", *The Journal of Fixed Income*, September, 78–84.

Sharpe, W.F., 1978, "Investments", Prentice-Hall, Englewood Cliffs, New Jersey.

Smith, G.D., (1975), "Numerical Solution of Partial Differential Equations", Oxford Mathematical Books, Oxford University Press.

Strickland, C.R., 1992a, "An Analysis of Interest Rate Volatility and the Term Structure of Interest Rates", *Financial Options Research Centre Preprint 92/37.*

Strickland, C.R., 1992b, "The Delivery Option in Bond Futures Contracts: An Empirical Analysis of the LIFFE Long Gilt Futures Contract", *The Review of Futures Markets*, **11**, 84–102.

Strickland, C.R., 1996a, "A Comparison of Diffusion Models of the Term Structure", *The European Journal of Finance*, **2**, 103–123.

Strickland, C.R., 1996b, "A Comparison of Models for Pricing Interest Rate Derivatives", *The European Journal of Finance*, **2**, 261–287.

Trigeorgis, L., 1991, "A Log-transformed Binomial Numerical Analysis Method for Valuing Complex Multi-option Investments", *Journal of Financial and Quantitative Analysis*, **26**(3), 309–326.

Vasicek, O., 1977, "An Equilibrium Characterisation of the Term Structure", *Journal of Financial Economics*, No. 5, 177–188.

Index

Index compiled by Geoffrey Jones

Printed in the USA/Agawam, MA
September 19, 2013
580140.013